The Reign
of
Napoleon
Bonaparte

Also by Robert B. Asprey

The Reign

of

Napoleon Bonaparte

Robert B. Asprey

BASIC
BOOKS

A Member of the Perseus Books Group

Published by Basic Books,
A Member of the Perseus Books Group

The Reign of Napoleon Bonaparte was
originally published in the United Kingdom by Little, Brown as
The Rise and Fall of Napoleon Bonaparte: Volume Two.
The Basic Books edition is published by
arrangement with Little, Brown.

A CIP catalog record for this book is available
from the Library of Congress.
ISBN 0-465-00481-4

01 02 03 04 / 10 9 8 7 6 5 4 3 2 1

To Tim
with gratitude, respect and love

CONTENTS

List of Illustrations

C. Sutherland. London: Weidenfeld & Nicholson, 1979.
Countess Marie Walewska. Portrait attributed to Jacques-Louis David
from Christine, Sutherland. With kind permission of C. Sutherland.   52

Victoria and Albert Museum   309
Madame George

MAPS

A NOTE TO THE READER

Ever since his untimely death at the age of 51 on the forlorn island of St. Helena in 1821, Napoleon Bonaparte has too often been the victim of biographical and historical exuberance, of unhealthy literary passions that treat him either as demi-god (mainly French authors) or as devil incarnate (mainly British authors). The interpretive pendulum continues to swing, most recently toward devil incarnate in three lengthy books by American, British and French authors.

I object to either interpretation which, by distorting either his achievements or failures, gives the reader a lopsided view of one of the most fascinating persons of all time who dominated one of the most contradictory periods of the world's history.

Napoleon's relatively short life is a story of massive successes and disastrous failures, intense loves and violent hatreds, genius and stupidity, vision and cupidity, arrogance and ignorance, intrigue and treachery, short-term satisfactions and long-term frustrations – of unfettered power once intended for the public good but in time diluted by overweening ambition and conceit.

Napoleon was not the father of chaos, as his detractors would have us believe. He was heir to chaos both at home and abroad. We tend to forget the appalling conditions of abject human servitude that fomented the French Revolution; the devastating period of terror invoked by Robespierre and his Jacobin followers; the inept and corrupt administration of the Directorate which followed the overthrow of the Jacobins. These miserable and chaotic years shaped the young Bonaparte's thinking to bring forth his active participation in a *coup d'etat* followed by the creation of the Consulate and the Empire – and a reasonably successful attempt by the new ruler to restore order in a torn nation while leading it to what he believed was its rightful role in the consolidation of Europe.

Neither was Napoleon the father of the wars that accompanied the process, as his detractors would also have us believe. Almost constant warfare was a legacy of the revolutionary chaos, a series of wars invoked by European and English rulers determined to topple the dangerous interloper and restore Bourbon feudalistic rule to France.

As European armies suffered repeated defeats owing to Napoleon's military mastery, the desire of their governments for revenge continued to grow. It was fueled on the one hand by Napoleon's determination to build a French empire in an attempt to unify a discordant Europe, on the other hand to force the English government to share its control of the seas: too often overlooked is the singular fact that in the first decade of the nineteenth century Britain controlled five-eighths of the world's surface – its oceans – compared to Napoleon's relatively slight and always tenuous European holdings.

The long Anglo-American alliance has tended to make many Americans forget the humiliations suffered by our colonial forefathers, the painful war that gave birth to our nation, the subsequent maritime insults to our fledgling navy and merchant ships, the war of 1812 and the burning of Washington. In Napoleon's day the Royal Navy indisputably ruled the seas to provide its masters with a virtual monopoly of colonial trade that Napoleon was determined to break.

Since the English government had no intention of relinquishing its rule of the seas the results were inevitable. It was the English crown which dishonored its signing of the Treaty of Amiens to declare war on France in 1803; that bankrolled numerous Bourbon *émigré* attempts on Napoleon's life; that subsequently spent millions of pounds sterling in subsidizing a series of armed coalitions to make war on the French tyrant. And, because of Napoleon's strategic errors, both military and political, it was the English crown that emerged the winner to continue enlarging its vast overseas empire throughout the nineteenth and twentieth centuries.

If Napoleon ultimately failed in his grand design to make the seas neutral and to form Europe into a cohesive union of non-warring states, he nevertheless accomplished a great deal in his short reign. His legal reforms embodied in the famous Code Napoléon were alone sufficient to bring lasting fame. Add to that his insistence on the revolutionary principle of equality, one example being his dictum of promotion on grounds of performance rather than birth; his founding of the Bank of France and a national university, of schools, hospitals, orphanages, workhouses; building of roads, tunnels, canals, ports and extension of the primitive telegraph system; his encouragement of and contribution to the arts and sciences – his alleged geometric theorem remains well known; his sponsorship of smallpox vaccination and other unpopular public health measures; his attempts to introduce a unified coinage in his empire; his repeated experiments and successes in agrarian and animal husbandry; his beautification of Paris and other cities.

Militarily he introduced tactical mobility so necessary to battlefield improvisation of which he was a master. Napoleon used time as a precious clock: "We don't march, we fly," General Berthier wrote early in the first Italian campaign. But rapid movement depended on willing troops, and here was Napoleon's real secret of success. No commander in history has so inspired his troops to march, often without adequate food or wine, on occasion without shoes, frequently with meager clothing in dreadful weather. Time and again, in Italy, Egypt, Austria, Germany, Prussia, Russia, and finally France, he asked his men to do what often appeared to be impossible – and they did it. His tricks were many, their sum spelled unexcelled leadership.

His political contributions were real enough even if some were accidentally inspired. Our United States as we know them would never have emerged but for his providential sale of the immense Louisiana territory – an act calculated to strengthen America against England. His creation of the Cispadane and Cisalpine republics planted the seeds of a future Italian nation. His Egyptian campaign, although a strategic failure, resulted in the discovery of the Rosetta Stone and, ultimately, in the building of the Suez Canal. His admittedly nebulous plans for a cohesive Europe, had they been realized, might possibly have led to two centuries of peace as opposed to body- and soul-destroying wars.

Such however was the scope of his ambition, such his unbridled belief in physical force, such his arrogance derived from igno-rance of naval strategy and the potential of guerrilla warfare, such his error in confusing his country's destiny with his own, such the strength and determined resistance of aristocratic and oligarchic rule, that in the end his own ambitious dreams fell victim to the nightmare of defeat followed by abdication, exile and six years of very cruel imprisonment on St. Helena island.

As with all of us, Napoleon was a sum of his parts which is why I have treated him, warts and all, as a human being, as child, stu-dent, man, soldier, general, lover, husband, father, ruler, emperor, conqueror and statesman. His story is an intensely dramatic saga, presented in terms not of our day but of his. I hope you enjoy the result.

ACKNOWLEDGEMENTS

I am greatly indebted to a number of people and institutions for helping me with this book. I want to thank the staffs of the Bodleian Library, the Codrington Library of All Souls College and the New College Library, all at Oxford; the London Library and the British Museum Library; the Library of Congress; the Army and Navy Club Library in Washington, D.C.; the New York City Library; the Vassar College Library; the Bibliothéque Nationale in Paris; and the Biblioteca Nacional in Madrid.

Among many friends who aided my work in one way or another are Gordon and Sheila Seaver, David and Christine Sutherland and Jacques W. Kleynhans in England; Philippe and Danièle Delamare in France; Edward and Irma Sommer in Spain; Robert Andreen, David Bradford, Elle Gohl; Caroline Gifford; Lila and David De Campo; my literary agent, Matthew Bialer, of the William Morris Agency; the "fathers" of the book, two fine editors, John Hermann and Stephen Fraser; my publishers, Jack McKeown of Basic Books and Alan Samson of Little Brown, London; my American editor, Donald Fehr, and my English editors, Becky Quintavalle and Jean Maund.

My old friend, Graham Rosser, has spent many hours during the last several years in correcting and often improving my translations from a wide variety of French sources, and I am grateful. I am equally indebted to my sister, Winifred Asprey, to whom this book is dedicated, for the many hours devoted to the careful proofing of a long manuscript. The maps are the work of the English cartographer, Samantha A. Kirby, to whose talent, care, patience and good temper I pay deep homage.

Robert Asprey

PERMISSIONS

Grateful acknowledgment is made for permission to quote from the following sources:

Chandler, David G. *The Campaigns of Napoleon*, Weidenfeld & Nicolson, 1967.

Bruce, Evangeline. *Napoleon & Josephine – An Improbable Marriage*, Weidenfeld & Nicolson, 1996.

Thomazi, August Antoine, *Napoléon et ses marins*, Berger-Levrault, 1950.

Sutherland, Christine. *Marie Walewska – Napoleon's Great Love*, Weidenfeld & Nicolson, 1979.

Bertrand, Henri-Gratien. *Napoleon at St. Helena – The Journals of General Bertrand*, Doubleday, 1952.

Craig, Gordon. *The Politics of the Prussian Army 1640–1945*, Oxford University Press, 1955.

Thiry, Jean. *Napoléon et Italie*, Berger-Levrault, 1973.

Thiry, Jean. *Les Années de la Jeunesse de Napoléon Bonaparte*, Berger-Levrault, 1975.

Clearchos was a true soldier and war was his passion . . .
When he could have kept at peace without shame or
damage, he chose war; when he could have been idle, he
wished for hard work that he might have war; when he
could have kept wealth without danger, he chose to make it
less by making war; there was a man who spent upon war
as if it were a darling lover, or some other pleasure.

Xenophon

Clisson was born for war. While yet a child he knew the
lives of the great captains. He thought out the principles of
the military art at a time when those of his age were at
school and were running after girls. As soon as he was old
enough to carry arms he marked every step by brilliant
actions. He had reached the first rank in the army though
but a youth. Fortune constantly favored his genius. His
victories followed one another and his name was known to
the people as one of their dearest defenders.

The opening lines of Napoleon's novella,
Clisson et Eugénie, written after the breakup
of his romance with Eugénie Désirée Clary.

CHAPTER ONE

THE "GLORIOUS PEACE"
DECEMBER 1805–JANUARY 1806

Peace is not obtained by shouting Peace . . . *Peace is a word
devoid of meaning; we must make a glorious peace.*

Napoleon to Prince Joseph Bonaparte, Schönbrunn,
13 December 1805[1]

NAPOLEON DEEMED AUSTERLITZ a "decisive victory" without perhaps realizing that *decisive* is a finite adjective with a limited
lifespan. Victory did leave him in a powerful position *vis-à-vis*
wavering Prussia and the members of the now moribund Third
Coalition, but it would not provide the answer to potentially
dangerous political problems. This was a task for intelligent
and astute diplomacy not fully appreciated by the French
emperor.

Dead and dying soldiers still littered the battlefield when
Napoleon met with Emperor Francis. Although the victor agreed
to an armistice and the opening of peace negotiations, he excori-
ated Austrian duplicity in having sent peace envoys to the French
camp while simultaneously preparing to attack. He also scorned
Austria's foreign minister, Count Johann Cobenzl, who "sold
himself to England to pay his debts and who has ruined his master
and his nation."[2] Although Cobenzl was soon to be dismissed, the
price of his misjudgment was suggested in an earlier letter from
Napoleon to Talleyrand: the enemy having gambled and lost
everything "must now expect harsh conditions," an early one of
which was a levy of an enormous sum, 100 million francs, in
"contributions".[3]

The Russians had already paid their contributions, so to speak, in the form of heavy losses of men, all of their huge artillery park, supply and baggage trains along with much of their pride. Before sneaking off with the wounded General Kutusov in tow, Czar Alexander had asked Francis to request an armistice from Napoleon on his behalf. Informed that Alexander had agreed to evacuate all Russian troops from Germany and Galicia and that he wanted a separate peace devoid of English participation, Napoleon called off his pursuit.

Napoleon's gentle if contemptuous treatment of Czar Alexander is curious, as if regarding the Russians as visitors from another planet. He disparaged Russian arms, having noted even before Austerlitz that the cavalry although splendidly turned out had not yet learned to use sabers effectively. "The Russian troops are brave," he commented after Austerlitz, "their generals inexperienced, their soldiers ignorant and sluggish which in truth makes their armies to be little feared."[4] He regarded Alexander as an ambitious but inexperienced and impetuous young man surrounded and controlled by firebrand courtiers such as Prince Dolgoruky who were in English pay. Alexander's participation in the Third Coalition was a temporary aberration, an unwise intrusion in European affairs. "Russia is the sole power in Europe able to make a war of fantasy," he wrote. "After a battle lost or won, the Russians vanish; France, Austria, Prussia, to the contrary, must live a long time with the results of the war."[5]

Napoleon's desire to obtain a "glorious peace", by which he meant a profitable but permanent peace with Austria, was not a simple matter. One Austrian army had been decimated but there remained Prince Charles with some 90,000 troops not far distant. There also remained a Prussian army 190,000 strong, elements of which were reportedly in Silesia. Napoleon's past experience with these courts had taught him to trust neither ruler, weak men who bent too easily under the weight of anti-French advisers. "Until the peace," Napoleon warned corps and division commanders, "the armistice should be regarded only as a moment of repose, a means of preparing for new battles." Commanders were to repair the ravages of battle as quickly as possible while keeping their units on the alert, ready to march within two hours.[6]

Peace negotiations dragged on through most of December. Those with the Prussian envoy, Count Haugwitz, proceeded rapidly and favorably. Unlike Prussia's foreign minister, Prince Karl von Hardenberg, Haugwitz was an admirer of Napoleon, a Francophile who proudly wore the cordon of the French Legion of Honor. Haugwitz had arrived in Vienna shortly before the battle of Austerlitz to convince Talleyrand of Prussia's desire to cooperate with France, even going so far as to deny the validity of Prussia's recent treaty with Russia. "I am very content with Count Haugwitz," Talleyrand informed his master at the time.[7]

After a considerable delay Napoleon received the Prussian envoy in mid December at Schönbrunn palace, a formal and tense meeting that resulted in the signing of preliminaries to what would become the treaty of Schönbrunn. Once Russian and English troops had evacuated German territory Prussia would occupy Hanover in return for yielding substantial territories in central Germany to Bavaria and France. Napoleon also proposed an offensive and defensive military alliance – and a satisfied Haugwitz departed for Berlin.[8] "There is nothing to fear from the North," Napoleon informed Joseph Bonaparte (prematurely as it turned out), "our disagreements with Prussia have been cleared up to our mutual satisfaction."[9]

Negotiations with Austria did not progress so smoothly, mainly because of Napoleon's stringent demands. The treaty of Pressburg, signed two days after Christmas, cost the Vienna court all of its Venetian territories (absorbed into the Italian kingdom which Austria now recognized); Istria and Dalmatia in the Balkans which went to France (see map, Chapter 13, Vol. I); all of the Tyrol and Vorarlberg to Bavaria; and all of its diverse Swabian holdings to Bavaria, Württemberg and Baden, thus yielding its dominant role in southern Germany to Napoleon.

That was for starters. A good many millions in cash already had
been seized by the French. Under treaty terms another 8 million
would be handed over before French troops evacuated Pressburg,
and 40 million more would follow. Under the expert tutelage of
Vivant Denon, who had perfected his art in the Italian and
Egyptian campaigns, museums, libraries and palaces had been
stripped of artistic and cultural treasures. Over 2,000 cannon were
shipped from the famous Vienna arsenal – some to Venetian and
Dalmatian fortresses, some to Paris to embellish a hall in the
Musée Napoléon (later the Louvre) along with "some curious
things" also found in Vienna.[10] The land had been stripped of
provisions and horses, Murat alone having more than doubled
the size of his cavalry corps.

This "glorious peace" was one of vengeance just as had been
those of Lunéville and Campo Formio several years earlier.
Although justified at least in part by the Austrian court's enduring hostility and duplicity and its failure to heed Napoleon's
warning in favor of spearheading the Third Coalition's war
against France, it was perhaps not his wisest move – though this is
certainly debatable. Talleyrand had argued against the harsh terms
on grounds that Austria instead of being humbled should remain
a great power and should be strengthened as "a needful bulwark
against the barbarians, the Russians." He even suggested giving
Hanover to Austria in order to break the Anglo-Austrian
alliance.[11] (In view of subsequent events Talleyrand's advice was
perhaps biased – he was probably in Austrian pay even at this
point.)

However, it is clear that Napoleon wanted none of it. A number
of reasons have been posited for his stand: that he needed alliance
with Prussia and Russia in order to close European ports to British
goods (the embryo of what would become his Continental
System); that once again he was looking eastward toward Turkey
and India (that Charlemagne had again given ground to Alexander
the Great in this teeming, fecund mind). More probably it
stemmed partly from his understandable distrust of the Austrian
court and from his resentment of its invasion of Bavaria which

forced him to abandon his cross-Channel expedition. He was also in urgent need of money, owing to the financial crisis that was rocking Paris. Having humbled the Austrian court he could discard it, content that, like Russia, it would remain militarily impotent for some time. He had warned the Vienna court not to make war against him. Having ignored the warning, it would now pay the price.

Napoleon left Vienna at the end of December for a stay of several weeks in Munich in order to await ratification of the treaty and to oversee a dynastic marriage. The electors of Bavaria, Württemberg and Baden had been well paid for their recent alliance with France. Each received new territories, the electors of Bavaria and Württemberg were promoted to kingly status and the Elector of Baden was made a grand duke.

Bavaria was the most important member of the burgeoning edifice and as such saw its territory increased by a third. In gratitude for its military assistance Napoleon awarded the 9 million livres paid in contributions by the Tyrol to the new king, Maximilian I, and gave him 40 places in the Legion of Honor to be divided between officers and men; General Deroy gained a lifetime pension and General Wrede a high rank (with pension) in the Legion of Honor. The alliance was now to be cemented by a propitious marriage.

The bride was Princess Amelia Augusta, young daughter of the Bavarian elector who earlier had attracted Napoleon by her good looks and innate charm. The groom was his stepson, Prince Eugène Beauharnais, viceroy of Italy. Eugène was 24 years old, a soldier and ruler whose competence had considerably increased during the last six years owing in large part to Napoleon's almost constant tutelage.

As was customary neither bride nor groom had been consulted. "I have arrived in Munich," Napoleon informed Eugène on the last day of December. "I have arranged your marriage with Princess Augusta . . . This morning the princess visited me and we

had a long conversation. She is very pretty. You will find her portrait on the enclosed cup, but she is much prettier."[12] In early
January, Eugène learned that he was to leave Milan within twelve
hours to travel incognito to Munich as rapidly as possible.

Napoleon remained rapturous over the forthcoming marriage,
"the union of a princess as perfect as Princess Augusta with a
child [sic] for whom everyone knows my tender sentiments," as he
expressed it to Prince Cambacérès. A day prior to the wedding he
informed the senate in Paris that he was formally adopting
Eugène, which constitutionally made him heir to the Italian
throne.

The French emperor was very much concerned with Italy's
future. Eugène was to establish a new administration in the
recently acquired Venetian lands and arrange for the military
occupation of the Frioul by General Marmont. The general
would also send a division to Istria and Dalmatia which would be
governed by General Lauriston.[13] Meanwhile General Junot
would put down an insurrection in the duchies of Parma and
Piacenza: "Peace in Italy is not maintained by words," he
informed Junot. "Do what I did at Binasco [in 1796]: burn a large
village, shoot a dozen insurgents and send out mobile columns to
seize brigands wherever they may be to give an example to the
people."[14]

Napoleon was equally concerned with the situation in Naples.
Ruled by King Ferdinand IV and Queen Caroline who were dominated by their prime minister, the Englishman Sir John Acton,
that kingdom had become virtually an English colony (under
feudal rule), a mainstay in British domination of the
Mediterranean. Despite repeated promises of neutrality, the court
and particularly its queen had remained under Acton's influence
to the extent that a frustrated Napoleon had militarily occupied
the country. This led to still another promise of future neutrality
in return for the departure of French troops. Early in 1805
Napoleon warned Queen Caroline that "if she were the cause of
another war, she and her children would beg their bread all
through Europe."[15]

Undaunted, in the autumn of 1805 the good queen had welcomed an Anglo-Russian expedition some 20,000 strong which landed to challenge the French presence in Italy. This was part of England's peripheral strategy which was complemented by an Anglo-Russian-Swedish expedition that was to occupy North Germany simultaneously with Austria's invasion of Bavaria. The French victory at Austerlitz quickly dissolved the southern expedition, the Russians decamping for Corfu and the English across the straits to Sicily, the Naples court having re-established itself in Palermo.

While negotiating the peace with Austria, Napoleon had sent Gouvion St. Cyr with a large force to seize Naples and formally depose its royal rulers: "The dynasty of Naples has ceased to reign . . . Its existence is incompatible with peace in Europe and the honor of my crown."[16] The job was to be done by St. Cyr, Masséna and Reynier's corps operating under command of Prince Joseph Bonaparte. "Attach yourself to General Reynier," Napoleon ordered his brother. "He is cold but of the three he is the most capable of making a good plan of campaign and giving you good advice." Joseph should not worry about the Anglo-Russian force: "An army composed of men of different nations will not take long to make some blunders. The art will be to wait and profit from them." If reinforcements should reach the enemy, Napoleon would immediately join Joseph. Finally, he was to "speak seriously to Masséna and St. Cyr, and tell them you do not want thieving. Masséna has stolen plenty in the Venetian countries." Joseph would remain in Naples, eventually to be crowned king. In the interim he was to administer the country with the help of Ségur, Roederer and Saliceti.[17]

While these events played out, the French army began an evacuation from Austria minutely prescribed by its commander. No unit was to march until local contributions had been paid. Marches were to be short so as not to tire the men unnecessarily and create laggards to give the evacuation "the appearance of a disorderly retreat."[18]

Some units had begun the journey home by the time Napoleon left Munich. An indication of future problems appeared when

Berthier was informed in late January that "my affairs with Prussia are not entirely terminated, and my intention is to keep forty thousand men at Frankfurt until the Russians have evacuated Silesia."[19]

Notes

1   Corr. XI. Nr. 9561, Schönbrunn, 13 December 1805.

2   Corr. XI. Nr. 9546, Austerlitz, 5 December 1805. See also Méneval, I, 401; Savary, II, 478–80.

3   Corr. XI. Nr. 9542, Austerlitz, 4 December 1805. See also Nr. 9566, Schönbrunn, 13 December 1805; Bertrand (Pierre), Talleyrand to Napoleon, Lettre CXL, 13 December 1805.

4   Corr. XI. Nr. 9550, Austerlitz, 7 December 1805.

5   Corr. XI. Nr. 9556, Brünn, 10 December 1805.

6   Corr. XI. Nr. 9572, Schönbrunn, 14 December 1805.

7   Bertrand (Pierre), Talleyrand to Napoleon, Lettres CXXXV, Vienna, 1 December 1805; CXXXVII, Vienna, 2 December 1805.

8   Rose (*Life*), II, 44.

9   Corr. XI. Nr. 9592, Schönbrunn, 20 December 1805.

10 Corr. XI. Nr. 9616, Schönbrunn, 26 December 1805.

11 Bertrand (Pierre), Talleyrand to Napoleon, Lettre CXXXVIII, Vienna, 5 December 1805. See also Rose (*Life*), II, 46–9; Vandal (*Alexander*), I, 8–9.

12 Corr. XI. Nr. 9636, Munich, 31 December 1805.

13 Corr. XI, Nr. 9663, Munich, 12 January 1806.

14 Corr. XI, Nr. 9678, Stuttgart, 19 January 1806.

15 Rose (*Life*), II, 62.

16 Corr. XI. Nr. 9625, Schönbrunn, 27 December 1805. See also Flayhart ("United Kingdom"), 115–18.

17 Corr. XI. Nr. 9665, Munich, 12 January 1806.

18 Corr. XI. Nr. 9657, Munich, 7 January 1806.

19 Corr. XI. Nr. 9702, Strasbourg, 24 January 1806.

CHAPTER TWO

THE NEW CHARLEMAGNE
JANUARY–JULY 1806

My intention is to place the kingdom of Naples in my family.
This will be along with Italy, Switzerland, Holland and the
three German kingdoms my federated States, or in truth the
French empire.

Napoleon to Prince Joseph Bonaparte, Paris,
27 January 1806.[1]

NAPOLEON ARRIVED INCOGNITO in Paris on a night in late January 1806. His first official but secret act was to summon the principals of what had become a serious financial crisis; we noted its first makings in 1804. Finance minister Gaudin's reforms were only beginning to produce satisfactory results at a time when Napoleon needed vast sums for grandiose civil and military projects. To raise the money the treasury minister, François de Barbé-Marbois, had foolishly involved himself with a company of merchant-speculators headed by Gabriel Julien Ouvrard (with whom Joséphine and her lover, Hippolyte Charles, had earlier been involved in a series of shady dealings with army contractors). This necessitated borrowing money from the Bank of France and other banks to finance various speculative ventures, the security being the large Spanish debt to France which was to have been paid with gold and silver brought from Mexico. Unfortunately the English blockade nullified this arrangement, to everyone's embarrassment.

That was the situation when Napoleon had gone to war five months earlier. Barbé-Marbois meanwhile kept borrowing and Ouvrard's hold on the treasury kept growing as he siphoned off the cash. Accurate rumors that the Bank of France was running out of gold had brought a rush of withdrawals met by issuing paper money, which soon declined sharply in value. Napoleon had learned details of the growing crisis in mid campaign and had promised to settle matters upon his return.

He did so. He immediately replaced Barbé-Marbois with a no-nonsense state councillor, an experienced financial administrator named Nicolas François Mollien (a man of energy, talent and probity who would serve him well until the end). Although Napoleon deplored Barbé-Marbois' naïve stupidities, he did not regard him as criminally involved. Not so with Ouvrard and his cronies whom he forced to return 87 million francs to the treasury, a wise surrender since the emperor otherwise "had resolved to have them shot without a trial."[2] This cash infusion taken with the loot of the recent campaign and other income partially restored financial stability and in a month the crisis had passed though the treasury was anything but full.

Although Napoleon had hoped to continue civil programs begun during the Consulate and carried into the Empire, these were not to regain their former impetus. Neither desire nor imagination was lacking. In early March the minister of interior, Jean Baptiste Champagny, read a lengthy "State of the Empire" paper to the legislative corps. This work included a review of diverse accomplishments in every facet of national life as well as an impressive list of future intentions.

The government would continue to subsidize new factories, encourage such counter-measures to the English blockade as home refining of beet sugar and manufacture of ersatz coffee, saltpeter (necessary for the manufacture of gunpowder) and indigo dye (vital to the textile industry); it would also fund plans for new buildings, erect new statues and monuments, open additional schools, stage another industrial exhibition in Paris, repair old roads, bridges, canals and ports and build new ones. But where once many millions were devoted to such projects, now it was a matter of a few hundred thousand here and there with work to be spread over years to come.

The villain was limited income trying to finance an expansive foreign policy dependent on a large, costly and ever-growing military establishment. We see at this stage an unfortunate transition from a ruler of France to a man intending to rule Europe. Ulm and Austerlitz had dangerously increased the imperial ego, as a study of pertinent letters, decrees and memoirs shows only too clearly.

Napoleon's political position at home was secure enough. He was immensely popular with the ordinary citizen. Minister of police Joseph Fouché kept a careful eye on dissidents conspiring in the cafés of the *faubourg* St. Germain and in elegant private salons. Editors of journals and newspapers perforce took a careful line as did authors, playwrights, artists and composers. Virtually no overt criticism of the regime was tolerated. Fouché's agents were seemingly everywhere enforcing petty censorships – one decree ordered newspapers to confine coverage of military affairs to what appeared in the official *Moniteur*. Napoleon continued to cosset the Catholic clergy and was rewarded with impressive fealty. A cowed and bored tribunate offered hardly any obstruction to his new laws, nor did the legislative corps or the senate, all of which were becoming increasingly moribund. His ministers with one or two exceptions, his councillors of state dared not challenge sometimes imperfect imperial *ukases*. Those who did, either civil or military, usually regretted their rashness. Infrequent queries or suggestions more often than not drew negative replies and sometimes scoldings. So long as Napoleon was present the machinery of government functioned reasonably well, a matter of extreme vigilance on his part. It was in his absence that major cracks appeared in the structure, owing mainly to the fear of cowed lieutenants who rarely dared to act without imperial orders.

That the emperor's political position abroad was infinitely more complex and far less secure than his domestic situation was largely his own doing. Recent military successes had caused him to conjure up a false picture of Europe. In his mind Austria was moribund, no longer a major influence in Germany, its future confined to a few motley feudal states. He had created the nucleus of a new Germanic confederation which would soon tie 16 German rulers into a confederation of the Rhine with himself as protector – thus the demise of the Holy Roman Empire, no great loss since in Voltaire's classic remark it was neither holy, Roman nor empire.

He had brought Russia to task, nothing to fear there. He controlled Holland's fate – Louis Bonaparte would soon become its king. He believed that the defeated and dishonored Russians would remain quiet for years to come. Spain, or rather Prince Manuel Godoy, was again under the French thumb and would cooperate in the conquest of Portugal if that power did not accept French hegemony and close its ports to English ships. Prince Eugène de Beauharnais was well established as Viceroy of Italy, a kingdom about to be enlarged by Venice and the Venetian states. French troops already had raised the flag in Istria and Dalmatia in the Balkans. Prince Joseph Bonaparte would soon wear the crown of Naples. New expeditions were preparing to sail (in theory) for Martinique, South America, Africa and elsewhere. England was still a threat but in late January his *bête-noir*, William Pitt, had died (it was said from the final shock of Austerlitz). The government was now headed by Lord Grenville and included Sir Charles James Fox as foreign affairs minister. The roly-poly, rubicund and immensely common-sensical Fox was a proponent of the peace of Amiens. Openly sympathetic to French aspirations, his new presence suggested the possibility of achieving the long-desired peace.

From Napoleon's standpoint it was a pretty enough canvas. Unfortunately it had the major defect that its colors would retain luster only by repeated coats of costly force.

Prussia was typical. The Berlin court had refused to ratify the treaty of Schönbrunn worked out with Count Haugwitz. Influenced by a strong anti-French and English-bribed faction headed by the foreign minister, Count Hardenberg, King Frederick William submitted a list of modifications, one of which would postpone his cession of territories until a general peace – to be mediated by Prussia.[3]

But Prussia was in no position to mediate anything. Prussia was alone, bitterly resented by England, Russia and Austria for not having joined the Third Coalition, scorned by France for its divisive fatuities, its army reverting to peacetime status, its ministers and generals quarreling over future plans.

Count Haugwitz brought the new demands to Paris in early February 1806 where they were spurned by Napoleon in a lengthy and often unpleasant audience. Haugwitz returned to Berlin with the draft of a new treaty that, in line with the original, would turn Hanover over to Prussia in return for some Prussian lands. Prussia was now to close its northern seaports and the Sound (between the Baltic and North seas) to English ships which, as Napoleon gleefully informed Talleyrand, taken with Portugal sealing its ports, would deal a terrible blow to England.

Despite his earlier and impulsive bravado, Frederick William had little choice but to sign. Large numbers of French troops remained in Germany uncomfortably close to Prussian borders, and Napoleon had left no doubt in Haugwitz's mind that they would be used if necessary. "I imagine that Ney, Soult [and] Davout have their corps concentrated . . . ready for a campaign," he wrote Berthier in early February. The chief of staff was to inform the marshals that "all is not finished with Prussia."[4]

Staring at the neighboring glitter of French eagles and privy to the hostile sentiments of their handlers, the Berlin court accepted the new treaty. Count Hardenberg was relieved of his duties as foreign minister, most of them being taken over by the more pliant Haugwitz. A few weeks later England declared war on Prussia.

The new English foreign minister, Charles James Fox, meanwhile had decided that England and Russia must make peace with France. Fox had wanted a peace all along and now, old and seriously ill, it became his chief goal. In early March he opened the door to negotiations by informing the French government of a new plot to assassinate Napoleon, naming the individual and providing "details as to its intended accomplishment."[5] A grateful emperor responded by releasing several English political prisoners. Among them was Lord Yarmouth who subsequently represented Fox in peace talks with Talleyrand and General Clarke.

This well-intentioned effort soon ran aground owing to obstacles past and present. The French unsuccessfully tried to revive the treaty of Amiens, stressing the clause calling for English evacuation of Malta. Whitehall unsuccessfully demanded Russia's participation in the negotiations. Napoleon did agree that Hanover should be restored to England (having recently bestowed it on Prussia) and Talleyrand seemed amenable to England retaining control of Sicily (this at a time when Napoleon was urging King Joseph to seize the island and depose the old Bourbon dynasty).

By midsummer little progress had been made in dissipating the heavy cloud of mutual suspicions and conflicting interests. Napoleon summed up his view of the situation to Talleyrand in early July, pinpointing the stumbling-blocks as Malta and Sicily. If the English controlled these islands they would own an "impassable barrier" to French communications with the Adriatic and Constantinople.

England must either renounce Malta, he insisted, or refuse to guarantee Sicily to its present rulers. If it renounced Malta then the island's fortifications could be razed, which would make it a neuter, or it could be entrusted to a neutral nation such as Denmark. As for Sicily, the old king and queen must abdicate in favor of the young prince royal who in turn would permit neither foreign troops on the island nor foreign ships in the harbor. Once this problem was settled England could work out an arrangement with Prussia concerning Hanover. If necessary Russia could be enlisted to guarantee Sicily to the present Bourbon rulers if that were finally needed to remove England from Malta.[6]

This pragmatic solution to the impasse contained some defects, however. Despite the failure of the Third Coalition armies, England had run up a number of naval successes against the

French. In January an expedition had seized Capetown on the southwestern tip of Africa to ensure communications with India; an English fleet had almost neutralized Admiral Linois' earlier successful campaign in the Indian Ocean; in February another English fleet had seized five French warships at San Domingo. As Napoleon was dictating his summary to Talleyrand, an Anglo-Neapolitan force commanded by Sir John Stuart was landing on a Naples beach and would soon win a stunning if minor victory over General Reynier's corps at Maïda. Nor could England overlook the empty meaning of a neutral Sicily, for as Napoleon had pointed out to Talleyrand, "Sicily would be conquered any time we wanted and certainly at the first sign of hostilities between [England and France]."[7]

Perhaps the most important defect however was Napoleon's demonstrated desire to control continental Europe and, judging from his naval construction program, his desire to contest English naval supremacy in the Mediterranean and eventually the world.

Napoleon's vaunted ambition at this point must be briefly examined. He had long since fallen in love with force, which he continued to rely on during these months after Austerlitz. Having seen his summary treatment of Prussia, we are not surprised by his threat to renew war with Austria if it did not withdraw its troops from Würzburg and thereafter keep them within Austrian borders, and if it did not open a land route to Istria and Dalmatia for French troops.

He was equally firm when it came to Italy and its viceroy, Prince Eugène. His personal concerns were two, the first being absorption of the newly acquired Venetian lands into the Italian kingdom and consolidation of French control of Istria and Dalmatia. These were major tasks and in carrying them out Eugène was frequently and sometimes hotly criticized but on occasion also praised.

The other concern was Italy's internal security. General Junot, dispatched to quell an uprising in Parma, was not to concern himself with its cause, only with its cure. "Burn five or six villages," Napoleon again ordered, "shoot sixty people; make some extremely severe examples for the consequences of what has happened at Parma for a month are incalculable for the security of Italy."[8]

A negative report from Junot elicited a reply as stern as it was disturbing:

> The Italians . . . are false. Seditious under a weak government, they fear and respect only a strong and vigorous government. My intention is that the insurgent village . . . be burned, that the priest who is in the hands of the bishop at Placentia be shot, and that three or four hundred of the guilty be sent to the galleys. We do not share the same idea of clemency. You will be clement only in being severe, lacking which this unfortunate country and the Piedmont are lost . . . I do not share your opinion as to the innocence of Parmese peasants. These are great scoundrels who are guilty of the greatest excesses; and I am astonished that one of my oldest soldiers regards resistance to my arms and lack of respect for my standards a minor offense. My wish is that they be religiously revered . . . Believe in my former experience with Italians. Your conduct during the next month will influence greatly the respect of my Italian peoples for my government. Burn one or two big villages, leaving no trace. Say that this is my order. When one has great states, one can maintain them only by severe acts. Nothing absolves the inhabitants of the Parma states.[9]

Prince Joseph Bonaparte was also to use a heavy hand in governing Naples. This was a curious appointment but entirely in keeping with family loyalty (no matter the price). Joseph had left Paris before his brother's return. "I am thoroughly satisfied with everything you have done while you were in Paris," Napoleon wrote Joseph (under whose quasi-regency France had nearly become bankrupt). "Receive my thanks and as a token of gratitude, my portrait." There followed the first of a long string of orders that probably made the indolent Joseph wish he were back on his beautiful Mortefontaine estate:

> Take the right tone with the army. Do not suffer thieves. I hope that you will be content with [Marshal] Masséna; if you are not, discharge him . . . Don't let Saliceti steal . . . my intention is to place the kingdom of Naples in my family. This will be, along with Italy, Switzerland, Holland, the three German kingdoms, my federated States or truly the French empire.[10]

Once master of Naples and all forts, Joseph was to publicly proclaim "that the dynasty of Naples has ceased to reign." He was then to send a strong corps to Reggio to prepare for the invasion of Sicily. "No half-measures, no weakness. I want my blood to reign in Naples for as long as [it does] in France."[11] Joseph next learned, possibly to his discomfiture, that "[you are not] to listen to those who would wish to keep you far from battle; you have need to prove yourself. If there are some opportunities, expose yourself ostentatiously."[12]

Numerous letters and directives followed, dealing mainly with the handling of his new subjects and the invasion of Sicily. He was sending Miot de Milo who would make a good minister of war, also some auditors (no doubt to check rapacious generals such as Masséna and civil officials such as Saliceti). Joseph was to remember his position and maintain his dignity. He was also to send the emperor exact strength reports of his army: "The situation reports of the armies are for me the most agreeable books in my library, and those that I read with the most pleasure in moments of relaxation."[13]

Pope Pius VII also fell victim to the firm hand. Prior to Austerlitz the pope had objected to a French military occupation of Ancona. Napoleon replied only when he was back in Munich, and only to scold him for papal obstructionism owning to pro-British councillors. To set the record straight, he wrote, "God had demonstrated by the success with which He has favored my arms the protection that He has accorded to my cause." He regarded himself "as the protector of the Holy See, and as such I have occupied Ancona . . . It is to your Holiness' interest to see this fortress in my hands rather than in those of the English or the Turks."[14]

Napoleon received the pope's ambivalent reply in Paris and responded: "All of Italy will be subject to my law. I will never threaten the independence of the Holy See . . . on condition that your Holiness will have for me in temporal affairs the same respect I have for him in spiritual affairs, and . . . will cease useless accommodation with heretical enemies of the church and toward the powers which can do him no good. Your Holiness is sovereign of Rome, but I am the emperor. All my enemies must be yours." The pope was to forbid any agent from the courts of Sardinia, England, Russia or Sweden to reside in Rome or the papal states, nor would their ships be allowed to enter Roman ports. He also took the pope to task for the delay in approving newly appointed bishoprics in various German states, which was causing religious anarchy. "Six months are required before the bishops take up their duties, which can be done in eight days."[15]

Napoleon's envoy in Rome, his uncle Cardinal Fesch, was part of the problem. "You are not firm enough on my behalf," he was bluntly informed. Fesch was to rid the papal lands of hostile foreign agents and close its ports to enemy ships – he could rely on military assistance from Joseph Bonaparte in Naples if necessary. The pope must be made to understand that "I am Charlemagne, the sword of the church, their emperor; that I must be treated as such . . . if he does not acquiesce, I shall reduce the papacy to the state that it occupied before Charlemagne."[16]

Notes

1   Corr. XI. Nr. 9713, Paris, 27 January 1806.
2   Corr. XII. Nr. 9764, Palais des Tuileries, 6 February 1806. See also Mollien, I, xii–xiii, 316–30, 407–440; Madelin (*Consulate*), 234, 272–4.

3   Rose (*Life*), II, 64–6.
4   Corr. XII. Nr. 9777, Paris, 8 February 1806. See also Corr. XII, Nr. 9771, Paris, 7 February 1806.
5   Corr. XII. Nr. 9944, Paris, 8 March 1806.
6   Corr. XII. Nr. 10448, St. Cloud, 4 July 1806.
7   Corr. XII. Nr. 10448, St. Cloud, 4 July 1806.
8   Corr. XII. Nr. 9744, Paris, 4 February 1806.
9   Corr. XII. Nr. 9772, Paris, 7 February 1806.
10 Corr. XI. Nr. 9713, Paris, 27 January 1806.
11 Corr. XI. Nr. 9724, Paris, 31 January 1806.
12 Corr. XI. Nr. 9738, Paris, 2 February 1806.
13 Corr. XII. Nr. 9788, Paris, 9 February 1806.
14 Corr. XI. Nr. 9655, Munich, 7 January 1806.
15 Corr. XII. Nr. 9805, Paris, 13 February 1806.
16 Corr. XII. Nr. 9806, Paris, 13 February 1806.

CHAPTER THREE

Prussia Goes to War:
The Battles of Jena and Auerstädt
June–October 1806

*My darling, I have made some beautiful maneuvers against the
Prussians. Yesterday I obtained a great victory . . . I have
taken 20,000 prisoners, a hundred cannon and some
standards . . . I am in marvelous health. Adieu, my darling,
keep well and love me.*

Napoleon to Empress Joséphine, Jena, 15 October 1806.[1]

PEACE NEGOTIATIONS BETWEEN France and England somehow managed to stay alive during winter and spring of 1806, but little
progress was made. The irresistible force was still meeting the
immovable object. Neither nation was negotiating on a basis of
goodwill or even common sense. English and French ships around
the world were doing everything possible to sink each other.
England was reinforcing Sicily with the intention of landing more
troops on the Neapolitan coast. English warships and small craft
were making predatory attacks on the French Channel coast.
Napoleon was almost daily adjuring Prince Joseph to seize the
Anglo-Sicilian fort of Gaëta about 50 miles up the coast from
Naples and to send a strong force across the Messina straits to
seize Sicily. Prince Eugène was to close as many Italian and papal
ports as possible to English ships, and General Lauriston on the
Balkan coast was to do the same.

To complicate matters Napoleon in May received a friendly
letter from the Russian foreign minister, Prince Czartoryski,
which seemed to be a peace tentative. Czar Alexander followed up

The Jena–Auerstädt Campaign September – October 1806

by agreeing to remove his troops from Cattaro on the Montenegrin coast (which to Napoleon's fury the Austrians had recently permitted them to occupy). Alexander next dispatched a special envoy, one Oubril, to Paris to open peace negotiations (much to England's alarm). Napoleon meanwhile was secretly urging the Turkish sultan to close the Bosphorus to Russian ships in order to isolate the Russian garrison on Corfu, and he also urged Selim to regain control of the lower Danube principalities of Moldavia and Valachia recently occupied by the Russians, promising as much support as possible.[2] Russia simultaneously was carrying on secret negotiations with Prussia and Austria in order to fashion a new anti-French coalition.

Napoleon soon charmed Oubril into signing a secret treaty that ended the war between the two powers. Under its terms Russia was to retain Corfu but was to support the abdication of the Neapolitan Bourbons and to recognize Joseph Bonaparte as King of the Two Sicilies. Oubril departed for St. Petersburg and a jubilant Napoleon ordered Joseph to publish the treaty in Naples – henceforth all Russian ships in French ports would be treated as friends.[3]

Lord Yarmouth meanwhile continued meeting with Monsieur Talleyrand and General Clarke to draft still another treaty. Thanks to a crafty bit of blackmail on Talleyrand's part, England would give Sicily to France in return for Hanover. Charles James Fox refused to accept any such arrangement, Yarmouth was replaced by Lord Lauderdale and another draft treaty was presented to the French in early August.

At Fox's insistence this was based on the diplomatic principle of *uti possidetis* – each side to keep what it had won. As General Clarke was quick to point out, this was ludicrous since it would allow France to retain all of Austria, Moravia and Hanover. Napoleon agreed and the draft was returned with modifications unacceptable to England. Impasse once again. In early August poor old Fox, an increasingly ill victim of dropsy, admitted to Lord Holland that "he had not the slightest expectation of peace."[4]

Clarke's derisive reply to the English draft validated Fox's pessimism and Lauderdale was recalled. Talleyrand however refused to grant the necessary passports, evidently hoping to learn that the Russian court had accepted the new treaty with France which would give England second thoughts. In early September however news reached Paris that an angry Russian Czar had rejected the proposed treaty. This brought renewed negotiations with Lauderdale, but Fox's death in mid September again changed matters. When Napoleon still refused to accept British control of Sicily, Lauderdale returned to England. With the pro-war faction back in Whitehall any hope of peace with France ceased.

French relations with Prussia were also deteriorating. First had come an ugly scuffle when Marshal Joachim (Murat), the newly named grand-duke of Cleves and Berg, had tried to absorb some nearby territory, an effort effectively challenged by old General Blücher whose troops tore down Murat's proclamation. Murat worsened matters by complaining to King Frederick William whom he addressed in the regal style as "my brother" (which brought a stinging rebuke from Napoleon). Then, in mid July, Napoleon announced the formation of a new confederation of the Rhine composed of 16 German rulers with himself as protector, an unsettling development for Berlin only partially ameliorated by his willingness for Prussia to form a North German confederation.

These affairs were being exploited by the vocal anti-French war party in Berlin – the militant Count Hardenberg had been reinstituted as foreign minister – when the Prussian king learned that Talleyrand had secretly agreed to restore Hanover to England. This was too much even for the vapid Frederick William who now gained Czar Alexander's promise of military aid if Prussia went to war against France. He followed this *démarche* by opening the blocked North Sea river mouths to British ships and by asking England to sign a peace treaty and provide money while he mobilized his army.

Napoleon paid little attention to what he termed bizarre Prussian behavior. He repeatedly stressed to his ministers that he did not want a war with Prussia, and he ordered his marshals in Germany to avoid offending Prussian officials and to always speak highly of the Prussian king. On the other hand, he kept his corps uncomfortably close to Prussian borders and continued to convert Wesel, which many Prussians considered the key to North Germany, into a strongly defended garrison town.

Nor did he make any secret of his control of southern Germany. Annoyed at the spread of anti-French inflammatory pamphlets he warned of harsh measures if these were not suppressed. In late August he made his point by the arrest of a Nuremburg bookseller named Palm who was tried by a French military court for selling seditious literature and shot as a traitor. Palm's sudden demise caused much head-shaking among members of the new Rhenish confederation, and it also provided the Berlin war party with further proof of what it termed French barbarism.

King Frederick William meanwhile, having won Russia's promise of military support, was persuaded by the militant Queen Louise and her bellicose courtiers to demand evacuation of French troops from Germany. Taken with the Russian court's rejection of the proposed treaty with France, this development brought a change of mind at St. Cloud. Plans to evacuate these troops were canceled, a new class of conscripts was called up and troop commanders were ordered to make detailed reconnaissances of Germany and Prussia from Bamberg to Berlin.

Napoleon still did not want war with Prussia but daily it became more likely. "Prussian movements continue to be very extraordinary," he wrote Berthier on 10 September. "They want to be taught a lesson."[5] But two days later he wrote to the Prussian monarch, pointing to the evil lies offered up by the Berlin war party in order to bring on a "sacrilegious war" that could only serve the purpose of "our enemies."[6] At the same time however he warned the departing Prussian ambassador that "if your young officers and your women at Berlin want war, I am preparing to satisfy them." He also warned the Berlin and Saxon courts that Saxony must not mobilize and Prussian troops must not enter Saxony.[7]

Upon learning a week later that Prussian troops had moved into Saxony, he ordered his marshals in Germany to carry out battle deployments that would stretch from Mainz on the Rhine eastward up the twisting Main river some 200 miles to Bamberg. Master of the Horse General Caulaincourt was to prepare the imperial equipage – "my small cabriolet of war", several wagon-loads of clothes and equipment that included his "strong tent with iron cot and carpets", and an assortment of field glasses.[8] At end of September he and Joséphine departed for Mainz.

Wars generally begin because of irrational acts by one or both of the opponents. King Frederick William's decision to make war on France in autumn of 1806 was so irrational as to defy belief. It might have seemed reasonable prior to the battle of Austerlitz when the Grand Army was heavily committed in Austria, though considering the obsolete state of the Prussian army that would have been far from certain. Now, nine months later, it was a fore-ordained disaster.

The Prussian army's tactical decadence had begun even before Frederick the Great's death.[9] It was ingloriously exposed at Valmy in 1792 when a French revolutionary army of mostly untrained volunteers forced the old duke of Brunswick to yield all his gains in favor of hurried retreat back to Belgium.

Fourteen years on, the army was still too big and too heavy, its columns like those of Austria and Russia marching only a few miles a day, their existence tied to thousands of cumbersome supply wagons. Tactically it was living in the dark ages, its recruits armed with obsolete muskets and drilled in automated rhythms following rigid geometrical precepts that took forever and a day to move from location A to location B, then to deploy in stiff, inflexible lines before firing volleys against volleys fired from an enemy's equally stiff, inflexible lines. Since this was a costly business in lives most commanders preferred to remain in reasonably safe cantonments remote from the battlefield.

Senior Prussian commanders were a sorry lot. King Frederick William, 36 years old, was commander in chief, but knew nothing of war except that he hadn't wanted one against Napoleon. He had been supported in this pacific intention by his senior field commander, the 71-year-old duke of Brunswick. Other commanders, the 64-year-old Blücher, Prince Hohenlohe, General von Schmettau (and Queen Louise) did want war with France as did foreign minister Count Hardenberg. Hohenlohe, Prince Louis Ferdinand (who nightly was carried to bed drunk), Kalkreuth and others not only wanted war, they demanded it and took every opportunity to persuade their king to become the liberator of Germany, pointing to Frederick the Great's victories – in particular at Rossbach where the Prussians eliminated an entire French army. They were supported by hosts of colonels, majors, captains and lieutenants (no one else counted in Prussia) who for the most part were tactical marionettes, poorly schooled both in general and in their *métier*, far more interested in flaunting elegant uniforms and chased swords in Berlin's high society than in coming to grips with a proper study of war. This did not hinder a pathetic belief in the superiority of their arms; thus one stupid colonel who preferred cudgels to sabers, thus officious lieutenants who noisily sharpened their swords on the stone steps of the French embassy in Berlin.[10]

These patriots were assisted in their desire for war by Napoleon's arrogance, by his inept execution of the Nuremburg bookseller, Palm, by the magic effect of English gold, by the presumed promise of Russian troops and by their king's flaccid character which made him bend like a reluctant willow in bellicose winds.

So Prussia went to war with an obsolete army, its marshals and generals at each other's throats, each insisting on his own convoluted plan of operations though none with the slightest notion of Napoleon's plans. With Brunswick not wanting to march, and the hawks screaming for action, the quarrels became so intense that the king took field command – his adviser the 82-year-old Field

Marshal von Möllendorf, his chief of staff a quarrelsome tripartite effort by generals Schwarzenberg, Phull and Massenbach (each of whom held the others in contempt), his division staffs virtually non-existent.

The king's army which a few months earlier counted 190,000 now mustered around 150,000 effectives (soon to be augmented by 20,000 Saxons) since for political reasons he refused to call up East Prussian reserves. He might have fended off a French attack with this force had he remained behind the Elbe river to wait for Russian help or promised aid from England. Fox's death however postponed positive English action. A Prussian officer sent to St. Petersburg to coordinate army movements brought no operations plan which caused Alexander to back off from his commitment. The Austrian court revenged itself on Prussian refusal to earlier join the Third Coalition by refusing to even consider a supporting move until a Prussian-Russian army had won a victory.

That was the situation when the Prussian army deployed *west* of the Elbe with the apparent intention of attacking the French corps in central Germany. In late September, Brunswick with 70,000 men was deployed between Leipzig and Naumburg, Hohenlohe with 50,000 around Dresden; Rüchel with 30,000 at Mühlhausen, with Blücher's cavalry at Göttingen.

What now?

Brunswick wanted "to move by Erfurt on Würzburg" to cut French communications. Hohenlohe "violently" opposed this plan, opting instead for a push on Bamberg, having already sent Tauenzien's Saxony division to Hof as an advance guard. The argument went on for several days with no real conclusion, one council of war after another submitting conflicting plans.[11] One of Prussia's few qualified generals, Gerhard von Scharnhorst, Hohenlohe's 51-year-old chief of staff, said it all: "What we ought to do I know right well, what we shall do only the gods know."[12]

The French army moved out in early October, Napoleon's aim being "to debouch into Saxony . . . in three columns" through the dense forest, the *Thüringerwald*: Murat's cavalry in the lead; on the right Soult's corps followed by Ney's and a Bavarian division, some 50,000 troops, target, Hof; in the center Bernadotte and Davout's corps and the Guard, more than 70,000 strong, target, Saalburg-Schleiz; on the left Lannes followed by Augereau's corps, over 40,000 men, target, Coburg-Gräfenthal-Saalfeld – altogether a massive advance on a northeast axis, destination Dresden, but with a new and very inventive tactical innovation, 200,000 men marching, in Napoleon's term, *à la bataillon carré* – like a battalion square.[13]

To no one's great surprise the various movements came off more or less as ordered although Napoleon, briefly out of touch with Lannes and Augereau on his left, suffered anxious moments since he correctly believed the bulk of Prussian strength to center on Erfurt. After Soult on the right overran some enemy outposts while moving on Hof, the first real blood was drawn by Murat and Bernadotte who crossed the Saale to fall on Tauenzien's mixed command of Saxons and Prussians near Schleiz, taking a good many prisoners while forcing this division to fall back on Hohenlohe's corps at Mittel-Pölnitz. Meanwhile the elusive Lannes drove his corps through thick woods to fall on Prince Louis Ferdinand's corps at Saalfeld, a short and vicious battle (in which General Suchet once again distinguished himself) and a major defeat for Prussia with the prince's death and heavy casualties including nearly 10,000 men taken prisoner.

The enemy, as perhaps Napoleon guessed, was as confused as ever and even more discouraged by recent losses, Prince Louis' death and the continuing French advance. Hohenlohe on the left retreated from Kahla to Jena. The king and the duke of Brunswick, still with most of the army at Erfurt, learned on 12 October that the French had occupied Naumburg northeast of Auerstädt. A council of war now decided on a general retreat to the Elbe via Auerstädt and Halle. Hohenlohe and Rüchel's corps were to form the rearguard west of Jena – a purely defensive mission that prevented Hohenlohe from occupying the Landgrafenberg (the high ground overlooking Jena) in force.[14]

Napoleon had hoped to be attacked by the enemy north of Schleiz, but when events outpaced this, he pushed Soult followed by his other columns toward Gera where he believed the enemy would try to shift its main force. Informed that the Prussians were still at Erfurt, it was a matter of making slight adjustments in case they gave battle there or retired north on Magdeburg fortress. Accordingly Murat's cavalry and Davout and Bernadotte's corps were ordered to Naumburg on the Salle from where they could either block a Prussian movement to the north or, in case of battle at Erfurt, turn the Prussian left wing.

Shortly before departing from Auma on 12 October, Napoleon wrote Talleyrand that things were going exactly as he had calculated two months ago in Paris: "The [Prussian] generals are great imbeciles. One can not conceive how the supposedly talented duke of Brunswick can have directed the operations of this army in such a ridiculous manner." Davout's advance guard had now reached Naumburg, Murat was at Zeitz, Lannes at Jena and other corps were closing on the area. From Gera, Napoleon replied to a letter from the Prussian king at Erfurt, once again pointing to the idiocy of this war and begging the king to back off.[15]

Here at Gera he received reports from Augereau at Kahla south of Jena, from Davout at Naumburg (where he had captured the Prussian supply magazines and a magnificent pontoon bridge train) and from Murat at Zeitz that the Prussian columns were all falling back on Erfurt. "The curtain is finally drawn," he wrote Murat, "the enemy begins his retreat on Magdeburg." Murat was to join Bernadotte at Dornburg as soon as possible while sending his heavy cavalry to support Lannes. If Lannes were attacked, as Napoleon supposed he would be, Murat and Bernadotte were to come to his aid from Dornburg while Soult and Ney hurried up from the southeast.[16]

Napoleon arrived at Jena in mid afternoon to find Hohenlohe's rearguard, anywhere from 12–15,000 men according to Lannes, occupying the plateau of the Landgrafenberg above the town. Responding to this development and hoping to have his big battle at last, Napoleon decided to deploy Lannes' corps and the Guard on the plateau, the idea being to hold the enemy center while Augereau hit Tauenzien's right flank from Kahla, and Soult followed by Ney his left flank. Davout meanwhile was to march on Apolda to complete the encirclement. If Bernadotte were at Naumburg he could march with Davout, but Napoleon hoped that he was at Dornburg from where he could easily support Lannes and the Guard if necessary.[17] Napoleon's letter to the Prussian king was handed over to General Prince Hohenlohe in late afternoon – the king would not receive it until battle had started the next morning.[18]

Getting troops onto the plateau was not easy. A narrow trail up the steep slope had to be widened (shades of Switzerland-Italy) to allow the artillery to pass. Napoleon spent part of the night, lantern in hand, supervising this work which would result in several thousand troops occupying an area scarcely large enough for a battalion. Other troops spent the night boiling sugar and wine found in the deserted town, getting steadily drunker with each sardonic toast to the Prussian king – each grenadier would carry three bottles into battle, two in the folds of his headgear and one in his pack.

14 October, dawn: in thick, cold fog Napoleon rode the line, drawing some fire before the first regiments debouched onto the plain, Suchet on the right, Gazan on the left. They were greeted by artillery fire. "The Prussians have a cold and are coughing," growled one veteran, "we must take them some sugared wine."[19] Soult's advance guard came up on Suchet's right and Augereau on Gazan's left to form about a mile and a half of front, room enough for the center corps to take up attack positions on the flat ground.

Hohenlohe had been fooled. Believing that the main French army was marching north and that he was facing a flank guard, he was rudely surprised when the fog lifted in mid morning to see

Tauenzien's fleeing Saxons emerging from the mist in full flight from French troops on his front and flanks. Bringing up what reinforcements he commanded, he sent for help from Rüchel and in waiting for it to arrive held the bulk of his force in open ground to be shattered by the French firing from cover. With the enemy everywhere reeling, in early afternoon Napoleon ordered a general advance joined by his reserve of over 40,000 troops – an infantry-cavalry-artillery behemoth over 90,000 strong that soon put Hohenlohe's surviving units in full retreat. Rüchel's corps arrived only in mid afternoon and bravely defied all tactical odds by proceeding to counter-attack, a brief effort horribly shattered, Rüchel himself mortally wounded, his legacy a desperate situation beyond repair.

The battle was over by 4 p.m. before half the French soldiers had even fired their muskets. It was a matter now of pursuit, Murat's cavalry in the lead. By nightfall Augereau and Ney's divisions were in Weimar, Soult's corps in Schwabsdorf four miles to the northeast. Napoleon meanwhile had policed the battlefield tending to evacuation of the wounded before returning to Jena from where he could scarcely wait to spread the news. At last, he believed, he had fought his "decisive battle" to win an enormous victory in crushing the *entire* Prussian army. The intoxication lasted only until an officer arrived with sobering news from Marshal Davout's headquarters: Napoleon had fought but one portion of the enemy, leaving Davout to cope with the remainder.

Neither Napoleon nor Davout knew that on the day prior to the battle of Jena, King Frederick William, his militant queen (riding the line garbed as a hussar), the duke of Brunswick and some 70,000 soldiers had departed from Weimar to begin a withdrawal to Magdeburg fortress, the first stop having been Auerstädt, a town about 22 miles southwest of Davout's camp at Naumburg.

That evening a brush with Prussian cavalry patrols gained Davout a few prisoners from whom he learned of the massive

Prussian presence not far away. This intelligence obviously voided Napoleon's earlier orders to march on Apolda. Davout and Bernadotte's mission was now to block or at least contest the enemy march northward. Bernadotte's headquarters were just south of Naumburg with his divisions spread further south along the road to Dornburg. Despite Davout's frantic pleas for support, Bernadotte refused to join him in marching on Auerstädt, preferring instead to move his headquarters to Dornburg where he arrived the next morning.

Davout's corps, only 26,000 strong including 1,500 horse and a mere 44 cannon, marched early on 14 October, three divisions commanded by Gudin in the lead, followed by Friant and Morant, each of whose name deserves respect. They met the enemy on Hassenhausen plain around 8 a.m. when from out of the fog galloped 600 of Blücher's cavalry followed by Schmettau's infantry with Wartensleben's division still in the rear. While the Prussian king conferred with old Marshal Möllendorf (soon to be taken prisoner), his staff and generals, the fog lifted to reveal Gudin's demi-brigades which immediately became the target of an impulsive and ill-timed assault by Blücher's cavalry. Gudin's men, hastily formed into battalion squares, repulsed not one but four charges each 2,500 strong.

Friant's division meanwhile came up on Gudin's right. Enemy divisions also arrived to attack left of the village to force Davout to commit his only reserve, a single regiment. It performed well. Schmettau was killed and the duke of Brunswick mortally wounded. The Prussians never recovered. Although fighting remained intense there was probably no force in the world that could have withstood the frantic fury of the French as they routed battalion after battalion, division after division.

King Frederick William still held sufficient troops to have kept on with the battle, but shortly before noon he decided to fall back on Hohenlohe's army to fight again the following day. Great was his surprise to find only panic-stricken fugitives instead of whole Prussian regiments. Perhaps with Napoleon's warnings ringing secretly in the royal ears, the king ordered a general retreat northward. He left behind 10,000 dead soldiers, another 3,000 taken prisoner.[20]

There are several postscripts. Davout's corps wrote one of the most brilliant chapters in military history, Bernadotte's one of the most dismal. Attacked by an enemy nearly three times his strength, in just 4½ hours Davout put that enemy in flight. Success cost dearly: 40 per cent casualties in Gudin's division, a total corps loss of 7,000 men.[21] Bernadotte's corps suffered no casualties. Although his orders were, should he find himself at Dornburg, to march to the sound of cannon, he marched to support neither Davout nor Napoleon but rather to Apolda where he arrived after the two battles were over. Napoleon praised the one and damned the other,[22] but in so doing added yet another footnote. Never ever would he refer to the battle as other than that of Jena.

Notes

1   Corr. XIII. Nr. 11005, Jena, 15 October 1806.
2   Corr. XII. Nr. 10339, St. Cloud, 9 June 1806.
3   Corr. XII. Nrs. 10528, St. Cloud, 20 July 1806; 10529, 10536, St. Cloud, 21 July 1806; 10539, St. Cloud, 22 July 1806. See also Rose (*Life*), II, 71 ff.
4   Bryant (*Victory*), 200; Rose (*Life*), II, 81–2.
5   Corr. XIII. Nr. 10757, St. Cloud, 10 September 1806.
6   Corr. XIII. Nr. 10764, St. Cloud, 12 September 1806.
7   Rose (*Life*), II, 88. See also Corr. XIII, Nrs. 10765, 10766, St. Cloud, 12 September 1806.
8   Corr. XIII. Nr. 10759, St. Cloud, 10 September 1806.
9   Asprey (*Frederick the Great*), 629 ff.
10   Görlitz, 26.
11   Fuller, II, 419–21.
12   Fuller, II, 420–4. See also Lettow-Vorbeck, 163; Wartenburg, I, 275–6, whose figures of Prussian strength are considerably less; Chandler (*Napoleon*), 454–6.

13   Corr. XIII. Nr. 10941, Würzburg, 5 October 1806. See also
     Wartenburg, I, 273–7; Chandler (*Napoleon*), 467 ff.
14   Fuller, II, 429.
15   Corr. XIII. Nrs. 10989, Auma, 12 October 1806; 10990, Gera, 12
     October 1806.
16   Corr. XIII. Nr. 11000, Gera, 13 October 1806.
17   Fuller, II, 430–1.
18   Corr. XIII. Nr. 11064, Wittenberg, 23 October 1806.
19   Marbot, I, 296–8; Coignet, 83–5.
20   Savary, II, 269–83; Fuller, 420–3; Wartenburg, I, 267–302;
     Chandler (*Napoleon*), 467–506.
21   Fuller, II, 440.
22   Corr. XIII. Nrs. 11009, Jena, 15 October 1806; 11041, Halle, 21
     October 1806; 11060, Wittenberg, 23 October 1806. See also
     Savary, II, 292; Marbot, I, 302–4.

CHAPTER FOUR

THE POLISH ADVENTURE – I:
THE BATTLE OF PULTUSK
OCTOBER–DECEMBER 1806

*It rained and snowed incessantly. Provisions became very
scarce; no more wine, hardly any beer . . . muddy water, no
bread, and quarters for which we had to fight with the pigs
and the cows.*

Captain Marcellin Bon de Marbot[1]

NAPOLEON WAS NOT yet finished with Prussia. A fast and furious
pursuit in all directions captured thousands of stunned troops.
Erfurt fell almost immediately, then Halle where the Prussian
reserve commanded by Prince Eugène of Württemberg was all
but destroyed. Dessau was seized, the ancient fortress of
Magdeburg surrounded, then Wittenberg, Berlin, Spandau,
Stettin. Davout's corps seized Leipzig, bridged the Elbe and
marched on toward the Oder. Far to the west King Louis Bonaparte
marched from Weser to Hameln as prelude to occupying
Hanover.

The emperor was in seventh heaven, almost daily sending exuberant victory bulletins to Paris, stopping briefly to tour the
ancient battlefield of Rossbach and to avenge Frederick the
Great's humiliating victory over the French in 1757 by having
the Prussian commemorative column torn down and sent to
Paris.[2] Following hard on the whirlwind advance of his various
corps he kept a stable of aides galloping off with fresh orders,
encouraging words, punishments for marauding troops and camp
followers, cautions not to run horses to death and, in Bernadotte's

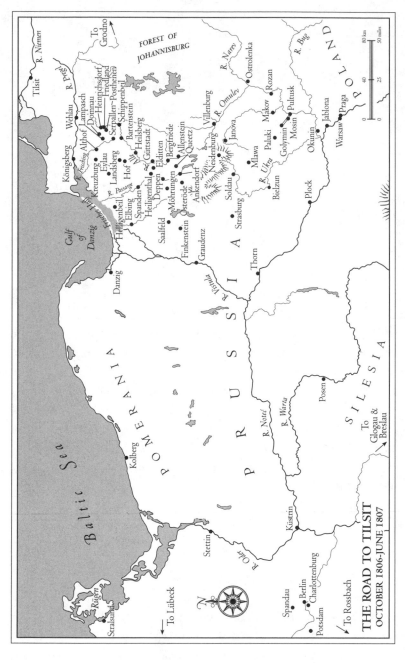

The Road to Tilsit October 1806 – June 1807

THE ROAD TO TILSIT
OCTOBER 1806-JUNE 1807

case, a burning chastisement for his failure to act during the battle of Jena and for not carrying out the more recent orders.[3] He replied sympathetically to a request for peace from the elector of Saxony but brusquely refused the Prussian king's request for an armistice in order to bury his dead: "Deal with the living and leave us the job of burying the dead. There is no need of a truce for that."[4]

In just over a week Napoleon was in Potsdam paying reverence to Frederick the Great's tomb which Czar Alexander had blessed with a kiss a year earlier – the visit that turned Queen Louise of Prussia into a female Mars whose mission was to eliminate France from planet Earth. Napoleon quickly transferred reverence to Frederick's *schloss* and to Sans Souci from where he pilfered the royal sword, the Order of the Black Eagle and the standards of the Potsdam Guards, all of which went to Paris for inspirational display in the Invalides.[5] (He also snitched Frederick's silver alarm clock which many years later would tinkle away in his bedroom on St. Helena island.) He was thoroughly enjoying himself, the weather was beautiful, a delegation of Berlin's most important civilians presented him with the keys of the city while swearing their innocence and pinning the war on Queen Louise, Prince Louis Ferdinand, Blücher, Schmettau, Rüchel and others. He soon left Potsdam for Charlottenburg palace and a triumphal entry into Berlin, stopping to salute a statue of the great Frederick. King Frederick William meanwhile had crossed the Vistula river with 10–20,000 survivors to establish his court in Graudenz and face the extent of his defeat.

It was enormous. By month's end the French claimed tens of thousands of prisoners including more than twenty generals. The duke of Weimar was on the run, as was General Blücher. Over 100 standards had been captured, 600 cannon, numerous strong-boxes of hard cash, several thousand horses with saddles, millions of francs' worth of food, wine, brandy, beer, supplies, munitions and equipment.[6] English merchandise seized at Leipzig brought an offer from local merchants of 60 million francs; so plentiful was English cloth that Napoleon ordered new uniforms made for the entire army.[7]

In early November, General Blücher who had inherited the duke of Weimar's fugitive corps (the duke wisely having retired to his estates) and who was locked in Lübeck would succumb to the combined storm of Bernadotte and Soult's corps to surrender 20,000 more soldiers, not to mention untold treasures to the French troops. A few days later Magdeburg, the last important fortress west of the Oder river, surrendered its garrison of 16,000 troops and hundreds of cannon plus an immense amount of treasure to Marshal Ney. This prize brought the tally of prisoners to 140,000, of whom Napoleon planned to send half to France to work on the roads and in the fields and as many others to Spain as Prince Godoy would like.

Napoleon meanwhile had received scores of couriers from around the empire, issued dozens of new orders, reviewed numerous divisions, promoted many worthy soldiers. With great delight he announced the obliteration of Hesse-Cassel and the addition of its states and treasury to the French crown. A plea from captured officers of the Prussian Guard – those who a few weeks earlier had sharpened their swords on the steps of the French embassy in Berlin – to avoid being paraded through Berlin was maliciously if understandably denied; indeed they were marched past the French embassy to the secret delight of those Berlin citizens who had not wanted war.[8] He also ordered the courtmartial of Count Hatzfeld who, having been appointed interim governor of Berlin, had foolishly informed General Hohenlohe of French army activities. The man was within hours of being shot when his attractive wife gained a suppliant audience with the emperor. Falling victim to her abundant tears, Napoleon gave her the only hard evidence against her husband, a letter, and told her to throw it in the fire. Hatzfeld went free and Napoleon felt better for it.

He was not so sympathetic concerning Queen Louise – "how unfortunate are princes who allow women to influence political affairs."[9] Not unnaturally Joséphine took exception to this sentiment and was rewarded with a semi-placatory, semi-warning reply: "It is true that I hate intriguing females above all else. I am accustomed to nice women, gentle and conciliatory. They are the ones I love." In his defense he cited his submission to the Countess Hatzfeld: "You see, then, that I love good women, naïve and gentle, those alone who resemble you." Joséphine probably did not appreciate the flattery. Bored to death in Mainz she wished either for them to return to Paris or that she come to Berlin. Napoleon sympathized with her but claimed that the trip would be too arduous and dangerous. Paris was out of the question for him, he explained in mid November, because he had too much to do where he was.[10]

This was an understatement. Two weeks earlier he had ordered Marshal Davout to march on Posen, the first step on the road to the Vistula river where he proposed to meet and defeat the Russian army.

Prussia's almost total demise brought the makings of a fourth coalition against the French barbarians. Once again Austria was secretly arming. Archduke Charles at Prague commanded a force estimated at 60–80,000 strong and Viennese officials were sending letters to St. Petersburg announcing that all of Naples and Italy had risen in insurrection, that Marshal Masséna had been killed and other such imaginative tidbits, a propaganda campaign that drew a warning from Napoleon to Emperor Francis to cease and desist.[11] War with Austria was possible, Napoleon informed King Joseph in Naples, adding that Russia would concentrate its forces in Poland while England supported its ally Sweden.[12]

Russia was the immediate threat. Napoleon had learned that the commander in chief of the Russian army, a 61-year-old trans-planted Brunswickian, General Leonty von Bennigsen, was leading a force of four columns into Poland. Each column, marching on a separate route, consisted of 14,000 infantry, cavalry and artillery, a total 56,000 men (which Napoleon reckoned would be reduced to no more than 50,000 by attrition from a 40-day march). If news of the French victory of Jena-Auerstädt did not upset the Russian plan, Napoleon expected the columns to converge on Thorn by 18 November at the earliest. Meanwhile he would concentrate the rest of his army at Posen on the Warta river from where if necessary he could easily retire on Stettin or Küstrin which were hurriedly being fortified.

Napoleon's position vis-à-vis Russia strengthened during November. Davout's advance guard, a regiment of chasseurs, was received in Posen "with an enthusiasm difficult to portray."[13] Polish patriots from the richest nobles to the poorest peasants were rebelling against Prussian and Russian rule and were allegedly raising an army 60,000 strong. Prussian resistance having vanished, Murat's cavalry and three infantry corps commanded by Ney, Soult and Bernadotte were freed for a new campaign. Davout's corps had reached Posen on 10 November. Jérôme Bonaparte's corps on Davout's right was preparing to march on and besiege Silesian fortresses. Lannes' corps on his left was marching on Thorn northeast of Posen. Marshal Mortier's corps occupied Hamburg and would soon control the rich Hanseatic ports.

French diplomats meanwhile had met with their Prussian opposites to hammer out an armistice sent to King Frederick William (now in Königsberg) for ratification.[14] Napoleon with good reason regarded the Prussian campaign as finished, a magnificent victory earlier celebrated by slapping a contribution of 150 million francs on the Prussian states.[15]

Why was Napoleon not content to enjoy his striking victory, place his deserving army in winter quarters, send for Joséphine and spend a few relaxing months in Berlin?

The suggested answer is complex, consisting as it does of diverse political, strategic, tactical and personal factors. Napoleon could not afford to sit still until he had obtained a general peace. Everything was subordinate to this overall objective which was stated in an army bulletin of mid November published in Paris and elsewhere: "The French army will leave Berlin only when the colonial possessions of the Spanish, Dutch and French are returned to them, and total peace reigns."[16]

To emphasize this demand he startled Europe and especially England by publishing a decree that prohibited France, its satellite states and by indirection its allies from engaging in "all commerce and all correspondence with the British Isles." As England was blockading France, so France would blockade England. All English ships in French ports would be seized with their cargoes, all English merchandise in countries controlled by France would be confiscated as legitimate prizes and all Englishmen arrested and held as prisoners-of-war. Henceforth continental ports were closed to English ships or to vessels carrying English merchandise.[17]

This was the etiology of what is historically known as the "Continental System" – in Napoleon's words, "I wish to conquer the sea by the land."[18] But so long as Russia, Sweden and Prussia remained at war with France, Napoleon did not command the land. Since Sweden and Prussia would count for nothing without Russia, it was necessary to defeat Russia militarily.

All well and good, but why forsake the comforts of Berlin for the discomforts of inhospitable Poland? To remain in Berlin, Napoleon reasoned, would allow Bennigsen's Russians to fortify the line of the Vistula river which would greatly hinder a new campaign, not only from the resistance standpoint but because hungry Russians would eat the land bare. A delay would also free Russian troops in Moldavia and Valachia, the Danube principalities, to move against a weak and indecisive Turkish sultan.

Napoleon was aware of numerous disadvantages in continuing the campaign. He held only a vague notion of Russian intentions and strength. He was warned of treacherous weather, far worse than anything experienced in Moravia; of innumerable rivers, lakes, ponds, marshes and forests that had to be crossed; of sudden vicious frosts followed by thaws and heavy rains that turned crude roads into impassable seas of mud; of a generally barren land. He was also warned of a high human attrition rate; his own supply lines were attenuated, the new provinces not yet organized to feed the maw of war. Some units lacked proper uniforms for war in a cold climate, most units lacked sufficient shoes

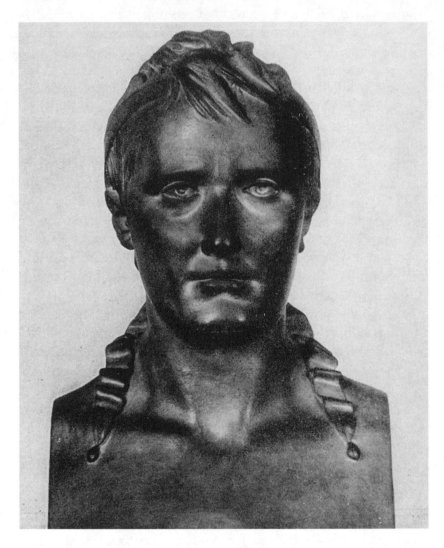

Napoleon as Emperor

for the slog ahead. "We have passed the most beautiful season," Napoleon wrote Lannes, "and henceforth a pair of shoes will not last ten days."[19] The troops were already short of shoes, the divisions needed physicians, surgeons, orderlies and medicines. The army was still tired – not only soldiers but officers and generals for the most part did not want to go into Poland, particularly in winter.

Napoleon paid scant attention to these and other potential pitfalls. He had decided on a mission and that was that. Bad weather? The late October days were beautiful, obviously a prolonged autumn. Tired soldiers? Over half of them had not fired a round in the recent campaign. High attrition rate? Nothing that new conscripts could not repair – he would call up the 100,000 men slated for 1807 in January instead of in autumn. Bad roads? The French soldier could march anywhere. He had 200,000 of the best, *capotes* would somehow be provided, shoes would be made, the troops would eat off the land; his cavalry were remounted on Prussian horses, he had just added 1,000 more troopers to Murat's columns, eight regiments of horse were coming from Italy. The enemy? Fifty thousand at most, poorly trained and armed soldiers commanded by inefficient and lazy officers. To cap matters he did not expect battle, all he wanted was to reach the Vistula, take up winter quarters and rest the troops until the opening of the spring campaign.

Napoleon left Berlin in late November. Three days later he learned that King Frederick William had rejected the proposed armistice on grounds that he was allied with Russia whose troops were already in Poland and that he was powerless to intervene. This decision was more annoying than surprising – the king's last hope rested on a Russian victory. Regarding it as still another nail in Prussia's coffin, Napoleon blithely continued on to Posen where in early December he established imperial headquarters.

His advance corps had met few enemy and those few had retired as the French approached. The weather admittedly had been capricious. Beautiful autumnal days had suddenly given way to heavy rain that predictably converted crude roads into swamps to slow and often halt marches. Murat's cavalry none the less reached Warsaw in late November, the Russians hastily retiring to the northeast without destroying the bridge over the Vistula. Davout immediately set up a strong bridgehead at the suburb of Praga while Milhaud's light cavalry moved on the river Bug. Davout's engineers bridged this river at Okunin, set up another strong bridgehead and established outposts on the right bank of the Bug, the Russian General Bennigsen having reached Pultusk.

Soult's corps meanwhile closed on Thorn, a fortress about 120 miles downstream on the right bank of the Vistula defended by General Lestocq's greatly weakened corps, perhaps 6,000 troops, the only remaining force of the Prussian army. As Augereau and Lannes' corps arrived to be followed by Ney and Bernadotte, Soult and Augereau marched upstream. Thorn soon fell to Lannes who moved on Strasburg 35 miles to the northeast. By mid December the right bank of the Vistula was secure.

Napoleon's initial intention was to place the army in winter quarters *behind* the Vistula. But now he decided to bring Bennigsen to battle. A powerful corps of heavy cavalry led by Marshal Bessières and followed by Ney's corps moved to support Soult's march up the Vistula to clear the way to the Ukra river and set the stage for the final act, the encirclement of Bennigsen's Russians. The plan looked good on paper. While Soult and Bernadotte cut enemy communications with fortress Königsberg, Augereau's corps would attack Bennigsen from the west as Davout's infantry and Murat's cavalry struck from the east.

This was roughly the situation in mid December when Napoleon left Posen for Warsaw.

From Napoleon's standpoint everything seemed to be going quite well. Unlike his wet, tired and hungry soldiers he had not yet come to grips with the terrain and weather other than to grumble about the rain in letters to Joséphine.

The Empress Joséphine

He had been rapturously received in Posen. An important Polish delegation had called on him from Warsaw, "animated with the best will," he informed Prince Cambacérès. ". . . They show a great desire to recover their independence: the nobility, the clergy, the peasants are as one."[20] Life in Posen was passable. Some Milanese musicians were on hand to perform evening concerts, the kind citizens had honored him with a ball on the anniversary of Austerlitz.

Joséphine was very much on his mind. "I love you and want you . . . These nights here are long all alone."[21] He now agreed that she could come to Berlin once he returned from "a tour" of Poland.[22]

This tour was becoming considerably more complicated by the day. The Vistula country was not rich and could not feed his huge army. He had soon ordered chief quartermaster Daru to buy 2.5 million pounds of wheat and 100,000 bushels of oats in Galicia, along with livestock and other provisions. The troops lacked heavy clothing and, as he had been warned, above all shoes. "Shoes! Shoes!" he frantically wrote General Clarke, governor of Berlin. ". . . Pay the closest attention to this matter."[23] Similar orders went to Daru and Bertrand. "We very much need blankets and mattresses," he wrote Bertrand. "Make new arrangements for shoes before you depart."[24] Surgeons and hospital orderlies were in short supply, he complained to Daru. "There is not one doctor here . . . It seems that they [physicians and surgeons] are on one side and the army on the other."[25]

These serious shortages were understandably telling on troop morale. Once departed from Posen, Napoleon heard numerous complaints from the troops that would become a litany. He had heard them all before, in Italy, Egypt, Austria, Moravia, Germany. Grumblers, he good-naturedly called them – les grognards – a name that would stick: they would just have to put up with the situation until the army took up winter quarters.[26]

Winter quarters were still far distant. Napoleon's knowledge of the enemy remained sketchy at best. A second Russian army, some

35,000 troops commanded by General Buxhöwden, had meanwhile joined Bennigsen's army at Pultusk – as had a new commander in chief, the 76-year-old Marshal Kamenski who was rapidly fading in mind and body.[27] He nevertheless moved his divisions west and south of Pultusk to defend the triangle northwest of Warsaw, an area bordered by the Ukra, Narev and Omulev rivers.

Finally aware of the Russian concentration, Napoleon ordered a somewhat modified offensive: Davout's corps to attack from the south across the Ukra while Augereau on his left struck about 20 miles upstream. Soult's corps was approaching on Augereau's left but was still considerably distant. Bessières' cavalry followed by Ney's infantry was to clear a front of some 40 miles defended by Lestocq's Prussians west of the river.

Bessières and Ney had the easiest task. Although the Prussians fought well they were greatly outnumbered and terribly alone. Driven from Bielzun by General Grouchy's aggressive cavalry while Ney struck Bülow's rearguard, they fell back on Soldau on the Ukra and then, pressed by Ney, began a final retreat to Neidenburg, having suffered heavy casualties and having lost contact with the Russians on their left.

The dirt end of the operational stick went to Davout and Augereau, each corps suffering heavy casualties in crossing the Ukra and pushing the defenders back on Pultusk. Davout's night attack ordered by Napoleon cost over an estimated 1,300 casualties while Augereau in forcing a crossing against Barclay de Tolly's Russians lost perhaps 500 men (including General Savary's brother, Colonel Savary of the grenadiers).[28]

By Christmas night the Prussians were in retreat to Neidenburg, the Russians to Golymin and Pultusk. Alarmed by the French advance and aware of his own losses Marshal Kamenski ordered a general retreat on Ostrolenka. Bennigsen with several divisions plus cavalry and Cossacks at Pultusk – 40–45,000 heads – refused the order. The old marshal shuffled off to Grodno, leaving his subordinate to establish a main line of defense about 2½ miles long between Pultusk on the left and Mosin wood on the right along the Pultusk-Golymin road.[29]

Lannes' corps of Suchet and Gazzan's divisions marched at 7 a.m., about an hour before daylight, on 26 December. Road conditions were horrible. "The country was clayish and cut by marshes . . . the cavalry, infantry and artillery were lost in the depths of mud," General Rapp later wrote.[30] A recent thaw followed by rain, sleet and snowstorms had turned the earth into a living hell. The troops slogged through freezing muck up to their knees, often hard put to escape from sucking marshes as they advanced slightly over a mile an hour. Cannon and caissons pulled by four times the usual number of horses slipped this way and that, often overturning to halt already snail-like movements.

Once Bennigsen's outposts had fallen back Lannes personally reconnoitered the enemy position. Such was the terrain configuration that he saw only Barclay de Tolly's cavalry on a ridge and the front of Bennigsen's wings, "the whole covered by the line of Cossacks in the intervening depression."[31] He saw neither the town nor the main defensive lines, nor had he any notion of Russian strength. Napoleon was under the impression that Pultusk was lightly held, thus Berthier's dispatch which Lannes received in mid morning stating that "the enemy's center is pierced." Lannes was to seize the Pultusk bridge and establish a bridgehead on the opposite side.[32]

Lannes attacked about an hour later to open a battle that no soldier on either side could ever forget. It was more a series of inconclusive individual struggles than a coordinated effort, the left, center and right being victorious one moment, doomed at another, lost in snowstorms, slaughtered by cavalry charges and blown to bits by cannon case shot – a horrible, ghastly day that did not end with darkness at 4 p.m. but continued for another four hours. Lannes might well have lost his entire corps but for the timely arrival of one of Davout's divisions on his left. As it was, what was left of the corps limped back to pre-attack lines while Bennigsen's Russians slipped off to begin a 22-mile retreat on Rozan.[33]

There was no victory. Lannes was believed to have suffered 7–10,000 casualties (he admitted to more than 2,200 and insisted that the Russians had lost 7,000). But neither Lannes nor Bennigsen nor their troops had anything to apologize for and plenty to be proud of. Both had grounds for complaint. Bennigsen blamed Buxhöwden for holding up reinforcements from Makov only 9 miles away, but this scarcely holds water in that Buxhöwden was obeying Marshal Kamenski's orders to retreat. Lannes had a better case since Napoleon had failed to realize that Pultusk was defended in strength.

Napoleon was the real loser because he had badly miscalculated. Believing the enemy to be on the run, he had ordered Soult to push in on Makov and Augereau and Murat to move on Golymin 12 miles northwest of Pultusk in order to seal off the Narev river from the Russian retreat. Owing to the weather and terrible condition of the roads Soult's advance guard got no further than Paluki. General Galitzin was defending Golymin not from choice but because his troops were too tired to march on to Makov. Although greatly outnumbered he fought hard and well, aided not least by the weather which prevented Augereau from bringing up his artillery.

This battle too lasted into darkness. "We thought the enemy had fifty thousand men," Murat wrote Napoleon.[34] As at Pultusk no one won. Napoleon had had enough. After announcing that the army would move into winter quarters north of the Vistula he returned to Warsaw, arriving late on the first day of the new year, 1807.

Notes

1 Petre, 54.
2 Corr. XIII. Nrs. 11029, Merseburg, 19 October 1806; 11060, Wittenberg, 23 October 1806; Savary, II, 292–3. See also Asprey (*Frederick the Great*), 468–73, for a brief account of the battle of Rossbach.
3 Corr. XIII. Nr. 11041, Halle, 21 October 1806. See also Chandler (*Napoleon*), 499.

 4   Corr. XIII. Nr. 11053, Dessau, 22 October 1806.

 5   Corr. XIII. Nr. 11094, Potsdam, 26 October 1806.

 6   Corr. XIII. Nrs. 11093, Potsdam, 26 October 1806; 11145, Berlin, 2 November 1806.

 7   Corr. XIII. Nrs. 11064, 11065, Wittenberg, 23 October 1806.

 8   Marbot, I, 307–8.

 9   Corr. XIII. Nr. 11097, Charlottenburg, 27 October 1806.

10   Corr. XIII. Nrs. 11191, Berlin, 6 November 1806; 11261, Berlin, 16 November 1806.

11   Corr. XIII. Nrs. 11088, Potsdam, 26 October 1806; 11194, Berlin, 7 November 1806.

12   Corr. XIII. Nr. 11173, Berlin, 4 November 1806.

13   Corr. XIII. Nr. 11200, Berlin, 7 November 1806.

14   Corr. XIII. Nr. 11277, Berlin, 17 November 1806.

15   Corr. XIII. Nr. 11223, Berlin, 9 November 1806.

16   Corr. XIII. Nr. 11283, Berlin, 21 November 1806.

17   Corr. XIII. Nr. 11283, Berlin, 21 November 1806. See also Savary, III, 15–19.

18   Corr. XIV. Nr. 11379, Posen, 3 December 1806.

19   Corr. XIII. Nr. 11182, Berlin, 5 November 1806.

20   Corr. XIII. Nr. 11318, Posen, 29 November 1806.

21   Corr. XIV. Nr. 11365, Posen, 2 December 1806.

22   Corr. XIV. Nr. 11310, Meseritz, 27 November 1806.

23   Corr. XIV. Nr. 11431, Posen, 10 December 1806.

24   Corr. XIV. Nr. 11451, Posen, 12 December 1806.

25   Corr. XIV. Nr. 11452, Posen, 12 December 1806.

26   Marbot, I, 288–9; Savary, III, 22–3; Coignet, 190–7.

27   Wartenburg, I, 321.

28   Marbot, I, 322–3; Petre, 82–7.

29   Petre, 90–115.

30   Marbot, I, 323–30; Petre, 93.

31   Petre, 94.

32   Petre, 95.

33   Petre, 96–103; Wartenburg, I, 317–26.

34   Petre, 115.

CHAPTER FIVE

THE POLISH ADVENTURE – II:
THE BATTLE OF EYLAU
FEBRUARY–MARCH 1807

What a massacre! And for nothing.

Marshal Michel Ney after inspecting the
battlefield at Eylau, 9 February 1807[1]

HER NAME WAS Marie Walewska, a 20-year-old Polish countess.
Her father had been killed in a rebellion against Russian rule when
she was 8; she was raised on a small country estate near Warsaw.
As Christine Sutherland tells us in her well-researched and
charming biography, times were exceptionally hard for her mother
who nevertheless educated her children as best she could. Marie
was tutored at home by a transplanted Lorrainer named Nicolas
Chopin (the father-to-be of the brilliant composer) who taught
her French, music, geography and history, a good education
topped off by a private school in Warsaw.[2]

At 16 she was, like hundreds of thousands of Poles, a firm
patriot incensed by the three partitions that earlier had eliminated Poland as a state, hating Prussia, Austria and Russia for
their crimes, seeing in Napoleon Bonaparte a savior who would
restore the country's independence. She was also a raving beauty,
blonde with beguiling blue eyes set off by exceptionally white
skin and dark curling eyelashes, soft inviting lips and an exquis-
itely slim, full-bosomed body. At her mother and brother's
insistence she had married a rich and powerful neighbor, Count
Anastase Walewski, the 71-year-old owner of a large estate, twice
married but widowed for ten years, and had borne him a boy, "a

Countess Marie Walewska

puny, delicate and sickly child who was immediately swept away from his mother by a crowd of elderly female relatives."[3]

Marie and Anastase were at their Warsaw mansion when Napoleon arrived in the capital. Despite Marie's voluntary work in hospitals now filling up with French sick and wounded, they led an active social life. Talleyrand and his dashing illegitimate son, Lieutenant Charles de Flahaut, had earlier been struck by the girl's beauty and her fervent patriotism and trust in France. Talleyrand wanted an independent Poland, just as he had wanted a peaceful relationship with Austria, as a bulwark against Russia. Perhaps he believed that this lovely young lady could steer Napoleon toward this goal – at any rate he went to considerable trouble to ensure that the Waleswskis were invited to the imperial reception in January.

Upon her being presented, Napoleon complimented her beauty. At a ball a few nights later he arranged for her to partner him in a formal French *contre-danse* after which he did not take his eyes off her. Napoleon was smitten. The past months had been lonely, Joséphine was in Mainz. He was 36 years old. The recent campaign had been disappointing. Things were not going well with the army. There were difficult supply problems, the Poles were beginning to resent French requisitions. Napoleon needed love and solace in the soft arms of a beautiful woman and he turned to a courtship of juvenile love letters, heaps of flowers and expensive jewelry, all formally delivered by the stern and unbending Marshal Duroc. Marie at first rebuffed his approaches but, pressed by her family, women friends and even her husband, soon gave in and began spending nights in an apartment in the old castle, conveniently next to the emperor's quarters.

What started as an exciting tryst became an exquisite romance as much of the minds as of the body. Napoleon perhaps had never been as much in love since the early days with either Désirée Clary or Joséphine. Only a few of their letters have survived. "Marie, my sweet Marie," Napoleon wrote early in the courtship, "my first thought is for you – my first desire of the day is to see you again . . . Love me, my sweet Marie." Love him she did: "You were so beautiful yesterday," he wrote, "that for long in the night I could still see you in my mind . . . *mio dolce amore* . . . I kiss your charming mouth and your hands." A few days later: "I beg to know how you spent the rest of the night . . . the memory of last night will never leave me. Marie, remember that I love you, that you have done me the favor of sharing my feelings. Will you promise to remain constant?"[4]

Indeed she would. She worshiped him and their hours together when the talk centered on history, politics, war – and in Marie's case Polish independence (not a popular subject with her lover). The idyll lasted for three gorgeous weeks when it was broken by Napoleon's sudden return to war.

Napoleon had deluded himself as to Russian losses and weakness. Bennigsen had retreated but was determined to continue the campaign, a sentiment shared by Czar Alexander who now placed him in command of all armies in Poland. Bennigsen decided to leave three divisions to contain the French right wing while the remainder of his army, seven divisions, marched northeast to the far side of Johannisburg forest. There they would wheel left, march west to the Alle river, the move concealed by woods, then up the western bank of the Alle to be joined by General Lestocq's Prussians before falling on the exposed French left wing.

Napoleon had spread his corps across the wintry landscape from the Vistula to the Omulev rivers, Ney on the left, Lannes on the right, Bernadotte north at Osteröde with units pushed out to Elbing and Frisches Haff, the remaining corps sharing the void from left to right. Major supply depots were left *behind* the Vistula in case of a retreat, but such was the shortage of food and clothing, such the confused distribution arrangements, that they might as well have been in Timbuctoo. Most of the corps commanders went along with Napoleon's planned defensive positions even though their troops were trying to survive on potatoes culled from frozen ground and little else.[5]

Not so Michel Ney, who preferred action to words. Where the majority of marshals respected Napoleon's demands for constant information Ney supplied the minimum necessary, if even that. Berthier's dispatch to Ney in early January informed him that "the Emperor, not wishing to make any offensive movements . . . during the winter, desires you to take such cantonments as will protect Marshal Soult's left and Marshal Bernadotte's right." A few days later he was instructed to move his cantonments to the area around Soldau.[6] Ney however was already on the march toward Königsberg before Berthier had *written* the first set of orders. In less than two weeks he had reached the upper Alle from where he notified Berthier of abundant provisions, adding that he was negotiating an armistice with the Prussian General Lestocq. Napoleon furiously ordered him to fall back immediately on Soldau and Mlawa as per earlier orders.

Napoleon's anger was completely justified. Although he had no definite word on Russian movements, he presciently feared the exact maneuver that Bennigsen was making in order to cut off the French left. Having seen the light, so to speak, he acted quickly to move his center and right forward to attack Bennigsen between the lower Vistula and the Frisches Haff. Meanwhile Bennigsen's Russians had been joined by Lestocq's Prussians and Russian cavalry had moved on Ney's outposts, forcing a hurried retreat to Neidenburg not without some losses. Ney now had Bernadotte on his left and Soult on his right.

The emperor was still shifting his corps when in late January Bernadotte's divisions marching on Möhrungen clashed with the oncoming Russians, an indecisive but hard-fought action with each side suffering perhaps 2,000 casualties and Bernadotte falling back on Strasburg. By month's end Bennigsen believed himself ready to attack what he reckoned was the exposed French left flank.

He reckoned wrongly. Having made preliminary preparations and having decided that Bennigsen was moving on the French left, Napoleon kissed Marie Walewska goodbye and traveled to Villenburg from where he would spring his tactical trap. On the last day of January he ordered Bernadotte to come up on the army's left by a secret night march if possible. "It is unnecessary for me to tell you," wrote Berthier, "that the Emperor, desiring to cut off the enemy, would prefer your joining his left."[7] This uncoded message was carried by a young subaltern who was captured by the Cossacks before he could destroy the paper. Bennigsen read it the following day, a paper bomb that blew his great operational plan into the stuff of dreams, in this case the nightmarish realization that he was walking into a cunning trap. He immediately ordered a general retreat.

The French right, Murat's cavalry followed by Soult's infantry, had already marched as had Ney on their left. Bennigsen continued to fall back, hotly pursued by Murat and Soult, a retreat that led to a fierce battle at Hof before culminating at Eylau just over 20 miles south of Königsberg.

The action had been fast, furious and fruitless. Bennigsen's main body marched through the night from Landsberg to the village of Eylau, arriving only in the morning of 7 February to be hastily deployed in a defensive position. Having decided to fight, Bennigsen sent word to Lestocq to bring his Prussians up to Althof on the right. While Murat's cavalry spent the day pushing back the Russian rearguard, the French corps steadily advanced. By evening Soult and Augereau's troops along with the Guard had reached the outskirts of the village, Davout's corps was approaching from Bartenstein on the right and Ney's force was marching on Kreuzburg, the first step in a clever enveloping maneuver.

Dawn, 8 February, two degrees above zero. Bennigsen opened the action with a heavy cannonade. Standing by a church on Cemetery hill, Napoleon carefully placed his guns, sent an order to Ney to return to Althof and waited for word from Davout. Davout's task was to block Bennigsen's retreat while Augereau's right wing reinforced by St. Hilaire's division fell on the Russian left.

Nothing was wrong with Napoleon's tactics (despite the censures of some future historians). Had Augereau and St. Hilaire's attack succeeded and had Davout reached the rear of the Russian left flank, Soult's corps and the Guard were on hand to deliver a probable *coup de grâce* with the aid of Ney's corps advancing on the Russian right.

It did not succeed mainly because of capricious winter weather. If Napoleon is to be faulted, it is for continuing the winter offensive after he had countered the Russian threat by forcing Bennigsen to retreat. That aside, the attack at Eylau was going well when a sudden snowstorm blew in from the west to blind Augereau and St. Hilaire's troops and to slow Davout's march from Bartenstein. St. Hilaire's division went off track in the direction of Serpallen where it was struck by Russian cavalry and forced to fall back. With vision reduced to 15 yards, Augereau's divisions made a false turn to the left that exposed them to devastating canister fire from both Russian and French cannon. Augereau, already stricken with rheumatism so painful that he could scarcely mount his horse, was hit by a ball and most of his regiments knocked out while blindly floundering about in the snow. Russian horse moved in followed by infantry for the kill and almost reached Napoleon's headquarters on Cemetery hill before falling back from the fire of the Foot Guard. "I never was so much struck by anything in my life," General Bertrand recalled many years later, "as by the emperor at Eylau when he was almost trodden underfoot by the Russian column. He kept his ground as the Russians advanced, saying frequently, 'What boldness.'"[8]

Shortly before noon Napoleon sent in Murat and Bessières' cavalry which after several hours of the most vicious fighting pushed back the Russian left to clear the way for St. Hilaire and Davout's advance. By late afternoon the tattered Russian left was giving way. The arrival of Lestocq's Prussians temporarily balanced matters, but shortly after dark Ney's corps closed the field to threaten the Russian right as Davout was threatening the left and rear. Recognizing the danger of envelopment Bennigsen ordered a night retreat, leaving the field to the French.[9]

According to extant accounts Napoleon had remained calm throughout this terrible day, but his letters written immediately after the battle reveal his mixed feelings and disappointment with the day's results. Although he held the field he could not claim the decisive victory that he so badly wanted and needed, nor could he ignore the carnage that lay before him.

"There was a great battle yesterday which I won," he wrote Joséphine in the early hours of the morning, ". . . but I have lost a great many men; enemy losses are greater but that is no consolation to me." In writing to Duroc he called it "a very bloody battle . . . it is possible that, to have winter quarters safe from the Cossacks and this swarm of light troops, I shall move to the right bank of the Vistula."[10]

Daylight brought a more positive attitude arising from the discovery that Bennigsen had departed, leaving only a screen of Cossacks to discourage pursuit. "The enemy has retired in full rout," Napoleon informed Prince Cambacérès in Paris. ". . . The results will be forty cannon and 12,000 prisoners. Enemy losses are calculated at 10,000 wounded and 4,000 dead; this is not to exaggerate. Unfortunately our loss is severe enough, above all in soldiers of distinction. I reckon it as 1,500 dead and 4,000 wounded." Cambacérès was to have an account of the battle, "one of the most memorable of the war," published in the *Moniteur*.[11] "To put the enemy's loss at 30,000," Napoleon wrote General Clarke in Berlin, "is to underestimate it."[12] And to Talleyrand in Warsaw: "The affair has been very hot, very lively and risky enough."[13]

Almost all authorities agree that French losses were far higher, even after Napoleon revised his figures upward. Augereau's corps alone had been so shredded that it was broken up, its remnants going to other regiments, the badly wounded Augereau to France for a lengthy and not entirely successful treatment, all its generals, all its colonels dead or wounded. Scores of other officers were dead or wounded, field hospitals jammed, surgeons working around the clock, too few wagons to evacuate the luckless victims over roads nearly impassable owing to a sudden thaw. Captain Marbot later estimated French casualties at 20,000.[14] The Russians put their own losses at 20,000 including 8 generals and 400 other officers,[15] (Marbot later estimated 25,000, Napoleon 30,000) and Lestocq's Prussians must also have suffered considerably.

The exact numbers will never be known and are not very significant. Napoleon would go on claiming victory until blue in the face, but the army knew there had been no victory. The day after the battle Marshal Ney threaded his way through thousands of frozen bodies lying twisted on blood-stained snow, many of them to be eaten by beasts and birds before the ground thawed sufficiently for burial.[16] Marshal Michel Ney, the red-headed, hard-charging, 38-year-old veteran of more battles than he had years, listened to the cries and pleas of the wounded, turned to an aide and said bitterly: *"Quel massacre! Et sans résultat."*[17]

In headquarters at Osteröde, Napoleon faced the enormous task of rebuilding a shattered army, of forming new alliances and, not least, of mollifying Joséphine who had learned of his affair with Marie Walewska and whose weepy letters apparently brought pangs of remorse to the emperor.

His first concern was the security of the army which perforce had taken up winter quarters. The tactical task now was to cover Marshal Lefebvre's sieges of Danzig and Kolberg.[18] He distributed his corps in a line running southeast from Frisches Haff behind the river Passarge and on to Villenburg on the Omulev. A Polish corps of observation commanded by General Zajonchek (who had made his name in Egypt) was based on Neidenburg. Cavalry covered the area from Osteröde to Thorn, and Lannes' corps, commanded by Savary during the marshal's illness, defended Warsaw and Pultusk. On the extreme left Mortier's corps defended Swedish Pomerania, on his right Marshal Brune's army of observation held Germany in thrall while on the extreme right Jérôme Bonaparte's corps occupied Silesia where it had seized all fortresses except Glogau, currently under siege.

There was little to fear from the enemy. Savary and Suchet had recently fought the extreme Russian left wing at Ostrolenka, a lively action that won Savary the Grand Cross of the Legion of Honor (with an annual life pension of 20,000 francs). Reported movements of Bennigsen's army followed by a hot skirmish in which Dupont's division thrashed a mixed Russian-Prussian force worried Napoleon not a whit, particularly when a captured Russian general informed him of the weakened and tired Russian soldiers who were as starved as the French.[19]

The main security concern centered on omnipresent Cossacks whose irregular infiltration tactics continued to disrupt army communications. Avoiding set battles, these fierce horsemen descended in swarms on such rewarding targets as baggage depots, striking quickly, killing mercilessly and departing hurriedly with the loot. During the battle of Eylau both officers and men in the rear echelons fled at the panic cry, "The Cossacks are coming," running back to Thorn and even the Oder.[20] So nimble and fast were Cossack horses and so attenuated their operations that French cavalry repeatedly failed to check them. In desperation Napoleon asked General Poniatowski to send him several thousand Polish cavalry who "will be my Cossacks."[21]

Neither was manpower lacking. The conscription of 1807 levied earlier than usual had brought 140,000 bodies into training depots, and Napoleon would soon decree a premature levy of the 1808 class to bring in another 80,000.[22] Poniatowski and Dumbrowski were raising a Polish legion though not as rapidly nor in the quantity Napoleon had hoped for. Infantry and cavalry replacements were marching from Naples and Italy, and 15,000 Spanish regulars would soon arrive to defend the northern ports in conjunction with French forces.

The immediate problem was to feed, clothe and rearm about 95,000 troops, most of whom were living on potatoes culled from frozen ground. "Nothing new here," Napoleon laconically informed General Duroc in late February, "except that I have great difficulty in surviving."[23] To Talleyrand in Warsaw: "My position would be very beautiful if I had some provisions. The lack of food makes it mediocre."[24]

Napoleon had hoped to ease matters by replacing Warsaw with Thorn as the major supply depot on what was now a new line of communications stretching back through Landsberg to Berlin. Provisions still had to come from Silesia and Warsaw, transport was in short supply, the roads remained in terrible condition. Ney's corps at Güttstadt, only about 30 miles northeast of Osteröde on the river Alle, was going hungry as was Davout's corps at Allenstein only 20 miles away. "I am upset by your suffering," Napoleon wrote Ney. "We must be a little patient."[25]

General Caulaincourt later wrote rather critically of Napoleon's severity during this trying period, complaining that he fended off complaints by citing the stoic and noble behavior of the Roman legions in time of want.[26] But this was mere bluster while Napoleon frantically tried to alleviate the situation. He had turned the elegant Talleyrand in Warsaw into a virtual quartermaster, ordering him to get help from Poniatowski. Prince Jérôme in Silesia was to send 100,000 pints of brandy, 330 tons of grain and 3,000 cows without delay.[27] Talleyrand was to dispatch 80 wagons a day carrying 50,000 rations of biscuit and 2,000 pints of brandy. "If I have bread, beating the Russians is child's play . . . Three hundred thousand rations of biscuit and eighteen to twenty thousand pints of brandy will thwart the plans of all [our] enemies."[28]

Although Napoleon noted a considerable improvement in the food (and drink) supply by late March, he was still upset to learn that Ney's corps, lacking transport, was on half rations. The situation would continue to improve however as spring approached to clear roads and waterways for the passage of the precious wagons.

Notes

1   Lucas-Dubreton, 69.
2   Sutherland, 21.
3   Sutherland, 37.
4   Sutherland, 78, 81.
5   Savary, III, 27–8, 45–6.
6   Petre, 131.
7   Petre, 148.
8   Rose (*Life*), II, 113.

9 Corr. XIV. Nr. 11796, Preussisch-Eylau, 9 February 1807. See also Marbot, II, 337–41; Coignet, 200–3; Rose (*Life*), II, 111–15; Wartenburg, I, 337–42; Chandler (*Napoleon*), 535–55.

10 Corr. XIV. Nrs. 11787, Eylau, 9 February 1807, 3 a.m. 11789, Eylau, 9 February 1807.

11 Corr. XIV. Nr. 11791, Eylau, 9 February 1807.

12 Corr. XIV. Nr. 11792, Eylau, 9 February 1807.

13 Corr. XIV. Nr. 11790, Eylau, 9 February 1807.

14 Marbot, I, 339–40.

15 Corr. XIV. Nr. 11815, Preussisch-Eylau (footnote), 14 February 1807; Marbot, I, 340.

16 Petre, 220.

17 Lucas-Dubreton, 69.

18 Corr. XIV. Nr. 11804, Eylau, 12 February 1807.

19 Corr. XIV. Nr. 11895, Osteröde, 27 February 1807; Savary, III, 54–8.

20 Corr. XIV. Nr. 11955, Osteröde, 6 March 1807.

21 Corr. XIV. Nrs. 11843, Liebstadt, 20 February 1807; 11864, Osteröde, 23 February 1807.

22 Corr. XIV. Nrs. 12080, 12082, Osteröde, 19 March 1807; 12100, Osteröde, 20 March 1807.

23 Corr. XIV. Nr. 11824, Osteröde, 25 February 1807.

24 Corr. XIV. Nr. 11897, Osteröde, 27 February 1807.

25 Corr. XIV. Nr. 11967, Osteröde, 7 March 1807.

26 Caulaincourt, II, 378–9.

27 Corr. XIV. Nr. 12006, Osteröde, 12 March 1807.

28 Corr. XIV. Nr. 12015, Osteröde, 12 March 1807.

CHAPTER SIX

THE POLISH ADVENTURE – III:
THE BATTLE OF FRIEDLAND
FEBRUARY–JUNE 1807

It was a hideous sight. The position of Russian squares was
marked by the lines of piled up bodies, that of their cannons
by dead horses.

General Savary on the battlefield of Friedland,
14 June 1807[1]

CORPSES STRIPPED NAKED by scavenging camp followers and local
peasants still covered Eylausian fields when Napoleon in a sharp
reversal of policy informed King Frederick William that he
wished to make a separate and generous peace with Prussia
"whose intermediary power is necessary to the tranquility of all
Europe."[2] Prussia would regain all its land east of the Elbe and
would participate in a future conference to ensure the peace of
Europe.[3]

Austria forced another consideration. "What does the house of
Austria want? I don't know," he wrote plaintively to Talleyrand
from Osteröde. If he could not forge a separate peace with
Prussia, perhaps Austria would ally with him in return for a portion of its beloved Silesia? On the other hand an alliance with
Russia would be "very advantageous" but it was still necessary to
keep Austria quiet, perhaps by accepting its mediation between
France and Russia. In any case, Austria must not arm, and if it
continued to do so Napoleon would march 40,000 troops into
Bavaria. His suspicions that Russia was trying to bring Austria
into a new anti-French coalition increased when he learned that

England had ordered a levy of 200,000 conscripts for its army. But he also believed that Archduke Charles and other Austrian generals wanted to remain at peace.[4]

He continued to court Turkey and Persia, offering men, money and arms (along with a great deal of advice on how to fight the Russians). He was delighted when the Turks, greatly aided by French artillery officers, forced a British squadron intent on bombarding Constantinople to hastily leave the Dardanelles. His diplomatic initiative suffered a major setback however when Sultan Selim was overthrown by Sultan Mustafa, a soldier who did not want French advice and who sent the French military advisers home.

Try as he did to favorably influence the political situation in Europe, Napoleon eventually had to return to square one: the immediate solution was to defeat Russia militarily.

It was not England's most brilliant winter. A military expedition to South America had ended in disaster and various operations in the Caribbean had produced little of value. Compounding the failure to bombard Constantinople was a landing in Egypt that resulted in a great many dead English soldiers and the remainder blocked in Alexandria. Holland Rose summed up the performance nicely: the Grenville ministry "clung to its old plan of doing nothing and doing it expensively."[5] Little wonder that it remained lukewarm regarding a diversionary landing in northern Germany in support of the Prussian-Russian effort against France.

At this point, March 1807, the government tripped up on the enduring Irish question when Lord Grenville favored an increase in political and military rights for upper-class Irish landowners. Although crown and public reaction caused a hasty reversal of the notion the damage was done, the Whigs were out, the Tories headed by the duke of Portland were in.[6]

The new government was still organizing itself when Czar Alexander and King Frederick William signed an alliance at Bartenstein designed to drive Napoleon from Germany and restore French boundaries to their pre-revolutionary state. Portland's new government returned to Pitt's former continental policy by joining the convention, paying Prussia a subsidy of 2.5 million pounds sterling, promising Russia a loan of twice that amount, twisting the Vienna court with still more gold and agreeing to land a corps in Swedish Pomerania in conjunction with a Swedish army.

Thus heartened, Russia and Prussia spent the rest of the winter in repairing their armies for a new campaign. Bennigsen was not a great nor even a good general, but he was a *persistent* general. His reputation had been soiled at Eylau but at least he denied Napoleon his accustomed outright victory. After a brief retreat he revived and in March with only minimum reinforcements began moving against the French. A series of inconclusive if sometimes bloody attacks produced only more dead and wounded. After an unfortunate attempt to relieve besieged Danzig by land, in mid May he posted Lestocq's Prussians behind the Passarge river and his own Russians on the banks of the lower Alle, determined to open a new campaign, weather permitting.[7]

This plan was encouraged by England joining the alliance, but it should have been discouraged when English troops failed to land in Pomerania during the allied attacks designed to save Danzig. This splendid fortress would fall to the French in late May (as will be seen), to release at least 20,000 French soldiers involved in the siege. Bennigsen must have had some idea of French strength, he must have known that Napoleon's army was much stronger than his, and he must have realized that he was up against not one but several supreme tacticians, not to mention some very skillful and determined veteran troops.

These and other adverse factors apparently did not register. By early June he had concentrated his army at Heilsberg on the right bank of the Alle. Platov's Cossacks shielded his front and Lestocq's Prussians and General Kamenski's Russians formed his right flank north of the Passarge river. His ambitious plan was for Lestocq and Kamenski to attack the enemy on the Passarge while six columns converged on Ney and Soult's corps spread west of the Alle river in the area of Güttstadt-Queetz-Elditten, with posts extending down to the river's left bank.

Owing to command confusion Lestocq prematurely opened the action on 4 June by an unsuccessful attack on Spanden south of the Passarge. The following day Bennigsen's advance guard marched to strike Ney.

Once the food crisis had passed, Napoleon moved imperial head-quarters from Osteröde to the château of Finkenstein pleasantly isolated in the midst of Poland's famous lakes and birch forests. The old *schloss* or castle had been built by one of Frederick the Great's noblemen. A massive two-winged structure of about 100 rooms, its oak-paneled salons, an enormous library and numerous large fireplaces were to Napoleon's taste – "very agreeable to me," he informed Joséphine, "when I get up during the night I love to watch the fire."[8]

But not alone. One night in mid April an elegant carriage pulled up to a secluded rear entrance of the castle to be met by Napoleon's valet, Constant Wairy. Marie Walewska was quickly hustled to apartments next to Napoleon's, there to remain in seclusion for the next six weeks, her presence allegedly known only to her brother Benedict who had accompanied her, valet Constant, secretary Méneval and body servant Roustan. According to her biographer there followed six weeks of bliss, a questionable surmise from Marie's standpoint since she was not allowed outside their apartments, she could entertain no one and could only peek through curtains to watch daily military reviews – but love is a powerful blanket and it may have been so.[9]

There is little doubt of Napoleon's bliss, of the relaxing hours of love-making, awakening with this beautiful woman in his arms, returning to her after a day of running an empire, of absorbing myriad lengthy dispatches and dictating long replies, sending scores of orders to his diverse corps in preparation for a spring offensive, inspecting regiment after regiment and trying to divine enemy plans and how best to demolish them. Napoleon was apparently not the greatest lover in the world. According to Marie's biographer he frequently doubted his virility but Marie, although inexperienced, constantly reassured him, showering him with tenderness and love.[10] He must have been as sad to see her depart for Warsaw as he was glad to return to war. Both were heartened by their desire to resume the romance once circumstances permitted.

When Bennigsen opened his offensive in early June, Napoleon was surprised by his stupidity. Another attempt to save Danzig, this time by the entire Russian army, with the fortress in French hands was ludicrous. French strength moreover had increased by the day as Napoleon shaped his army for a spring offensive, once Danzig had fallen and crops were sufficiently ripe to provide forage for his horses – probably in the first two weeks of June, he informed General Clarke in early May.[11]

Danzig capitulated in late May, a fantastic prize that yielded enough wheat to feed the French army for two years, quantities of wine and diverse provisions, cloth, 800 cannon and thousands of small arms. (Each soldier of the siege force received a bottle of wine; half a million bottles were sent to the Elbing depot along with 20,000 pints of brandy and the same of rum.)[12] In a week or two the fields would be green with forage. Napoleon planned to attack on 10 June, but as we have seen was pre-empted by the enemy on 4 June.

Lestocq's determined but futile attempts to seize villages on the left bank of the Passarge during 5 and 6 June resulted only in heavy Prussian casualties compared with light French losses (Marshall Bernadotte suffered a head wound and was replaced by Victor). The main Russian effort on Lestocq's left was not much more successful though bloody enough. Outnumbered as he was, Ney made a fighting withdrawal from Güttstadt to reach Ankendorf and Heiligenthal. Although he suffered 400 casualties and lost 1,600 men taken prisoner, he inflicted some 2,000 casualties on the Russian columns. After some hard fighting in his new positions he retreated across the Passarge to Deppen while Soult withdrew on Möhrungen. Bennigsen's advance guard reached Heiligenthal by the evening of 6 June, but now the considerable French presence made him fear for his communications. Late the next day he ordered a general retreat down the Alle to his fortified camp at Heilsberg.[13]

Napoleon meanwhile had reached Saalfeld from where he called up rear-area corps in anticipation of a counter-attack, his intention being to outflank Bennigsen's right, thereby cutting him from Lestocq's force and from Königsberg before delivering the mortal blow. On 8 June he joined Ney at Deppen from where he ordered Murat and Soult to march on Heilsberg with Lannes in tow. Davout followed by Mortier's corps (earlier summoned from Swedish Pomerania and replaced by a Spanish force) would make an end run past Heilsberg to threaten Bennigsen's right while Victor crossed the Passarge to pin down Lestocq's force. Ney and the Guard would remain in reserve.

Murat and Soult, with Lannes some miles in the rear, were closing on Heilsberg when Napoleon joined them on 10 June. Seeing the Russians in retreat along the line Napoleon ordered a hot pursuit toward the town. The pursuit ended abruptly that evening with Soult's near-fatal attack on Russian redoubts backed by 150 cannon firing from heights on either side and behind the infantry. Having stopped short the French, the Russians leaped from their positions to drive them from the field, an appalling five-hour action joined by Lannes' corps which also lost heavily in an unsuccessful counter-attack.

Dawn revealed the most ghastly carnage, thousands of naked dead and wounded on both sides who as usual had been stripped bare by hordes of camp-followers.[14] French losses including men taken prisoner have been estimated at over 12,000 including 1,400 dead. Soult's corps alone suffered more than 8,000 casualties. The Russians were believed to have lost 2–3,000 killed and 5–6,000 wounded.[15]

Refusing to accept defeat, Napoleon prepared to fight what he still hoped would be a "decisive battle . . . that would put an end to the war."[16] Bennigsen would have none of it. He was aware that Davout's corps was on the march, that his own right wing was vulnerable and that his rations were rapidly shrinking – he was said to have less than two days of bread left. On the night of 11 June he slipped his troops across the Alle for a further retreat on Bartenstein. Kamenski with 9,000 men went to join Lestocq behind the Frisching river and fall back on Königsberg while the main army marched on Wehlau "to support the line of the Pregel [river]."[17]

Napoleon has been justly criticized for fighting the battle of Heilsberg. A frontal assault on a prepared position is without doubt the most costly tactic in the world even with a preponderance of strength – and Napoleon on the night of 10 June was greatly inferior in numbers. He had only to wait for Lannes, Ney and the Guard to come up to give him a reasonable parity. But why did he want to attack a prepared position instead of waiting for a better opportunity? Bennigsen could not have remained at Heilsberg once Davout and Mortier gained his right flank. Savary and Lannes were highly critical, not only of the impetuous attacks but also of Murat's aggressive behavior, Savary condemning him for causing unnecessary casualties: Murat was a "show-off who one day would make us lose an important battle," he angrily told Napoleon, "and that in short it would be better for us if he were less gallant and had a bit more common sense."[18]

The action was described all too favorably in a subsequent bulletin that claimed the attacks had been successful. As for the losses (not specified), "the spirit of the troops was such that several light infantry companies assaulted the prepared Russian defenses. Some brave men died in the ditches of the redoubts and at the foot of the palisades."[19]

Napoleon did not want his enemy to escape. Sending some cavalry to follow the Russians down the right or eastern bank of the Alle, he fanned out his corps to the west and north. By 13 June Murat's cavalry and Davout and Soult's infantry – altogether some 60,000 troops – were marching toward the Pregel to protect the French left and proceed on to Königsberg if the situation permitted. Ney and Mortier were moving on Eylau, Lannes on Lampasch. Napoleon was still in doubt as to Bennigsen's position but, as he wrote Soult, "indications suggest that they wish to meet at Domnau."[20] Learning a few hours later that Bennigsen had reached Schippenbeil, he ordered Lannes to occupy Domnau and send out patrols toward Friedland.

Lannes' hussars closed on Friedland that afternoon to chase out some Russian troops guarding supply magazines. But that evening General Galitzin's advance guard of cavalry arrived to cross the river, capture a number of hussars and send the rest running back to Domnau. Informed of this development Napoleon ordered Grouchy's dragoons, Nansouty's cuirassiers and Ney's corps to hurry to Lannes' assistance, with the rest of Mortier's corps, Victor's corps and the Guard to follow. Lannes had already started Oudinot's division toward Friedland and he now followed with the rest of the corps. Oudinot reached the plain about 3 a.m. on 14 June.

The small village of Friedland on the left bank of the Alle was fronted by a large fertile plain now green with rye and wheat, backed by a semi-circle of thick woods interspersed with small farm villages. A millstream ran through the village of Posthenen about three miles southwest of Friedland, then curled north and east to cut through the plain before spilling into a pond in Friedland.

Bennigsen's original plan had been to continue his retreat down the Alle to Wehlau and beyond, having no intention (contrary to Napoleon's belief) of crossing the Alle at either Schippenbeil or Friedland. As counter to Napoleon's error however Bennigsen believed that the main French army was marching directly on Königsberg and was considerably west of the Alle.

Bennigsen reached Friedland only an hour or two after Galitzin's cavalry had chased out Lannes' hussars. He now concluded that Lannes was on his own and could easily and quickly be defeated before the Russian march resumed. Accordingly he shunted his arriving troops, men who had marched 34 miles in 48 hours in oppressively hot weather, across the bridge to form a semi-arc, there to be reinforced as more regiments arrived to cross on hastily constructed pontoon bridges.

This decision placed Lannes in considerable danger. He counted only about 9,000 infantry and 3,000 cavalry, although Grouchy and Nansouty's imminent arrival would soon give him another 5,000 cavalry. Even with that the best he could do until more help arrived was to fight a holding action. The battle began somewhat desultorily shortly after first light, about 3.30 a.m., but soon heated up as more Russian regiments crossed the river, covered by a fearsome shield of artillery fire. Grouchy and Nansouty's cavalry arrived with infantry close behind. Grouchy soon noticed that the bulk of Russians crossing the river was moving on Heinrichsdorf some two miles northwest of Friedland on the Königsberg road and with Nansouty's cuirassiers in tow raced his dragoons to seize the village which would be fought over for the rest of the day.

By mid morning Lannes commanded about 17,000 men against Bennigsen's nearly 50,000, the latter deploying from left to right across the plain. But now Mortier's division and the advance guards of other units arrived to raise French strength to 40,000, a drastic improvement that cut short Bennigsen's plan to attack.

Napoleon reached the scene somewhere around noon, reminding one and all that this was the anniversary of the battle of Marengo. He liked the battlefield as viewed through a field-glass from a hillock close to his bivouac at Posthenen, particularly the Russian left wing which was holding a triangular-shaped area semi-isolated by the millstream on one side and the river Alle on the other. His mind turned the triangle into a funnel, a perfect receptacle, once further troops arrived, into which he would pour his army to crush the enemy into the small end, thereby turning Bennigsen's left while other French corps, aided by massive artillery fire, held the Russian center and right.[21]

Ney's corps won the task of filling the funnel, with Lannes holding the center from Posthenen to Heinrichsdorf and Mortier, supported by Espagne and Grouchy's cavalry, the left, the base on which Ney would pivot. Napoleon's lengthy order is extant and is perfect, yet it was dictated before he was aware of enemy strength. Although Oudinot reported that he was facing the main army, Napoleon could scarcely believe that Bennigsen would be so foolish as to fight with his back to an inadequately bridged river. Convinced at last, he waited only until the Guard and Victor's corps arrived. At 5 p.m. he signaled the attack.

Ney's advance started well but the enemy, not liking the small end of the funnel, opened a vicious fire followed by a sudden and murderous cavalry charge. This halted and then shattered the French advance. But at this critical moment Dupont's divison of Victor's corps plugged the hole until General Sénarmont's artillery – 36 guns – hurried in from the left to smash the Russian horse with murderous grapeshot fired finally from only 60 yards' range. This sounded the death knell for the Russian left, pressed now into the small end of the funnel by Ney's revitalized battalions. Spewed out in the bombarded chaos of Friedland's corpse-covered streets, trapped by the French from the west and by the Alle's burning bridges, the Russians found either surrender or death by bayonet or drowning: thousands surrendered, thousands died.

Furious unrelenting artillery fire meanwhile had taken an horrendous toll of the Russian center and right. Had the French cavalry posted around Heinrichsdorf attacked as ordered hardly anyone could have escaped. As it turned out, a considerable number including Bennigsen and staff fled downstream to save themselves by crossing a ford to the right bank and making a final retreat across the Pregel to the Niemen river – and Russia.

They left a sad, savage legacy as indicated by General Savary's observations quoted at the beginning of this chapter. The toll was probably at least 15,000 dead and perhaps as many if not more wounded. French casualties approached 10,000. Many thousands of Russians were taken prisoner, including a score of generals. Thousands of horses were killed or maimed. The field would not be cleaned for several days and we can only feel pity for the burial parties working in the stinking, sordid squalor of grotesquely mutilated bodies, man and beast.

Napoleon at once proclaimed a great victory, ordering *Te Deums* to be sung from one end of his empire to the other. While working parties evacuated thousands of the wounded to rear-area hospitals, French cavalry pursued Bennigsen's remnants down the right bank of the Alle. The main French army, once reorganized, moved down the left bank, crossed the Pregel and continued northward. News of the battle caused Lestocq and Kamenski to evacuate Königsberg, whereupon Soult's corps at once occupied the ancient port to find rich booty including 200 Russian ships loaded with cargo – "enough provisions to feed the Grand Army for at least four months."[22]

Five days after the battle Murat's cavalry entered Tilsit. Czar Alexander now asked for an armistice to be followed by a meeting of the two emperors and the opening of peace negotiations. Sensing that he was about to win a new and immensely valuable ally, Napoleon agreed.

Notes

1 Savary, III, 92.
2 Corr. XIV. Nr. 11890, Osteröde, 26 February 1807.
3 Corr. XIV. Nr. 11810, Eylau, 13 February 1807.
4 Corr. XIV. Nrs. 11918, Osteröde, 3 March 1807; 12181, Osteröde, 26 March 1807.
5 Rose (*Life*), II, 115–16.
6 Bryant (*Victory*), 209–11.
7 Corr. XV. Nr. 12604, Finkenstein, 18 May 1807.
8 Corr. XV. Nr. 12263, Finkenstein, 2 April 1807.
9 Sutherland, 90–1.
10 Sutherland, 93–6.
11 Corr. XV. Nr. 12557, Elbing, 8 May 1807.
12 Corr. XV. Nr. 12686, Finkenstein, 29 May 1807.
13 Corr. XV. Nr. 12747, Heilsberg, 12 June 1807.
14 Marbot, I, 351. See also Petre, 302.

15   Petre, 302–3.
16   Corr. XV. Nr. 12747, Heilsberg, 12 June 1807.
17   Petre, 303–5.
18   Petre, 304.
19   Corr. XV. Nr. 12747, Heilsberg, 12 June 1807.
20   Corr. XV. Nr. 12750, Preussisch-Eylau, 13 June 1807.
21   Corr. XV. Nr. 12756, Posthenen, 14 June 1807. See also Savary, III, 83–92; Marbot, I, 362–7; Coignet, 210–12.
22   Corr. XV. Nr. 12775, Tilsit, 19 June 1807; Savary, III, 95.

CHAPTER SEVEN

THE PEACE OF TILSIT
JUNE–JULY 1807

"I hate the English as much as you do, and I will second you in
all your actions against them," Czar Alexander told Napoleon
upon their meeting.
"In that case," Napoleon responded, "all can be arranged and
peace is made."[1]

THE MEETING OF the emperors took place in an elegant tent raised
on a hastily constructed raft anchored midstream in the Niemen
river. French troops lined the left bank, Russian Cossacks the
right bank as the rulers were rowed to the imposing edifice where
they embraced each other and retired for two hours of private
talks.

Although not recorded their conversation can be surmised.
Alexander had grown steadily disillusioned with his English
ally. England's naval foray against Constantinople was just
short of farcical; Whitehall had reneged on its promise of a five
million pound loan; British ships had seized Russian vessels
sailing from French ports; the promised troop expedition to
the Baltic had not arrived (and would not arrive for several
more weeks).

The embryonic relationship prospered. "I never had more prej-
udices against anyone than against him," Alexander later said,
"but after three-quarters of an hour of conversation, they all disappeared like a dream."[2] Napoleon was equally pleased. "I have
just seen the Emperor Alexander," he wrote Joséphine. "I have
been very pleased with him: he has an excellent intellect above
which is commonly attributed to him."[3]

Czar Alexander of Russia 1775–1825

They met again the next day, this time with their poor relation, King Frederick William of Prussia, a beaten man who hastily agreed to Napoleon's terms for an armistice. Napoleon treated him with all possible scorn, telling him among other unpleasant things that he would have to get rid of his foreign minister, Count Hardenberg, before peace terms could be discussed.

The French emperor now moved to Tilsit close by the czar's lodgings. Negotiations ensued in an almost carnival atmosphere of military parades, fêtes, dinners and country outings, the two rulers frequently entertaining each other while redrawing the map of Europe.

In less than two weeks two treaties were signed between France and Russia. The public document stripped Prussia of all its Polish holdings gained from the last two partitions and converted them into the Grand Duchy of Warsaw which was given to the king of Saxony. Prussia also lost all lands west of the Elbe river which were formed into the kingdom of Westphalia (soon to be given over to Jérôme Bonaparte's rule). Owing only to Alexander's intercession Prussia retained its lands between the Elbe and the Niemen rivers as well as Silesia.

The young, attractive and vigorous Queen Louise, on whom Napoleon in large part blamed the war, unsuccessfully employed her beauty and wit to persuade him to allow Prussia to retain the fortress of Magdeburg on the left bank of the Elbe. "The queen of Prussia is truly charming," Napoleon wrote Joséphine, "forever flirting with me. But don't be jealous, I am an oil cloth on which all this only slides off. It would cost me too dearly to play the gentleman."[4] In short, as a result of neglecting Napoleon's earlier offer of an armistice Prussia lost an immense amount of territory holding half of its subjects, was forced to join the continental blockade and was left as little more than a buffer state between east and west.

A second secret treaty bound France and Russia "to make common cause in any war that either of them might undertake against any European power, employing, if need be, the whole of their respective forces . . . if England did not accept the czar's

mediation, or if it did not, by the 1st December 1807, recognize
the perfect equality of all flags at sea, and restore the conquests
made from France and its allies since 1805, then Russia would
make war on her." Should this come about, France and Russia
would ask Denmark, Sweden and Portugal to close their ports to
England and declare war; should one of them refuse, France and
Russia would declare war on the recalcitrant country. If on the
other hand England made peace it would receive Hanover in
return for restoring the colonies taken from France, Spain and
Holland. Should Turkey refuse French mediation then France and
Russia would seize Ottoman holdings in Europe. Alexander
wanted the right to seize Constantinople, but Napoleon refused to
consider it. Meanwhile Alexander was free to invade Finland and
Sweden, Napoleon to acquire Sicily.[5]

Despite all the *bonhomie* Alexander's position was not comfortable. He had not been conquered but he had been militarily
defeated twice within 18 months – first the humiliation at
Austerlitz, then his army shredded by the Polish campaign and
the dénouement at Friedland. Suddenly he was face to face with
the most famous man in the world, the conqueror of Europe, a
man as stern, decisive and forceful as Alexander was pliant,
wavering and feminine. Napoleon had read his character, a weak
ruler surrounded by scheming and corrupt courtiers, but also a
charming and intelligent man. Alexander was overwhelmed by
Napoleon's friendship and by his military genius. On their various
walks and ride he tossed a hundred tactical questions at the
master. "I explained matters to him," Napoleon later wrote, "and
I told him that, if I were ever again at war with Austria, he should
lead an army corps . . . under my orders, so that he could learn the
art of war."[6]

Thus ended the Polish campaign, a clear if costly victory for
France in lives, money and national spirit. It had also told on the
mental and physical resources of the emperor as he constantly
struggled with the vicissitudes of waging a bloody war in a frozen

wasteland. Added to the local political and military challenges were those of trying to govern a distant empire, not to mention the emotional complications inherent from his affair with Marie Walewska.

Napoleon has frequently been criticized for this romantic attachment, which is not altogether fair. Probably it would not have happened had Joséphine been on hand but neither Berlin nor Warsaw was a suitable place for her. Even before he met Marie he sympathized with Joséphine's boredom at Mainz and advised her to return to Paris and enjoy herself.

Joséphine did not take kindly to this advice and in short order became a nagging pest. We don't have her letters but judging from his replies they were scarcely soothing. "What you say to me of your sadness pains me," he wrote in mid January, ". . . I shall see you soon . . . show some character and fortitude. I am mortified that my wife can be suspicious of my destinies. *Adieu, mon amie*: I love you, I want to see you and I want you to be content and happy." Three days later: "I am told that you are always crying. For shame . . . I am very well and love you very much; but if you are always crying I shall believe that you have no courage or character; I do not like cowards; an empress should have courage." Joséphine was not one to give up easily. "Your heart is excellent and your judgment feeble," Napoleon wrote from Villenburg, probably annoyed by having had to leave Marie in Warsaw. ". . . I want you to be cheerful, content with your fate, and that you obey, not in grumbling and crying, but with a gaiety of heart and a little happiness. *Adieu, mon amie*, I leave tonight to inspect my advance posts."[7]

The battle of Eylau briefly interrupted the quarrel. A few days after the slaughter Napoleon wrote: "Don't be desolate, I beg you; all this will finish soon, and the joy of seeing you will make me promptly forget my weariness . . . *Adieu, ma bonne amie*; a thousand kisses."[8]

Joséphine had thrown in the towel and returned to Paris which considerably reduced the tension, at least for a while: "I see with pleasure that you have been to the opera and that you intend to hold weekly receptions. Go to the theater on occasion, [sit] always in the imperial box . . . I have put my army in billets to rest it. Don't ever be sad; love me, and believe in all my devotions." Two days later: "Try to pass the time agreeably; have no care, and never doubt of the love I hold for you."[9]

In response to Joséphine's expressed worries Napoleon wrote in early March from Osteröde: "I have never been so well; you will find me very fat . . . I have ordered what you wish for Malmaison. Be gay and happy, this is my wish . . . I embrace you from the heart." Similar notes followed but in mid March he wrote: "Don't believe the evil rumors that may be spreading. Never doubt my devotions, and have no inquietude."[10]

Evil rumors? Divorce? Possibly. Marie Walewska? Almost certainly. Although we read no more of evil rumors, Joséphine broke the wobbly truce in late March by expressing her wish to come to Poland that summer. Don't even think about it, she was told – "it is not possible." He desired a quiet life as much as she: ". . . I know how to do other things than make war but duty comes before all else. All my life I have sacrificed everything, tranquility, my own interest, happiness, to my destiny."[11]

He continued to write to her for the rest of the campaign, brief but generally warm notes reporting his victories, tidbits from the Tilsit negotiations and finally his relief that the campaign was over and that he was returning to her.

He was also writing to Marie Walewska, now at her family home outside Warsaw. Although like the majority of the Polish people she was disappointed by the results of the Tilsit peace – Poland wanted independence, not government by Saxons (or anyone else) – she reveled in his secretly delivered notes. Soon after his return to France he sent her a diamond and sapphire bracelet and a medallion with portrait, writing his intention of having her join him soon in Paris.[12]

Napoleon's relations with other family members varied. His letters to the satellite kings, Joseph of Naples and Louis of Holland, generally concerned administrative matters. One such is of particular interest. Written from *Schloss* Finkenstein in Poland, he asks them to have their coins minted in the same value as those of France, as was already being done in Italy and the confederation states. "In this way all Europe will have a uniform currency which will prove of tremendous advantage to commerce" in that it would eliminate false escalation of currency values.[13] Although King Joseph was spared the usual long sermons owing to the emperor's other cares, now and then Napoleon stuck in the needle, probably deservedly. He was very tender with Prince Eugène's wife who was upset by giving birth to a girl. "Tell her," he wrote his step-son, "that when one begins with a daughter one has at least a dozen children."[14] He treated Prince Jérôme, commanding a force in Silesia while being groomed for a kingship, with great patience and encouragement and was not displeased when under the guiding hand of General Vandamme he carried out the successful sieges of a series of forts. (When Jérôme complained of hemmorhoids Napoleon advised him "to apply three or four leeches. Since I used this remedy ten years ago I have never again been bothered.")[15]

King Louis of Holland had not fared so well. The general theme of a series of scolding letters was that "you act too lightly and quickly," the result of being surrounded by advisers in English pay. Louis claimed to have had 20,000 troops with the Grand Army, but according to Napoleon he didn't even furnish 10,000 and these were useless. "You rule this country like a mendicant friar . . . A king asks nothing from anyone, a king orders." He was creating marshals when he needed captains, he was treating Hortense badly, as one would manage a regiment, and he was showing prejudice against the Catholics in his administration. "All this shows little of force and character." Louis was trying to be popular, the worst failing of a king. "You move without thinking. You pay no attention to my advice . . . You have governed badly."[16] He probably would have come down harder but for his brother's ill-health, Hortense whom he adored and their baby, Charles Napoleon, a possible heir to the throne.

He was extremely solicitous when Charles Napoleon suddenly died from croup, a common child-killer at this time, but he became increasingly impatient when Joséphine, Hortense and Louis refused to modify their grief. Two weeks after the baby's death he wrote Hortense "that however legitimate your sorrow, it has to have limits. Do not spoil your health, take some distractions, and understand that life can be the source of so many evils that death is not the worst of all." This did not end matters. "Try to calm yourself and not make me upset," he wrote Joséphine. "One must find one's consolations for any ill without remedy."[17] The death of his presumed heir had actually upset him greatly and led him to order medical studies as to the nature and remedial treatment of the illness.[18]

Notes

1   Rose (*Life*), II, 128.
2   Rose (*Life*), II, 129.
3   Corr. XV. Nr. 12825, Tilsit, 25 June 1807. See also Vandal (*Alexander*), I, 51–111.
4   Corr. XV. Nr. 12875, Tilsit, 8 July 1807. See also Vandal (*Alexander*), I, 86–107.
5   Rose (*Life*), II, 135–6.
6   Ludwig, 271–3.
7   Corr. XIV. Nrs. 11641, Warsaw, 16 January 1807; 11653, Warsaw, 18 January 1807; 11749, Villenberg, 1 February 1807.
8   Corr. XIV. Nr. 11798, Eylau, 11 February 1807.
9   Corr. XIV. Nrs. 11846, Liebstadt, 21 February 1807; 11858, Osteröde, 23 February 1807.
10   Corr. XIV. Nrs. 11912, Osteröde, 2 March 1807; 12037, Osteröde, 15 March 1807.
11   Corr. XIV. Nr. 12192, Osteröde, 27 March 1807.
12   Sutherland, 103–4.
13   Corr. XV. Nr. 12544, Finkenstein, 6 May 1807.
14   Corr. XV. Nr. 12368, Finkenstein, 13 April 1807.
15   Corr. XV. Nr. 12656, Finkenstein, 26 May 1807.

16 Corr. XIV. Nr. 11580, Warsaw, 7 January 1807; Corr. XV. Nrs. 12294, Finkenstein, 4 April 1807; 12424, Finkenstein, 19 April 1807.

17 Corr. XV. Nrs. 12609, Finkenstein, 20 May 1807; 12636, Finkenstein, 24 May 1807.

18 Masson (*Famille*), IV, 2–7.

CHAPTER EIGHT

THE EMPEROR'S RETURN
JULY 1807–FEBRUARY 1808

*My minister of the interior will inform you of the public works
either in progress or completed. But what remains to be done is
still more important for I plan to increase the citizen's well-
being and the value of his property in all parts of my empire
down to the smallest hamlet.*

Napoleon's opening address to the legislative assembly,
Paris, 16 August 1807[1]

NAPOLEON ARRIVED AT St. Cloud in late July 1807, shortly before
his thirty-eighth birthday. He had survived a very strenuous six-
month campaign remarkably well. Letter after letter proclaimed
his good health although he admitted to growing fat. His mental
output was as prodigious as ever even if his tactical judgments
began to show the wear of time and strain as he became more
autocratic and aloof in dealing with subordinates.

His personal and professional relationships remained reasonably
constant considering the demands of greedy and quarrelsome family
members, marshals, generals and ministers. He continued to treat
old friends and even enemies generously. When the famous chemist
Claude Louis Berthollet was forced to borrow 150,000 francs to
meet his debts, Napoleon gave him the money "as a proof of my
esteem."[2] Other deserving officials were given valuable gifts, pro-
motions, honors, titles, in some cases houses and even estates. His
compassion frequently extended to people in trouble. Learning that
the mother of Joseph Sulkowski (killed in Egypt) had come on hard
times he awarded her an annual pension of 3,000 francs.[3] Probably
no veteran of a campaign who needed help was ever turned down.

Napoleon remained immensely popular with the army's rank and file although the soldiers were not quite so free with the cries of *Vive l'Empereur!* after the slaughters of Eylau, Heilsberg and Friedland. A certain tension also existed in his relations with some marshals and generals, particularly those who had not wanted a winter campaign in Poland. We see here the beginning of command cracks brought on by the weight of too many campaigns and battles, and by the ugly fact that Napoleon was showing himself entirely too prodigal with the lives of his *braves*.

He may have sensed this (although he would never admit it). He had issued more bulletins than ever for distribution in France, telling of the outstanding bravery and achievement of Ney, Lannes, Oudinot, Verdier, Mortier, Savary and many others. He was extremely generous to deserving commanders. Old Marshal Lefebvre, whose less than aggressive command at the siege of Danzig at times had driven Napoleon wild, was given the hereditary title of duke of Danzig. The ever-present Berthier would soon be appointed Vice Constable of the Empire. Davout was named the duke of Auerstädt.

He repeatedly rewarded the troops. Each soldier wounded at the battle of Ostrolenko had received one gold *Napoléon*, each wounded officer five of the coins (100 francs). He had done his best to get food, wine, brandy, tobacco and proper clothing to *les grondeurs*. He had established aid stations and hospitals wherever possible, and he often wrote personal notes to sick or wounded officers.

The emperor's *Correspondance* is full of letters of condolence to wives of officers killed in action, each of whom was promised the imperial favor for herself and children. After the peace of Tilsit he distributed hundreds, perhaps even thousands of silver eagles of the Legion of Honor to officers and men. He frequently congratulated satellite rulers on the performances of their corps. Generals Zajonchek and Dombromski each received one million francs' worth of crown property in Poland, with many other valuable portions going to deserving Polish officers.

Morale nonetheless suffered when the troops learned that they would remain in Germany until the Prussians paid every last *sou* of some 140 million francs still owed in contributions. Napoleon heard the rumblings. Soon after his return to Paris he distributed 11 million francs to his marshals and generals in gratitude for the victorious campaign. When the Imperial Guard later returned to Paris its soldiers were given a tremendous civic welcome as an honor to the entire army – but that scarcely rubbed off on men stuck in provincial Prussian garrison towns who wanted to return to their loved ones and who saw no sign of that happening. Most of the Grand Army remained in Prussia; other homesick troops were serving in Italy, Naples and Dalmatia and would soon be in Corfu – not to mention Spain and Portugal.

Seemingly confident that the treaty of Tilsit would soon bring England to the peace table, Napoleon called in his officials to whom he dictated a vast building program of canals, roads, bridges, harbors, drainage of marshes, city and town improvements, new schools, the resumption of all earlier projects so rudely interrupted by Prussia and Russia's military exuberance. This was followed by a "state of the empire" speech, a 28-page presentation that called for enormous improvements in cities, towns, schools, prisons, hospitals, farms, factories and the arts.

Napoleon probably intended to carry out this comprehensive plan (followed by more such). When in Prussia and Poland he had remained in constant touch with the Tuileries and on occasion had ordered various embellishments for Paris (mostly military monuments). From the depths of Poland he had sent a long dissertation on the need for expanded educational disciplines (some of his principles are in practice today) and he had prescribed in detail a strict regimen for a new girls' school. There is some evidence however that his earlier zeal for elaborate public works programs had been blunted by what he regarded as necessary continuing military adventures, as witness his official correspondence for the remainder of 1807.

Whatever the truth of his desires, several hindrances opposed the commencement, much less the completion, of these grandiose plans. One was lack of money, another Napoleon's ego and ambitions greatly enlarged by the last campaign and the treaty of Tilsit, a third an adverse effect of the continental system.

The French economy was wilting in the doldrums. The British blockade had brought maritime trade almost to a standstill. French, Russian, Danish, Spanish and American ships filled French ports, unable to sail through the screen of lurking British cruisers. French warehouses bulged with manufactures of all sorts, thousands of small factories had shut down, thousands of people were unemployed, beggars filled city streets, coffee, spices, sugar, tobacco and other colonial commodities had disappeared from store shelves. The situation was so serious that any neutral ship discharging cargo in a French port had to take on French goods of equivalent value, not the most enticing prospect for foreign shipowners and at any rate only a drop in a very big bucket of economic despair.

Trade stagnation had greatly reduced state and private incomes. Customs and tax collections dropped radically. Although money contributions from and financial impositions on conquered kingdoms and cities in the recent campaign were enormous – Savary later offered a figure of over 600 million francs[4] – large amounts still had not (and would not) be paid. Far from being able to support lavish domestic programs Napoleon had all he could do to maintain his army, even with numerous corps being fed and clothed at foreign expense.

That army had become the *sine qua non* of his foreign policy which was designed ultimately to bring England to its knees once the war on land had won the war at sea. The peace of Tilsit had made him master of almost all of western and southern Europe. He felt himself invincible, it was a matter now of closing the few remaining holes in the coastal curtain, and certainly no time for military economies.

This was a Catch-22 situation brought about by the villain of the piece, the continental system, which was hurting France and its allies nearly as much as it was hurting England. The peace of

Tilsit which so entranced its creator was an invidious trap. Napoleon failed to realize that he had guaranteed himself perpetual conflict by his insistence on expanding the blockade to neutral countries. It was moreover a dubious strategy at best in view of the diverse nature of European countries, long coastlines, thousands of small ports and hidden coves, the universal appeal, indeed necessity, of trade, the basic element of human greed and the tenacious character of the English nation supported by two mighty weapons, warships and money. Napoleon's imagination had conjured up a false picture of a starving island that soon would come begging for peace.

The fallacy of the system had almost immediately been suggested by increasingly effective smuggling. English merchandise was freely circulating in the Hanseatic towns, in Holland, Italy, the papal states, Etruria, Austria, Naples and elsewhere.[5] Enforcement of the blockade in these areas was already causing a great deal of discontent while not eliminating the flow of contraband goods.

This was only one drawback. The curtain had yet to be drawn. Owing to hostile pressures financed by England in the St. Petersburg court, Czar Alexander had held off from closing his ports while he attempted to mediate a peace between France and England. The key to the Baltic, Denmark, was still neutral, its ports open to English ships as were those of Portugal. Here was fertile ground for conflict – and conflict there would be.

Despite deluding himself that the continental system would swiftly bring his enemy to its knees, Napoleon was correct in his belief that it was seriously hurting England: its warehouses were also jammed with merchandise, its factories frequently closed, workers idle and angry. It was also suffering from the loss of merchant ships captured by enemy corsairs, not to mention expensive and humiliating military failures in South America. This bleak but scarcely hopeless state of affairs was inherited but not respected by the incoming Portland government. In the best Pittish tradition the new minister of foreign affairs, George Canning, seconded by the minister of war, Lord Castlereagh, was determined to rid the world of the monster Napoleon.

Their opening move was not impressive, the landing of a small force at Stralsund a month *after* the battle of Friedland. But now Canning decided to bring Denmark with its weighty battle fleet under his wing before Napoleon and Alexander moved in. Canning's offer to "rent" the Danish fleet for £100,000 a year was not only rejected but caused Denmark, cowed by neighboring French and allied forces, to declare war on England.

England responded by landing troops near Copenhagen and summoning the city to surrender. Refusal brought a heavy bombardment and submission. England walked away with 15 warships and numerous smaller vessels, but in a peace negotiated by Sir Arthur Wellesley agreed to evacuate its troops. These included the corps at Stralsund which the French now occupied along with Rügen island, hastily ceded by frightened Sweden.

The sudden English action caught France and Russia by surprise. In late August, Napoleon asked Alexander to persuade Sweden to come to Denmark's aid, adding that he would gladly commit his large force stationed at Hamburg. This came to nothing owing to the evacuation of British troops, but without doubt the assault proved that the old English lion could still pounce if sufficiently provoked. If its fleet could move on Denmark it could also move on Portugal – which Napoleon now decided to prevent.

He had long had his eye on Portugal. As First Consul seven years earlier he had suggested to the Spanish court that since Portugal refused to make peace the two countries should seize a few of its provinces.[6] Other matters interfered with this conquest which was revived a few years later when Napoleon and Manuel Godoy, the Prince of the Peace, worked out a combined plan to seize the entire country. This too was deferred by Napoleon's new war in the north and by his quarrel with Godoy who behind the emperor's back, so to speak, mustered a large Spanish militia uncomfortably close to the French border, a threat hastily removed when Austerlitz made Napoleon the master of Europe.

The emperor was still in Poland when he ordered General Junot, who had been misbehaving, to leave his lucrative post as governor of Paris and take command of a new Army of Observation in the Gironde. The reason became clear in July 1807 when Napoleon ordered Prince Regent Jean of Portugal to close his ports to English ships by the first of September or face a French invasion.[7]

The prince avoided the ultimatum by engaging in a series of diplomatic talks during which he seemed willing to cooperate. Correctly reading this as a ploy to gain time until England could extricate itself from Denmark and come to the rescue, Napoleon in early September sent him a sharp message to ally either with France or with England. King Charles of Spain was informed on the same day that only "carefully concerted and faithfully executed measures between the two courts could lead Prince Jean to make the right choice."[8]

These negotiations were no longer in foreign minister Talleyrand's hands. Whether because of his disapproval of Napoleon's foreign policy or because he had been caught out in subversive dealings with foreign governments, Talleyrand abruptly resigned in August and was replaced by the more complaisant if less able Jean-Baptiste Champagny to deal with the Portuguese crisis.

To aid Prince Jean in making the right choice, Napoleon sent General Junot with 25,000 troops from Bayonne across the Spanish border to march on Lisbon. Jean, a very weak man in his strongest moments, continued to vacillate between French and English demands, the one calling for dismissal of the English ambassador, a strong man named Lord Strangford, and closing of ports to English ships; the other for the royal family, the Portuguese battle fleet and treasury to sail for Rio de Janeiro, capital of the Portuguese colony of Brazil.

The prince regent hesitated too long. At a diplomatic reception in Paris in mid September, Napoleon coldly informed the Portuguese ambassador that the house of Braganza was finished. "My minister has left Portugal," Napoleon wrote Marshal Duroc

Junot, Andoche 1771–1813 French General

in late October. "I consider war declared on this power."[9] Junot was to march on Lisbon to seize the Portuguese fleet while a Spanish corps moved into the Algarve.

The French and Spanish courts signed the secret treaty of Fontainebleau in November. This called for the partition of Portugal, Prince Godoy to gain the southern third, a smaller portion to go to the infant king of Etruria and his mother, Queen Regent Marie Louise (in return for the kingdom of Italy absorbing Etruria), France to retain control of the remainder until the general peace. Junot in addition was to levy public and private contributions where possible. A second Army of Observation, 40,000 strong, was to be formed in Bayonne.[10]

Napoleon's bellicose actions had already frightened Prince Jean nearly to death and had caused him to renew frantic peace overtures to France.[11] Lashed by Napoleonic exhortations Junot's army was simultaneously slogging over mountains, through valleys and across barren plains in forced marches that were tearing his corps to pieces in an attempt to beat England to Lisbon.[12]

All in vain.

He was on the point of crossing the Portuguese border when Lord Strangford supported by Napoleon's old nemesis of Egypt days, Sir Sidney Smith, persuaded Prince Jean to load family and treasure on his flagship and sail the fleet to Brazil. Junot reached Lisbon a few days later with only a few thousand men, but no matter – Portugal was now held by French and Spanish troops, to close the last patch of curtain on the continent (at least in theory).

Notes

1   Corr. XV. Nr. 13034, Paris, 16 August 1807.
2   Corr. XV. Nr. 12502, Finkenstein, 1 May 1807.
3   Corr. XVI. Nr. 13133, Rambouillet, 8 September 1807.
4   Savary, III, 143–4.
5   Corr. XV. Nr. 12962, St. Cloud, 31 July 1807; Corr. XVI. Nr. 13196, Fontainebleau, 29 September 1807.
6   Corr. VI. Nr. 4727, Paris, 23 April 1800.
7   Corr. XV. Nr. 12928, Dresden, 19 July 1807.
8   Corr. XVI. Nrs. 13131, 13132, Rambouillet, 8 September 1807.
9   Corr. XVI. Nr. 13237, Fontainebleau, 12 October 1807.
10 Corr. XVI. Nrs. 13247, 13258, Fontainebleau, 16 October 1807; 13287, Fontainebleau, 23 October 1807; 13300, 13301, Fontainebleau, 27 October 1807.
11 Corr. XVI. Nr. 13340, Fontainebleau, 8 November 1807.
12 Corr. XVI, Nr. 13314, Fontainebleau, 31 October 1807. See also Thiébault, II, 196–9.

CHAPTER NINE

THE SPANISH ADVENTURE – I: NOVEMBER 1807–MAY 1808

Spain is a great nation [but] the indolence and ineptness of the Spanish court [and] the debasement of the people make its [military] attacks little to be feared. But the patient character of this nation, the pride and superstition which predominates, the resources offered by a large land will render it formidable if it is attacked.

Excerpt from General Napoleon Buonaparte's "A Note on the Political and Military Position of our Armies of Piedmont and of Spain . . .", Antibes, 19 July 1794, submitted to Maximilien Robespierre's Committee of Public Safety in Paris[1]

JUST WHEN NAPOLEON decided to steal the Spanish throne is difficult to say. Spain had been subordinated to French policy off and on since the 1795 treaty of Basle, the negotiation that brought peace with France and earned Manuel Godoy, the lover of Queen Marie Louise, the title of Prince of the Peace.[2]

Two years older than Napoleon, Godoy came from a noble but impoverished family and began his career in the royal guard. Young, virile, handsome, shrewd and ambitious, he soon became the royal favorite and, as prime minister, the virtual ruler of Spain.

Napoleon as First Consul had cosseted Godoy and his secret agent, Eugenio Izquierda, to increasingly suck troops, ships and money from this kingdom of disparate provinces peopled by deeply superstitious, religious, ignorant and impoverished peasants governed by independent and ultra-conservative provincial *juntas* or councils of nobles and priests. Godoy allied Spain with

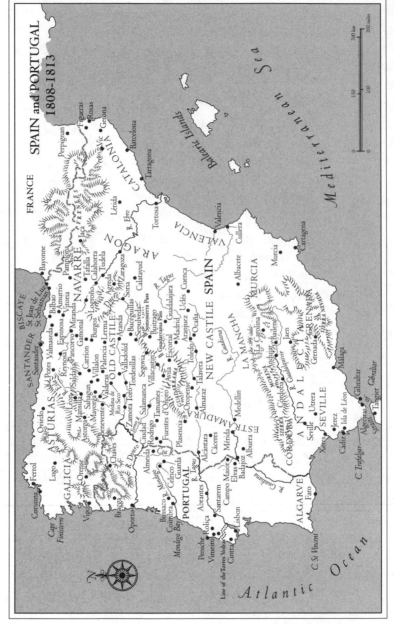

Spain and Portugal 1808–1813

France in the brief conquest of Portugal in 1801 (the treaty of Amiens restored its independence). He next allied with France in 1804, a disaster that cost Spain most of its fleet sunk at Trafalgar, another major blow to its diminishing influence in South America. In early 1806 he joined Napoleon in still another conquest of Portugal, a plan interrupted when the emperor marched the army off to war in the north.

Bribed by English gold Godoy now seriously erred by mobilizing a large militia army in northern Spain when the Grand Army was hundreds of miles distant in Germany. This watery show of defiance evaporated in the uncomfortable heat produced by French victories at Austerlitz and Jena-Auerstädt. Although Napoleon capitalized on Godoy's repentance by persuading the Spanish court to send 15,000 of its best regular troops to join the French army in occupying Swedish Pomerania, he never forgave Godoy's insolence which may have been a catalyst in his final decision to invade Spain.

Tantalizing hints foreshadow this decision. Manuel Godoy's usurpation of royal power had alienated the legitimate heir, Ferdinand, the prince of Asturias, around whom a strong opposition *junta* had formed. In October 1807 the 24-year-old prince, widowed the previous year, wrote to Napoleon asking permission to marry a Bonaparte princess in order to make "an alliance [that] was the ardent wish of all Spaniards."[3] Napoleon did not reply since he knew that Ferdinand was under strong English influence. King Charles got wind of the affair and complained to Napoleon who denied all. Charles nonetheless charged his son with high treason but then let the matter drop, even asking Napoleon to provide Ferdinand with a suitable bride (to which Napoleon eventually agreed).

Never one to overlook neighboring weakness, Napoleon now made discreet inquiries as to the political situation in Spain: "if opinion is in favor of the prince of Asturias or the prince of the Peace?" This question was variously pursued over the next two months, even to Marshal Bernadotte who was commanding the recently arrived Spanish troops in Pomerania.[4]

Also in autumn of 1807, Napoleon asked General Junot to send him detailed reports on Spanish roads, rivers, climate and striking terrain features noted while his troops crossed the peninsula. General Dupont's army, which began entering Spain in November under pretext of reinforcing Junot should the English attempt to seize Lisbon, was also charged with detailed reconnaissance of the area including Bilbao, Burgos and Pamplona "to determine the attitude of these places on the events which are passing in Spain."[5] Similar orders went to General Duhesme who led his division into Barcelona.

Even in aggregate these indications are scarcely incriminating. In Napoleon's mind nothing must come in the way of occupying Portugal. The only way he could guarantee this major blow to the English was to safeguard his line of communications through Spain, and he should not be professionally faulted for making adequate preparations to do this. The morality of his actions was another matter, but was consonant with his aggressive determination not only to seal the European coalition from English ships but also to achieve mastery of Europe and possibly points beyond. This was the real disadvantage of the treaty of Tilsit and alliance with Russia – it had opened to him the almost unlimited prospect of power not yet achieved.

His behaviour was scarcely subtle. Having kept his troops in Prussia as we have seen, he further flexed his muscles in Austria's direction to cause that court to declare war on England and to join the continental system. He steadily and heatedly encouraged King Joseph to seize Sicily, but even more important he ordered Viceroy Eugène to fortify the Dalmatian coast and particularly the island of Corfu (gained from Russia by the treaty of Tilsit), not only to control Adriatic waters but also to form a springboard for his earlier plan of a large Franco-Russian force descending on India. In December he annexed Etruria to his Italian kingdom (as agreed by the treaty of Fontainebleau), thus closing the port of Leghorn to the English.

*

Contrary to Napoleon's hopes, these and other extreme measures did not bring a contrite English government to the peace table. That enemy, though allied now only with a weak Sweden, was as determined as Napoleon to carry on the war. The old adage of an irresistible force meeting an immovable object remained as valid as ever. Not being able to fight on the ground in Europe, England fired a heavy naval salvo in November in the form of an Orders in Council decree: neutral ships could no longer enter continental ports without first either being searched by English cruisers at sea – and taken as prize if their cargoes were not properly certi-fied – or docking in an English port and paying a significant duty on their cargoes in order to be released.[6]

This surprise *ukase* infuriated Napoleon who was making a tour of Italy. Emboldened by his obvious strength on the conti-nent, Russia having recently declared war on England, he at once accused England of invalidating the age-old maritime respect for national flags by "denationalizing" all the ships of all nations. Henceforth, he announced in what would become famous as the "Milan decree", any neutral ship arriving in a French port which had allowed itself to be searched or had docked in an English port would be embargoed and its cargo seized; any ship sailing to or from English ports or its colonial ports would be considered a lawful prize for French corsairs.[7]

The English decree also angered the United States govern-ment, long since resentful of England's maritime arrogance. The Non-Intervention Act passed by Congress in December called for U.S.-registered ships to remain in American harbors, a sort of "plague on both your houses" action that backfired to bring severe repercussions and great hardship to American trade. Napoleon welcomed the move and in January 1808 informed the American minister in Paris that he "regarded America at war with England from the day the English pub-lished its decrees."[8] He would shortly follow this however by holding all American ships in French ports, in some cases con-fiscating and selling their cargoes, until further events, but this was softened somewhat by offering to persuade Spain to cede the

Spanish Floridas to America should the latter go to war against England.[9]

Napoleon returned to Paris in early January 1808. His aggressive foreign policy remained unchanged. Italy was to be heavily fortified. If the Sardinian court did not stop insulting French shipping the island would be invaded. If Pope Pius VII failed to join the continental system and send provocative pro-English bishops and Neapolitan rebels back to Naples, Rome would be militarily occupied – a rash act soon to be carried out by General Miollis. Soothing letters were sent to the shah of Persia whose cooperation would be important for a French march on India. King Joseph received numerous directives concerning the desired invasion of Sicily. Holland was to declare war on Sweden, arrest all Swedish agents and confiscate all Swedish boats and merchandise. Admiral Ganteaume was to reinforce the Corfu garrison and send several small expeditions to the colonies. Additional troops were to go to Spain, but in January of the new year the spotlight was more on Italy than on Spain.

That spotlight shifted quite suddenly in February when dissension in the Spanish court began coming to a head. The last thing Napoleon wanted was to break with this court, but now he found himself in a quandary. Manuel Godoy was so unpopular with the Spaniards, not least for being blamed for the presence of French troops, that he had to go; indeed articles in the *Moniteur* began attacking him in early February. King Charles and Queen Marie Louise were almost as unpopular and could not guarantee the surety of their country at this critical time. This left Prince Ferdinand, a lightweight at best, surrounded by a coterie of *seigneurs* in English pay. For the moment Napoleon would play both sides, offering one of Lucien's daughters to Ferdinand while making sure that the king, queen and treasury did not debunk to the New World.

On the pretext of supporting Junot in Portugal, Dupont's reserve corps had been deployed in the northwest and Duhesme's division in the northeast at Barcelona while a squadron of ships cruised off Cádiz to prevent the Spanish court from sailing.[10]

Murat, Joachim 1767–1815 Marshal of France

In mid February Dupont and Duhesme seized important fortified towns in their areas while more French reinforcements arrived in Bayonne and Perpignan. Marshal Joachim Murat (the grand-duke of Cleves and Berg) was named the emperor's lieutenant in Spain and was to have a vanguard of 50,000 troops at Burgos by mid March as preliminary to occupying Madrid. Dupont's corps now advanced to Valladolid and Moncey's to Aranda to shield Murat's right from a Spanish division in Galicia during his march on Madrid.

Napoleon nevertheless was taking numerous precautions to keep the peace. If Godoy questioned Murat's presence he was to be told that the marshal had come to inspect French troops. Two million gold francs were sent to Bayonne to ensure that the troops were paid so that they would not pillage: "The soldier should treat the Spanish as they would treat the French themselves."[11] Troop discipline was of paramount importance: "The most strict order should be observed during the march."[12] Napoleon informed the French minister in Madrid, François de Beauharnais, that Murat's army would enter the capital in late March. He was to ask the court's permission, explaining to the partisans of both Godoy and Ferdinand "that my project is to march on Cádiz in order to besiege Gibraltar [held by the British] and proceed on to Africa, and in passing to arrange affairs in Spain so as to leave no doubt as to the succession of the throne." If either Godoy or Ferdinand wished to meet the emperor at Burgos, that would be fine.[13]

At this point Napoleon appeared confident that he would peacefully settle his differences with the Spanish court. "I hope that there will be no war," he wrote Murat. ". . . If I take so many precautions it is because I am used to leaving nothing to chance . . . I want to remain friends with Spain and fulfill my political goal without hostilities, but I have to be able if necessary to overcome any resistance by force."[14]

He was about to receive a nasty shock. On 19 March he had written Murat that "I very much hope to learn that my troops have entered Madrid peacefully and with the consent of the king."[15] A few days later he wrote to explain that his departure for Spain had been delayed: Russia had invaded Finland and he was sending Bernadotte's corps into Sweden to assist the Russians. Murat was to hold steady until Napoleon arrived: "Have nothing to do with the different factions that divide the country and do not anticipate which side I shall take."[16]

But now he learned that Prince Ferdinand's clique, suspecting Godoy and the court at Aranjuez (about 25 miles south of Madrid) of plotting to kidnap the prince, had arranged an attack on Godoy's mansion. Godoy escaped the furious mob only by wrapping himself in a rush carpet in his attic where with the help of servants he remained for three days. In finally trying to escape he was intercepted and nearly beaten to death before Prince Ferdinand personally intervened. After several weeks in horrible jails – his blooded shirt remained unchanged and his beard grew to 7 inches in length – he arrived more dead than alive in Bayonne from where Napoleon would shunt him off to comfortable exile in France.[17]

The mob had also forced King Charles to abdicate in favor of Ferdinand, which was the situation when Murat's advance guard reached Madrid. Following orders Murat did not recognize Ferdinand as king. He placed the deposed monarch and his queen under French protection and installed them in the Escorial in the country outside Madrid with appropriate security. Murat's army was to remain in Madrid to keep the peace while ambassador Beauharnais met with the principals to settle "this affair."[18] This was not going to be easy since King Charles had meanwhile accused his son of forcing him to abdicate by threat of death and had reclaimed the crown – a crown respected by the French emperor.

Upon learning further details of the insurrection Napoleon suddenly awakened to the complexity of the situation which he examined in a long, somewhat bewildered and in part inaccurate appraisal written to Murat: "I fear that you have deceived me as to the situation in Spain along with yourself. The affair of March 20th has singularly complicated matters. I am left greatly perplexed." Perhaps the awkward turn of events brought to mind his cautionary words of nearly 14 years earlier – an excerpt is quoted at the beginning of this chapter – when he had warned the government not to carry the war across the Pyrenees, for now he continued in ruminative and disturbing thought:

Don't think that you attacked a disarmed nation which will submit merely at the sight of our troops. The revolution of March 20th proves that the Spanish have some strength. You are dealing with a newly awakened, courageous and enthusiastic people who have not worn out their political passions . . . Spain has more than 100,000 men under arms, more than enough to favorably support an internal war. They are strategically located and can serve as nuclei for a

total insurrection . . . The English will not fail to exploit
our difficulties. Their frigates are daily supplying their
forces on the Portuguese and Mediterranean coasts.[19]

This delicate situation demanded careful treatment. Little could
be hoped from the Spanish king and queen who were so unpopular that "they could not hold out for three months." Ferdinand as
king would be only the mouthpiece for factions that had wished to
destroy France for a quarter of a century. On the other hand both
Charles and Godoy controlled local supporters – Napoleon was
sending General Savary to Madrid to discuss the matter with King
Charles. "I don't believe we should precipitate anything; instead
we should deal with events as they arise. We must reinforce our
troops on the Portuguese frontier and see what happens."[20]

This was probably the most reasonable course of action but it
was based on a fallacy that would prove disastrous. "The aristocracy
and clergy are the masters of Spain," Napoleon proclaimed. He
was thinking in terms of an homogenous Spain ruled by a central
junta composed of court, nobles, clergy and generals. This was not
the case. Spain, as mentioned earlier, was a country of disparate
provinces and dialects loosely ruled by provincial *juntas* whose often
ignorant leaders held a bewildering variety of divergent views
except when it came to meddling foreigners. Extreme xenophobia
ruled the land, be it against the French, be it against the English.

Napoleon regarded Spain as another Egypt, another Italy, fit
only for colonization to be accomplished through this hypotheti-
cal ruling faction: Murat was to

impress on the nobles and clergy that if France should
intervene in the affairs of Spain their privileges and tax
exemptions will be respected. Tell them that the [French]
emperor wants their political institutions improved to put
them on a level with European civilization in order to
abolish the reign of favoritism. Tell the magistrates, the
middle-class citizens and the educated gentlemen that
Spain needs to recreate its governmental machinery; that

laws are necessary to protect its subjects from arbitrary feudal rule, that institutions are needed to revive industry, agriculture and the arts. Describe the state of tranquility and freedom enjoyed by France despite its unending wars, the magnificence of its religion resulting from the Concordat that I signed with the pope. Explain the advantages to be gained from a political regeneration: internal order and peace, external respect and power. This should be the subject of your speeches and writings.[21]

Murat was only too pleased to preach Napoleon's sermon to the *grandees*. His arrival in Madrid had been widely applauded by diverse Spanish delegations, to the extent that he fancied himself on the verge of obtaining what he had so long desired: his own crown. Napoleon obviously had heard unsettling rumors to this effect for in this same letter he warned the marshal of the dangers of personal ambition, and again exhorted him to avoid any engagement with Spanish forces: "If war comes all would be lost."[22]

Napoleon had still not decided on a specific course of action as he prepared to leave for the journey to Madrid where Murat was to find him suitable quarters: "I do not know if the Prado, the king's country house, is big enough for me. If it is not perhaps it would be convenient for me to go to the Escorial."[23]

He did not seem unduly worried, nor was he in any great hurry. He spent eight days in Bordeaux from where he informed Murat that he wanted to see Ferdinand – the now self-titled King Ferdinand VII – at Bayonne before deciding the future of the Spanish crown.

Security meanwhile was a major concern. He had already ordered Dupont to move headquarters to Toledo, southwest of Madrid, from where he could easily block the Badajoz and Cádiz roads to the capital in case a Spanish division approached from the Portuguese border. Additional reinforcements were reaching

Duhesme in Barcelona and Marshal Bessières, now commanding the French rearguard in Burgos. Murat was to keep a close eye on Prince (King) Ferdinand and explain to him that Napoleon's only desire was to conciliate all parties in establishing a government "that will maintain the integrity and independence of the Spanish monarchy."[24]

The emperor reached Bayonne in mid April. "I am in a horrible lodging," he complained to Joséphine, who was to follow him from Bordeaux, "but I'm moving shortly to a country house outside the city."[25] Anticipating Ferdinand's arrival he wrote to offer him a royal bride (one of Lucien's daughters) and recognition as king of Spain so long as his father's abdication "was not forced by the insurrection and mutiny of Aranjuez."[26] General Savary delivered this letter which was designed to test Ferdinand: either he would accept the invitation or would try to return to Madrid in which case he would be arrested and forcefully brought to Bayonne.[27]

Ferdinand accepted the invitation but in the interim the emperor, at King Charles' request, had agreed to arbitrate the quarrel. The meeting with Ferdinand was a non-event. "I had received him very well," Bessières was informed. ". . . I don't think that I should recognize him [as king]."[28] To Talleyrand: "The prince of Asturias is very stupid, very disagreeable, very much the enemy of France . . . The king of Prussia is a hero compared to the prince of Asturias. He has yet to say one word to me; he is indifferent to everything, very materialistic, eats four times a day and has no idea of anything."[29] As the day arrived for the reception of the king and queen Napoleon ceased relations with Ferdinand and had his correspondence with the Madrid *junta* intercepted. "I am continuing my military preparations in Spain," Talleyrand was informed. "If I do not deceive myself this tragedy is in the last act; the end is in sight."[30]

The curtain went up on the last act with a 60-gun salute to greet King Charles and Queen Marie Louise who were formally escorted to their fully staffed and well guarded palace, courtesy of Napoleon. The king was ill and senile, "a gallant man," Napoleon over-generously described him to Talleyrand, "with the sincere and good air of a patriarch." Queen Marie Louise "wears her heart and her history on her face – enough said. It surpasses anything that one could imagine."[31] (The reader will appreciate his remarks by taking a look at the Goya portrait of the royal family in the Prado.)

During the royal couple's brief stay the break with Ferdinand became final, the son at Napoleon's insistence writing a detailed apology for his behavior, the father a lengthy condemnation of his son, both pieces appearing in the Paris *Moniteur* and the *Gazette de Madrid* with copies sent to numerous foreign courts and embassies.

The time had come for Napoleon to end the affair. After forcing Ferdinand to return the crown to his father and "signing away his rights in return for a castle and a pension," he sent him and his brothers to enjoy life (under genteel house arrest) at Talleyrand's elegant estate of Valençay. Ferdinand was to receive an annual allowance of 500,000 francs, each of his brothers 400,000. King Charles formally ceded "all of his rights to the throne of Spain" in return for two French estates and an annual pension of about 7.5 million francs.[32]

These details out of the way Napoleon formally announced to the Spanish people and the supreme *junta* that Marshal Joachim (Murat) would command the kingdom and preside over all councils until a new king was chosen.[33]

Murat simultaneously opened a blitz campaign in Madrid to prepare the nation for the royal family's turnover of the crown and exile. Napoleon had toyed with taking the crown himself but finally offered it to King Louis of Holland. When Louis refused it Napoleon settled on King Joseph of Naples. "Spain is entirely different from the kingdom of Naples," Joseph was told. "It has eleven million inhabitants, more than 150 million [francs] of income without counting the immense revenues from its possessions in the Americas. In Madrid you are in France, Naples is at the end of the world."[34]

Napoleon now received another rude shock. He had several

times warned Murat against lodging his army in Madrid instead of keeping it together in the suburbs. Despite his exhortations discipline had deteriorated, with officers and men stealing money and valuables and otherwise acting as arrogant conquerors. This behavior had created a fertile field of discontent for Ferdinand's supporters to exploit. On 2 May a mob 30–40,000 strong rose against the French, firing on troops from windows and spilling into the streets to hunt down and slaughter 150–200 isolated soldiers.[35] Murat recovered quickly to declare martial law and a few hours later some 2,000 insurgents had been shot down or bayoneted – Goya's famous *Dos de Mayo* depicts the brutal beginning of a horrible war.

Notes

1   Colin, 443–7.

2   Carr, 82.

3   Rose (*Life*), II, 111–12.

4   Corr. XVI. Nrs. 13354, Fontainebleau, 13 November 1807; 13473, Paris, 19 January 1808.

5   Corr. XVI. Nr. 13353, Fontainebleau, 13 November 1807.

6   Rose (*Life*), II, 155–6.

7   Corr. XVI. Nr. 13391, Milan, 17 December 1807. See also Rose (*Life*), II, 155–7.

8   Corr. XVI. Nr. 13446, Paris, 12 January 1808. See also Adams, I, 1037–53, 1063–4, 1098–1103.

9   Corr. XVI. Nr. 13516, 2 February 1808.

10   Rose (*Life*), II, 163.

11   Corr. XVI. Nr. 13628, Paris, 8 March 1808.

12   Corr. XVI. Nr. 13632, Paris, 9 March 1808.

13   Corr. XVI. Nrs. 13629, 13632, Paris, 9 March 1808.

14   Corr. XVI. Nr. 13652, Paris, 14 March 1808.

15   Corr. XVI. Nr. 13664, Paris, 19 March 1808.

16   Corr. XVI. Nr. 13682, St. Cloud, 25 March 1808.

17   Corr. XVII. Nrs. 13780, Bayonne, 25 April 1808; 13793, Château de Marracq, 29 April 1808.

18 Corr. XVI. Nrs. 13695, St. Cloud, 27 March 1808; 13702, St. Cloud, 30 March 1808.

19 Corr. XVI. Nr. 13696, n.p., 29 March 1808.

20 Corr. XVI. Nr. 13696, n.p., 29 March 1808.

21 Corr. XVI. Nr. 13696, n.p., 29 March 1808. See also Roederer (*Journal*), 264–80.

22 Corr. XVI. Nr. 13696, n.p., 29 March 1808.

23 Corr. XVI. Nr. 13711, St. Cloud, 1 April 1808.

24 Corr. XVI. Nrs. 13730, Bordeaux, 9 April 1808; 13733, Bordeaux, 10 April 1808.

25 Corr. XVII. Nr. 13752, Bayonne, 17 April 1808.

26 Corr. XVII. Nr. 13750, Bayonne, 16 April 1808.

27 Corr. XVII. Nr. 13756, Bayonne, 17 April 1808. See also Savary, III, 287–8.

28 Corr. XVII. Nr. 13773, Bayonne, 22 April 1808. See also Savary, III, 336.

29 Corr. XVII. Nr. 13778, Bayonne, 25 April 1808.

30 Corr. XVII. Nr. 13778, Bayonne, 25 April 1808.

31 Corr. XVII. Nrs. 13794, Bayonne, 30 April 1808; 13797, Bayonne, 1 May 1808.

32 Corr. XVII. Nr. 13834, Bayonne, 9 May 1808.

33 Corr. XVII. Nr. 13813, Bayonne, 5 May 1808.

34 Corr. XVII. Nr. 13844, Bayonne, 10 May 1808.

35 Corr. XVII. Nrs. 13821, Bayonne, 6 May 1808; 13894, Bayonne, 15 May 1808.

CHAPTER TEN

THE SPANISH ADVENTURE – II: INSURRECTION MAY–AUGUST 1808

*Your monarchy is old: my mission is to rejuvenate it . . . Trust
in me for I want your descendants to preserve my memory and
say:* he restored our country.

Napoleon's proclamation to the Spanish people,
Bayonne, 25 May 1808[1]

NEWS OF UPRISINGS in Madrid and Burgos did not greatly disturb
Napoleon. "I am very pleased with the force that you have
shown," he wrote Marshal Murat three days after the event. "I
hope that you will proceed to disarm the people as rapidly as
possible."[2] As with Italian and Egyptian rebels those of Spain had
been severely punished to end the trouble. Intercepted correspondence showed the instigators to have been Prince Ferdinand's
junta but since that prince and his brothers were about to be
exiled to France, Napoleon reasoned that the problem should be
solved.[3]

A few days later however he learned of "fermentations" in
Valladolid, Ciudad Rodrigo and Salamanca which were on his line
of communications to Portugal. At the first sign of real trouble, he
wrote Marshal Bessières, the rebels must be given a severe lesson:
"It is in speaking firmly that you will prevent those people there
from doing foolish things."[4] Murat meanwhile had slackened his
efforts, displaying the false confidence "of a child," which could
only lead to another and far more serious uprising: "Fortify the
New Palace," he was ordered, "the arsenal and the casernes."[5]

The emperor's mild alarm soon vanished as more French troops arrived and as various *juntas*, suitably massaged by Murat, formally requested Joseph Bonaparte to take the Spanish crown. Napoleon next called for an assembly of provincial deputies to meet at Bayonne in mid June to put a popular seal of approval on the appointment.[6] Meanwhile he concerned himself with meeting the costs of occupying both Spain and Portugal. General Junot was to send him 6 million francs in cash from Lisbon and raise another 50 million by sequestering private and church properties. Murat was busily raising money in Madrid, where Napoleon thought he could easily come up with 25 million francs by borrowing on the royal diamonds.[7]

"Public opinion is coming around to my wishes," Napoleon informed Prince Cambacérès. "Peace will reign everywhere."[8] And to Talleyrand, "The affairs of Spain are going well and are on the way of being terminated."[9]

In preparing for the Bayonne assembly Napoleon sent the draft of a new constitution to Murat who was to ask for comments from leading Spanish officials. He accompanied this with the proclamation to the Spanish people cited in part at the beginning of this chapter: "Your monarchy is old: my mission is to rejuvenate it. I will improve your institutions and will make you happy, if you support me, with the benefits of reform without annoyances, disorders or convulsions." After announcing the convocation of a general assembly and a new constitution, he concluded: "Spaniards, recall what your fathers have been: see what you have become. This is not your fault but rather that of a bad government. Trust in me for I want your descendants to preserve my memory and say: *he restored our country.*"[10]

By early June then the French position in the Iberian peninsula seemed to Napoleon to be more than satisfactory. The Army of Spain had increased to 80,000 men with more units arriving daily. As he confidently asserted to General Junot, the Spanish affair would be finished by November.[11]

*

The emperor's optimistic prognosis was already being challenged by events, unwanted symptoms of a dangerous illness that in time would become a malignancy impossible to cure. The brutal repression of the Madrid uprising taken with the forced exile of the royal family had brought fresh rebellions led by revolutionary *juntas* throughout the country. Pro-French governors and mayors in Badajoz, Cartagena, Jaen, Cádiz and elsewhere had been hunted down and murdered by armed mobs. Several areas in the provinces of Valencia and the Navarre were up in arms, rebellion had broken out in Seville, a revolutionary council in Oviedo in the northern province of the Asturias had voted to raise a large insurgent army. Although Spain was still at war with England the Seville *junta* had asked the English governor of Gibraltar for arms and money, while a deputation from the Asturias would soon appear in London with hats in hand – appeals that would result in a hastily contrived peace and the formation of a British expeditionary corps to land in Portugal.[12]

In early June a serious uprising in the port of Santander had caused Bessières to commit a corps several thousand strong, his generals "to impose prompt and severe justice" in order to prevent the English from exploiting the situation. Bessières was also to send "two or three good priests" in advance "to make the inhabitants realize how much their infatuation with the English was pushing them to total ruin." The troops were to disarm the inhabitants, shooting anyone found with arms. Bessières was to ask important officials including the captain-general of Old Castile, Cuesta, to issue proclamations "to make the people know the misery that the rebellion will bring."[13]

Other French corps were dispatched to Aragon province where 12,000 rebels were holding the lovely old city of Zaragoza. Still other divisions marched to put down disturbances in Pamplona and Logroño in the north, Valladolid, Salamanca and Segovia in the west and Córdoba and Seville in the south. The extent of what Napoleon euphemistically termed "fermentations" should have triggered a warning of things to come, the more so since rebellions in Portugal had severed French communications by forcing Junot's divisions to retreat behind Lisbon defenses.[14]

Napoleon had misread the political and military aspects of his new conquest. He had supposed that the supine and sympathetic behavior of the Spanish *grandees* would guarantee the introduction of his wide-ranging reforms. While French troops were marching to trouble spots around the kingdom the deputies of the Castile *junta* arrived in Bayonne. One of their early acts, prompted by Napoleon, was to issue a proclamation that welcomed the French presence. This was widely distributed throughout the country as were appeals to various rebel forces to put down their arms and end the anarchy that would destroy Spain if unchecked. They then met with Napoleon to discuss the proposed constitution that was to awaken Spain from its century-long torpor. Such was their cooperative attitude that Napoleon could not conceive of their people failing to welcome his intercession and his intention of ridding the land of rapacious priests and dangerous inquisitors.

His next failure resulted from an innate disrespect for Spanish arms whether regular army, militia or irregular "rabble". The Spanish army was not a formidable force. The captains-general of Old Castile and Andalucia, Cuesta and Castaños, had declared for the French. Disorganized militia groups though numerous were scattered about the country and represented little cohesive threat. Irregular troops who would become famous as guerrillas were still few and widely dispersed.* Order had easily been restored to Santander. General Verdier attacked 2,000 insurgents at Logroño, killed 3–400 and captured their seven cannon. "Order is entirely restored," Napoleon reported to Murat, "at a cost of three or four wounded French." Lasalle's cavalry fell on a strong force north of Valladolid and put it to flight after sabering some fifty unfortunates. Marshal Bessiérés had already collected 16,000 weapons in Castile and Palencia,

---

*The Spanish word *guerrilla* translates to "little war" which was fought by *guerrilleros*, a word corrupted into guerrilla in the English language.

Marshall Lefebvre confiscated 20,000 muskets in the Aragon – "everywhere the patrols entered, the people submitted," Napoleon noted. In pacifying Catalonia, General Duhesme attacked a force a few miles from Barcelona, killed over 1,800 rebels and burned nine villages at a cost of six French killed and twelve wounded. Among the Spanish dead, Napoleon wrote, were "a great number of army officers, priests and monks," a fact that did not disturb him (even though generals Cuesta and Castaños had recently gone over to the insurgents and taken their corps into Galicia). Approaching Zaragoza, Marshal Lefebvre found the heights of the town defended by 12,000 irregulars, two Spanish line regiments and some cavalry. A French charge killed 2,000 men and captured 10 cannon at a cost of five French dead and eight wounded – of his entire force only three companies of light infantry fired their weapons.[15]

So it was that give or take a few setbacks Napoleon had no reason to question his tactics. His troops everywhere had put down insurrections, his line of communications seemed to be re-established, King Joseph had been well received by the Spanish delegations, the most powerful *juntas* seemed to be at one with the French.

None the less a few weak spots existed. Army morale was not all it should have been. The troops loathed the country, the long marches often in extreme heat over narrow twisting mountain trails, primitive accommodations in barns, the hay teeming with lice, poor rations and dreadful wine. They hated the people and the people hated them. They had constantly to be alert. Loiterers were often tortured before being killed. Couriers were ambushed, their parcels taken, their throats slit. Marshal Murat was ill in Madrid of an undefined "serious malady" (said to be of the mind) which left field commanders at loose ends until Napoleon sent General Savary to act in his place.

As Napoleon might have foreseen, Joseph had soon become a nervous wreck, forever tilting at windmills, forever needing pampering and reassurance that all was going well. Napoleon's adjurations became a virtual litany: "Don't worry, you shall lack nothing," letter after letter the same, "Be happy and content, take care of your health"; "Be gay, let nothing bother you, and don't for a moment doubt that everything will finish better and more promptly than you think."[16]

A final weakness stemmed from Napoleon himself. His diplomacy was atrocious. The exclusion of either King Charles or Prince Ferdinand from rule was doomed from the beginning, as anyone with the slightest knowledge of the Spanish character would have realized. The center of power envisaged by Napoleon did not exist. The *grandees* who had propped up the throne were as despised as the French. Military occupation had turned into a war of pacification that neither Napoleon nor his generals knew how to fight. It was a fast-moving series of small wars in a big country, not a war of corps and divisions. Early successes, a few hundred insurgents shot here, a few thousand there, villages burned, arms collected, private properties and fortunes sequestered, officials and priests forced to swear allegiance to the new crown, cities and towns required to pay enormous "contributions" – all these were ingredients for a massive civil explosion.

Napoleon was a "big battle" general. Nothing shows this more clearly than a lengthy analysis of the military situation that he dictated for Joseph's benefit in mid July. His key player was Marshal Bessières who with some 17,000 troops was to attack Cuesta's army, hopefully to push it back into Galicia and break its communications with the Estremadura, Madrid and Andalucia, thus ensuring French communications with Junot in Portugal.[17]

Bessières came on Cuesta's large army at Medina de Rio Seco to win a victory by an early morning attack made more daring in view of his limited numbers against 35,000 Spanish occupying "a superb position defended by four cannon." Cuesta lost 5–6,000 killed, several thousand taken prisoner and all of his artillery against French casualties of 30 dead and 250 wounded. Once reinforced, Bessières was to march into Galicia, eliminate Cuesta's remnants and close the sea coasts to the English.

Napoleon was delirious with joy: "This affair will give us all of Galicia and will decide the affairs of Spain." General Dupont who meanwhile had defeated rebel forces at Córdoba and Jaen in Andalucia would now be reinforced sufficiently to eliminate General Castaños' army.[18] King Joseph would shortly enter Madrid in triumph to begin what Napoleon foresaw as "a beautiful and glorious task" of rebuilding the country.[19]

The victory came at a good time. Napoleon could no longer ignore matters in his northern ramparts. He had become increasingly concerned by reports that Austria once again was arming, and he was also displeased with Czar Alexander's refusal to remove his troops from the lower Danube provinces, as agreed upon at Tilsit. In early June he had written Alexander that once affairs were settled in Spain, "I shall be able to meet you at your convenience in order to reconcile the different interests of our empires."[20]

Napoleon's optimism did not last long. At Bordeaux on his return journey to Paris he learned that General Dupont's reinforced corps in Andalucia had been attacked by General Castaños and forced to retreat. "This is inconceivable," he wrote Joseph, but scarcely crucial in that Dupont's losses could easily be replaced. However, the gory details arrived two days later. Under pressure from the Spaniards Dupont had retreated from Córdoba to Andujar on the Guadalquivir river from where the general planned to recross the Sierra Morena range into La Mancha.

Dupont's position was precarious. He himself was seriously ill. Most of his generals were more intent on saving wagonloads of loot pilfered from churches, convents and rich *fincas* than on fighting Castaños. As one result the overloaded columns had moved like snails and the divisions and brigades had become separated.

Castaños caught up with Dupont's lead division in the area of Bailen. Here Dupont fought only briefly before accepting an armistice, the first step in surrendering his entire corps under allegedly honorable conditions so that the officers could save their plunder (which ironically, owing to a *cambo de sentido* or change of mind on Castaños' part, they soon lost).

Twenty thousand French soldiers taken prisoner with arms in hand, cannon ready to fire: a humiliation comparable only with the disastrous battle of Rossbach in 1757 when Frederick the Great's Prussians captured an entire French army. "Never since the world existed has there been anything so stupid, so inept, so cowardly," Napoleon explosively wrote General Clarke in Paris. "One sees from General Dupont's report exactly what happened." How could Dupont have done this to him? Dupont whose troops nearly ten years earlier had saved the day of 19 *brumaire* at St. Cloud. Dupont whom Napoleon was training for a marshal's baton – "He had seemed to do well in commanding a division," Napoleon went on. "He has been dreadful in commanding a corps."[21]

This "horrible catastrophe" which exposed Madrid to attack from the south caused a panic-stricken Joseph to evacuate the government after only nine days in the capital and, deserted by most of his Spanish ministers and advisers, fall back with his troops to the line of the Duero river. As Miot de Melito (now Count de Melito soon to join Joseph's staff) later wrote: "On leaving Madrid the monarch ceased to exist; there remained only a general and an army in retreat."[22] Marshal Bessières on the verge of marching into Galicia now had to withdraw to the Duero while General Verdier was forced to raise the siege of Zaragoza. General Duhesme's troops perforce retired into Barcelona fortresses, thus yielding all of Catalonia to rebel movements. The psychological results were incalculable both in Spain and throughout Europe.

The deed being done, the damage had to be repaired. Napoleon was sending Marshal Ney, one of his most aggressive commanders, to Spain along with an infantry corps and some cavalry. "Almost all the Grand Army is on the march, by autumn Spain will be inundated with troops," he informed a shaken Joseph a few days later. "Try to defend the line of the Duero in order to maintain communications with Portugal. The English don't amount to anything . . . Lord [sic] Wellesley does not have 4,000 troops and these moreover are headed for Portugal, I believe."[23]

Notes

1   Corr. XVII. Nr. 13989, Bayonne, 25 May 1808.
2   Corr. XVII. Nr. 13813, Bayonne, 5 May 1808.
3   Corr. XVII. Nr. 13894, Bayonne, 15 May 1808.
4   Corr. XVII. Nr. 13860, Bayonne, 11 May 1808.
5   Corr. XVII. Nr. 13879, Bayonne, 13 May 1808.
6   Corr. XVII. Nr. 14051, Bayonne, 2 June 1808.
7   Corr. XVII. Nrs. 13896, Bayonne, 15 May 1808; 14013, Bayonne, 28 May 1808; 14052, Bayonne, 3 June 1808.
8   Corr. XVII. Nr. 13888, Bayonne, 15 May 1808.
9   Corr. XVII. Nr. 13899, Bayonne, 16 May 1808.
10   Corr. XVII. Nr. 13989, Bayonne, 25 May 1808.
11   Corr. XVII. Nr. 14053, Bayonne, 3 June 1808.
12   Bryant (*Victory*), 226.
13   Corr. XVII. Nrs. 14054, 14055, Bayonne, 3 June 1808.
14   Bryant (*Victory*), 239.
15   Corr. XVII. Nrs. 14072, Bayonne, 8 June 1808; 14089, Bayonne, 13 June 1808; 14102, 14103, Bayonne, 16 June 1808. See also Bartel, 93–5.
16   Corr. XVII. Nrs. 14191, Bayonne, 13 July 1808; 14195, Bayonne, 14 July 1808; 14218, Bayonne, 19 July 1808; 14222, Bayonne, 21 July 1808; 14240, Bordeaux, 1 August 1808. See also Miot de Melito, II, 245–9.
17   Corr. XVII. Nr. 14196, Marracq, 14 July 1808.
18   Corr. XVII. Nrs. 14212, 14213, Bayonne, 17 July 1808; 14215, Bayonne, 18 July 1808.
19   Corr. XVII. Nr. 14218, Bayonne, 19 July 1808.
20   Corr. XVII. Nr. 14059, Bayonne, 3 June 1808.
21   Corr. XVII. Nr. 14242, Bordeaux, 3 August 1808. See also Miot de Melito, II, 262–7; Savary, III, 384–402.
22   Miot de Melito, II, 257.
23   Corr. XVII. Nr. 14247, Nantes, 9 August 1808.

CHAPTER ELEVEN

BETRAYAL AT ERFURT
AUGUST–OCTOBER 1808

*Sire, what are you coming here for? It is for you to save
Europe, and you will only succeed in that by resisting
Napoleon. The French are civilized, their sovereign is not. The
sovereign of Russia is civilized, his people are not. Therefore
the sovereign of Russia must be the ally of the French people.*

Talleyrand to Czar Alexander, Erfurt, August 1808[1]

St. Cloud, mid August, 1808:

NAPOLEON FOUND HIMSELF strategically between two stools, one
the war in Spain, the other the situation in the north. Recent
information from the peninsula was especially upsetting. How
could Joseph authorize his army to retreat "without having seen
the enemy, without attempting to give battle?" he asked Berthier.
Such a precipitous move without reason showed a complete ignorance of war. How could Marshal Bessières be ordered to leave
highly favorable ground and withdraw to unfavorable terrain
"without knowing the location of the enemy?" How could
Verdier's corps be pulled out of Zaragoza, then returned without
support to expose it to ruin when it was vital for the defense of
Pamplona and the Navarre? It would appear, he angrily wrote
Berthier, that the army had fallen into the stupid trap of waging
cordon warfare as if the enemy were a bunch of smugglers rather
than soldiers.[2]

Upsetting reports continued to arrive. Almost all of the Spanish
corps sent to Pomerania, some 15,000 first-line troops, had

deserted Marshal Bernadotte's command to sail for Spain on English ships. Wellesley's force meanwhile had worked down the Portuguese coast toward Lisbon. Junot had sent General Laborde's division to hold the British advance until Loison's division could attack the English left flank. This having failed, Junot prematurely attacked only to be sent reeling with a loss of 2,000 men, a shock that caused him to ask for surrender under honorable conditions. The subsequent convention of Cintra allowed him to embark his army including weapons, cannon and plunder on British ships for transport back to France. This idiotic agreement, the work of Wellesley's two old and incompetent superiors, not unnaturally caused an uproar in England, the principals including Wellesley being ordered home to face an inquiry. General Sir John Moore with 30,000 troops remained in possession of Portugal.[3]

Napoleon was still fuming over Dupont's capitulation at Bailen: Dupont "has shown as much ineptness as pusillanimity," he wrote Marshal Davout. "When you learn the details your hairs will stand up on your head."[4] General Clarke, minister of war, was to compile a dossier on which to base courtmartials of the culpable generals who were to be arrested upon their arrival in France.[5]

The emperor meanwhile tried to control the damage by sending reams of "observations" to Joseph along with a new chief of staff, Marshal Jourdan, and additional troops from Germany. The Army of Spain was henceforth to consist of six corps commanded by Victor, Bessières, Moncey, Lefebvre, Gouvion St. Cyr and Ney, and was to hold the line of the Ebro river until ready for a new campaign. Once reinforcements arrived, Joseph was to open a second siege of Zaragoza, occupy the port of Santander and win the kingdom of Léon. Berthier meanwhile was to press hard on the new chief of staff, Jourdan: "It appears that in the Burgos theater of war the army is without purpose . . . It is only with vigorous and positive plans that one succeeds at war."[6]

Napoleon now took another knock when he learned of Junot's capitulation in Portugal followed by Sir John Moore's march to join Cuesta's army in Galicia. "The English are landing nearly 40,000 men in Spain and Portugal," he wrote Jérôme. "I shall soon march there myself."[7]

There remained the situation in the north. In early September, Napoleon informed the senate that he was going to destroy the English forces in Spain – that "my alliance with the Russian emperor leaves England with no hope for its projects." He mentioned Austria only by inference: "I believe the continent to be at peace . . . [but] because my neighbors increase their arms, it is my duty to increase mine."[8]

This last sentence was somewhat clarified in a lengthy "report" to Napoleon by his minister of foreign affairs, Champagny, a few days earlier. This work, believed to have been written by Napoleon, touched lightly on Austria's seemingly friendly behavior in recalling its minister from London, dismissing the English minister from Vienna and closing its ports to English and other ships suspected of carrying English merchandise. But "this power having increased its army beyond all measure in proportion to its population and finances," it would have to be checked. Prussia was mentioned only in passing.[9]

Prussia nevertheless formed a worrisome factor as it slowly recovered from battered impotence – the work of two men, a civilian and a soldier. The civilian was a fireball named Baron Heinrich Friedrich vom und zum Stein. Ironically he had become prime minister in summer of 1807 owing to Napoleon having forced King Frederick William to sack Count Hardenberg. Stein had persuaded the king to institute some major reforms which were announced in autumn of 1807, the main one being the elimination of serfdom. "The chief idea was to arouse a moral, religious and patriotic spirit in the nation," Stein wrote, "to instil into it again courage, confidence, readiness for every sacrifice in behalf of independence from foreigners and for the national honor, and to seize the first favorable opportunity to begin the bloody and hazardous struggle."[10]

The soldier was General Gerhardt Johann von Scharnhorst who headed a royal commission charged with investigating the recent defeat of Prussian arms. Scharnhorst had been preaching the need for military reform for years and had attracted a following of enlightened officers that included August von Gneisenau. Well aware of the army's unpopularity, the legacy of the Junkers' unbelievable aristocratic arrogance, Scharnhorst called for military reforms that would "raise and inspire the spirit of the army . . . bring the army and nation into a more intimate union and . . . guide it to its characteristic and exalted destiny."[11] Civilian and soldier were obviously not far apart and their desire to bridge the gulf between governors and governed by creating a new national spirit was emphasized early in 1808 by the famous philosopher, Johann Gottlieb Fichte, in his chauvinistic *Address to the German Nation*.

In attempting to implement military reforms Scharnhorst would fight a long and in many ways unsuccessful battle; however he did push through a decree in August 1808 that allowed commoners to enter the heretofore sacrosanct Junker officer corps and also abolished, at least in theory, the brutal punishments for which the Prussian army was famous.[12]

Napoleon received some inkling of this resurgent spirit when French forces in Brunswick were fired on in September, but he seems to have missed the motivation: "I see there a popular insurrection which is a result of the discontent that I am assured exists in Westphalia and in several German states," he informed King Jérôme. "I am told that you have few police in your kingdom and that the agents of the old princes are striking out in all directions . . . You must identify the instigators of this mutiny at all costs and publicly punish them or you will soon have more serious uprisings."[13]

In several flattering letters Napoleon had been very careful to keep Czar Alexander informed of the French presence in Spain. In early July he had sent the czar a copy of the proposed new Spanish constitution, explaining that

the disorders of this country have reached a degree difficult
to conceive. Forced to intervene by the persistent decline in
affairs, I have introduced a system which, in assuring the
well-being of Spain, assures the peace of my states. Under
the new system Spain in reality will be more independent
of me than it has ever been, but I shall have the advantage
in that, finding itself in a congenial position and having not
to worry from the land standpoint, it will employ all its
means in reestablishing its navy. I am very satisfied with all
persons of rank, fortune or education. The monks alone,
who occupy half the land, foresee in the new order of
things the elimination of abuses, and the numerous agents
of the Inquisition who fear for their extinction are agitating
the country.[14]

While traveling back to France, Napoleon received a note from the
czar who "made me know that if I have war with Austria he will
ally with me, and he shows me much understanding on the affairs
of Spain, the news of which is beginning to reach him."[15]
Arrangements were subsequently made for a meeting of the two
rulers at Erfurt in Saxony come late September.

Napoleon was not so sanguine about Austria. Although in his
correspondence he continued to insist that relations were never
more pacific, reports that Emperor Francis had reorganized his
army and was rearming had upset him. "Does Austria wish then
to make war or does it wish to frighten us?" he bluntly asked the
Austrian ambassador in Paris, Count Metternich. When
Metternich stressed the pacific intentions of his government,
Napoleon continued. "If that is so then why your immense preparations?" Purely defensive, Metternich smoothly replied. "Who is
threatening you?" Napoleon demanded. "What makes you think
that you will soon be attacked?" He then delivered a lengthy lecture to the ambassador, leaving little doubt in pointing to the evils
of a new war. "If your dispositions are as peaceful as you say, you
must announce it . . . all Europe must be convinced that you wish
peace."[16]

It was not an easy situation and Napoleon's ambiguity was plain:

> Austria arms, but it arms from fear [he wrote Davout in Warsaw]. Our relations with this power are of the best, but the fact remains that she is building up her army and I have begun to demand some firm explanations. I am sure of Prussia which prevents me from fearing anything from Austria, however it is necessary to hold steady and keep one's eyes open. I intend to evacuate Prussia and execute the treaty of Tilsit . . . All the [German] confederation troops are under arms and would march at the slightest sign of a threat from Austria. Reassure people where you are that I want nothing from Austria.[17]

Two weeks later he wrote King Jérôme: "I am certain of Russia's feelings. Austria's pacific language is contradicted by its armaments."[18]

How certain was he of Russia? Shortly after the Tilsit meeting he had sent General Savary to St. Petersburg to report on the political climate. From Savary's letters and from subsequent reports of his new ambassador to Russia, General Caulaincourt, he knew that Czar Alexander had experienced a less than triumphal return from Tilsit. Influential court elders in St. Petersburg, many of them in English pay, correctly argued that he had given away too much and gained too little. Alexander himself was annoyed with the French emperor for his harsh treatment of Prussia, his insistence on clinging to the Oder fortresses, his retaining Silesia so long as Russian troops remained in the lower Danube provinces, and he deeply resented Napoleon's refusal to allow Russia free play with the Ottoman Porte. Napoleon also realized that Alexander was not endowed with a strong character and, like Emperor Francis of Austria and King Frederick William of Prussia, was apt to be easily swayed by advisers hostile to France, by pernicious propaganda and other activities of English agents and by adverse reports from the new Russian ambassador in Paris, Count Pierre Tolstoy. He had hoped to counter these noxious influences, at least in part, by Savary and Caulaincourt's diplomacy – not the wisest choices in view of their known connections with the d'Enghien execution* – and by his own direct correspondence with the czar.

Napoleon was playing for high stakes. The success of his grand strategy designed to bring England to the peace table rested on the successful outcome of the war in Spain. To secure victory in the peninsula he would need to transfer units from the Grand Army in Germany. This left the danger of an Austrian attack unless the czar proved good for his word given at Tilsit.

The time had come to reaffirm the Tilsit pledges by a grand conference at Erfurt, a glittering demonstration of solidarity among France, Russia and the German courts, a display that the Austrian court would have to respect.

General Savary later described Napoleon's elaborate preparations for the Erfurt meeting: the most minute arrangements for guards, escorts, lodgings furnished with the richest tapestries, paintings and sculptures brought from Paris, ornate dining tables covered with linens, gold and silver dishes, the finest china and crystal, elaborate menus prepared by French chefs, the most precious wines, beautiful carriages, superb horses, the best professional entertainment. A battalion of chefs, *maîtres d'hôtel*, liveried ser- vants and coachmen would ensure everyone's comfort as they were regally entertained by the great tragedian Talma and the entire troupe of the *Comédie Française* along with top singers and musicians from the *Opéra*.[19]

The extravaganza opened in late September when Napoleon's carriage accompanied by outriders and glittering cavalry thun- dered into the old Thuringian town. The next day Napoleon and

---

*See Chapter 42, Vol. I, *The Rise*.

his staff rode to meet Czar Alexander at Weimar and escort him
to Erfurt, the road bordered by brilliantly uniformed French hussars who presented arms as the monarchs trotted past on brightly
caparisoned horses.

The diplomatic social whirl had already begun. Erfurt citizens
had never seen the like. The town was jammed with royalty, Czar
Alexander and his elegant martial brother, the towering grand-
duke Constantine, the kings of Bavaria, Württemberg and
Westphalia, the reigning princes and dukes of Germany, hosts of
other princes and princesses, dukes and duchesses, counts and
countesses, barons and baronesses, each wearing their most elegant garb and most expensive jewels, each with their court
minions and lackeys. "I found all Erfurt astir," Talleyrand later
wrote, "there was not a decent house that did not lodge some
ruler and his retinue."[20]

Talks between Napoleon and Alexander began the next day
and continued for two weeks. In view of the social schedule one
wonders how any business was conducted. This was a calendar of
hedonism, of elegant luncheons, prolonged dinners, all-night
balls, moving dramatic performances, beautiful concerts, illicit
liaisons, enchanting operas, exciting hunts, quiet walks and long
horseback rides as Napoleon attempted to revive his political and
personal dominance over the younger Russian ruler. In view of the
divisive issues at work this would not be easy. Astute diplomacy
possibly could have brought Alexander back to the comfortable
fold of Tilsit, but here Napoleon seriously erred by entrusting
Talleyrand with the task.

It was a strange decision. Talleyrand later wrote that Napoleon
took him along because of his good relationship with Alexander at
Tilsit and because of minister Champagny's ineptness – in
Napoleon's words, "arriving zealously every morning in order to
excuse his blunders of the previous day" – and also because of
Talleyrand's close relationship with General Caulaincourt, the
French ambassador at St. Petersburg.[21]

None of these qualifications seems sufficient to have overridden
Talleyrand's recent eclipse. Perhaps Napoleon believed that his

Talleyrand-Périgard, Charles Maurice de 1754–1838 Grand Chamberlain

past contributions to Talleyrand's welfare – and they were many and generous – would ensure his loyalty. Or perhaps he knew that if negotiations proved to be unsatisfactory he could always over ride them. We don't know.

Talleyrand's first official mission was political. If the czar joined Napoleon in objecting to Austrian preparations for war, Emperor Francis would back down thus freeing the French hand in Spain. The second mission was personal and dynastic. Napoleon had almost decided to divorce Joséphine and wanted the czar's permission to marry one of his sisters.

According to Talleyrand's memoirs he met with Alexander almost daily, not to further the French cause but to report Napoleon's reaction to his own talks with the czar. Talleyrand later argued that this behavior was necessary to save Europe from a man going mad with unbridled ambition. The latter-day observer can argue that it was treachery of the highest degree, undoubtedly well paid for by Russian, Austrian and English gold.[22]

Whatever the case, Alexander dug in his heels. Despite continuing mutual bonhomie interrupted on occasion by Napoleonic temper, the czar refused to be either cajoled or threatened. When Talleyrand suggested that Napoleon marry one of his sisters, Alexander replied that he had no power over such matters which were up to his mother (known to be hostile to Napoleon), and there the matter rested. (Napoleon got a little of his own back when Alexander asked his advice on seducing an actress who had caught his eye. "Go right ahead," Napoleon told him, "but keep in mind that such are the gossips here it will soon appear in every newspaper in Europe." The planned seduction was quickly abandoned.)[23]

Meanwhile the social whirl intensified. "I want to astonish Germany by my splendor," Napoleon had told Duroc when planning the festivities.[24] On occasion his over-generous hospitality was reciprocated. The duke of Saxe-Weimar hosted a commemorative rabbit shoot on the nearby battlefield of Jena as well as a glittering ball at Weimar. "I hunted on the battlefield of Jena," Napoleon wrote Joséphine. ". . . I attended a ball at Weimar. Emperor Alexander danced a lot, but not I: forty years are forty years. My health on the whole is good except for some minor problems."[25]

Neither of these events ended in Napoleon's favor, although he probably didn't realize it. The hunt at Jena brought an outcry from Prussian patriots who criticized it as a revolting disregard of hallowed ground in view of the thousands of dead buried there but two years earlier. This was somewhat unfair because it was not Napoleon's idea, and it would have been a severe breach of etiquette on his part not to have accepted.[26]

The ball was marked by the presence of the famous 59-year-old German poet and dramatist, Johann Wolfgang von Goethe, and the septuagenarian German author, Christoph Martin Weiland.

Napoleon later granted each an audience: the reader will have to decide who came out on top, judging from the following brief excerpts. In talking with Weiland, whom he addressed as "the Voltaire of Germany", Napoleon criticized several of his writings that intermingled fiction with history and vice-versa. Weiland replied:

> I wanted to give my readers some useful lessons and for this I needed historical authentication. I wanted the examples which I borrowed from history to be easy and pleasant to imitate, and for that it was necessary to mix the ideal in with the romantic. The thoughts of humans are sometimes better than their actions, and good works of fiction are worth more than human behavior.

Goethe was no more yielding. At one point Napoleon suggested that if he wrote a treatment of the Erfurt meeting he should dedicate it to the Russian emperor:

> *Goethe:* This is not my practice . . . I have made it a principle never to dedicate a work so that I shall never have cause to regret it.
> *Napoleon:* The great writers of Louis XIV's day have not agreed.
> *Goethe:* True, Sire, but your Majesty would not guarantee that they have never regretted it.

Napoleon seemed oblivious to the put-down and invited Goethe to Paris, an invitation refused on account of age.[27]

The conference terminated in mid October after the mutual signing of a convention of alliance which designated England as "their common enemy and the enemy of the [European] continent." Neither ruler was to make a separate peace with England, plenipotentiaries however would go to England for peace talks.

Peace would be conditional on England recognizing Russia's possession of Finland, the Danube principalities of Moldavia and Valachia and French possession of Spain. Alexander agreed to respect the integrity of the Ottoman empire (minus Moldavia and Valachia). Napoleon withdrew as mediator between Russia and Turkey, but if Austria or any other power allied with Turkey then France would support Russia. Alexander equally agreed to support Napoleon militarily should Austria declare war on France.[28]

'All goes well, I am satisfied with Alexander as he should be with me," Napoleon wrote Joséphine, adding somewhat cryptically, "If he were a woman I believe I would make him my mistress."[29]

Despite the formal convention, neither ruler had much to be content with although Napoleon would continue for a time to put a brave face on the results. A joint letter sent to King George of England pointed not only to the need for a prompt peace but also to attendant advantages, but this was more form than substance. Alexander remained suspicious of Napoleon's future intentions in Poland, and was annoyed that Napoleon had prevented the partition of Turkey. Nor was he pleased that the French would retain the Oder fortresses in Prussia, despite Napoleon's agreement to reduce the still unpaid Prussian contributions by 20 million francs.[30] Napoleon was upset by Alexander's refusal to object to Austrian preparations for war, and by not being immediately welcomed as a future brother-in-law.

As for Emperor Francis' claimed desire for peace:

I have never doubted your Majesty's upright intentions [Napoleon wrote] but I was for a moment still afraid that we might renew hostilities. There is in Vienna a faction which pretends to be frightened in order to urge your cabinet to violent measures which would be the beginning of disasters greater than those of the past . . . your Majesty should not reopen discussion of what fifteen years of war have terminated. You must forbid any proclamation or

move that would provoke war. The last *levée en masse*
would have infallibly brought war if I had feared that this
levy and those preparations were made in conjunction with
Russia . . . Let your Majesty permit me a last word: that he
be guided by his own judgment, his own feeling, which are
infinitely superior to those of his advisers.[31]

Notes

1   Rose (*Life*), II, 180. See also Metternich, II, 298 (English edition).
2   Corr. XVII. Nr. 14253, St. Cloud, 16 August 1808.
3   Thiébault, II, 203–16. See also Bryant (*Victory*), 242 ff.; Napier;
    Oman; Longford; Asprey ("The Peninsular War").
4   Corr. XVII. Nr. 14269, St. Cloud, 23 August 1808.
5   Corr. XVII. Nr. 14274, St. Cloud, 27 August 1808.
6   Corr. XVII. Nrs. 14300, 14301, St. Cloud, 7 September 1808;
    14307, St. Cloud, 8 September 1808.
7   Corr. XVII. Nr. 14259, St. Cloud, 17 August 1808.
8   Corr. XVII. Nr. 14293, St. Cloud, 4 September 1808.
9   Corr. XVII. Nr. 14289, Paris, 1 September 1808.
10   Craig, 40.
11   Craig, 41. See also Showalter, 364–80.
12   Craig, 46–9. See also Shanahan, 178 ff.
13   Corr. XVII. Nr. 14319, St. Cloud, 14 September 1808.
14   Corr. XVII. Nr. 14170, Bayonne, 8 July 1808.
15   Corr. XVII. Nr. 14248, Nantes, 10 August 1808.
16   Corr. XVII. Nr. 14254, Paris, 16 August 1808.
17   Corr. XVII. Nr. 14269, St. Cloud, 23 August 1808.
18   Corr. XVII. Nr. 14300, St. Cloud, 7 September 1808.
19   Savary, III, 154–205. See also Vandal, I, 112–44, 152–65, 197–203;
    Metternich, II, 151–9, Caulaincourt, I, 243–302; Seton-Watson,
    116–17.
20   Talleyrand (*Mémoires*), I, 414, 420–22; Savary, III, 452 ff.; Vandal,
    I, 410–16. Generals Savary and Lauriston were Napoleon's aides-
    de-camp at Erfurt.
21   Talleyrand (*Mémoires*), I, 401–25. See also Vandal, I, 203–14,
    401–2; Caulaincourt, I, 32.

22 Rose (*Life*), II, 180–1. See also Vandal, I, 419–40.

23 Gourgaud, II, 53; Las Cases, IV, 238–9.

24 Talleyrand (*Mémoires*), I, 401–2.

25 Napoleon *Lettres* (Tulard), 312.

26 Savary, III, 465–7.

27 Talleyrand (*Mémoires*), I, 426–90, 436–7. See also Rose (*Life*), II, 183–4.

28 Corr. XVII. Nr. 14372, Erfurt, 12 October 1808. See also Savary, III, 166 ff.; Vandal, I, 464–8, 474–83; Caulaincourt, I, 266–75.

29 Napoleon *Lettres* (Tulard), 313.

30 Corr. XVII. Nr. 14379, Erfurt, 14 October 1808.

31 Corr. XVII. Nr. 14380, Erfurt, 14 October 1808. See also Savary, III, 460–7; Corr. XVII. Nrs. 14373, Erfurt, 12 October 1808, 14379, Erfurt, 14 October 1808.

CHAPTER TWELVE

THE SPANISH ADVENTURE – III:
OCTOBER 1808–JANUARY 1809

*I shall be in Bayonne within a month . . . At present the
enemy's boldness makes me think that he will remain in his
present positions. The longer he does so, the better for us. The
war can be ended in a single blow by a skillfully coordinated
maneuver, and for that I must be on hand.*

Napoleon to King Joseph, Erfurt, 13 October 1808[1]

THE UNLEASHED LION reached Paris in a few bounds. Despite the
elegant trappings of Erfurt, its challenges and pleasures,
Napoleon's thoughts had frequently reverted to the deteriorating
situation in Spain. En route to the conference he had written
Joseph a lengthy instruction on the necessity of ensuring his line
of communications: "any general who loses his line of communications deserves to be shot."[2] Shortly before leaving the conference
he again wrote to Joseph as quoted above.

General Junot and his surrendered troops meanwhile had been
returned to France by their English captors. Undoubtedly anticipating a rough reception from the emperor, Junot must have been
grateful when instead he was sent to command a new corps des-
tined for Spain. In view of General Dupont's disgrace Napoleon's
handling of Junot is curious. "You have done nothing dishonorable," Napoleon informed him after reading his report, "you
returned with my troops, my eagles and my cannon. I had hoped
however that you would do better." This mild scolding was private: Napoleon publicly approved Junot's conduct. The task at
present was to shape up his new command for a triumphal return

to the Portuguese capital: "A man such as you should either perish or return to Paris only as master of Lisbon . . . You will lead the advance guard and I shall be behind you . . . Do not lose a moment . . . overcome the difficulties."[3]

Considering King Joseph's position in Spain this was not going to be easy. "All I can see is that you have evacuated the entire right bank [of the Ebro river]," Napoleon complained to his brother, who the previous month had withdrawn to Vitoria, "therefore your position is bad. No longer fearing that you can take the offensive at Burgos, the enemy can move on Bilbao without fear . . . no longer fearing that you will debouch by the right bank on Zaragoza he can equally move against your extreme left flank. None of this would have been possible if you had aggressively occupied Burgos and Tudela in force . . . I know absolutely nothing of what you have done except that this is regrettable."[4]

Matters elsewhere seemed somewhat more favorable. Murat in Naples was about to seize the fort of Capri island as prelude to a winter landing in Sicily. Things were quiet in the north: "I am on the best terms with Russia," he wrote Marshal Davout in Berlin. "I have nothing to fear from the Austrians, but in any case I intend to concentrate more and more of my troops . . . I leave for Spain in a few days."[5]

His annual "discourse" at the opening of the legislature was far less detailed than usual, merely touching on various affairs – the satisfactory condition of the empire, the beneficial effects of the new legal code, the sound state of finances, the progress in public works. He mentioned the Erfurt meeting only briefly, assuring the deputies that his and Czar Alexander's "primary thought was that of peace. We have likewise determined on some sacrifices necessary to bring, if possible, our millions of people all the benefits of maritime commerce. We stand united concerning both peace and war." He mentioned nothing of his plans to seize Sicily. "I leave in a few days to take command of my army and, with God's help, to crown the king of Spain in Madrid and plant my eagles on the forts of Lisbon."[6]

War with England showed no signs of ending. Napoleon and Alexander's letter from Erfurt to King George drew a less than satisfactory response, not from the king but from Whitehall whose mandarins insisted that Spanish insurgents would participate in any peace conference, a condition that effectively terminated the effort.[7]

The Army of Spain now consisted of seven corps plus the Guard and reserve cavalry, a total of about 190,000 troops. Marshal Lefebvre's corps occupied Bilbao, having recently defeated General Blake's force which retreated to Valmaseda. Marshal Victor's corps was at Amurrio, Bessières at Miranda on the Ebro river, Ney had seized Logroño on the Ebro and Moncey was at Tafalla. Further east General Duhesme was locked in Barcelona but could easily hold out while Gouvion St. Cyr's division worked down from the border to seize Gerona and eventually relieve him. Mortier and Junot's two corps would soon arrive to be followed by additional regiments as needed.

The troops were in general sufficiently well fed but their uniforms were worn out. They desperately needed jackets, vests, trousers, cloaks and shoes, the result of the usual supply inefficiency and corruption. Perhaps a more important deficiency stemmed from lack of troop discipline. Conscripts who had made up the initial corps had not been properly trained. Ugly incidents occured almost daily to increase local resistance and hatred. Pillage was rife and it worsened with the arrival of Grand Army veterans who were specialists in the art. In but a short time Napoleon was hurling out orders reminiscent of those published during his Italian campaign. Any soldier who arrested or maltreated a peasant bringing his crops to market would be courtmartialed and shot as would anyone who indulged in pillage. Unfortunately the pillage, often violent, continued to escalate.[8]

The Spanish army numbered about 115,000, mostly untrained and poorly disciplined peasant conscripts and volunteers (also intent on pillaging). Lacking a commander in chief, the generals received individual and often conflicting orders from the central *junta* in Aranjuez and were frequently at swordspoint with each other. They were also dispersed over some 200 miles stretching from Drake and Romana's left flank, about 50,000 strong at Valmaseda, then Castaños with some 25,000 holding the line Calahorra-Tudela on the right bank of the Ebro, and Palafox's smaller corps on the right between Zaragoza and the Aragon. Vives' army of 20,000 stood just south of Barcelona, and Belvedere's 13,000 men remained in reserve at Burgos.[9]

Napoleon was not pleased with what he discovered. Orders were soon flying hither and yon to procure proper uniforms, improve conditions in the hospitals and strengthen fortress defenses. The army lacked intelligence on enemy locations and strengths (one result of pillage), communications between French corps were poor. Marshal Lefebvre had pre-empted his plan to roll up Drake's corps before turning on Castaños and had only pushed Drake and Romana to Valmaseda without having eliminated them.

The emperor now decided on a three-pronged attack, a movement that collided with a simultaneous enemy advance, a brief but sharp action that put the Spanish in retreat and, a few days later, Napoleon in Burgos.

He next ordered Marshal Lannes to lead Moncey's corps in an attack on Palafox while Ney, who had taken command of Bessières' corps, would simultaneously march north from Soria to strike Castaños. Lannes as usual attacked furiously and brilliantly, an action well described by his young aide, Captain Marbot, to throw Palafox in retreat.[10] Ney's cavalry meanwhile forced Castaños to retreat on Calatayud, but for reasons unknown (Ney's actions were often problematical), Ney held his grenadiers at Soria which permitted Castaños to slip away. Napoleon did not seem particularly upset, writing to Prince de Cambacérès in Paris that "affairs are moving very fast", and to Joseph that "the provinces of Santander, Biscay and Soria have already submitted." General Clarke in Paris learned that the Spanish armies in Andalucia, Aragon, Valencia and New Castile were "scattered and destroyed."[11]

The way now lay open to Madrid, a priority march since Joseph, for some time little more than a rear-area figurehead, had yet to be formally crowned. The army moved out from Aranda in late November. Two days and 35 miles later Victor's corps, preceded by Napoleon and a Polish legion of light horse, began the steep ascent of the Guadarrama mountains – the border between Old and New Castile – to the key pass of Somosierra, a tight defile defended by 9,000 troops and a ring of 16 cannon. The Polish cavaliers attacked immediately, bravely but recklessly. Repulsed at considerable cost, their squadrons were reorganized by General Montbrun who led them at full gallop up the steep rocky trail. The amazed defenders fired only one salvo before running away, leaving their cannon, 10 standards, 50 wagons and a great many troops to be taken prisoner. "We lost very few men," Napoleon falsely informed Joseph. A few days later the army held the heights of Chamartin overlooking the defended capital whose 30,000 inhabitants surrendered after brief resistance, the central *junta* having fled Aranjuez eventually to set up shop in Cádiz.[12]

Napoleon thought to consolidate this victory by issuing a number of decrees that abolished feudal rights and the dreaded court of inquisition. One-third of the monasteries in Spain were to be closed, their properties seized. Errant rebels were promised clemency, the people regeneration of the torn country, expulsion of the English villains and future prosperity and greatness – provided they fully cooperated with the French authorities.

Overall the French position had considerably improved. Mortier's corps had arrived to reinforce the troops besieging Palafox at Zaragoza, Junot's corps was *en route*, St. Cyr had captured Rosas and was moving on Gerona toward Barcelona, Soult was marching on Léon between the Duero river and the sea. General Castaños, whose force now numbered only about 8,000, was retreating on Cuenca southeast of Madrid. French troops occupied the capital, the people seemed to welcome their presence, and Joseph would soon arrive to be established as ruler. The good news traveled to Paris in a special bulletin: "Dissolution of Spanish troops continues everywhere. The new levies have all dispersed, the men returning to their homes," the central *junta* (allied with England) hated and despised in all of Spain.[13]

Napoleon was unduly optimistic. Such was his scorn for irregular warfare that he was attaching too much importance to the Spanish armies and not enough to nascent insurgent bands that were forming throughout the land. The Spanish armies may have been on the run but many of their fugitive soldiers had joined guerrilla forces in the hills and mountains. Captain Marbot (in carrying an important message to Napoleon) was horrified to come on two mutilated bodies of French soldiers who had strayed too far from an advance post as had a young French lieutenant, crucified upside down on a barn door, his roasted head a few inches above a defunct fire.[14] Numerous French commercial residents in the cities had been beheaded. As in Egypt more and more troops were necessary to escort couriers and guard mail-relay posts, yet Napoleon had already spread himself thinly and was facing a shortage of 135,000 men. Half of these were being raised by extraordinary levies, but 63,000 would have to be called up prematurely from the conscription pool of 1810.[15]

Having neutralized the Spanish armies, at least for the moment, Napoleon was far more concerned with fighting the English to "hang the eagles on the Lisbon forts." But where was Sir John Moore's army? Napoleon did not know and a hostile countryside prevented him from finding out. Assuming that the English would advance on Madrid, "the only possible place for them,"[16] he pushed Victor's corps to Talavera on the Tagus river and Ney's corps to Avila northwest of Madrid.

He was on the right track. Moore with some 25,000 troops had meanwhile marched from Portugal to reach Salamanca in mid November. Here Moore learned that 10,000 reinforcements had been landed at Corunna and would shortly arrive at Astorga. Notified of Napoleon's victorious march to Madrid, he toyed with returning to Lisbon but instead was persuaded by his staff to march north and, reinforced, break the French line of communications with Burgos, an excellent plan but overly ambitious in view of his limited strength. He next learned by an intercepted message that Soult was to advance into Galicia to cut the English line of communications with the Atlantic port of El Ferrol. To block Soult he concentrated his force at Sahagun. Soult in turn marched his corps on Carríon de los Condes, some 25 miles east of Sahagun, these moves having been accomplished by late December.

Napoleon now had a much clearer idea of the situation. "The maneuver of the English is unusual," he informed Joseph on 22 December. "It is certain that they have evacuated Salamanca. Everything leads me to think that they will evacuate Portugal and fix their line of operations on El Ferrol . . . By making this rear movement, they can [also] hope to inflict a defeat upon Marshal Soult's corps."[17] Napoleon in turn could hope to attack Moore's exposed flank, *if* he could march his army north fast enough.

Leaving half his force, Victor and Lefebvre's corps, under Joseph's command with the all-important mission of screening Madrid, he ordered Ney to march on Valladolid as advance guard. "I am leaving at once to handle the English who appear to have been reinforced and wish to step out," he wrote Joséphine on 22 December. "The weather is beautiful, my health perfect; do not worry."[18]

The beautiful weather suddenly vanished to turn the ensuing march into a nightmare. It would have been strenuous in fair weather, but this was winter, very cold, the rude road to the Guadarrama mountains dangerously slick with ice. What Napoleon described as "disagreeable enough weather" was a considerable understatement. Midway up the mountain a howling blizzard struck so fiercely that officers and men had to dismount and link arms to prevent being blown away. The march quickened upon reaching the plains, the exhausted troops sometimes almost miraculously making over 20 miles a day. Four days distant from

Madrid, Marshal Berthier informed Joseph "that we have captured some English stragglers. The English position is not yet clear but everything suggests that they are retiring on Corunna. We are hoping to catch up with them. All goes well. We are in a country abundant in bread and wine."[19]

They were also in a country over-abundant with rain that turned the miserable roads into almost impassable quagmires. But the march went on, the troops stripping to ford icy streams whose bridges had been destroyed by the enemy, carrying their packs and muskets overhead, falling to the muddy ground come dark, munching a bit of bread or biscuit and sipping some wine if fortunate, sleeping in half-frozen mud. The pace quickened as they encountered more English stragglers, cold, hungry men as pitiable as the emaciated, abandoned English horses that had been hamstrung to prevent the French from using them. Now it was only a matter of time before they came to grips. For some the pace was too fast. Captain Marbot watched three old grenadiers, veterans of countless battles, blow their brains out because they could not go on and were afraid of being tortured by lurking guerrillas.[20]

Suddenly the tactical position became clear. On 26 December, Napoleon wrote Ney that Marshal Soult was at Carrión with two of his divisions, that the English right rested on Villalon, the left on Sahagun, while Romana's Spanish force was marching south from Léon. Soult expected to be attacked the next day. Ney was to concentrate his corps at Medina de Rio Seco, ready to march in support of Soult if he heard gunfire.[21]

The following day Napoleon informed Joseph that he believed the English to be 36,000 strong. "I shall be at Medina de Rio Seco today and probably today or tomorrow great events will take place. If the English have not already begun to retreat they are lost, and if they do retreat they will be pursued to their ships so forcefully that half will not escape."[22]

Napoleon's decisive battle failed to materalize. On the day before Christmas, Moore was marching to attack Soult when he learned that Napoleon was approaching from the south. Moore at once ordered a general retreat to Corunna and the waiting fleet.

Napoleon reached Valderas on 28 December intending to close the trap, but Moore was already evacuating Benevente to begin the long march to Astorga and Corunna.

Ney was at Astorga on 31 December and Napoleon was with the bulk of the army at Benevente from where he wrote Joséphine: "I have been pursuing the English for some days, but they were scared off. They have abandoned the debris of La Romana's army in order not to delay their retreat even half a day. We have taken more than a hundred baggage wagons. The weather is awful." To Joseph on the same day: "The English move out at top speed, abandoning their munitions and baggage . . . They have not only cut the bridges but have blown up the arches, barbarous and useless conduct . . . unnecessary harm to the country. All the Spanish hold them in horror. They have taken everything, cattle, mattresses, blankets, and in addition abused and beaten everybody." A day later he again wrote Joseph: "The English have abandoned fifteen hundred tents and four thousand blankets, all their rum, an immense quantity of wagons and many stragglers . . . we are hurrying after them . . . General La Romana does not have six thousand troops, and they are without clothing, raw conscripts, and he does not dare take them to battle because they are completely fed up with him."[23]

It was a complete rout. It lasted for 18 days and nights, a morbid saga of the hunters and the hunted played out in some of the most difficult terrain in the world. The heretofore gently undulating land sharply changed character at Benevente which lies nearly 200 miles southeast of Corunna. Here began wild, fierce, mountainous country traversed only by primitive narrow roads, more often trails, deep gulleys, unbridged streams wild in flood, tight twisting defiles with 90-degree turns; bread and wine sparse at best and often none at all, sudden blinding snowstorms turned to blizzards by shrieking mountain winds, then thaws and frequent rain to transform roads and trails into impassable mud – 200 miles of insult to human fortitude already severely tested.

The officers were generally mounted, that is until their horses wore through their shoes and collapsed from want of forage –

there were no spare mounts. The men walked. The English had the worst of it because they were on the run, they were scared, their ranks thinned, supply wagons non-existent, yet they had only to wrestle a few field cannon up and down snow-covered trails with chasms yawning for victims. The French lacked this advantage. Their columns were frequently held up until the big guns were manhandled across flooded streams, through tight defiles and up steep slopes and down again, an exhausting and remorseless pattern broken only by nightfall and secret tears.[24]

What magnificent troops were these Frenchmen! Many were conscripted youngsters serving in their first campaign and nearly all were fed to the teeth with their war in Spain. But now they were on the verge of coming to grips with the real enemy, and they responded well. Each carried at least a 60 lb pack, a bulky ammunition *giberne*, a clumsy stoneware water bottle and an awkward very heavy musket topped with pointed bayonet; yet they marched on, more often hungry than not, sometimes 15 miles a day, sometimes even an unbelievable 25 miles. There have probably been no tougher soldiers in the world.

Many of the English units contrarily all but disintegrated, the famished, frozen, disillusioned, ill-disciplined and often dregs of society deserting in droves to sack villages and towns with a savagery that appalled even veteran officers. An English officer later wrote of one village where "every door and window was broken . . . Rivers of wine ran through the houses and the streets, where soldiers, women, children, runaway Spaniards and muleteers lay in fantastic groups with wine oozing from their lips and nostrils."[25]

Had it not been for Sir John Moore's presence, his most able commanders, a few crack regiments, the gallows and the lash, there would no longer have been a British army. That army owed its life to those diehard veterans who somehow held off Soult's pursuing cavalry until the weary and disorganized columns, reduced now to 15,000 men, reached Corunna – and the transports. The crisis was not yet over. As troops began loading, Soult's advance guard appeared on the heights overlooking the harbor and with the arrival of their guns launched a final attack. A furious rearguard action personally commanded by Sir John held them off until the troops were aboard. Sir John was killed by a cannon-ball shortly before the action ended and what was left of the army was saved. English losses were immense, an estimated 10,000 troops dead or captured, several thousand more wounded, thousands of horses abandoned, thousands of carts and wagons lost, at least one of which contained a fortune in gold.

News of the exodus reached Napoleon in Valladolid. Once again he had been cheated of a decisive victory, the "single coup" that he believed, perhaps accurately, would have ended the war. That hope vanished with the departure of the English fleet. The enemy no doubt would return. Meanwhile the insurgency would grow, there would be no peace.

Very well, his plan had failed. "I can no longer hope that Europe will be pacified this year," he wrote Joseph. "I doubt it so much that yesterday I signed a decree to conscript [another] 100,000 men. England's hatred, events in Constantinople, all presage that the hour of peace and tranquility has not yet struck." Nevertheless he was optimistic concerning Spain: "The provinces of Léon, the Asturias and New Castile want only peace." He expected that Gerona in the northeast would soon fall and that General Duhesme in Barcelona would receive sufficient reinforcements to control Catalonia. Joseph was now to set up court in Madrid, "hang a dozen citizens" to eliminate any opposition and send 50 valuable paintings (taken from private homes and convents) to Paris. In a few weeks or so he should lead an expedition to occupy Seville and Mérida in Andalucia while Soult invaded Portugal from the north. "This is the operation that will conclude affairs in Spain. I reserve to you the glory."[26]

In mid January he informed Joseph that "circumstances in Europe force me to be in Paris . . . The situation permitting, I shall return toward the end of February."[27]

Notes

1   Corr. XVII. Nr. 14378, Erfurt, 13 October 1808.
2   Corr. XVII. Nr. 14347, Kaiserlautern, 24 September 1808.
3   Corr. XVIII. Nr. 14386, St. Cloud, 19 October 1808.
4   Corr. XVIII. Nr. 14387, St. Cloud, 19 October 1808. See also Roederer (*Journal*), 235–9, 243–51.
5   Corr. XVIII. Nr. 14410, Paris, 25 October 1808.
6   Corr. XVIII. Nr. 14419, the Tuileries, 27 October 1808.
7   Corr. XVIII. Nrs. 14488, Burgos, 18 November 1808; 14491, Burgos, 19 November 1808.
8   Corr. XVIII. Nr. 14552, Chamartin, 12 December 1808. See also Miot de Melito, II, 279–81.
9   Wartenburg, II, 10–11.
10 Corr. XVIII. Nr. 14489, Burgos, 18 November 1808; Marbot, II, 63 ff.
11 Corr. XVIII. Nrs. 14486, Burgos, 18 November 1808; 14499, Burgos, 20 November 1808; 14512, Aranda, 26 November 1808.
12 Corr. XVIII. Nrs. 14522, Buitrago, 30 November 1808; 14524, Chamartin, *près* Madrid, 2 December 1808; 14530, Madrid, 5 December 1808. See also Miot de Melito, II, 286–92 (English edition here and following).
13 Corr. XVIII. Nr. 14558, Madrid, 13 December 1808. See also Roederer (*Journal*), 275.
14 Marbot, II, 67–9.
15 Corr. XVIII. Nrs. 14583, 14591, Chamartin, 18 December 1808; 14601, 14604, Madrid, 21 December 1808.
16 Wartenburg, II, 17.
17 Corr. XVIII. Nr. 14609, Chamartin, 22 December 1808.
18 Corr. XVIII. Nr. 14606, Madrid, 22 December 1808.
19 Corr. XVIII, Nr. 14618, Tordesillas, 25 December 1808.
20 Marbot, II, 91–2.
21 Corr. XVIII. Nr. 14619, Tordesillas, 26 December 1808.
22 Corr. XVIII. Nr. 14620, Tordesillas, 27 December 1808.
23 Corr. XVIII. Nrs. 14623, 14626, Benevente, 31 December 1808; 14637, Benevente, 1 January 1809.
24 The writer recently retraced the march of the English and French corps from Benevente to Corunna, and Soult's subsequent march

through northern Portugal to Oporto. The rugged but beautiful terrain has to be seen to be believed. This is not an onerous task and makes for a good holiday. For the most part the provinces of Asturias and Galicia, as well as northern Portugal, are not yet popular tourist attractions. Numerous new and small two- and three-star hotels are very clean, comfortable with most amenities and, along with hearty, delicious meals and excellent wine, very reasonably priced.

25 Bryant (*Victory*), 280. Bryant gives a moving account of the retreat from the British perspective, 277–94.

26 Corr. XVIII. Nrs. 14684, Valladolid, 11 January 1809; 14716, Valladolid, 15 January 1809.

27 Corr. XVIII. Nr. 14717, Valladolid, 15 January 1809.

CHAPTER THIRTEEN

WAR ON THE DANUBE – I: THE BATTLE OF EGGMÜHL JANUARY–APRIL 1809

Austria apparently wants war; if it wants it, it shall have it.

Napoleon to Viceroy Eugène in Italy, 21 February 1809[1]

THE IMPERIAL CARRIAGE rolled into the grounds of St. Cloud in late January 1809. A day or two later Napoleon was in his *cabinet* in the Tuileries, desk heaped high with priority papers of the empire. After briskly dealing with a host of domestic and foreign affairs he faced the unpleasant problem of mutiny in the ranks, in this case strong rumors that police minister Joseph Fouché was conspiring with former foreign affairs minister Talleyrand to overthrow the imperial throne, as Ambassador Metternich reported to Vienna.[2]

Fouché got off lightly. Serious trouble was brewing in the interior not only from the usual shenanigans of disloyal *émigrés* and dissident priests supported by English gold. All but the most deaf heard rumblings of discontent from average citizens suffering from increased hardships brought on by the English blockade and the continental system, as well as by enforced military conscriptions and continuing warfare. Fouché was certainly a scoundrel, but a very able and intelligent scoundrel with a powerful network of informants and police agents who over the years had served Napoleon well. Now, with war in Spain and probably war with Austria, was not the time to discharge him. He was said to have received a private tongue-lashing, not the first and not the last,

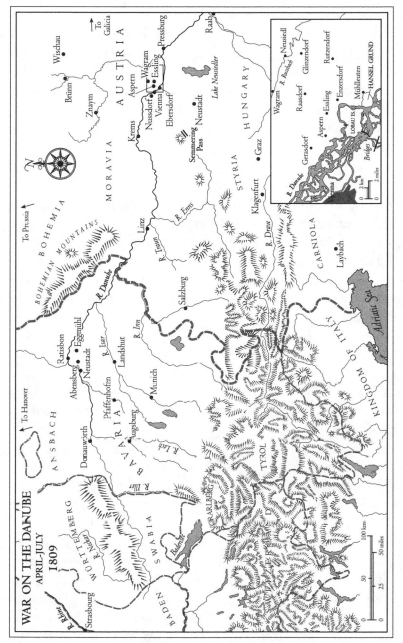

War on the Danube April – July 1809

WAR ON THE DANUBE
APRIL-JULY
1809

and, if so, he probably returned chastened to his office to sort through the lucrative bribes on his desk.

Talleyrand was not so fortunate. Napoleon summoned him to a special meeting of senior councillors and ministers which was prefaced by a short lecture on loyalty. According to one account he then turned to Talleyrand who, "in a characteristically graceful and negligent attitude, was half-leaning against a small table by the fire." Probably not to the diplomat's surprise he listened for the next 30 minutes to a catalogue of his crimes as "a thief, a coward, and a traitor." Among other evils he was accused "of responsibility for the execution of the duke d'Enghien and for the peninsular war." As if this were not sufficient Napoleon allegedly taunted him "with his lameness" and "the infidelity of his wife." Shaking his fist in near-maniacal rage Napoleon concluded the meeting by describing his victim "as so much shit in a silk stocking." Talleyrand had listened as if deaf, his dignified countenance unchanged. Limping from the room he was said to have remarked to a companion, "What a pity that such a great man should be so ill-bred."[3]

Although Napoleon stripped Talleyrand of the title of Grand Chamberlain he retained that of Vice Grand Elector. Moreover he gained the last word by appearing at the next two court receptions, finally forcing Napoleon to acknowledge his presence and make a peace of sorts.

The incident is curious. If Napoleon were convinced of treachery, as appeared to be the case, his treatments of Fouché and Talleyrand were lenient enough. Some historians have wondered why he did not imprison or even execute Talleyrand, but as we pointed out earlier such was not his style. It would have been an admission of failure in that Napoleon was responsible for his ascendancy in the empire. In addition both he and Fouché held considerable followings in military and civilian circles. Talleyrand probably never forgot the humiliating dressing-down but it didn't much matter. He already had turned against his master, he had betrayed him to Czar Alexander and was currently in Austrian and English pay, and he would continue to thwart his policies to the best of his considerable ability.

Napoleon faced other severe vexations. The treasury was dangerously low. To a request for funds from King Jérôme of Westphalia, Napoleon replied: "[This] request is unwelcome at a time when I do not know how to meet the immense expenses occasioned by my armies in Spain and elsewhere which cost me heavily and return nothing. Cut your luxurious standard of living by half and reduce part of your civil list in order to increase your army."[4] He should have taken his own advice. A few days later he complained to his court administrator, Count Daru, that "my household is full of corruption . . . The stables alone cost me 450,000 francs [annually] in wages."[5] He would continue to complain about a shortage of funds and would soon order sharp cuts in an already anaemic public works program and in army expenditures.

Admiral Decrès and the navy had let him down once again. An expedition that was supposed to sail from Toulon remained in port. "When I am not on the scene nothing goes right," he complained to the naval minister; no ships were being built, and there were fewer naval workshops than ever.[6]

The situation in Spain was anything but encouraging. Ney had suffered a serious setback in Galicia. Jourdan, King Joseph's chief of staff, now had to send Soult's corps into Galicia to mop up the remnants of Romana's Spanish army and re-establish communication with Ney. Victor's march on Seville must be only a prelude to re-establishing contact with Soult: "the first task of the army is to destroy the rest of Romana's corps and reign supreme in the north." Should Romana bring Galicia into rebellion the English could then land at Vigo to seriously threaten Ney's isolated force.[7]

Napoleon's primary concern however remained the Damocletian sword of Austria that could fall on him at any moment. He initially had been optimistic, writing to Joseph: "My prompt arrival in Paris has already changed Austria's attitude;

arrogance and extreme confidence have given way to fear."[8] Napoleon had fallen victim to enemy deception (just as the enemy had fallen victim to *his* deception prior to Austerlitz). The Austrian army was continuing to mobilize and Emperor Francis and the Aulic Council soon would decide on war with France. Some inkling of this probably reached the Tuileries: in late February, Napoleon wrote his stepson, Viceroy Eugène, in Italy, "Austria apparently wants war; if it wants it, it shall have it."[9]

Employing a studied somnolence tinged with abject subordination, the Austrian court for some time had convinced Napoleon that it genuinely intended to respect the terms of what he called the "glorious peace" – the 1805 treaty of Pressburg which again had humbled the once mighty Habsburg empire. Austria had remained neutral during Napoleon's war with Prussia and Russia, playing for time to rebuild its army.

This was the work of Archduke Charles who had been appointed head of the *Hofkriegsrat* (Aulic Council) but who (as a modern and very able historian, Gunther Rothenberg, has pointed out) "spent most of his time in administrative and bureaucratic reforms."[10] Eventually Charles made some progress in transforming disparate and independent regiments of a half-dozen non-German nationalities into single corps on the Napoleonic model while recruiting, arming, equipping and training new cadres of infantry, cavalry and artillery. But, unable to wean himself from the slavish concepts of eighteenth-century slow-motion warfare, and frightened to death at the thought of raising a people's national army, his strategic and tactical concepts did not greatly differ from those of old.

So matters stood when Count Johann Philipp Stadion became Austrian minister of foreign affairs in 1805, soon to begin secretly looking for a new anti-French coalition with London and St. Petersburg.[11] The trick now was to preach a policy of peace until Charles had built a strong army, until England had agreed to a new coalition and – most important – until Napoleon had moved a large portion of the Grand Army from Germany to Spain. By August 1808, Charles commanded a partially revitalized army 300,000 strong, while Stadion had gained the covert sympathy of Prussia as well as the support of Tyrolean leaders groaning under French-Bavarian rule.

As we have seen, Napoleon was clearly puzzled, informing Davout in October that "I have nothing to fear from the Austrians," but nevertheless he was continuing to concentrate his troops for any contingency.[12]

In one sense Napoleon had *little* to fear from the Austrians in view of his own troop strength in France and Germany and his knowledge that neither Charles nor anyone else could ever produce an inspired national army from the heterogeneous makeup of the multi-lingual Austrian army of unwilling serfs. Neither could Charles nor old and inept Austrian marshals and generals, not to mention lesser fry, adapt to the Napoleonic system of warfare within a few years, if ever. The Austrian character did not lend itself to military daring and efficiency. A feudal command arrogance and a gross *schlamperei* or sloppiness could not be eliminated. As Charles would shortly learn, numbers were one consideration, performance another.

Napoleon's intelligence service was not very good, nor were those of his Rhenish allies. A lengthy discussion between his foreign affairs minister, Champagny, and the Austrian ambassador in Paris, Count Metternich, in early March 1809 further confused matters. A master of duplicity, that is to say a skilled diplomat, Metternich smoothly countered Champagny's list of grievances by citing counter-grievances and denials while insisting that Austrian armed forces had remained on a peacetime footing.[13] After sending copies of Champagny's lengthy report to Czar Alexander and King Frederick August of Saxony, Napoleon directed members of the confederation to mobilize their armies. "Will all this lead to war?" he plaintively asked the Saxon king. "This is still doubtful. As for me, I have no desire to attack for it

is not my style to fight without reason. I shall wait for an expla-
nation of Austria's mysterious conduct before deciding on a
course of action."[14]

The situation heated up a few days later when Metternich suddenly informed Champagny that Vienna was putting its armies on
a war footing. Napoleon responded by ordering his troops in
France to cross the Rhine to join confederate forces. "The emperor
of Russia is shocked by Austria's behavior," he informed the
Bavarian king, "and is [also] deploying some troops."[15] Eugène in
Italy had been alerted and was to deploy his five divisions defen-
sively – he could expect to be attacked by some 50–70,000
Austrians. General Marmont in Dalmatia was to build an
entrenched camp on the Croatian frontier and prepare to attack
Austrian outposts, while Murat, the king of Naples, was to keep a
division ready to march on Rome.

Napoleon was still uncertain of Austrian intentions. "I find it
difficult to believe that Austria has decided to attack," he wrote
one of his allies; but, he went on, if so it would probably not be
before the end of April. By the first of April, Napoleon would
have 200,000 troops ready to march, and that did not include
Bernadotte's corps, the Saxon army, a Polish corps nor 60,000
Russians camped on the Galician border which Czar Alexander
had pledged to personally lead into battle.[16]

In addition he was calling in from Spain such tried and spirited
officers as 33-year-old General Antoine Charles Lasalle of the
cavalry, one of the heroes of the battle of Medellin. Lasalle's
ebullience at being ordered to join Masséna's corps in Germany
was made clear in a chance meeting with Roederer and Thiébault
at Burgos. To Roederer's question if he were traveling via Paris,
Lasalle replied, "Yes, it's the shortest way. I shall arrive at five
a.m.; I shall order a pair of boots; I shall make my wife pregnant,
and I shall depart."[17]

At the end of March, Napoleon informed Berthier: "The
Austrians have not yet declared war. They probably will not attack
without first recalling their ambassador . . . However war is without doubt imminent because Austria cannot feed such a large

quantity of mobilized troops for a long period. Everything indi-
cates that toward mid April their army will be ready to march."[18]

Napoleon was almost right. Archduke Charles after issuing a
stirring proclamation to his new army crossed the Inn river into
Bavaria on 9 April. Simultaneously the Tyroleans unfurled the
flag of insurrection. The Austrian ambassador was still in Paris.

Napoleon had planned initially to fan out his forces around
Ratisbon (Regensburg) on the Danube river to meet an enemy
advance from western Bohemia. This deployment was directed by
Marshal Berthier from Augsburg while the emperor remained in
Paris to arrange the machinery of government in his absence. He
had intended to leave Joséphine behind but at the last minute she
threw herself into his carriage, reportedly kicking and screaming
until he agreed to take her along to Strasbourg.[19] He remained
there only briefly before moving on to Donauwörth from where he
made a dramatic proclamation to his troops: "Soldiers, the territory of the confederation has been violated. The Austrian general
wants us to flee at the sight of his arms and abandon the territory
of our allies. I am coming to you with the speed of an eagle."[20]

It was just as well that he had wings. Poor Berthier, an efficient
chief of staff but no tactician, had stuck to his master's original
orders by reinforcing Davout in Ratisbon and stringing out the
other corps behind the Lech river. But these orders had been given
before Charles showed his hand. Had Charles moved more rapidly
(which was asking the impossible) he probably could have cut off
Davout to turn the allied left. As it was, Napoleon instantly recognized Berthier's error, ordered Davout to march southwest
toward the main army and deployed his other corps to meet the
approaching enemy. "The army maneuvers in every sense of the
word," Napoleon informed Viceroy Eugène on 18 April, "some
important events will soon take place."[21]

They did so the next day when Masséna's advance guard,
Oudinot's corps, marching northeast from Augsburg on
Pfaffenhofen drew first blood. Davout's five divisions marching

southwest on Neustadt simultaneously struck four enemy corps which were unpleasantly surprised to find a French army in the area, and were even more upset to be attacked from the rear by Lefebvre's Bavarians. Davout was now ordered to hold his line while Napoleon hit two other enemy corps – some 60,000 troops – advancing from Landshut. This action was brilliantly carried out by Marshal Lannes commanding two French divisions on the left while Wrede's Bavarians and Vandamme's Württembergers struck the enemy right so fiercely that after one hour the Austrians retreated, yielding 8 standards, 12 cannon and 18,000 prisoners at a relatively small French cost.

Having uncovered the Austrian flank, on 21 April Napoleon marched on Landshut which was taken by a coordinated attack in which Bessières, Mouton and Masséna distinguished themselves, their troops capturing 30 cannon, 9,000 prisoners, several thousand baggage wagons, three "superb pontoon bridge trains" and most of the Austrian supply dumps.

Archduke Charles meanwhile had seized Ratisbon to join Rosenberg, Hohenzollern and Liechtenstein's corps – about 110,000 troops – which were being blocked by Davout and Lefebvre about 15 miles south of Ratisbon at Eggmühl. Marching early on 22 April, Napoleon reached the area in mid afternoon. Lannes immediately attacked the enemy's left while Davout and Lefebvre supported by Montbrun's light horse struck the whole line – a fierce, coordinated action that produced what Napoleon later termed "one of the most beautiful spectacles that war has offered"; an enormous outflanked army in full retreat to Ratisbon, its guns abandoned, thousands of soldiers throwing down their arms in surrender as Nansouty and St. Sulpice's cuirassiers swept the field, a furious cavalry action that continued throughout the night.[22]

A minor crisis developed the following day during the French assault of Ratisbon in which Marshal Lannes and his aide, Marbot, distinguished themselves. Surrounded by his staff Napoleon was struck by a spent ball that grazed his ankle, news that sent an immediate shock through the army. Although in momentary pain he insisted on mounting his horse to gallop through the ranks as proof of his well-being. The ball "scarcely grazed the Achilles tendon," he later informed Joséphine. "My health is excellent, you have no reason for concern."[23]

A special army bulletin at once proclaimed the tremendous victory to all of Europe: in five days the Grand Army had captured 50,000 Austrians, 100 cannon, 40 standards, over 600 caissons with their ammunition, 3,000 baggage wagons and all the regimental pay chests."[24] Numerous officers (including Berthier) and men were publicly praised for great and selfless deeds – Davout's courageous stand won him a second, well-deserved title, the prince of Eggmühl.

If enemy losses were perhaps exaggerated, there is no doubt that they were severe, both physical and psychological, the survivors trudging into Moravia and down both sides of the Danube. Nor is there any doubt that Charles returned to Austria with sufficient forces that, once reinforced, would soon be ready to fight again. Had Czar Alexander lived up to his promises, had he actively joined the campaign, Austria would have had to sue for peace. Alexander however stood still, his eyes resting only on Warsaw. Napoleon now had little choice but to march on Vienna, if he wanted to end the war.

Notes

1 Corr. XVIII. Nr. 14797, Paris, 21 February 1809.
2 Metternich, II, 261–3.
3 Cooper, 187. See also Metternich, II, 268–9.
4 Corr. XVIII. Nr. 14764, Paris, 7 February 1809.
5 Corr. XVIII. Nr. 14783, Paris, 16 February 1809.
6 Corr. XVIII. Nr. 14746, Paris, 27 January 1809.
7 Corr. XVIII. Nrs. 14955, Paris, 26 March 1809; 14989, Paris, 1 April 1809. See also Roederer (*Mémoires*), 213–47; Thiébault, II, 242 ff.
8 Corr. XVIII. Nr. 14749, Paris, 27 January 1809.
9 Corr. XVIII. Nr. 14797, Paris, 21 February 1809. See also Vandal (*Alexander*), I, 495–6; Metternich, II, 280–1.

10   Rothenberg ("Archduke Charles"), 214–25. See also Epstein (*Napoleon*), 22–3.

11   Falk, 290–305.

12   Corr. XVIII. Nr. 14410, Paris, 25 October 1808.

13   Corr. XVIII. Nr. 14843, Paris, 4 March 1809. Champagny's report of the meeting is attached under the date of 2 March 1809. See also Botzenhart, 587–8.

14   Corr. XVIII. Nr. 14864, Paris, 6 March 1809.

15   Corr. XVIII. Nrs. 14893, 14901, Rambouillet, 14 March 1809.

16   Corr. XVIII. Nr. 14920, Paris, 17 March 1809.

17   Roederer (*Mémoires*), 240–1.

18   Corr. XVIII. Nr. 14975, Paris, 30 March 1809.

19   Bruce, 436.

20   Corr. XVIII. Nr. 15083, Donauwörth, 17 April 1809.

21   Corr. XVIII. Nr. 15088, Donauwörth, 18 April 1809. For details of these events, see Corr. XVIII. Nrs. 15075–15112, 17–24 April 1809; Wartenburg, II, 31–57; Chandler (*Napoleon*), 677–94.

22   Corr. XVIII. Nr. 15112, Ratisbon, 24 April 1809.

23   Corr. XVIII. Nr. 15163, Enns, 6 May 1809. See also Marbot, II, 144–55.

24   Corr. XVIII. Nr. 15111, Ratisbon, 24 April 1809.

CHAPTER FOURTEEN

WAR ON THE DANUBE – II:
THE BATTLE OF WAGRAM
MAY–JULY 1809

The crossing of a river such as the Danube, in the face of an enemy knowing every inch of the terrain and supported by its inhabitants, is one of the greatest military actions that it is possible to conceive.

Tenth Bulletin of the Army of Germany,
Ebersdorf, 23 May 1809[1]

WHY DID NAPOLEON march on Vienna at a time when his forces were divided, and his situation in Spain problematical, when there were rumors of a British landing in Holland and Czar Alexander's alliance was in question, when there were local insurrections in Prussia and Germany and a major uprising in the Tyrol?

The answer is complex.

Napoleon desired above all to wreak vengeance on Austria (and indirectly on England) for what he regarded as a base betrayal of the 1805 treaty of Pressburg. He also believed that he had just dealt the Austrians a blow so severe that they would not risk falling easy prey to his own splendid army and might even surrender before another battle. Less than half his soldiers had fired a shot in the recent battles – "My army has never been so beautiful and numerous," he wrote Murat.[2] A "decisive victory" over the Austrian army would without question ensure his power position in Germany, would possibly bring Czar Alexander to his senses, and would allow him to swiftly finish off the war in Spain before bringing England to its knees by sealing all of Europe from its ships and goods. Tactically he had reason to believe that the Austrians intended to defend Vienna, thus all the more urgency to seize this valuable prize before it was heavily defended, a necessary prelude to crossing the Danube before the usual June flooding.

On the surface his reasoning seemed valid enough. He unquestionably held that valuable asset of tactical impetus. The Austrians had suffered heavy losses and were retreating in disparate and discouraged columns, the French and allied forces in hot pursuit, suffering a setback here and there but nevertheless keeping up the pressure on the capital.

Marshal Lannes' advance guard reached the suburbs of Vienna exactly one month after Austria had declared war on France. The old walled city was defended by Archduke Maximilian commanding a few army and militia battalions. A brief artillery bombardment sent the defenders scurrying across the Danube but did not prevent their destruction of the vital bridge, a misfortune that immediately caused Napoleon to order General Bertrand's engineers to find "the most propitious place to build a bridge below Vienna."[3]

The propitious place was Ebersdorf, a village about 5 miles down the Danube. Here two islands divided the sluggish river into three channels, altogether a width of about 900 yards of water. The stretch from Ebersdorf to the first island measured almost 500 yards; the second stretch to the big island of Lobau about 250 yards; the final stretch to the river's left bank approximately 150 yards. The islands were heavily wooded, which it was hoped would shield the bridging effort from enemy eyes as well as the final crossing to the left bank – the flat ground between two villages, Aspern on the left and Essling on the right. Construction of a decoy bridge was simultaneously begun a few miles from Vienna at Nussdorf. Although Napoleon still did not know the enemy's location he had learned that Archduke Charles intended to give battle either on the left side of the Danube or, by crossing the river at Krems, to strike the French left flank.[4]

Bertrand meanwhile had collected the necessary boats which had to be securely anchored, then planked over, the work of several days. On 19 May the advance guards of Masséna and Lannes' corps crossed on the new bridges. Napoleon and Berthier followed two days later to watch the final bridge put in place from Lobau island to the left bank, a matter of 15 pontoons planked over for some 150 yards. That night Molitor and Boudet's infantry crossed to the left bank along with Lasalle's division of light cavalry, and was followed the next day by Masséna and Lannes' corps, the first occupying Aspern on the left, the second Essling on the right, with Bessières and Espagne's cavalry covering the middle ground. Lannes was not a happy man. "Don't be slow following me," his officers heard him call out to his chief surgeon. "I shall probably need you today. This is going to be my last battle."[5]

Charles meanwhile had brought together about 90,000 troops who, supported by some 200 cannon, fell on the new arrivals in late afternoon. Attack after attack was repulsed during the next few hours with Bessières, Espagne and St. Germain's cavalry performing brilliantly, broaching the Austrian squares that bristled with bayonets, sharp, hot actions which closed at dark but not before the brave Espagne was killed. During the night Oudinot's corps, St. Hilaire's division, two brigades of light cavalry and an artillery train reinforced the bridgehead.

Fighting began again at 4 a.m. with massive attacks on Masséna's corps which not only held but suddenly counterattacked, a fierce charge that sent the enemy running. Noting that Charles had deployed most of his strength opposite the French flanks, Napoleon ordered Lannes to attack the enemy center, Oudinot on the left, Boudet on the right, St. Hilaire in the middle with Bessières' cuirassiers in support.

This effort was succeeding brilliantly when the French suddenly became unwelcome hosts to an adverse fortune of war, unseasonably warm weather. Tributary rivers hugely pregnant with waters released by a premature melt-off in the mountains delivered their children into the Danube. Rising in its wrath the

Lannes, Jean 1769–1809 Marshal of France

mighty river tore whole trees from its banks, battering rams that smashed into the two main boat bridges.

Napoleon learned the bad news about 7 a.m. when he believed himself on the verge of a great victory. The enemy left, center and right were in rout, cannons reversed as gunners hurried from the already blood-soaked field. Suddenly aides galloped to Masséna, Lannes and Bessières: draw in your troops, conserve your ammunition, Lannes to hold the field while the army fell back on Essling. Soon noticing the tactical shift the enemy turned its ranks, swiveled its cannon and during the next ten hours fired 40,000 lethal iron balls while its infantry tried in vain to break through the thin protective rearguard. The French, hoarding cartridges with the care of Croesus clutching a gold coin, somehow managed to hold the village despite repeated enemy attacks.

No one knows the true extent of the carnage. The French claimed to have killed 12,000 Austrians and to have killed or wounded 23 generals and 60 senior officers. French losses were put at 1,100 dead and 3,000 wounded, a ridiculously low figure. A cannon-ball tore away half of Marshal Lannes' thigh, St. Hilaire was seriously wounded, General Durosnel fell and was captured. Communication with the right bank was lost, leaving Davout's corps, most of the cavalry, the bulk of the guns and nearly all the ammunition on the wrong side of the river.

The orphans limped back to Lobau island the next day as angry waters continued to grow and the army to mourn its human losses.

Napoleon returned to Ebersdorf by boat to pick up the pieces of what should fairly be regarded as an unfortunate reverse – what Carl von Clausewitz, then a 28-year-old Prussian officer, would later term the "X factor" in war. Napoleon accepted it as the work of "General Danube," a rebuff rather than a disaster, and mustered his remaining resources accordingly.

He had lost heavily but the bulk of his advance corps was safe on Lobau, defending what he called a bridgehead to the left bank. The troops were tired and hungry, they lacked wine and brandy, many were wounded, others sick, the turbulent river kept rising. The bridges were repaired within two days but supplies and troops had no sooner begun arriving than an enterprising Austrian officer loaded some heavy grain mills on barges which easily smashed through the repaired structures. Undeterred, the French engineers began construction of permanent bridges while convoys of boats supplied the bridge-wrecked survivors on Lobau.

Napoleon meanwhile was calling various units from rear areas for another attempt against the enemy. His overall situation was excellent. Eugène had finally reported: on 16 April he had given battle to Archduke Jean's Austrians at Sacile, was defeated and retreated to his earlier prepared defensive positions on the Adige river. Here he reorganized his army into three corps, one of which was commanded by General Macdonald (who had been in "retirement" for five years as a result of his suspected connection with the Moreau conspiracy) and who in his later memoirs claimed credit for the successful retrieval of fortunes, a claim variously respected by careless or prejudiced historians. A distinguished modern historian, Robert Epstein, has effectively narrowed Macdonald's self-fancied role to what he actually was, a good corps commander in Eugène's army. Eugène's own direction of this campaign was however exemplary and greatly to his credit – Epstein tells the exciting story in his recent book.[6] "Eugène has joined me with all his army," Napoleon wrote Joséphine, "[and] has completely fulfilled his mission . . . He has almost entirely destroyed the enemy army before him."[7] Marmont's corps (also under Eugène's command) was marching from Dalmatia, a further 12,000 men which, taken with Eugène's other corps, would make a welcome addition of over 70,000 troops.

Bernadotte's corps was at Linz with reconnaissance parties probing into Bohemia. King Jérôme's army was in the process of terminating General Schill's brief insurrection in Germany. General Jellachich's Austrian corps had been forced from the Tyrol by Lefebvre's Bavarian corps, only to be shattered by advance units of Eugène's army.

An ebullient army bulletin in late May stated that "the Tyrol and Vorarlberg are completely subjugated. Carniola, Styria, Carinthia, the Salzburg area, Upper and Lower Austria are pacified and disarmed" – optimistic but inaccurate statements repeated by the emperor to private correspondents.[8] But now another blow struck. Marshal Lannes, who had been wounded thirteen times in his career, had survived amputation of his leg and was recovering nicely when suddenly stricken with severe fever. Napoleon at once summoned a Viennese specialist who could do no more than preside over a painful death. Napoleon grieved deeply if briefly – they had been through a lot together and now Lannes was gone. His body would be shipped to France and buried with full honors.

*

The chief problem remained General Danube's tumescence. Napoleon had ordered his engineers to build two permanent bridges supplemented by a boat bridge and a fourth bridge of rafts. No fewer than seven pile-drivers were working in waters so turbulent that slipping anchors caused frustrating delays. Work continued however under protection of a squadron summoned from the Boulogne flotilla whose gunboats patrolled the waters while piles were driven both for the bridges and for a protective iron chain to be strung upstream. This immense project would take over a month to accomplish.

Napoleon used the time well. Lobau had soon become a fortified camp with its own bake-ovens and other conveniences brought over by boat. Macdonald's corps, operating independently, had arrived at Graz and would shortly attack Archduke Jean's force at St. Gotthard. Marmont had reached Laybach from where he was to go after General Chasteler, the condemned villain of the Tyrolean uprising, who was now organizing local insurrections against the French. Archduke Jean retreated to Raab (today's Györ), about 70 miles southeast of Vienna, which capitulated after an 8-day bombardment by Eugène's cannon. Davout now attacked Pressburg (today's Bratislava), some 30 miles east of Vienna, to further cut enemy communications.

As these diverse operations played out, Napoleon prepared for the final act. Lobau, renamed "l'île de Napoléon" by the engineers, bristled with hundreds of cannon. Four portable bridges, including a unique single-piece structure of Napoleon's design, and a cable ferry to be protected by armed skiffs were being constructed for the assault of the mainland. In late June the new stationary bridges across the Danube were completed, "as wide and as beautiful as those of Wittenberg," Napoleon excitedly informed the Saxon king, "each being 880 yards long."9

It had been an exhausting month for the emperor. Uncertainty as to Archduke Charles' whereabouts and intentions was one problem, administrative and operational snags another. Marmont was performing badly, having turned up at Graz four days later than ordered: "You have committed the greatest blunder a general can make . . . Marmont, you have the best corps of my army; I want you to join me for an important battle and you hold me back for several days."[10] Macdonald had failed to seize the treasuries of Graz and Klagenfurt, a matter of several millions down the drain. The troops on Lobau island were dry – Berthier was to send 300,000 bottles of wine and 600,000 rations of brandy at once.[11] Bread was becoming scarce in Vienna, the result of the enemy having smashed the grinding mills. More serious, powder was in short supply as one result of prolonged bombardments of Raab and Pressburg.

These were relatively niggling problems that caused only minor delays in final preparations for the new assault. The emperor moved to the big island on the first day of July to oversee final artillery preparations, which were impressive. Besides extensive batteries on Lobau, guns, howitzers and mortars were deployed on small neighboring islands. After a day of heavy cannonades a task force of light infantry preceded by gunboats was landed downstream on the left bank, seizing the *Hansel-Grund* on the extreme right of the target area. Oudinot's corps then crossed on a hastily laid pontoon bridge to clear the woods of enemy and form a protective bridgehead with its right on Mühlleuten. Meanwhile Masséna's troops began landing upstream to form another protective bridgehead on the left, his cavalry and artillery following on a pontoon bridge, the rest of the infantry either carried on the cable ferry or crossing on Napoleon's innovative one-piece bridge. The way was now clear for Eugène's corps followed by Bessières' heavy cavalry and the artillery and supply wagons coming from Ebersdorf.

This was a superbly planned and executed operation, albeit eased by minimal and quickly overcome resistance. By daybreak Napoleon had deployed the bulk of the army in battle order. His corps formed three lines: the first consisted of Masséna's four infantry divisions and Lasalle's cavalry on the left; Oudinot's three infantry divisions and Colbert's cavalry in the center; and on the right Davout's four infantry divisions and Montbrun's cavalry reinforced by some squadrons of Eugène's dragoons. The second line was formed by Bernadotte's corps on the left; the Guard, Marmont's corps and one Bavarian division in the center; Eugène's Army of Italy on the right. Bessières' heavy cavalry comprised the third line. One division of each corps faced left, one center, and one right. The line of attack, right to left, would pivot on Enzersdorf.

Here was an army of about 160,000 men, its water flanks protected by gunboats, its soldiers carrying a two-day supply of bread and brandy for themselves, grass for the horses. It faced an enemy that for over a month had been fortifying a line stretching from Aspern on its right just over 4 miles to Enzersdorf on the left, the villages and flatlands covered with palisaded forts defended by over 150 cannon and held by nearly 200,000 regular, militia and irregular troops. Realizing the fatuity of a conventional attack Napoleon instead chose to strike the enemy left which, once turned, would force Archduke Charles to leave prepared positions to fight in open country.

This is what happened:

Following the opening bombardment, a detachment of Masséna's corps under General St. Croix cleared Enzersdorf of a few remaining enemy to open the plain to the debouching corps. Archduke Charles responded by sending several columns of infantry supported by artillery and all of his cavalry at top speed toward Rutzendorf in an attempt to outflank the potential out-flankers. Oudinot's people beat the Austrians to this village while Davout's corps on the right marched on, hoping to overrun Charles' headquarters.

Masséna meanwhile overran Essling and Aspern while Bernadotte's Saxons chased the enemy from Raasdorf. Hard fighting continued throughout afternoon and evening, the enemy retreating northeast to a defensive line, its center on Wagram, its left reaching to Neusiedl and its right to Gerasdorf. By late evening Napoleon's left rested on Aspern, his center on Raasdorf and his right on Glinzendorf. It had been an exhausting two days for the soldiers, first in marching to debarkation areas, then crossing the final channel, then fighting 5 or 6 miles inland with considerable losses. In crossing the Russbach stream and seizing the plateau in an attempt to gain the enemy's left, Macdonald's corps alone suffered nearly 2,000 casualties (including those taken prisoner). Napoleon however correctly judged his enemy to have been badly hurt, his corps weakened and confused. If he could seize Wagram by a night attack, he reasoned, he would cut this enemy in half (one of his favorite tactics) and thus void the difficult battle looming for the next day.

It was a bold concept but Napoleon was a bold commander – and it almost succeeded. The surprise attack was on the verge of entering Wagram when a French column, mistaking the white uniforms of the Saxon allies for the enemy, opened a disastrous fire-fight that caused the operation to fail with severe losses.

There remained the conventional attack the following morning. Sensing that Charles had deployed the bulk of his strength on his flanks, Napoleon accordingly concentrated his forces opposite the enemy center. While Bernadotte and Masséna guarded the French left with Montbrun's cavalry screening the right, Eugène and Macdonald supported by Oudinot with Bessières' cavalry in reserve would attack the enemy corps between Wagram and Neusiedl.

Rosenberg's Austrian corps started the action at daybreak by falling on Davout's regiments. Napoleon hastily sent a cuirassier division in support along with 12 cannon to take Rosenberg in flanking fire. In less than an hour Davout had pushed the Austrians northeast of Neusiedl to bend in the Austrian left flank, inflicting heavy casualties in the process. An artillery duel meanwhile commenced along the line as Napoleon tried to figure out what Charles was up to: "This enemy deployment appeared so insane," a bulletin later stated, "that one feared some trap."[12] Finally deciding that his enemy was inept rather than clever Napoleon ordered Masséna to seize a village on the left while Davout pushed in from the right. Once Davout's troops appeared, Marmont and Macdonald would attack from the front.

Macdonald, Jacques 1765–1840 Marshal of France

Masséna seized the village as ordered but was suddenly struck by a powerful counter-attack that outflanked his left to drive several miles southwest and threaten the lightly held village of Aspern. Meanwhile Bernadotte's Saxons were repulsed before Wagram and fell back to leave the army's center exposed – a movement that led to a sharp quarrel between Napoleon and Bernadotte and resulted in the latter's being sent from the field in disgrace. Macdonald was now ordered to fill the gap. But the four Austrian corps, in pushing back Masséna, had not only exposed their flanks but had left Wagram held only by Hohenzollern's corps and Rosenberg's weakened corps.

Napoleon acted quickly (while Charles failed to act at all). While Masséna moved southwest to cope with the advancing Austrians, Macdonald's heavily reinforced corps, with Eugène on his right and preceded by over 100 cannon fielded by Lauriston, fell on the prolonged enemy flank. Simultaneously Masséna attacked its head to send the entire force in disorganized retreat. On the other side of the battlefield, Davout after seizing Neusiedl was marching on Wagram which Oudinot was preparing to strike from the front.

The emperor later wrote that by 10 a.m. even "the less clair-voyant observers saw that we had won the battle."[13] His point was dramatically made two hours later when Oudinot and Davout pushed into Wagram to send its defenders in retreat with the other corps. By evening there was no sign of the enemy who, having been cut from Moravia and Hungary, retreated into Bohemia.[14]

It was an enormous but very expensive victory. At least 40,000 Austrians including a large number of officers had been killed, wounded or taken prisoner. The French admitted to 1,500 killed and 3–4,000 wounded, but more likely the figure was at least five times greater. General Lasalle was killed and a number of gener-als, Bessières among them, wounded. Macdonald, Marmont and Oudinot who had fought brilliantly for two days were promoted to marshal.

Although the French were in no position to pursue the enemy in strength, late the next day Napoleon sent Marmont with a strong force of infantry and cavalry to attack the rearguard "and do as much damage as possible."[15] Eugène's light cavalry was to patrol toward Hungary.

The action however was effectively ended. A few days later Napoleon was in camp in front of Znaym when the Austrians asked for an armistice. A line of demarcation between the armies was quickly drawn, the Austrians agreed to turn over key fortresses and evacuate the Tyrol and Vorarlberg. The armistice would be valid for 30 days – each side agreed to give 15 days' notice before resuming hostilities.

With that Napoleon returned to Schönbrunn.

Notes

1 Corr. XIX. Nr. 15246, Ebersdorf, 23 May 1809.

2 Corr. XVIII. Nr. 15193, Schönbrunn, 12 May 1809.

3 Corr. XVIII. Nr. 15189, Schönbrunn, 11 May 1809. See also Horward ("Beethoven"), 7: the noise of the exploding shells caused Beethoven to leave his quarters for refuge in a friend's cellar "where he buried his head in a pillow to protect his ears from the concussion of the exploding shells."

4 Corr. XIX. Nr. 15212, Schönbrunn, 15 May 1809. See also Epstein (*Napoleon*), 97–118.

5 Macdonell, 165.

6 Epstein ("Eugene"), 117–25, (*Napoleon*), 74–96.

7 Corr. XIX, Nr. 15261, Ebersdorf, 27 May 1809. See also Macdonald, 130–56.

8 Corr. XIX. Nr. 15272, Ebersdorf, 28 May 1809.

9 Corr. XIX. Nr. 15432, Schönbrunn, 24 June 1809.

10 Corr. XIX. Nr. 15453, Schönbrunn, 26 June 1809.

11 Corr. XIX. Nr. 15443, Schönbrunn, 26 June 1809.

12 Corr. XIX. Nr. 15505, Wolkersdorf, 8 July 1809.

13 Corr. XIX. Nr. 15505, Wolkersdorf, 8 July 1809.

14 Macdonald, 159–69; Epstein (*Napoleon*), 150–65.

15 Corr. XIX. Nr. 15496, Wolkersdorf, 7 July 1809.

CHAPTER FIFTEEN

THE TREATY OF SCHÖNBRUNN
JULY–OCTOBER 1809

*Come to Vienna . . . I want to see you . . . You cannot imagine
what a tremendous importance I attach to everything that
concerns you . . . Many tender kisses on your lovely hands and
just one on your beautiful mouth. Napole.*

Napoleon to the Countess Marie Walewska,
Schönbrunn, May 1809[1]

THE BATTLEFIELD OF Wagram had to be cleaned, the thousands of
dead bloating in summer sun hurriedly buried in mass graves, the
thousands of wounded evacuated to Vienna and to makeshift
hospitals in neighboring towns and monasteries – a ghastly job
greatly impeded by lack of physicians and surgeons, orderlies,
medicines, bandages and transports. Battle-worn regiments had
to be sorted out and refitted, gaps filled with new bodies, units
deployed in ready defensive positions in case the armistice broke
down.

Contrary to revisionist outpourings of later historians,
Napoleon paid the closest attention to refurbishing his army. In
mid July he ordered Count Daru, his chief supply officer, to have
a million rations and thousands of pounds of flour and grain sent
to Vienna, to establish workshops at Graz, Linz and Vienna to
manufacture cloaks, jackets, vests, breeches, shirts and shoes.
Oudinot was to put his men in barracks and, incidentally, to pay
them 15 *sous* for each bayonet or broken musket, 30 *sous* for each
whole musket retrieved from the battlefield. Other commanders
were to encamp their troops as soon as possible, then get them on

the drillfield and target range, "the sole means of maintaining order and discipline."[2]

By month's end Napoleon was reviewing various of his rejuvenated divisions. In mid August he announced cash awards to all officers and soldiers who had lost a limb since the beginning of the campaign. Come chilly weather, commanders were to replace the men's linen breeches with heavier cloth garments and where necessary move to high ground to avoid outbreaks of fever.[3]

Marshals Berthier, Davout and Masséna won new titles and generous land holdings. Champagny, Clarke, Maret, Reynier, Gaudin, Oudinot, Macdonald and Fouché were granted dukedoms.[4] If Napoleon praised and rewarded, he also condemned. We have witnessed Prince Bernadotte's ignominious departure from the battlefield of Wagram, relieved of his command and sent back to France. Before his departure the errant marshal retaliated by publishing an illicit order of the day which credited him and his Saxons with the capture of Wagram. Learning of this only in late July, Napoleon ordered his minister of war, General Clarke, to reprimand the marshal on grounds of his and the Saxons' poor battle performance. "I should tell you that the prince of Ponte-Corvo [Bernadotte] has not done very well in this campaign. Here is a broken-down man who wants only money, pleasures and titles, but who does not wish to pay for them by the dangers and fatigues of war. The truth is that this 'column of granite' [Bernadotte's phrase for his command] was constantly routed."[5] Napoleon followed this order with an all-army bulletin that gave General Oudinot entire credit for seizing Wagram, and with a special order of the day restricted to his marshals. After contradicting Bernadotte's claims and criticizing the Saxon performance Napoleon added: "His Majesty desires that this expression of his displeasure serves as an example so that no marshal claims the glory that belongs to others."[6]

Preliminary peace negotiations meanwhile had opened in Raab. Foreign minister Champagny informed Austrian envoys Metternich, Stadion and Liechtenstein that the Austrian *Landwehr* or militia must be disbanded and the regular Austrian army reduced by 50 per cent. Once these conditions were met, negotiations would commence either on the basis of *uti possidetis* – each side to keep territory currently held – or on "a system of compensation." Whatever the case, the Austrian envoys were informed that Napoleon intended to display "the same moderation and generosity that he has shown with the peace of Pressburg"[7] – which meant that the Austrian court was going to pay through the nose, a matter that would take two and a half months to resolve.

This would be a trying ten weeks for an already tired man. He would be embarrassed by an English landing in Holland, a serious uprising in the Tyrol, the arrest of Pope Pius VII in Rome, a fluctuating and often unfavorable military situation in Spain, and another attempt on his life. There would be two compensations, one a final peace after many ups and downs, the other the loving presence of the beautiful Marie Walewska (also with many ups and downs).

After spending two months in Paris in winter of 1808, Marie Walewska had returned to Poland shortly before Napoleon departed for Spain. He had stayed in touch with her and the previous May had invited her to come to Vienna.[8]

The countess arrived soon after the armistice and was installed in a small house in a nearby village. "I used to go and collect her there in a closed, unmarked carriage," valet Constant Wairy later wrote, ". . . to bring her to the palace through a special door which was the Emperor's private entrance."[9]

It was possibly the happiest time in either of their lives. Marie was at a peak of youthful beauty, "her complexion of the most wonderful freshness," wrote a contemporary, ". . . she blushed easily, and then she became truly ravishing."[10] Napoleon was as smitten as he had been in castle Finkenstein some two years earlier. At first they spent only clandestine nights together but soon she appeared frequently in his quarters, the famous red-and-gold Japanese apartments, listening to him dictate orders in response to one or more crises, discussing Poland's future (always to Napoleon's distaste), coaxing him into long walks in the private parks or drives in an unmarked carriage through the magnificent Prater park on the Danube, sharing his bed and comforting him through an extremely difficult and frustrating period. Their cup of happiness was full but in September Marie realized that she was pregnant.[11]

A delighted emperor at once summoned Doctor Corvisart, the court physician, to Vienna. After confirming the pregnancy he announced that the child would be born in May. "I could not even begin to describe the loving care the Emperor lavished on Madame Walewska," Constant later wrote, "now he knew she was pregnant . . . He was reluctant to let her out of his sight for even a short time."[12]

The English government had promised Emperor Francis not only a large amount of gold for going to war against France but also simultaneous diversionary landings in Italy and Holland to tie down French troops and draw others from the Grand Army.

Other than £250,000 in silver bars the money did not materialize. The Austrian treasury remained empty as heaps of worthless paper money flooded the country. The intended landing in Italy remained a non-event, the fault of the lazy, inept and timid General Stuart whose 15,000 troops remained idle in Sicily.

The northern expedition also backfired. Organized with great political and patriotic fanfare, it was commanded by a political appointee, the 52-year-old Lord Chatham (the late William Pitt's brother). Ships and troops were duly gathered on the Kentish coast – where they remained while the Austrian army suffered its string of humiliating defeats. Transports loaded with some 12,000 troops finally sailed in late July, over two weeks *after* the battle of Wagram. The advance guard reached the western channel of the Scheldt river the same evening, its mission to seize Fort Flushing on Walcheren island and Fort Breskens on Cadzand island in order to clear the way for the advance up the Scheldt to Antwerp, its ultimate purpose the capture and destruction of Napoleon's flourishing naval base and shipyards.[13]

Napoleon learned of the British presence only in early August. Although he did not regard it as very serious, he was extremely upset by Cambacérès and Clarke's failure to immediately call out provincial national guards and send them to protect Antwerp. Clarke was to reinforce garrisons at Cadzand and Antwerp; if the Walcheren garrison could not cope with enemy landings the dikes were to be cut to flood the island. In view of the English effort in Spain, Napoleon reasoned, it was doubtful if the English could find reinforcements for the new expedition.[14] To besiege Antwerp would require a very large force which would be attacked by hastily deployed French and Dutch armies.

Napoleon's hasty orders failed to dispel the lassitude of Cambacérès, Clarke and other ministers – with one exception. Joseph Fouché took it upon himself to call out the national guard which was placed under command of the semi-disgraced Bernadotte, the first step in ensuring the defense of Antwerp.

Fortunately for the French, Lord Chatham and his commanders shared French hesitation. Fort Flushing was duly besieged however and fell after a 48-hour bombardment, its commandant, General Monnet, having failed to cut the dikes. Although Napoleon never forgave Monnet for the surrender of 6,000 French and Dutch soldiers, for the English it was a pyrrhic victory. During the siege soldiers had already begun falling ill with the notorious island fever, a scourge that would soon decimate the new owners. By the time the base was secured, the Antwerp defenses were manned by 25,000 troops commanded by Marshal Bernadotte while Marshal Moncey extended the defense to Cadzand island.

The result was stalemate. Leaving 18,000 men at Flushing, Chatham gave up and returned to England. Within weeks half of the garrison was dying under ghastly conditions in makeshift hospitals. The remainder would finally be evacuated in late

September to complete one of the least glorious chapters in England's military history.

Another important factor in the Austrian court's decision to declare war on France (for the fourth time) had been an agreed-upon uprising against Bavarian rule in the Vorarlberg and the Tyrol. A successful insurrection here would cut French communications with Italy and pose a flanking threat to French and allied forces in Germany.

Shortly after the Austrians crossed the Inn river to begin the new war, generals Chasteler and Jellachich had moved Austrian troops into the Tyrol to signal the uprising. In response to Chasteler's inflammatory proclamation the insurgents captured and then killed 700 French conscripts traveling through the territory and 1,800 Bavarian soldiers stationed there.

Napoleon sent in Lefebvre's corps which forced Chasteler to retreat into Austria. Cited as a war criminal by Napoleon, if captured by the French he would be courtmartialed and shot. Jellachich, as we earlier noted, in retreating with his division ran into Prince Eugène's advance guard coming up from Italy and was all but eliminated. Napoleon announced in late May that "the Tyrol and Vorarlberg are completely submissive," a short-lived optimism dispelled by a partisan uprising against General Wrede's small occupying force of Bavarians.[5]

The insurgents numbered something over 2,000 men, most of them hardy mountaineers only too familiar with this rugged (and very beautiful) country ideal for guerrilla warfare. They were led by four determined men: Andreas Hofer, an innkeeper and a giant of a man; Joachim "Redbeard" Haspinger, a Capuchin priest; Joseph Speckbacher, a peasant; and Peter Kemnater, also an innkeeper. After suffering several bloody ambushes General von Wrede's small Bavarian force evacuated the country.

Only in late July did Napoleon face up to the situation by sending in Lefebvre's corps from one side and a new corps under Wrede from the other side, a strong force that he hoped would be supported by several thousand Württemberg soldiers.[16] Once again he had underestimated the staying power of well-led, organized guerrillas whom he summarily dismissed as brigands fit only to be shot. By mid August he was again appealing to the Württemberg king for the troops which had not yet appeared: "My orders to disarm the people and take hostages were given long ago. But our enemies continue the revolt . . . in the hope that they can influence the peace negotiations, or strengthen themselves if hostilities recommence [with Austria]. That is their game. Ours is to completely cooperate and profit from the armistice in order to suppress these insurrections."[17]

Far from being suppressed the rebels continued to prosper. A large Bavarian relief corps walked into still another well-laid ambush and was almost annihilated. In late August, Napoleon notified Murat in Naples that "the Bavarians have failed in Tyrol, and it appears that these mountaineers will be difficult to over-come. If hostilities begin again [with Austria], I will need eight to ten thousand men . . . to hold Italy and Tyrol in check."[18] A few days later he ordered General Rusca to negotiate with insurgent chiefs "to see if there weren't some way to peacefully determine the fate of these peoples." If the insurgents remained attached to Austria they would face eternal war – they could choose between becoming Bavarians or part of Italy.[19]

The Tyrolean leaders were not in the least interested in Napoleon's propositions and continued to fight even after becom-ing isolated by the treaty of Schönbrunn. With Austria removed from the war and the Tyrol returned to Bavaria, the task of paci-fication was given to Prince Eugène whose troops soon rounded up most of the insurgents. "The Tyrol has submitted," Napoleon reported to Berthier in late November.[20] Andreas Hofer's guerril-las kept on fighting but he was soon betrayed, captured and shot.[21] Italian and Bavarian troops continued to occupy the unhappy but now docile country.

An equally awkward situation arose from Napoleon's shaky rela-tions with Pope Pius VII who, surrounded by bitterly anti-French cardinals, not only continued to assert himself in temporal as opposed to spiritual affairs, but also to refuse the consecration of Napoleon's appointed bishops in France and Germany as agreed upon in the Concordat. Napoleon's occupation of Rome and annexation of the papal lands culminated in his being excommunicated from the Catholic church, which did not in the least upset him.

Far more worrisome was obvious papal support of British agents in Rome, taken with steady violations of the continental system which allowed British merchandise to flow into Italy and beyond. Napoleon had repeatedly warned the pope of the dangerous game he was playing. In late July the French governor of Rome, General Miollis, sought to end the game by arresting the old man and moving him under guard to Genoa, then to Grenoble.

Napoleon learned of the pope's arrest in early August, at about the same time that he was notified of the British landing in Holland. He had ordered the arrest only if the papacy had become "a center of rebellion" (or so he insisted).[22] Cardinal Pacca should have been arrested, not the pope, he explained to Fouché: "The pope is a good man but an uninformed fanatic. Cardinal Pacca is an educated rogue, an enemy of France who does not deserve generous treatment."[23]

This was but slight consolation to the pope whose enforced *hegira* finally ended in Savona, a port a few miles west of Genoa. Other than suffering a loss of dignity he was quite well off. Napoleon gave him an allowance of 100,000 francs a month (in addition to official expenses) and three carriages with livery. He should not be made to think that he was in prison, Napoleon wrote; his guard should be headed by a general and have the appearance of a guard of honor. He was not however to return to Rome.[24]

Meanwhile peace negotiations with Austria had moved like cold molasses, much to the emperor's fury and frustration. The Austrians might well have run away from Wagram, but Prince Charles still commanded some 200,000 troops. "It is possible that hostilities will recommence," Napoleon warned his generals in early August when dictating a series of contingency battle orders.[25] The British landing in Holland, the uprising in the Tyrol, the fluctuating situation in Spain and the neutered behavior of Russia all combined to slow the Austrian hand in hopes that Napoleon would be forced to lower his demands.

But he was not to be coerced. Despite peripheral events, despite the Austrian force in Hungary, he remained in a strong bargaining position. He was the victor, his army was on battle alert; he had made his conditions clear and it was up to the Austrian court to meet them. As he later informed an Austrian diplomat, "I found myself in a good position because I ate and drank at [your] expense while [your] position was deplorable."[26]

Much of the difficulty, Napoleon realized, stemmed from disparate advice given to Francis by his closest councillors. Metternich was duplicitous, Stadion a fool, Bellegarde "does not see clearly" and Liechtenstein was a flitting opportunist. Kind words were awarded only to Prince Charles, but he had left the army and was out of favor with the court. Emperor Francis was a good man but with no will of his own: "He always shares the opinion of the last person who spoke with him," Napoleon complained to Metternich.[27]

As meeting after meeting produced no results, as events in the Tyrol and Holland began tilting in his favor, Napoleon grew more strident, even threatening a return to fighting. Several factors however dampened his bellicosity and his demands. He was eager to return to France whose internal affairs including finances were becoming increasingly shaky, and also to deal with the Spanish war which was not going well.

In mid September he suddenly cut his terms by nearly half: Austria to cede territory on the frontiers of the Inn river and Italy that held about 1.6 million subjects; Saxony and Russia to gain lands in Galicia and Bohemia that contained some 2 million persons. When this compromise produced no action, Napoleon presented the Austrian court with an ultimatum: either accept or face renewed battle. This time the court caved in and in mid October the peace was signed.[28]

Napoleon got what he wanted. The cession of Croatia, Carniola, Trieste and Carinthia (which became the new Illyrian states) would now connect Dalmatia to his Italian states to strengthen his presence on the Adriatic coast, a necessary prelude to France becoming a maritime power in the Mediterranean. Bavaria gained the bishopric of Salzburg and the upper Inn river valley, Saxony added western Galicia to the duchy of Warsaw and Russia was given a few provinces in eastern Galicia.

A secret clause called for Austria to pay France an indemnity of 100 million francs, not as much as his previous war with Austria had yielded, but it would be supplemented by 50 million francs from the sale of surplus food, ammunition and equipment, which was just as well since his army payroll in Austria amounted to 4 million francs a month.[29]

The emperor almost did not live to witness the signing of the peace. Two days prior to the event he and his officers were about to review a division gathered on the parade ground of Schönbrunn when a handsome young man approached, saying he had come from Germany to deliver a petition to the emperor. As he stepped forward his evident apprehension caused a suspicious aide to intercept him. He was found to be carrying a knife and calmly admitted that he wished to kill Napoleon "to deliver Austria from the French presence." Napoleon interrogated him at length to conclude that he was neither a religious nor political fanatic, but rather a person gripped in "the fever of exaltation." Further interrogation revealed no political connection but when he refused to recant, insisting that he would try again if released, he was tried by courtmartial and shot.[30]

Although the emperor quietly brushed off the attempt it no doubt brought to mind the frailty of his existence. His virility confirmed by Marie's pregnancy, his immortality challenged by Stapps' knife (how many other similarly inspired young men were waiting in the shadows to kill him?), his thoughts would logically have again turned to the need for an heir to preserve the dynasty. Judging from his few extant notes to Joséphine at this time, his orders to Paris functionaries to seal off staircases and doors connecting his apartment with Joséphine's in the Tuileries and their country châteaux, and from his actions upon his return to France, he probably had decided to divorce her, though dreading the thought of confrontation.

Who would replace her?

Marie Walewska, beautiful, intelligent and loving as she was, could not be considered. "Yes, I am in love," Napoleon had written King Joseph, "[but] I must look for ways to further my major aims."[31] Marie, who was already married, a mother and was only of minor nobility, could not fill the bill. She was to return to Paris under Doctor Corvisart's care and if she bore a son, Napoleon promised, he would one day become the king of Poland.[32] (After a month in Paris, probably realizing that she had been conquered by events, she would return to Poland to have her child – we meet her again.)

Notes

1   Sutherland, 123.
2   Corr. XIX. Nrs. 15542, Schönbrunn, 16 July 1809; 15586, Schönbrunn, 24 July 1809.
3   Corr. XIX. Nrs. 15659, 15663, Schönbrunn, 15 August 1809; 15845, 15846, Schönbrunn, 23 September 1809.
4   Corr. XIX. Nr. 15658, Schönbrunn, 15 August 1809.
5   Corr. XIX. Nr. 15595, Schönbrunn, 29 July 1809.
6   Corr. XIX. Nr. 15614, Schönbrunn, 5 August 1809.
7   Corr. XIX. Nr. 15584, Schönbrunn, 24 July 1809.
8   Sutherland, 123.
9   Sutherland, 127–8.
10 Sutherland, 132.
11 Sutherland, 128, 132–3.
12 Sutherland, 133.
13 Bryant (Victory), 324–34, for a good summary of the expedition from the English standpoint. Cadzand island is today part of the mainland.
14 Corr. XIX. Nrs. 15619, 15620, Schönbrunn, 6 August 1809; 15625, 16626, Schönbrunn, 8 August 1809.

15 Corr. XIX. Nrs. 15272, Ebersdorf, 28 May 1809; 15310, Schönbrunn, 7 June 1809. See also Harford, 704–19.

16 Corr. XIX. Nrs. 15583, Schönbrunn, 23 July 1809; 15591, Schönbrunn, 26 July 1809; 15599, Vienna, 30 July 1809.

17 Corr. XIX, Nr. 15675, Schönbrunn, 17 August 1809.

18 Corr. XIX. Nr. 15716, Schönbrunn, 26 August 1809.

19 Corr. XIX. Nr. 15725, Schönbrunn, 29 August 1809.

20 Corr. XX. Nr. 16018, Paris, 22 November 1809.

21 Asprey (*War in the Shadows*), II, 135–6. See also Corr. XX. Nr. 16172, Paris, 27 January 1810.

22 Corr. XIX. Nr. 15634, Schönbrunn, 10 August 1809.

23 Corr. XIX. Nr. 15615, Schönbrunn, 6 August 1809.

24 Corr. XIX. Nrs. 15712, Schönbrunn, 5 September 1809; 15812, Schönbrunn, 14 September 1809; 15819, Schönbrunn, 15 September 1809.

25 Corr. XIX. Nr. 15622, Schönbrunn, 7 August 1809.

26 Corr. XIX. Nr. 15816, Schönbrunn, 15 September 1809.

27 Corr. XIX. Nrs. 15778, Schönbrunn, 10 September 1809; 15832, Schönbrunn, 21 September 1809.

28 Corr. XIX, Nrs. 15822, Schönbrunn, 15 September 1809; 15901, Schönbrunn, 5 October 1809; 15903, Schönbrunn, 6 October 1809; 15937, Schönbrunn, 14 October 1809. See also Metternich, II, 304–5, who on 10 August 1809 urged Emperor Francis to yield to the French demands and then play a waiting game until strong enough to avenge the defeat.

29 Corr. XIX. Nrs. 15758, Schönbrunn, 5 September 1809; 15950, Schönbrunn, 14 October 1809.

30 Corr. XIX. Nr. 15935, Schönbrunn, 12 October 1809.

31 Horne, 286.

32 Bruce, 440.

CHAPTER SIXTEEN

THE SPANISH ADVENTURE – IV:
JUNE–DECEMBER 1809

*When I appear beyond the Pyrenees, the [English] leopard will
take to the ocean to escape disgrace, defeat and death.*

Napoleon to the *Corps législatif*, Paris, 3 December 1809.[1]

HAVING ONCE AGAIN humbled his old enemy, Austria, Napoleon
turned to his war in Spain. That matters had radically changed in
his absence was scarcely surprising in view of King Joseph's lack-
adaisical nature, his military inexperience, his mediocre chief of
staff, Marshal Jourdan, his jealous, greedy and quarrelsome corps
commanders and, not least, the vast and rugged expanse of Spain
which was rapidly turning into an extremely hostile and dangerous country for French soldiers.

Here briefly is what happened:

For a time events seemed to justify Napoleon's optimism upon
his departure from Spain to fight the Austrians. Marshal Soult,
after seeing off Sir John Moore's broken corps at Corunna in mid
January 1809, moved into northern Portugal, his 23,000 troops
worming through tortuous mountain ranges to the coastal town of
Oporto. When his summons to surrender was refused, his troops
successfully stormed the port to commit almost every known
excess on the defenders and the populace. In the Estremadura,
meanwhile, Marshal Victor had caught up and severely mauled
General Cuesta's army at Medellin.

Sir John Cradock in Lisbon, commanding the 10,000 British
troops left in Portugal, now faced a drive by Soult's corps from the

Victor Perrin 1766–1841 Marshal of France

north and Victor's corps from the east, a total of nearly 50,000 troops that Napoleon not unreasonably supposed would be sufficient to throw the British garrison into the sea. But neither Soult nor Victor in the field, neither Joseph nor Jourdan in Madrid, showed much enthusiasm for the final march on Lisbon. Soult, comfortably ensconced at Oporto, had decided to make himself king of northern Portugal, while Victor seemed equally content to remain inactive at Medellin.

Their indolence allowed a large reinforcement to arrive in Lisbon. Wellesley soon commanded 20,000 British, 3,000 Hanoverians and 16,000 Portuguese.[2] Almost at once and very daringly he marched a strong corps northward, crossed the Douro river and fell on Soult's people in Oporto, a total surprise which in a few hours forced the French to retreat eastward. Blocked by a small English corps, they took to the northern hills, abandoning all guns and wagons and losing several thousand troops, many of them tortured by Portuguese peasants revenging the sacking of Oporto, an altogether ghastly 9-day march back into Galicia.

Wellesley and the Spanish central *junta* next agreed on a combined offensive against Victor's corps which, having eaten out the Estremadura, had moved eastward to Talavera. The ensuing battle of Talavera was a disaster for each side, a stand-off that cost the French some 7,000 casualties, the British 5,000, with Cuesta's Spaniards escaping annihilation only by a determined British stand.

Wellesley was debating his next move when he learned that Soult's reorganized and reinforced corps was approaching from the north to cut his communications with Portugal. Now there was nothing for it but to reach the border as rapidly as possible, which meant abandoning 4,000 wounded at Talavera.

After enduring incredible hardships and narrow escape from capture the battered survivors finally reached the fortress haven of Badajoz on the border. A few weeks later, in early September 1809, they were settled more dead than alive in the Guadiana valley.

Napoleon's reaction to these events was curiously mixed, a dangerous foreshadowing of what was to come. His initial criticism centered on King Joseph and Marshal Jourdan for having left the remnants of Romana's Spanish army free on the Galician borders to reorganize and harass Ney and Soult's rearguards. "It pains me to see that the French army has no commander," he wrote General Clarke in Paris, "a fault that will produce grievous results . . . the greatest calamities can result from this apathy and this neglect of the first principles of war." Joseph's priority was to secure the north in order to prevent a general insurrection before attempting operations in the south.[3]

The subject remained dormant while Napoleon was caught up in the whirlwind events of the opening battles in Bavaria, the occupation of Vienna, the crossing of the Danube and the battles of Aspern-Essling. His attention turned to the other war only in mid June. Apparently ignorant of Soult's fatal march into Portugal, his humiliating defeat at Oporto and costly retreat into Galicia, Napoleon ordered Ney, Mortier and Soult's corps to form one army under Soult's command (as the senior marshal). This force, 50–60,000 strong, should "march on the English, pursue them relentlessly, bring them to battle and throw them into the sea . . . if the three corps promptly unite, the English are bound to be destroyed and the Spanish matter resolved, but they must be joined together and not march in small groups. This is a guiding principle anywhere but above all in a country where it is impossible to maintain communication."[4] He followed this order with another directive to his minister of war: "Inform the king [Joseph] that the north must be considered above all; that if Zaragoza is seized and if he loses the Aragon, he will find himself in the most unpleasant situation. Why does no one at Madrid do anything? . . . The English are apparently reinforcing their troops in Portugal; the danger will come from there if appropriate action is not taken at Madrid."[5]

His Spanish thoughts were again interrupted during the immense preparations that led to victory at Wagram, the post-battle confusion, Marie Walewska's enchanting presence, army reorganization and peace negotiations. Only in late July did Napoleon scold General Clarke for not having reported on Spain, noting in passing that "General Wellesley has arrived with twenty-five thousand English troops at Talavera and has joined [General] Cuesta." He regretted that Soult's newly formed army had failed to hook up with King Joseph's divisions to make a force 100,000 strong: "This would be a wonderful opportunity to teach the English a lesson and finish the war."[6]

A subsequent report from Joseph brought a stinging criticism for not having kept his corps united. Had he brought Soult's force to Madrid instead of ordering it to Plasencia, his combined strength would have conquered Spain and Portugal: "No one at Madrid understands anything about the great movements of war."[7] His temper flared upon learning of the battle of Talavera – "*Mon Dieu!*" he complained to Clarke, "what is an army without a commander?"[8] – but subsided a few days later when he informed foreign minister Champagny that "things are going very well in Spain. Marshal Soult has reached the rear of the English army which is in retreat . . . The English have lost a third of their army in the battle of Talavera."[9]

Having received more details of the battle he next accused Marshal Jourdan, Joseph's chief of staff, of submitting false reports: Talavera was not a victory, the French had seized neither the town nor the battlefield. Soult's march on Plasencia "was dangerous and above all useless: dangerous because our army could have been defeated at Talavera before receiving help which would have compromised all my armies in Spain, while the British had nothing to fear since within three hours they could have retreated behind the Tagus river . . . that my best troops and the fate of Spain have been compromised by ignorance of the rules of war without having been able to obtain a result, even if successful." Having torn Jourdan's strategy to bits he turned to Victor's tactics, blasting him for attacking the English without prior reconnaissance:

It was certainly obvious that, [the English] having deployed their right on Talavera . . . and their left on a plateau, it was necessary to determine if this plateau could have been outflanked; that the enemy's position demanded, then, preliminary reconnaissances, and that troops have been led with no preconceived plan, as animals to a slaughter house; that finally, having decided to give battle, they did so half-heartedly because my troops have been rebuffed while 12,000 reserve troops did not fire a shot.[10]

As Napoleon received more reports on the battle his disgust mounted for the song-and-dance nonsense of Joseph and Jourdan: "instead of reporting the true situation to me, you give me school-boy fantasies." He wanted a detailed and truthful account of this action that was taken "without due thought and with no knowledge of warfare; that the action took place without unity, without plans, without resolution." In his mind this was not merely a military defeat. A very important principle was involved: "Make all my commanders realize," he directed General Clarke, "how much they harm the government by hiding things that it learns from soldiers who have written home, and causes it to credit enemy accounts all the more."[11]

The anxious month of August finally ended on an optimistic note. "News from Spain is good," Napoleon informed his foreign minister. [Spanish General] Venégas has stupidly lost two marches and has been attacked and defeated. He has lost his baggage, forty cannons and 4,000 men taken prisoner and is being pursued into Andalucia. The English return to Portugal, having lost 10,000 men and thirty cannons."[12]

These gains were short-lived. By mid September the emperor was complaining that Marshal Mortier had not actively pursued the retreating British, and that Joseph had stopped work on the defenses of the vital Retiro and Somosierra mountain passes. At month's end he suddenly replaced Jourdan with Soult, who would not only serve as chief of staff but would command the other marshals in the Army of Spain.[13]

Soult's appointment was extraordinary. Not only had he made a hash of his Portugal campaign, he had earlier all but proclaimed himself king of Portugal. "This would have been a crime which would have forced me, whatever my liking for you, to consider you guilty of treason . . . of a criminal attempt on my authority," Napoleon wrote him in late September. After scorching him for the Oporto débâcle Napoleon continued: "However, after much hesitation on what action I should take, the friendship that I have for you and the memory of your deeds at Austerlitz and in other battles have decided me. I am overlooking the past . . . and am appointing you chief of staff to my Army of Spain . . . King Joseph not having experienced war, my intention is that, until my arrival, you will inform me of events. I want to reach Lisbon as soon as possible."[14]

Napoleon continued to scold King Joseph and various generals during October even though he was deeply involved in signing the final peace treaty with Austria. He probably sensed that matters

Soult, Nicolas Jean de Dieu 1769–1851 Marshal of France

were getting out of hand in Spain – he certainly had reason to do so – perhaps without realizing that he had violated one of his own basic tenets, that of avoiding split commands. He also had failed to identify the real enemy even at this relatively early stage, concentrating instead on defeating Spanish armies and seizing towns and cities which did him little or no good, more often than not aggravating matters by the necessity of feeding and paying the troops which meant increased contributions from already overburdened and hostile locals, not to mention a drain on his own treasury.

When force failed to produce other than momentarily favorable results he resorted to more force. Shortly after his return to France he resolved to send 85,000 reinforcements to Spain during the winter, with another 100,000 formed in reserve inside France.

A tactical setback in mid November brought another torrent of criticism and repetition of a worn lament: "There is neither direction nor consistency in the conduct of my armies in Spain."[15] A few days later he decided to personally lead part of his Guard and 6,000 conscripts into the country. "When I appear beyond the Pyrenees," he informed the *Corps législatif* in early December, "the [English] leopard will take to the ocean to escape disgrace, defeat and death."[16]

Notes

1   Corr. XX. Nr. 16031, Palais des Tuileries, 3 December 1809. See also Corr. XX. Nr. 16040, Paris, 9 December 1809.

2   Byrant (*Victory*), 302–5. See also Napier; Oman; Fortescue; Fuente, 142–4; Horward ("Portugal"), 95–6.

3   Corr. XVIII. Nrs. 15037, 9 April 1809; 15051, Paris, 10 April 1809.

4   Corr. XIX. Nr. 15340, Schönbrunn, 12 June 1809.

5   Corr. XIX. Nr. 15396, Schönbrunn, 21 June 1809.

6   Corr. XIX. Nr. 15621, Schönbrunn, 7 August 1809.

7   Corr. XIX. Nr. 15661, Schönbrunn, 15 August 1809.

8   Corr. XIX. Nr. 15680, Schönbrunn, 18 August 1809.

9   Corr. XIX. Nr. 15683, Schönbrunn, 19 August 1809.

10   Corr. XIX. Nrs. 15694, Schönbrunn, 21 August 1809; 15700, Schönbrunn, 22 August 1809.

11   Corr. XIX. Nr. 15711, Schönbrunn, 25 August 1809.

12   Corr. XIX. Nr. 15723, Schönbrunn, 29 August 1809.

13   Corr. XIX. Nrs. 15786, Schönbrunn, 11 September 1809; 15864, Schönbrunn, 26 September 1809.

14   Corr. XIX. Nr. 15864, Schönbrunn, 26 September 1809.

15   Corr. XX. Nr. 16016, Paris, 21 November 1809.

16   Corr. XX. Nr. 16031, Palais des Tuileries, 3 December 1809.

CHAPTER SEVENTEEN

JOSÉPHINE OUT, MARIE LOUISE IN
DECEMBER 1809–AUGUST 1811

I do not know if the Empress has told you that our hope of a
pregnancy daily increases insofar as we can be sure at two and
a half months. Your Majesty will easily understand how much
this adds to the feelings that his daughter inspires in me, and
how much these new bonds increase my desire to be on
good terms with him.

Napoleon to Emperor Francis II of Austria,
St. Cloud, 26 July 1810[1]

NAPOLEON DID NOT make it back to Spain and never would. Upon his return to Paris from Austria he faced far more urgent problems than what he still regarded as a simmering insurrection, annoying but scarcely calamitous. Perhaps the most urgent problem was that of divorcing Joséphine and finding a fertile replacement, but there were also others: the need to complete the subjugation of Pope Pius VII and the Catholic church; the need to stop the increasing flow of smuggled British merchandise into Europe; finally the need to cope with an enormous backlog of administrative demands attendant upon a large and not altogether pacific empire.

Prior to returning to France he had ordered Joséphine to meet him at Fontainebleau. There he received her very coldly and for the next few weeks practically ostracized her from the court.[2] He did not however broach the explosive subject until the court returned to the Tuileries, and then only after Hortense, Cambacérès and finally Eugène had refused the task.

The awkward moment arrived after a sullen dinner *à deux* when the principals were taking coffee by themselves in a drawing room. The court prefect, Baron Bausset stationed in the neighboring room, suddenly heard a series of piercing shrieks. Summoned by a pale Napoleon, he found Joséphine flat out on the carpet, "weeping and moaning" (at which she was an expert). Not without difficulty the two men trundled her to her apartments, a bizarre scene with Napoleon holding a dripping candle in one hand while trying to steer the body down a narrow flight of stairs, Bausset tripping over his baronial sword and Joséphine in a guarded moment whispering to him that he was holding her too tightly.[3]

The deed done, Napoleon left her to the care of Doctor Corvisart and eventually her children. Henceforth she was *persona non grata* at court, an extremely difficult period for her despite the loyalty of Hortense and Eugène.

The *dénouement* of the sad drama occurred in mid December when the court was summoned to the throne room in the Tuileries. Facing senior dignitaries including most of the Bonapartes, Napoleon officially announced the divorce, a moving scene in which, tears running down his cheeks, he paid homage to their thirteen years of married life. Equally moved, Joséphine broke down while accepting the decree. The register was duly signed and witnessed. According to Napoleon's valet, Joséphine in a state of *déshabille* came to the emperor's bedroom for an emotional final night where tears apparently alternated with sex.[4]

The next morning Napoleon saw her off for Malmaison, escorted by Hortense and a convoy of carriages carrying her court and possessions, a brief but emotional farewell before he departed for the Trianon at Versailles to be consoled by his current mistress. After a brief visit the following day he wrote to her:

I found you today more depressed than you should be . . .
You must be courageous and not fall into a fatal
melancholy. You must be happy and above all care for your
health which is so precious to me . . . You can not doubt

Joséphine at Malmaison

my constant and loving affection and you would be
ignorant of all my feeling for you if you suppose that I can
be happy if you are not happy, content if you are not at
peace. *Adieu*, my dear; sleep well and do as I wish.[5]

Joséphine's melancholy was undoubtedly assuaged by a generous
settlement. She retained the title and rank of empress-queen, the
richly furnished château of Malmaison, the Elysée palace in Paris
and the château of Navarre in Normandy. She took with her an
unimaginably rich wardrobe including 280 pairs of shoes, scores
of the most beautiful silk and cashmere blouses and shawls, a fortune in gowns and furs; add to that several million francs' worth of
paintings, books, jewels, gold and silver plate, exquisite china, the
finest furniture and carpets, a fortune in Gobelin tapestries, elegant carriages, the best horses. Napoleon paid her current debts
(astronomical as always), gave her an annual income of 2 million
francs and promised to treat Hortense and Eugène generously
(which he did).[6]

   Nor did he cut her off emotionally. Short but sympathetic, generally plaintive and tender notes followed one after the other for
the rest of December.[7] They continued at a slower rate during the
next three months. On occasion they met, he gave her a few
extravagant gifts, extra funds for the Malmaison gardens, and
invariably assured her of his undying devotion and wishes for her
happiness. Nor would he neglect her after acquiring a new wife –
as will be seen.

With Joséphine more or less disposed of, the time had come to
find a suitable replacement. A number of eligible brides were
available but the important contenders were Grandduchess Anna,
Czar Alexander's 15-year-old sister, and Archduchess Marie
Louise, Emperor Francis' 18-year-old daughter.

   The French ambassador in St. Petersburg, General
Caulaincourt, had already petitioned the czar for Anna's hand
with no better success than Napoleon's earlier overture to marry

Grandduchess Catherine, one reason being the execution of the duke d'Enghien (related to the royal family through marriage), the other the alleged tale of Napoleon's sexual impotence earlier spread by Joséphine. Annoyed by Alexander's procrastination, Napoleon had given him a short deadline for a decision. Meanwhile Count Metternich, now Austria's foreign minister, had secretly been sponsoring Marie Louise as mainstay of a very shrewd strategy. Metternich, along with Viscount Wellington and to a lesser degree Czar Alexander, believed that Napoleon had overstretched himself in Spain: "We must continue to maneuver," he advised Emperor Francis, "to avoid all military action and to flatter . . . until the day of deliverance."[8]

A special council of state that included most of the Bonapartes met in early January to decide the matter. Napoleon, probably longing for his luscious Marie Walewska or perhaps repentant for having ditched Joséphine, was in a bad temper. Czar Alexander had not respected the imposed deadline (his negative decision would arrive within a few days). After several lesser nominees had been summarily rejected, Marie Louise was proposed. Napoleon was not particularly excited. The candidate was no raving beauty, what with protruding eyes and the ugly Habsburg mouth and chin. But now an exasperated aide pointed out that one of her ancestors had borne 26 children, another 17 and her own mother 13. Struck by such an opulent display of fertility the emperor settled things with a brief statement: "That is just the kind of womb I want to marry."[9] Prince Eugène was hurriedly dispatched with an appropriate request to the Viennese ambassador who, forewarned, at once approved.

Everybody (with the possible exception of Marie Louise) was delighted. Marshal Berthier hurried to Vienna to present the bride-to-be with the emperor's miniature portrait set in diamonds and a million or two francs' worth of jewelry before standing proxy at the wedding in the Hofburg. During these preliminaries Napoleon occupied himself with scores of prenuptial celebrations and with almost every detail of providing the chosen one with a

Marie Louise 1791–1847 Empress of France, mother of Napoléon II

luxurious wardrobe that would await her arrival, along with countless exquisite gifts. The Tuileries apartments and the Compiègne
château were redecorated under his personal supervision but, contrary to later detractors, he did not neglect empire affairs during
these exciting months.[10]

In late March a magnificent equipage escorted Marie Louise to
Strasbourg where she was met by Napoleon's sister, Queen
Caroline of Naples. Caroline brusquely replaced the Austrian
attendants with French equivalents before the procession drove on
to rendezvous with Napoleon at Compiègne. Welcomed at every
stop with intimate letters and heaps of flowers from the emperor,
Marie Louise was surprised when her proxy husband defied a
heavy rainstorm to intercept her carriage outside the old city. The
planned program was forsaken in favor of an intimate supper and

the night with his virgin bride (the tasteless details of which he allegedly recounted years later to his coterie on St. Helena island). Napoleon was obviously pleased. "She fulfills all my hopes," he informed Emperor Francis. "For two days we have not stopped exchanging proofs of the mutual feelings which unite us. We suit each other perfectly . . . We leave tomorrow for St. Cloud and on April 2nd we shall solemnize our marriage in a ceremony at the Tuileries."[11]

Napoleon had earlier marked the new relationship by decorating the Austrian emperor ("my brother and father-in-law"), Prince Charles and ranking court officials with high orders of the Legion of Honor.[12] He would continue his favors by making it easy for Francis to receive large loans from European bankers, by sending him a specially manufactured Sèvres cup bearing his daughter's portrait, by a large shipment of valuable china, by expediting the exchange of Austrian prisoners-of-war and finally by the news of Marie Louise's pregnancy (as quoted in the chapter heading).

Napoleon confirmed the pregnancy in mid November: "It has advanced to nearly five months. The empress is very well and is experiencing none of the usual discomforts of pregnancy . . . No one could be more perfect than the wife that I owe to you."[13]

The baby was born in the Tuileries on 20 March 1811. It was not an easy birth. Napoleon stayed by her during a prolonged and painful labor. At one point the attending physician informed him that it could come to a choice between the mother or the child's life. "Save the mother," Napoleon instantly declared.[14]

Fortunately that hideous decision was unnecessary and the baby was delivered by forceps. Thousands of patient citizens were waiting outside the palace for the news when the cannon suddenly boomed. Twenty-one rounds were to be fired for a girl, 100 for a boy. The twenty-second round turned the crowd into a delirious frenzy of celebrations that continued for several days and greatly reassured the emperor of his public support.

Napoleon immediately informed family members and also Emperor Francis of the difficult birth, noting that the empress was rapidly regaining strength and the infant was in splendid health. "My son is large and is in very good health," he wrote Joséphine. "I do hope that he thrives. He has my chest, my mouth and my eyes. I hope that he will fulfill his destiny."[15]

A few weeks later the baby was christened François Charles Joseph, the King of Rome (the title came with the birth), in the presence of a glittering assembly at Notre Dame.

Early in 1810 Napoleon had come to grips with another difficult problem, the taming of a recalcitrant pope. We left the old gentleman under comfortable if humiliating house arrest in Savona. French troops continued to occupy Rome which was governed by General Miollis, his task to nullify subversive efforts of royalist agents and pro-English cardinals while keeping papal ports closed to ships carrying contraband English goods.

Napoleon now set the scene for permanent annexation of the papal states and the pope's continued exile unless he conformed to imperial wishes. "Papal sovereignty in Italy," he wrote his foreign affairs minister, Champagny, "is incompatible with the authority of the Empire . . . the interests of Italy and France require all of Italy to be part of the great Empire."[16] The act of annexation, as the senate learned in mid February, "is going to consecrate one of the greatest political events of our majestic epoch," by which the emperor meant that the activities of the pope and the church would be confined to spiritual spheres while remaining subordinate to temporal rule. Henceforth the Roman states would form two departments of France represented by 11 deputies in the *Corps législatif*. Rome would become the second city of the empire, an hereditary prince automatically becoming the King of Rome.[17]

The immediate purpose of this act was to curb the church's active role in fomenting provincial rebellions designed to restore Bourbon rule and a return to feudalism with all its evils. But it also

Emperor Napoleon I of France 1769–1821

represented an enormous first step toward the emancipation of millions of ignorant Europeans held in thrall to the bigoted and superstitious teachings of the church. In essence it was a splendid continuation of the fight waged by the founding fathers of the Enlightenment to promote "science and wisdom over superstition and ignorance." If papal-dictated obscurantinism could be reduced, even eventually eliminated, the way would be open for vitally needed secular education (if only to teach people to read, write and count).

Less than a month after gaining the *senatus-consultum* which approved the annexation, Napoleon began the task of eliminating the "vermin of monks" that infested Piedmont, Tuscany, Parma and Genoa. All foreign priests were to be expelled from the new departments, and numerous convents and monasteries were to be closed. Italian priests were to wear ecclesiastical habits only in their seminaries. Bishops, priests and lesser fry who did not swear allegiance to the new government would forfeit ecclesiastical and personal properties. Numerous bishoprics would be eliminated, the city of Rome limited to 20 parishes.[18]

Pope Pius understandably refused to accept these various *ukases* and a period of stonewalling ensued. But in late December, in a conference with Prince Borghese and the local prefect, the pope seemed willing to accept a limited authority in return for the revival of the defunct Concordat. If that were so, Napoleon replied, an accommodation could be reached in spiritual (but not temporal) affairs. Should the pope agree, he was to write the emperor "without rancor but with the benevolence of the Gospel . . . it could concern only spiritual interests."[19]

The potential negotiation ended abruptly in early January 1811 when police exposed a papal plan to spread sedition in Paris. Sequestered papers proved beyond doubt the pope's "most horrible conduct joined to the greatest hypocrisy." Napoleon now appointed a committee of French cardinals, archbishops and bishops to advise on the right of the pope to excommunicate kings and their ministers for activities in temporal affairs.[20] The committee's somewhat cautious findings in support of the imperial power in temporal affairs brought a long and enthusiastic response from the emperor that would have warmed the hearts of the *philosophes*:

> I am only too ready to acknowledge that, if the thunderbolts of Rome have had little effect, I owe it to the enlightened minds of the century, and perhaps to the extensive decline of religious feeling in the minds of the European peoples. I know that one must render unto God the things that are God's,* but the pope is not God. When one sees the popes constantly bestirring themselves and destroying Christianity for temporal interests of the small state of Rome . . . one deplores the condition of Catholicism, compromised by such petty interests.[21]

Napoleon next convoked a council of French and Italian bishops to meet in Paris come June. Meanwhile a deputation of three bishops carried the emperor's demands to the pope at Savona. If the Concordat were to be revived the pope would have to consecrate the list of bishops long since named by Napoleon. He could return to Rome only if he swore allegiance to the emperor. Otherwise he would be allowed to establish the Holy See at Avignon. There were to be no ands, ifs or buts – as he informed the *Corps législatif* in mid June, the arbitrary rule of Rome was at an end: "I have permanently ended this disgrace. I have reunited Rome to the Empire."[22]

Pope Pius did not quite see it that way and by one ruse or another postponed a definite answer (presumably playing for time as Napoleon's situation in Spain continued to deteriorate). The impasse would be broken only in spring of 1812 when the old man was brought to Fontainebleau, still not having agreed to the terms of the revised Concordat.[23]

---

*A play on Matthew, XXII, 14: "Render therefore unto Caesar the things which are Caesar's."

Notes

1 Corr. XX. Nr. 16725, St. Cloud, 26 July 1810.
2 Bruce, 441.
3 Bruce, 442–3.
4 Bruce, 466.
5 Corr. XX. Nr. 16058, Trianon, presumably 16 December 1809.
6 Corr. XX. Nr. 16050, Paris, 15 December 1809. See also Ludwig, 346–7; Bruce, 447; Napoleon *Lettres* (Tulard), 396.
7 Corr. XX. Nrs. 16022, Trianon, *c.* 22 December 1809; 16088, Paris, 27 December 1809; 16097, Paris, 31 December 1809.
8 Bruce, 449. See also Metternich, II, 312–24.
9 Ludwig, 350.
10 See, for example, Bruce, 451; McLynn, 470–1.
11 Corr. XX. Nr. 16361, Compiègne, 29 March 1810. See also Bausset, 20–6.
12 Corr. XX. Nr. 16363, Compiègne, 24 March 1810. See also Metternich, II, 325–9.
13 Corr. XXI. Nr. 17133, Fontainebleau, 14 November 1810.
14 Bruce, 458.
15 Corr. XXI. Nr. 17499, Paris, 22 March 1811.
16 Corr. XX. Nr. 16137, Paris, 14 January 1810.
17 Corr. XX. Nrs. 16263, 16264, Paris, 17 January 1810.
18 Corr. XX. Nrs. 16194, presumably Paris, early January 1810; 16196, Paris, 2 February 1810; 16323, Paris, 11 March 1810.
19 Corr. XXI. Nr. 17232, Paris, 23 December 1810.
20 Corr. XXI. Nrs. 17265, Paris, 3 January 1811; 17268, 17269, Paris, 5 January 1811.
21 Corr. XXI. Nr. 17478, Paris, 16 March 1811.
22 Corr. XXII. Nr. 17813, Paris, 16 June 1811. See also Markham, 152–3.
23 Corr. XXII. Nr. 18043, presumably St. Cloud, 17 August 1811.

CHAPTER EIGHTEEN

THE CONTINENTAL SYSTEM: DOUBLE-EDGED WEAPON JANUARY–DECEMBER 1810

What does Russia intend . . . by such language? Does it want war? Why these constant complaints? Why these insulting suspicions? . . . Does Russia want to prepare me for its defection from our alliance? I shall be at war with her the day she makes peace with England.

Napoleon to Ambassador Caulaincourt in St. Petersburg, Paris, (presumably late January) 1810[1]

A NUMBER OF historians have suggested that Napoleon's second marriage marked a personal slackening of effort, a harmful malaise complicated by poor health. Nothing could be further from the truth. Napoleon did have some health problems, most hyperactive people do when they reach the forties: he was too fat, he tired more easily, he continued to suffer from urinary difficulties and acute attacks of indigestion. He occasionally suffered symptoms of what possibly was an attack of epilepsy, he was emotionally drained after his divorce. But none of these conditions slowed him one whit. The years 1810 and 1811 stand among the most active of his life, at least away from the battlefield.

Six years of war had greatly impeded his ambitious but well-meant plans for internal improvements in France, but did not bring them to a stop. Here and there a new bridge or road appeared, Paris received more drinking fountains, sewers, markets, slaughter-houses and granaries,[2] a canal was planned from Mons to Charleroi; the weaving of a new type of linen, a *lin filé* with a special silky texture, was encouraged as were manufactures of ersatz cotton and other items no longer available owing to the English blockade. Napoleon would shortly establish a *Conseil général d'Administration du Commerce et des Manufactures* in an effort to relieve the adverse economic pressures of the blockade on private business and industry, and at the same time to better enforce the regulations of the continental system.

The first steps were also taken to preserve the national archives – the emperor had discovered a disorganized mass of papers in the *palais Soubise* and wondered if a central archive to house the records of the two previous reigns could not be established in the new galleries that were being constructed in the Tuileries; if not, could a new building be made of metal (against fire) in the rue de Rivoli and paid for by selling the dilapidated *palais?*[3]

Some new schools were opened, others improved, an orphanage founded. The Trianon, Tuileries and other palaces were considerably improved. Plans were drawn to mount statues on the Austerlitz bridge of generals and colonels killed at Wagram. Work was revived on the tortuous Mt. Cenis road to provide refuge houses for winter travelers and a barracks for the laborers necessary to keep the pass open in winter.[4] Marshal Lannes' body was returned to Paris and buried with great pomp and ceremony. Work continued on the Louvre and Arc de Triomphe, but none of this was comparable in scale with the massive projects of earlier years.

This was not by choice. Napoleon forever respected posterity and fully intended to make Paris, indeed all of France, a beautiful living monument to his memory. But despite his claim to the legislature that France was comfortably solvent, money remained in short supply. Forced to sharply reduce military expenditures – economies that would breed severe problems – he even had to renege on his promise of cash compensation to wounded veterans of Wagram. As one result, he sadly noted, "these unfortunates are dying without having received what I promised them."[5]

The reason for this parsimony was all too obvious. If he cut military expenses he also called up new conscriptions which meant more bodies to clothe, more mouths to feed, more soldiers to pay. He continued to spend enormous sums on permanent fortifications along the Channel, Atlantic, Adriatic and Mediterranean coasts, at Antwerp and along the Scheldt river, on Walcheren and Cadzand islands, on Elbe fortresses and those in Italy, Trieste and Illyria. At the same time, state income from taxes and customs duties drastically dropped because of economic stagnation brought on by the continental system and the English blockade.

As more than one councillor of state had foreseen, the continental system soon turned into a double-edged sword for very good reasons. Trade has always dominated and will always dominate the world. People everywhere want to export surplus goods and import the goods they lack. Napoleon's intention was to bring England to its knees, not by starving it to death but by economic bankruptcy brought on by closing foreign markets to its manufacturers and colonial products. This possibly could have succeeded had things gone as intended, but when it comes to depriving human beings of food and money things rarely do go as intended. Very shortly after its inception, unemployment markedly rose along with shortages of foodstuffs and other products, not only in France but throughout the empire and in Naples, Germany, Prussia, Saxony, Austria and Russia. One result was the practice of one of man's oldest professions, smuggling; another a growing chorus of complaints from disgruntled citizenry.

Smuggling started (or more likely continued) with the plain, old-fashioned technique of small craft landing covertly in hidden coves to unload illicit cargoes. This was soon complemented by neutral ships carrying cargoes of forbidden English goods to European ports under counterfeit certificates that showed them to be of non-English origin. England's mastery of the seas made it difficult to prevent these evasions, a frustrating situation which soon led to wholesale embargo of what Napoleon termed "denationalized ships," that is vessels controlled by England and carrying contraband merchandise, no matter their flag. By 1810 Italians, Dutchmen, Prussians, Germans, Austrians, Neapolitans, Spanish, Portuguese, Russians and Americans were caught up in the quasi-maritime war.

The United States had been hit particularly hard owing to its geographical position, burgeoning sea trade and military impotence. For several years American diplomats had been trying to wriggle their merchant ships free from the vice-like grip of both England and France (a futile, fascinating and sometimes lurid effort told in excruciating detail by Henry Adams in his seminal history of the Jefferson and Madison administrations).[6]

Relations between America and France had seriously deteriorated owing to the various harsh orders in council declared by England and countered by France with equally stringent measures.

As we saw earlier, the United States tried to avoid hostilities by a "plague on both your houses" approach as expressed in the Non-Intercourse or Embargo Act of December 1807. Such was the appalling effect on the fledgling American economy that the congress repealed the Act in early 1809, but now the released flood of American ships was utilized, at least in part, to carry English and colonial goods to European ports in contravention of Napoleon's prohibition.

In late 1809 the French emperor closed his ports to what he called "American ships," meaning that these were either British-owned or British-coerced vessels flying the American flag and carrying English cargoes.[7] A few weeks later he ordered General Loison in Spain to seize all American ships that arrived in St. Sebastian, Bilbao and Santander, and sell their cargoes as prizes, and similar orders were sent elsewhere.[8] He described his policy as "a violence opposed to a violence," but in his case it was a very profitable violence. An official French report of July 1810 listed income from the sale of cargoes taken from American ships at Antwerp at 10 million francs, those from ships more recently taken in Holland at 12 million, in Spain at 8 million, with another 15 million coming from contraband goods seized at various customs posts.[9]

Napoleon was not overly concerned about relations with the United States. His interest in America had slackened after the sale of Louisiana and, more recently, the loss of his West Indies possessions to England. Nevertheless in early 1810, viewing the United States as a potential threat to England, he set about mending fences in trying to determine "the best course to remedy the present situation." Having heard that England was slackening some of its more stern maritime measures, he agreed to call off his corsairs and open his ports to American ships "not having been boarded at sea [by the English] and not having landed in England."[10] If England would lift its blockade of French ports, or at least of those from the Elbe to Brest, Napoleon would even revoke the Berlin decrees.[11]

In late January 1810 he spelled out his position in a diplomatic note to the American minister, Brigadier General John Armstrong. If America now cut itself free from English bondage, France was eager for renewed trade.[12] His expectations of a settlement were probably slight due in part to his contempt for the minister, an inarticulate "imbecile" who could not speak French, as he impolitely informed President Jefferson, "a morose person with whom one can not negotiate,"[13] but due in larger part to America's inability to seriously challenge England's military dominance – its army counted about 2,000 regulars, its navy a few frigates and some useless gunboats. Armstrong's own expectations were nil, as he had earlier reported to secretary of state Madison: "With one hand the [French] offer us the blessings of equal alliance against Great Britain; with the other they menace us with war if we do not accept this kindness and with both they pick our pockets with all imaginable diligence, dexterity and impudence."[14]

Napoleon's note having brought no significant results, in March he restated his right to seize American vessels in French harbors so long as his own ships were being sequestered in American harbors. Lacking means to prevent the forging of counterfeit certificates of origin, he continued to rely on force. But he shortly informed the American minister that he was prepared to cancel the Berlin and Milan decrees on condition that the American congress imposed its restrictions on trade with England if Whitehall did not cancel its daemonic orders in council of 1807.[15]

The eventual response to this *démarche* was favorable since America, fed up with having its ships boarded and American sailors seized and impressed into the Royal Navy, was heading toward its own war with England. In December the new French ambassador to the United States, the elderly Marshal Count Sérurier, was informed that if America had decided to fight for the independence of its flag "it will find all sorts of support and privileges [in France] . . . I am not opposed to America taking possession of the Floridas," Napoleon continued, ". . . which may contribute to the independence of Spanish America." The American *chargé d'affaires* in Paris (Armstrong had been recalled) was to be informed that "not establishing our commerce on exclusive grounds, I will see with pleasure the [continued] independence of a great nation provided that it is not under England's influence." The Americans would have to understand why France could not receive American ships coming from England or recognize American ships in the Baltic since they would have been "denationalized" by contact with the English: "the difficulty is to recognize the genuine Americans," but nevertheless he considered that the American government had taken the first step necessary to reach a good result.[16]

Napoleon's determination to end contraband trade was not confined to America. Throughout 1810 he continued his efforts to force the northern countries to close their ports, often using harsh words with a threat to send in troops.

King Louis of Holland had stopped just short of open disobedience in turning a blind eye to trade with England. He was already unpopular with Napoleon for numerous reasons: his often cruel treatment of Queen Hortense, his lukewarm support of Napoleon's military campaigns, his bending over backwards to ingratiate himself with the Dutch people, his failure to act promptly in the defense of Antwerp, his reluctance to introduce the Napoleonic Code, his refusal to introduce conscription to replace his battalions serving in Germany and Spain – not to mention his ridiculous expenditures in maintaining a richly garbed military staff not fit for combat, and in buying expensive mansions only to forsake them, one after another, following brief residences.

When numerous warnings to crack down on smugglers had no effect, Napoleon threatened to occupy the Dutch lands known as the Brabant between the Meuse and Scheldt rivers. This brought Louis to heel: he promised to end all contact with England, cede the Brabant provinces to France, allow French troops to police his ports (at Holland's expense), provide 9 warships to France and turn over 21 American merchant ships which had been sequestered with their cargoes. As worked out in mid March, the treaty changed the quasi-independent status of the kingdom of Holland to that of a province under French administration and laws.[17]

Napoleon now chose to make Louis the instrument of a new peace tentative to England, the result of a report by a Dutch banker, one Labouchère, which seemed to indicate that Whitehall was ready to deal. In late March this man, acting on behalf of Louis, carried a note (written by Napoleon but signed by Louis) to the English government: in exchange for a repeal of the orders in council of 1807, France could perhaps be persuaded to evacuate Holland and possibly even the Hanseatic cities.[18]

In carrying out his mission Labouchère conducted secret talks with the marquis of Wellesley who had replaced Canning as foreign minister. Meanwhile, unknown to the emperor, his minister of police, Joseph Fouché, had also opened secret talks with Wellesley through the channel of the semi-disgraced financier and Napoleon's earlier nemesis, Julien Ouvrard. Despite a series of mysterious meetings and letters written in invisible ink, none of this came to anything except to cost Louis his throne and Fouché his ministry. Fouché was replaced by General Savary and shunted off to Italy – we shall meet him again.

Napoleon held Louis partially accountable for the failed negotiations and for not putting a halt to large-scale smuggling. In late
June, Marshal Oudinot was ordered to concentrate a strong force
at Utrecht, ready to march on Amsterdam. When Dutch officials
at Haarlem refused passage to French troops, Napoleon ordered
the occupation of Amsterdam, shortly followed by his annexing
Holland to the French empire.

This was too much for King Louis who deposed himself and
fled to a secret destination, leaving considerable confusion and
massive debts for Napoleon to pay. He was finally located at
Teplitz in Bohemia. "His conduct can only be explained,"
Napoleon wrote his mother Madame Mère, "by the state of his
[venereal] disease."[19]

Another difficult situation had meanwhile arisen when Napoleon
asked Sweden to break all diplomatic and commercial traffic with
England, sequester all colonial merchandise and arrest all British
agents under the threat of French military occupation of Swedish
Pomerania. Although this blew over (temporarily), a new compli-
cation arose with the unexpected death of the hereditary prince of
Sweden who was to be replaced by Prince Bernadotte. Napoleon
agreed to the appointment but Bernadotte had first to forfeit his
title and rank, a blow softened by the award of a million francs,
mainly out of consideration for Désirée (Clary) Bernadotte.[20]
Relations with Sweden improved when its government declared
war on England, in theory closing one more country to British
goods.

Napoleon and Czar Alexander of Russia had been playing a
double game for some time, each having recommenced trade
with England in his own way. Napoleon had been carrying on a
clandestine traffic by means of import-export licenses issued to
the chosen few, the idea being to import sugar, coffee, tobacco,
indigo and other scarce items and to export wine, brandy and
Lyons silks. This practice had spread to satellite ports where
less worthy French officials, such as Bourrienne in Hamburg,

made small fortunes in selling these licenses and otherwise permitting English imports in return for enormous bribes. Owing to
corrupt customs officials there was no problem in moving the
contraband inland; for every official arrested a hundred survived.
Since the process was costly only wealthier citizens could buy the
goods which made the lower classes all the more resentful of the
government.

Czar Alexander and his advisers were not blind to Napoleon's
duplicity, as evidenced from Ambassador Caulaincourt's long and
frequent reports of their complaints. Russia already had paid
dearly in accepting the continental system, notably in the loss of
the English market for immense quantities of timber, hemp and
tar essential to shipbuilding and maintenance. Although the czar
continued to claim allegiance to the system, his exuberant sentiments toward the French emperor had long since been eroded by
his councillors, many of them in English pay, by Talleyrand's
treachery and by various diplomatic conflicts. As one result Russia
had gradually become one of the biggest violators of the system,
permitting English and English-controlled ships to unload in its
ports and allowing Russian merchants to distribute the contraband merchandise at will.

This was only one source of friction. Alexander's lukewarm
efforts to aid France in its recent war with Austria had thoroughly
annoyed Napoleon. Another point of contention arose early in
1810 over Poland. Caulaincourt and the Russian foreign minister
had signed a convention designed to allay Russian fears that
Poland would be re-established as an independent kingdom under
French protection. Napoleon refused to ratify the document,
mainly on semantic grounds: "I cannot say that 'the kingdom of
Poland will never be re-established' for this would be to say that if
one day the Lithuanians . . . had to re-establish it, I would have to
send troops to oppose it. I can not promise something that I can't
guarantee and that does not conform to my code of ethics."[21] An
exchange of lengthy and tiresome counter-drafts solved nothing
despite Napoleon's forceful logic: "If the Emperor had wished to
re-establish Poland, at Tilsit, instead of making peace, he would

have crossed the Niemen [river]; if subsequently at Vienna he would have had this intention . . . he would have annexed all of Galicia to the Grand Duchy of Warsaw."[22]

The imperial marriage interrupted the quarrel which Napoleon did not want to come to a head. In thanking the czar for his nuptial good wishes he added, "I share most sincerely the desire of your Majesty to force England to [make] peace."[23]

Napoleon reckoned without the Russian foreign minister, Romanzov, who was in English pay and who continued his not so subtle insinuations of French perfidy which gave rise to the emperor's lament quoted at the beginning of this chapter. Was Napoleon being prescient? Did he realize that more trouble lay ahead when in late August he once again brought up Russian defiance of the continental system? What was on his mind that autumn when he told Count Metternich, "I shall have war with Russia on grounds that lie beyond human possibilities, because they are rooted in the cause itself."[24] Did he mean that a clash of wills stemming from two expansionist policies was inevitable? Was he thinking in terms of the present or the near or far future? It is difficult to suggest an answer but it is obvious from the written record that from autumn of 1810 onwards he was on a collision course with his eastern ally.

This was inevitable so long as Napoleon believed that England was on the verge of surrender and needed only a final push to bring it about, an effort that transcended boundaries and governments. "Insist strongly on the confiscation of all ships carrying colonial merchandise," Caulaincourt was ordered in mid October. If Alexander closed his ports and acted with a little energy, "he will collect more than forty million francs [from confiscated ships] and will give England a great blow. The merchants there who six weeks ago wanted war are already crying for peace."[25]

In thanking the czar for a gift of some beautiful horses in late October, Napoleon stressed that English finances were in dire straits with many business houses going bankrupt. "The factories are shut down, the warehouses crammed. In Frankfurt and Switzerland I have just seized immense quantities of English and colonial merchandise." He then put his cards on the table: "Six hundred English merchant ships sailing in the Baltic have been refused entry in Mecklenburg . . . and are sailing to Russia. If your Majesty admits them, the war will continue; if he seizes them and their cargoes . . . he will strike a severe counterblow . . . It is up to your Majesty to have peace or to let the war continue. Peace is and should be his desire."[26]

Despite such appeals, contraband continued to flood Russia, Saxony, Poland and Germany. In early November the Russian ambassador in Paris, Prince Kourakine, was informed "that the colonial merchandises sold at the last Leipzig fair have been brought there by 700 wagons coming from Russia, that today all trade in colonial products is made by Russia, that finally the 1,200 merchantmen escorted by twenty English warships and disguised under Swedish, Portuguese, Spanish and American flags have in part unloaded their cargoes in Russia." If Alexander failed his word, if he did not halt this illicit traffic, goods coming from Russia would be seized at the frontiers of Prussia and Germany.[27]

We do not know how much of this sharp language reached Czar Alexander, but it is very likely that Kourakine faithfully reported at least part if not all to Count Romanzov who would eagerly have disseminated it to czar and court. The situation could only deteriorate further. The Russians had no intention of stopping trade with the enemy, particularly since France and its satellites were equally guilty. Alexander was further angered by Napoleon's annexation of the Swiss canton, Valais, in late November, and Napoleon in turn was alarmed by Russia's peace with the Ottoman Porte and subsequent construction of forts on the Dvina and Dniester rivers.[28]

More notes were exchanged, words grew sharper, but each side held the peace. Napoleon still hoped for an English economic collapse. Alexander along with the rulers of Prussia and Austria was content to sit on the fence, waiting for Napoleon's war with Spain to take its toll.

Notes

1 Corr. XX. Nr. 16181, Paris, (presumably late January) 1810.
2 Corr. XXI. Nr. 16905, St. Cloud, 14 September 1810.
3 Corr. XX. Nrs. 16259, 16260, St. Cloud, 15 February 1810.
4 Corr. XX. Nr. 16283, Rambouillet, 22 February 1810.
5 Corr. XX. Nr. 16523, Le Havre, 29 May 1810.
6 Adams, *History of the United States of America*. See also Watson, 859–76; Lacour-Gayet, 289–302.
7 Corr. XX. Nr. 16025, Paris, 25 November 1809.
8 Corr. XX. Nr. 16072, Trianon, 19 December 1809.
9 Corr. XX. Nr. 16612, St. Cloud, 5 July 1810.
10 Corr. XX. Nrs. 16080, Trianon, 21 December 1809; 16127, Paris, 10 January 1810.
11 Corr. XX. Nr. 16168, Paris, 25 January 1810.
12 Corr. XX. Nr. 16169, Paris, 25 January 1810.
13 Corr. XX. Nr. 16147, 19 January 1810. Judging from Armstrong's performance as the U.S. secretary of war during the War of 1812, Napoleon had his mark – see Muller.
14 Adams, I, 1131.
15 Corr. XX. Nrs. 16713, St. Cloud, 25 July 1810; 16736, St. Cloud, 31 July 1810.
16 Corr. XXI. Nr. 17206, Paris, 31 December 1810.
17 Corr. XX. Nrs. 16173, Paris, 27 January 1810; 16184, Paris, 29 January 1810; 16189, Paris, 31 January 1810; 16243, Paris, 12 February 1810; 16266, Paris, 17 February 1810; 16277, Rambouillet, 22 February 1810; 16330, Paris, 13 March 1810. See also Bond, 141–53.
18 Corr. XX. Nr. 16362, Paris, 20 March 1810.
19 Corr. XX. Nr. 16688, St. Cloud, 20 July 1810. See also Bausset, 31–2.
20 Corr. XX. Nr. 16476, Laeken, 16 May 1810; Corr. XXI. Nrs. 16875, St. Cloud, 6 September 1810; 16890, St. Cloud, 10 September 1810; 16906, St. Cloud, 15 September 1810. See also Fain (*Mémoires*), 299.
21 Corr. XX. Nr. 16178, Paris, 6 February 1810. See also Seton-Watson, 119–22.
22 Corr. XX. Nr. 16180, Compiègne, (presumably late January) 1810.

23   Corr. XX. Nr. 16571, St. Cloud, 20 June 1810.

24   Bryant (*Victory*), 390.

25   Corr. XXI. Nr. 17040, Fontainebleau, 13 October 1810.

26   Corr. XXI. Nr. 17071, Fontainebleau, 23 October 1810.

27   Corr. XXI. Nr. 17099, Fontainebleau, 4 November 1810.

28   Corr. XXI. Nrs. 17176, Paris, 30 November 1810; 17179, Paris, 2
     December 1810; 17187, Paris, 5 December 1810.

CHAPTER NINETEEN

THE SPANISH ADVENTURE – V:
MARSHAL MASSÉNA'S MASSIVE FAILURE
JANUARY 1810–APRIL 1811

*Thus, on the whole, this troubled year [1809] ended more
auspiciously than it had commenced. The recent military
operations had come to a successful end . . . yet our troubles
were far from being over . . . Public feeling was still against
us . . . We had conquered, but not convinced.*

Miot de Melito, councillor of state and private
adviser to King Joseph of Spain[1]

NAPOLEON'S PRESENCE IN Spain probably would not have altered
matters unless he could have achieved some kind of command
cohesion, which was doubtful. He had misread the situation from
the beginning. He was still trying to fight a conventional war in an
unconventional environment against unconventional people. This
was a natural enough error. It had been committed more than
once prior to Napoleon's day and would be too often repeated
during the next 190 years.

Perhaps also, using his own standards of measurement, he
deemed his presence there unnecessary. If Victor had taken a
knock at Talavera, Soult and Ney had compensated by forcing
Wellesley's decimated army to take refuge in the unhealthy
Guadiana valley. Soult had next smashed two Spanish armies at
Ocaña, south of Madrid, to eliminate that premature threat to the
capital and open the way for King Joseph's invasion of Andalucia.
Augereau, who had replaced Suchet in Catalonia, followed Soult's
victory by seizing Gerona which had been under siege for months.

"It is regrettable that you were not in command from the beginning," Napoleon wrote Augereau, "my battles would have been better fought. Do your best to conquer all of Catalonia . . . march as soon as possible to raise the [enemy] blockade of Barcelona."[2]

Although guerrillas were increasingly active, several small bands had been severely hurt in Old Castile and Suchet was more than holding his own in the Navarre. Four thousand gendarmes and Junot's new corps were soon to arrive to further protect the changed line of operations, Burgos-Aranda-Buitrago, from enemy attack.[3]

The way was now clear, Napoleon believed, to strike the main target, Wellesley's (now Viscount Wellington's) English-Hanoverian-Portuguese army. This would be a two-pronged effort: a large expedition to Andalucia to counter "the expected English diversion on Madrid and Salamanca" and to seize the naval base of Cádiz; a second expedition would in turn invade Portugal and throw the English into the sea.

The dual offensive began well. King Joseph's army filed through the snow-covered Sierra Morena passes in early January 1810. Within a few weeks his divisions had seized the important towns of Jaen, Córdoba, Seville, Málaga and Murcia. Victor next led a strong corps south to Cádiz, but there the offensive floundered owing to a stout defense of the port by Spanish, British and Portuguese troops supported by British warships. Napoleon however believed it would be only a matter of weeks before Cádiz succumbed.

Meanwhile Marshal Augereau was to relieve the blockaded garrison in Barcelona and continue on to join with Suchet. That general was to put Lérida under siege and move a corps to the Valencian border. Once united, Augereau and Suchet would bring about the subjection of Catalonia.[4] Such was the emperor's confidence in his strategy that in late February he informed his sister-in-law, Queen Julie in Paris, that "the situation in Spain is so settled" that she and the children could return to Madrid.[5]

The affairs of Spain were anything but settled. French troops may have occupied some principal cities but they did not control the countryside. Communications between corps, divisions, brigades, regiments and hosts of smaller garrisons were anything but secure – as Joseph's civil aide, Miot de Melito, put it, "We had conquered, but not convinced."[6] Victor's blockade of Cádiz, which showed little promise of a favorable result, had considerably weakened the army and had created new supply problems. The expedition to invade Portugal would not even be formed until Andalucia was secure. In the interim Wellington would receive reinforcements by sea while Spanish guerrilla forces continued to expand with new groups being formed.

Nor were Joseph and his Spanish *junta* to be relied upon. The government was not funding its share of the war, Napoleon complained, the result of Joseph surrounding himself with a coterie of useless Spanish toadies living luxuriously at court and contributing nothing to French fortunes. The war to date had cost France 300 million francs. The French minister in Madrid, Laforest, was to inform the *junta* that henceforth the Spanish treasury would pay the major expenses of the French army.[7]

To show his displeasure Napoleon transferred control of the northern and eastern provinces to French army governors. In future they were to collect taxes and levy whatever extraordinary contributions were necessary to make their troops self-supporting.[8] Marshal Augereau's army was removed from the Army of Spain and renamed the Army of Catalonia which would fly only French and Catalan flags (the first move in the emperor's plan to annex Catalonia and Navarre to France). Augereau was "to allow no communication between the Catalonians and the king [Joseph]."[9] General Suchet received similar orders concerning those parts of Aragon "indispensable to the security of France."[10] Ney, Junot and Bonet's corps were also to become self-supporting with no funds going to Madrid, everything to their own paymasters.[11]

These radical measures were motivated more by Napoleon's pique against Joseph and the *junta*, however well justified, than by good sense. He was sadly mistaken, as he had been all along, in his comfortable belief that the Spanish provinces could support his army. Estremadura and Andalucia did not produce much food in winter and in many places had already been stripped bare by Spanish, French and English troops, as well as by the growing number of guerrillas. An already burdened people smoldered with hatred and desire for revenge, not so much the local *grandees* and propertied classes who more often than not came to terms with the French but the farmers and the peasants, that is the vast majority of people on whom guerrilla bands relied for support (either voluntary or coerced).

Corps commanders were now to revert to the old revolutionary concept that war must pay for itself by levying further exactions on the people, a draconian measure that could only create more problems, particularly since from the beginning a large number of French marshals, generals, officers and men had lined their pockets with money and stolen loot. The fallacy was soon exposed – in mid July, Napoleon ate crow by sending a strongly escorted shipment of 3 million francs to pay the Army of the South (with many more such convoys to come).[12]

Despite the continuing stand-off at Cádiz, Napoleon refused to yield the thought of ultimate victory by which he meant the elimination of Wellington's army. In mid April he formed the new Army of Portugal, three corps commanded by Ney, Reynier and Junot under overall command of Marshal Masséna. Once reinforced Masséna was to proceed *methodically* with the siege of the Spanish border fortress of Ciudad Rodrigo, "the key to Léon." He would next seize the neighboring Portuguese fortress of Almeida, cross the mountains to the coast and march on Lisbon after the autumn harvest. Marshal Ney's corps, about 30,000 strong, opened the siege of Ciudad Rodrigo in late May.[13]

We left General Wellesley (about to become Viscount Wellington) with his decimated and demoralized but undefeated army in the Guadiana valley. This was in November 1809 after its near disaster at Talavera and subsequent narrow escape from Soult and Ney's corps. His position was critical. He had lost at least a

Masséna, André 1758–1817 Marshal of France

quarter of his force, his men were on the verge of starvation, malaria and dysentery were daily ravaging the ranks, politicians and people at home were calling for England's only army to pack up and leave Portugal while there was time.

Wellington would have none of it. He was convinced that Napoleon was over-extended, that the longer the French remained in Spain the weaker they would become, the military version of the Jurassic dinosaur whose strength ebbed as its bulk increased. In his words, "If we can maintain ourselves in Portugal, the war will not cease in the Peninsula, and, if the war lasts in the Peninsula, Europe will be saved."[14] He could not defeat Napoleon with his present strength nor could the Spanish armies. Spanish guerrillas however could help Napoleon defeat himself while Wellington patiently prepared the *coup de grâce*.

By any count Wellington was a remarkable if not a very like-able human being. He had made his mark in India, fighting and defeating Tippoo Sahib. Now 40 years old, tall and wiry with penetrating eyes looking down over that long nose so familiar to history books, he was a taciturn character, very arrogant but militarily extremely able if not brilliant.

Few commanders would have survived the fiasco of Talavera and the costly and painful retreat to the Guadiana valley. His offi-cers were still in the process of sorting out what remained of the army when he appeared in Lisbon, briefly enjoyed the charms of his mistress, then called his engineers together at Torres Vedras about 30 miles north of the capital. As he crisply explained, their job was to corral as many thousand Portuguese laborers as neces-sary to build three complex, mutually supporting defensive lines across the 20–25 mile coastal strip bordered on the left by the sea, on the right by the Tagus river.

Correctly calculating that a French invasion force would choose the more passable and in theory easier supply route of Ciudad Rodrigo, Almeida, Guarda and Coïmbra before turning south, he next moved his recuperating army north to the healthy mountain country inland from Coïmbra from where he could keep an eye on French movements around Ciudad Rodrigo. Fortunately for his plan, interim French operations interspersed with command quarrels allowed time to whip the army back in shape, time for General Beresford to turn 25,000 Portuguese soldiers into a reasonable fighting force and, not least, time for his engineers to complete the Torres Vedras defenses.

Wellington did not intend to give battle. His strategy and tac-tics were essentially Fabian.[15] His army would slowly retreat before the French invaders while the Portuguese people, town and city dwellers, farmers and peasants, rude militia bands, turned green land into barren desert of no use to hungry French soldiers. If the invaders could be stopped at Torres Vedras, if these lines prevented the capture of Lisbon, then their offensive would fail. They would then face one of two choices, either to remain on the inhospitable Portuguese coast and starve to death or retreat back up the coast and over the mountains into Spain.

It was a diabolically cunning trap – and it worked.

Prolonged resistance of the Spanish garrison holding Ciudad Rodrigo prevented Ney's advance guard from crossing the frontier into Portugal only until September.

Wellington meanwhile had received reinforcements. Including the Portuguese contingent his total strength rose to some 75,000 men with about 30,000 camped along the Mondego river on Masséna's line of advance. But his plan to fall back without giving battle fell foul of parliamentary wrath in London and public opinion in Portugal – why was he running away?

Hoping to defuse criticism by a favorable battle, Wellington called up reinforcements from the south and chose to stand some 8 miles northeast of Coïmbra. Here he fashioned the 9-mile-long ridge of Bussaco into a strong and well-concealed defensive position manned by over 50,000 troops.[16]

Masséna was tactically blind and professionally careless. Spanish and Portuguese guerrillas had kept him ignorant of Wellington's strength and location. His general contempt for the enemy was such that, coming on the allied position at Bussaco and believing that he outnumbered Wellington three-to-one, he failed to make even a cursory reconnaissance before sending General Reynier's two divisions up the steep rocky slopes. The French never had a chance. Accurate musket and artillery fire shattered the assault divisions – an estimated 4,000 casualties in a few hours. Further assaults met no better fate. The battle was over by evening. Over 30,000 of Wellington's troops had not fired a round.

But Wellington was also aware that he could be outflanked on his exposed left and thus cut from the vital river crossing at Coïmbra. A day later his troops, surrounded by thousands of civilians pathetically clutching babies and meager possessions, crossed the Coïmbra bridge to begin a 70-mile march to Torres

Vedras, not an easy effort in view of limited rations and Ney's ever-threatening advance guard.

Torrential rains greeted their arrival in early October but where the English and Portuguese, greatly to their surprise, found shelter, food and a warm welcome from troops holding the Torres Vedras lines, the French found only cold and hunger in land stripped virtually bare and a supply line dogged by determined Portuguese guerrillas and local militias only too eager to slit French throats. Masséna and his officers could scarcely believe their eyes as they fathomed the intricate network of redoubts, trenches and mutually supporting artillery batteries that stretched over the undulating land, the gunboats and warships that guarded the flanks, the vast expanse of the defensive complex which, after one or two futile attempts to penetrate, they realized were impenetrable.

Masséna was in deep trouble. His line of communications cut by Portuguese irregulars, he was virtually isolated in a barren land. He could not complete his mission without major reinforcements. In late October he sent a brigade commander, General Foy, to Napoleon asking for help from Marshal Soult. Until it arrived he could only try to survive.

Early in 1810 Napoleon had assured chief of staff Berthier that "the only danger in Spain came from the English,"[17] a statement that showed his contempt for both Spanish armies and guerrillas who surely would come to terms once the English had been driven into the sea. Napoleon failed to look at the other side of the coin: until the English *were* driven into the sea the guerrillas would not only continue to fight but, aided by money and weapons brought on English ships, the movement would continue to grow.

His contempt for renegade "brigands" blinded him to a very important and in the end disastrous fact: while the French were shredding regular Spanish armies in orthodox operations, explosive nationalism had blown a variety of provincial guerrilla bands into existence.

These had begun to emerge early in 1809. One of the first leaders was Juan Martín Díaz, 34 years old, a former dragoon private, illiterate, married, a father, a farmer in Castile. He gathered together half a dozen trusted neighbors, a rude lot badly equipped, a deficiency repaired by the ambush of a few dozen French couriers. In Navarre a young student, Francisco Javier Mina, armed another small band. In La Mancha a doctor appeared as leader, Juan Paladea, soon called *El Médico*; in Soria the friar Sapia turned guerrilla leader; in Catalonia another doctor, Rovera, took up arms; in the Estremadura the famous Julian Sánchez arose in Salamanca, the priest Delíca (*El Capuchino*) near Valladolid.

These and other brave ones generally confined early operations to interrupting French communications. By May 1809 Soult in Portugal had been out of touch with King Joseph Bonaparte in Madrid for five months, receiving neither news nor supplies, as letters intercepted by *El Capuchino*'s small band show. Small successes bred expansion. Bands multiplied and began attacking convoys to seize arms, food and treasure. By spring of 1809 Ney's corps was forced from Galicia. As guerrilla missions and effectiveness increased, French commanders suddenly discovered that they owned no more than the ground occupied by their troops, an unsettling thought that the more active guerrilla leaders never let them forget. If the French weakened an outlying garrison, peasants invariably related the information to local guerrillas who then organized an attack, often seizing and sacking the objective before quickly departing.

From such actions the guerrillas progressed to attacking troop formations. In mid July 1810 a priest, Geronimo Merino, known as *El Cura*, led an attack against two battalions of marines *en route* to reinforce Soult and Masséna. The guerrillas killed 13 officers and some 200 men. As the British historian C.W.C. Oman later pointed out, French army archives list dozens of officers killed or wounded "in a reconnaissance in Navarre" or "in a skirmish with Mina's bands." At one point Mina was being hunted by troops from no less than six major commands, "yet none of the six generals, though they had 18,000 men marching through his special district, succeeded in catching him, or destroying any appreciable fraction of his band."[18]

An army cannot properly function without communications which the guerrillas either severely impeded or destroyed. To carry Masséna's plea to Napoleon, General Foy needed half a brigade of troops as escort and even then did not reach Paris until the end of November.

While the French remained blind the enemy continued to be well informed as to French strength and movements from local peasants. Mina financed his extensive operations by taking stolen treasures and payrolls from the French, collecting rents from national and church properties, fining "bad Spaniards" (collaborators, and there were many), even by collecting tribute from French custom houses in return for allowing the importation of goods.[19] Every penny exacted from the countryside, every bit of food or bottle of wine, was just that much less than the French could collect, no matter their rigorous measures. Already severe by mid 1810 the guerrilla menace would continue to grow.

Masséna held out in front of Torres Vedras until mid November, his cold and starving troops floundering in flooded fields while waiting for an enemy attack. In vain. Wellington was content to let nature fight his war – and he was right. Only when the French deserted pathetic makeshift shelters for the return march northward did he emerge from his defenses to follow them up the coast, the route marked by French bodies and slaughtered Portuguese civilians who had refused to leave homes and lands.

The French marshal was not one to give up too easily however. Having reached the town of Santarem on the Tagus river, 30 miles to the north, he placed his men in favorable defensive positions in the surrounding hills, hoping once again that Wellington could be persuaded to attack. But once again Wellington chose to play the waiting game. Masséna's army continued to grow weaker as the scant food provided by the rugged land was consumed. Masséna was a tough one however and so were his hardened survivors. Convinced that reinforcements were on their way, he somehow persuaded officers and men to carry on, again with the hope that the enemy would attack.

Masséna's belief in Napoleon was justified. General Foy's unexpected arrival in Paris convinced the emperor that the Portuguese dream was turning into a nightmare. Soult was now ordered to strike the southern frontier fortresses to draw troops away from Wellington. But these tasks forced him to bring up some of Victor's troops from the blockade of Cádiz. Seeing Victor thus weakened, the port's defenders mounted an encircling counter-attack survived only with difficulty by the remaining French troops. Although Soult's new effort produced several victories against Spanish forces, including the bloody battle of Albuera which led to the surrender of the important border fortress of Badajoz, the offensive had to be called off if the blockade of Cádiz were to be restored and Seville protected from a threatening Spanish force (Soult having no desire to lose a fortune in looted treasures).

While these diverse actions played out, General Foy with some 2,000 troops reached Masséna in early February 1811. Masséna and his men were literally on their last legs. No further reinforcements having arrived by early March, the old marshal ordered a retreat across the mountains. Harassed day and night, forced to fight a series of losing skirmishes, the half-crazed troops, abandoning stolen loot and most of their equipment, vented their fury in an orgy of murder and rape of those unfortunate Portuguese civilians who were in their way.

Masséna still refused to accept failure. Having reached Celrico some 30 miles from the frontier, he ordered his generals to march southeast to join Soult on the Tagus river for another strike at Lisbon. (Soult had already returned to Seville.) Marshal Ney refused the order and was arrested. Generals Reynier and Junot more wisely pointed to the pitiable condition of their men who could not undertake a new march over more mountains. Masséna necessarily gave in and the retreat continued into Spain with Wellington's advance guard still in hot pursuit.

The Portuguese expedition ended in early April 1811. Of an estimated invasion force of 70,000 bodies, considerably less than 50,000 returned to Spain.

Notes

1   Miot de Melito, II, 358.
2   Corr. XX. Nr. 16078, Trianon, 19 December 1809.
3   Corr. XX. Nrs. 16153, 16154, Paris, 20 January 1810; 16190, Paris, 31 January 1810.
4   Corr. XX. Nrs. 16267, Paris, 17 February 1810; 16272, Paris, 19 February 1810; 16276, Rambouillet, 21 February 1810; 16294, Paris, 26 February 1810.
5   Corr. XX. Nr. 16284, Rambouillet, 22 February 1810.
6   Miot de Melito, II, 358.
7   Corr. XX. Nrs. 16175, Paris, 28 January 1810; 16229, Paris, 8 February 1810.
8   Corr. XX. Nr. 16230, Paris, 8 February 1810.
9   Corr. XX. Nr. 16275, Rambouillet, 21 February 1810.
10 Corr. XX. Nr. 16276, Rambouillet, 21 February 1810.
11 Corr. XX. Nrs. 16328, Paris, 12 March 1810; 16343, Paris, 16 March 1810.
12 Corr. XX. Nr. 16678, St. Cloud, 19 July 1810.
13 Corr. XX. Nrs. 16504, Dieppe, 27 May 1810; 16519, Le Havre, 29 May 1810.
14 Bryant (*Victory*), 351.
15 Asprey (*War in the Shadows*), I, 36. See also Horward ("Portugal"), 97–103; Fuente, 143–4; Knight, 32–4.
16 Bryant (*Victory*), 379–85, for an excellent brief account of the ensuing battle. See also Fuente, 148–50; Thiébault, 308–18.
17 Corr. XX. Nr. 16192, Paris, 31 January 1810.
18 Oman, III, 489. See also Barahona, 108–13; Horta (*Capuchino*), 87–99; Thiébault, II, 260–75.
19 Oman, III, 488–90.

CHAPTER TWENTY

THUNDER IN THE NORTH – STORMS IN THE SOUTH FEBRUARY–NOVEMBER 1811

If the Russian czar does not wish war and if he does not promptly stop these hostile moves, he will have one next year, despite me, despite himself, despite the interests of France and Russia.

Napoleon to the king of Württemberg, Paris, 2 April 1811[1]

THE YEAR 1811 in many ways resembled the previous year. On the surface Napoleon continued to occupy a very strong position at home and abroad. As in 1810 he continued a modest program of internal improvements, the most ambitious being the embellishment of Versailles, "a work of ostentation" in the emperor's phrase that would require millions to restore its original grandeur.

He still had much to be proud of. "How wonderfully Paris had improved since my departure for Naples in January 1806," the diplomat Miot de Melito wrote during a brief visit in 1811:

Magnificent quays, open sites ornamented with the trophies of our conquests, fine bridges named after our victories, columns and statues have been constructed . . . new fountains had sprung up in all directions . . . The Louvre, that had been left unfinished by a long line of kings, was now nearly completed, a second gallery was rising from the ground to connect this ancient palace with the Tuileries. Spacious museums contained the *chefs-d'oeuvre* of ancient and modern Rome, of Italy and of Flanders. In every direction marble and bronze proclaimed that the man who had created so much in so short a space of time, was one who knew how to glorify the nation by the arts of peace as well as by those of war.[2]

Unfortunately the arts of peace had succumbed to the demands of war. If civil work slowed, military expenditures continued to soar. Millions of francs went to improving and expanding fortifications in France and the empire as additional convoys of gold francs rolled into Spain. The artillery budget for 1811 amounted to a staggering 22.5 million francs. Early in the year the emperor announced the beginning of a four-year naval construction program intended to provide a fleet of 103 warships and 76 frigates by 1814. Available warships were not to sail in 1811 but were to be kept on full alert status, fully provisioned, troops aboard for weeks at a time as officials leaked plans for expeditions to Ireland, Sardinia, Sicily, the Channel Islands, even the coast of England, all part of a deception plan intended to make England tire its sailors and ships by blockading French ports and to transfer troops from Portugal to the threatened areas. French corsairs would continue to disrupt British trade where possible.[3]

An increasingly bellicose Russia also demanded extensive and expensive counter-measures. Marshal Davout, commanding the Army of Germany, was to prepare his troops for any contingency. Davout would have 130,000 men by June, and these could be supplemented by 70,000 more from the grand duchy of Warsaw, Saxony, Westphalia and confederation states.

Napoleon's relations with Czar Alexander were rapidly deteriorating. Blaming foreign minister Champagny in part, he replaced him with Hugues Bernard Maret (duke of Bassano). He had increasingly regarded Caulaincourt's long-winded reports of the czar's friendship, loyalty and desire for peace as camouflage for intended evil – and he was right.

Caulaincourt was being duped. Alexander was not only trading openly with enemy England, he was also working with Prince Czartoryski in setting the scene for rebellion in his favor in the grand duchy of Warsaw; he was secretly sounding out Austrian and Prussian courts as to a military alliance; and he was secretly encouraging the Spanish central *junta* in Cádiz to carry on its struggle against France.

The czar's open animosity to France surfaced in December 1810 when his ambassador in Paris, the obese and senile Prince Kourakine, delivered an explosive *ukase* to the French foreign minister. Henceforth, contrary to previous trade agreements, all French textile and other luxury goods would be subject to enormous customs duties upon entering Russia or its territories. He followed this bombshell by sending a secret agent, the young Colonel Count Czernichev, to Paris as "special envoy," to work with Count Nesselrode of the Russian embassy and the turncoat Talleyrand in penetrating the highest levels of Parisian society while stealing secrets from the French war ministry. If Alexander still held reservations as to a collision course with his ally, they all but vanished upon his learning that Napoleon had annexed the duchy of Oldenburg (the duke was married to the czar's sister) which he occupied with French troops.[4]

In late February 1811, Napoleon notified the czar that he was recalling Ambassador Caulaincourt for reasons of poor health and was replacing him with General Count Lauriston. Never one to beat around the bush, he wrote that although his friendship for Alexander remained constant, "I have to believe that your Majesty is no longer friendly to me." Otherwise, he went on, the czar would not continue to object to French annexation of the Oldenburg duchy even though its duke had been offered a generous cash subsidy. Alexander's earlier prohibition of French goods entering the Danube principalities of Valachia and Moldavia – some merchandise was even burned – indicated a definite change of heart, as did the czar's incorrect belief that Napoleon intended to make Poland an independent country. These facts, taken with Russian construction of forts along the Dvina river and failure to enforce the continental system against England, made it difficult not to assume that the czar was abandoning the treaty of Tilsit for rapprochement with England; indeed "all of Europe sees that our alliance no longer exists." Napoleon then recalled Russia's extensive gains from this alliance: Finland, one-third the size of Sweden; Valachia and Moldavia, one-third of Turkish holdings in Europe. If Alexander were to desert the alliance with France and go over to England, Napoleon warned, "war would sooner or later follow." If Alexander did not intend to abandon the alliance then Napoleon would like a clear understanding to dissipate the divisive clouds.[5]

The clouds were already too thick to be blown away by rhetoric and now thunder was heard. Alexander's new fortifications and the announcement that England planned to send a battle fleet into the Baltic were causing Napoleon to spend two million francs upgrading Danzig's fortifications and reinforcing its garrison. Russia could scarcely object to that in view of its own fortress construction on the Dvina river and its transfer of infantry and cavalry divisions from Finland, Siberia and Moldavia to Polish frontiers. These and other moves were hostile to France, as opposed to his own moves designed solely to bring England to the peace table.

Shortly after the birth of his son in March, the emperor explained his position to Marshal Davout, commanding the Army of Germany. He did not believe that the Russians would attack France because they were too occupied with their war against the Turks. But once that war ended they would probably deploy more troops on the Polish frontiers with the eventual intention of falling on Warsaw (precisely what Alexander had in mind). Although he did not want war with Russia it was necessary to "take an offensive position which if done too late would cause war to break out . . . if these movements were made when the Russians had all their forces available they would no longer believe my explanations and would undoubtedly march on Warsaw."[6] Since Napoleon had no intention of meeting the czar's claims to two Polish districts as compensation for the duchy of Oldenburg, territories that would allow Russia to dominate the grand duchy of Warsaw, he foresaw a lengthy negotiation and was determined to negotiate from a position of strength. In short, as General Lauriston was to inform the czar, "we wish peace but we are ready for war."[7]

The first impression gained from reading Napoleon's extensive correspondence of this period is that of unlimited confidence and strength. Only upon close study do some ugly cracks appear. In view of England's naval preponderance, the preparations to launch various expeditions and scare England into recalling troops from Portugal were only a study in futility. His new conscriptions at home were immensely unpopular. At best they would furnish only mediocre and disgruntled soldiers to add to an already enormous payroll. Napoleon would not admit that he was beginning to run out of human flesh. The shortage of horseflesh was more obvious. In January 1811 the Army of Germany lacked some 18,000 horses. This deficit was partially repaired by buying remounts in France, but in late June the emperor notified Davout "that France is out of horses." By mid July the Army of Germany still lacked 9,000 of them.[8]

A more immediate failing was the continuing flow of English merchandise to the continent. Marshal Murat (King Joachim) was suspected of letting contraband goods into Naples. Spain was flooded with English products while more and more American grain was carried in American ships to Portugal and Spain – 835,000 barrels in 1811 – to feed Wellington's army. French merchants were dealing with the enemy, sometimes with court permission, sometimes surreptitiously, as were merchants in Holland, Prussia, Sweden and Russia. Bourrienne continued to build a fortune in Hamburg by selling import-export licenses. French police, as Napoleon discovered during an autumnal inspection of the coast, were selling import licenses that allowed millions of francs' worth of goods to enter at Dunkirk, Ostend and Boulogne. Although he harshly reprimanded police minister Savary, it was largely his own fault for originally condoning limited trade with the enemy.

Equally discouraging were his relations with the northern

countries. Despite his and Lauriston's adjurations to St. Petersburg, extensive Russian trade continued with England while Russian troops were being recalled from the Danube to threaten the grand duchy of Warsaw. At a diplomatic reception on his birthday the emperor loudly dressed down the Russian ambassador, Prince Kourakine, on these points, warning him that "even should the Russian army appear on the hills of Montmartre, I will not cede an inch of Warsaw's territory," and going on to vaunt his own military strength.[9]

Upon receiving reports in late August that 500 merchantmen sailing under false American flags had arrived in Russian ports, Napoleon threw up his hands, writing to foreign minister Maret "that Russian plans are now exposed; they wish to maintain trade with England."[10] Prussia was constructing suspicious fortifications at Kolberg and Spandau – in mid September, Davout was alerted to send in troops if this work did not stop.[11]

Sweden also remained troublesome. In early 1811, Prince Royal Bernadotte asked the French ambassador in Stockholm, Alquier, to support Sweden in recovering Norway and Denmark: if France went to war with Russia, Sweden would invade Finland to threaten St. Petersburg. Alquier received orders to ignore this tentative, indeed to have nothing to do with Bernadotte, but only with the king and his cabinet to whom he should make it clear that "France has no need of Sweden . . . France wants nothing from Sweden and asks for nothing."[12]

Relations worsened during the year, mainly because Sweden violated the continental system by furnishing armed escorts to ships carrying English merchandise, to a clash between Swedish and French troops in Swedish Pomerania, and by Sweden refusing to release some captured French corsairs. In early November, France was represented in Stockholm only by a *chargé d'affaires*. So tense was the situation that Napoleon wished Princess Bernadotte (Désirée Clary) to leave Paris and return to Sweden since war was imminent.[13]

*

There remained the war in Spain which even before Masséna's entry into Portugal had taken a turn for the worse. Marshal Augereau's splendid beginning in Catalonia had petered out which caused Napoleon to replace him with Marshal Macdonald (who soon had to be reinforced with 12,000 infantry and 1,300 cavalry).[14] Augereau's failure was somewhat balanced by General Suchet's capture of Lérida, but further preparations for a march on Valencia were stalled mainly because of the pervasive activity of Spanish guerrillas.

As the year 1810 drew to a close Napoleon was forced to take the guerrilla threat to his line of communications more seriously, but still without any real notion of its future tactical implications, much less any idea of how to counter it other than by traditional methods that to date had only encouraged it. In early January he sent Marshal Bessières to Bayonne "to take measures to promptly disperse and hunt down the brigands who infest Navarre . . . in order to safeguard the army's rear."[15]

Macdonald having done no better in Catalonia than Augereau, Napoleon relieved him in favor of the newly redeemed Suchet who with 40,000 men was "to proceed vigorously with the siege of Tarragona. This city taken, he will have really conquered Catalonia . . . It is in Tarragona that he will find his baton of marshal of France."[16] Suchet pushed as hard as possible, winning his baton in the process, but he would continue to be thwarted by guerrillas as would Bessières in the north and Victor, Soult and Masséna in Andalucia and the Estremadura.

Napoleon's brief effort to make the Spanish war pay for itself never got off the ground. Spain was too poor, its lands already scoured by French and Spanish armies, its guerrillas too active, and French commissaires, officers and soldiers too venal. He would soon learn from his treasurer that 29 million francs had been sent to the peninsula in 1810, another 24 million already in 1811, and that it would be necessary to draw on reserve funds to make payments due in the next four months.[17]

He might still have salvaged something had he divined the type of war being fought. Had he paid even a flying visit to the

Suchet, Louis Gabriel 1770–1826 Marshal of France

country he probably would have faced up to the truth of dispersed and isolated armies, divisions, regiments and battalions, troops low in morale and combat effectiveness, their sullen and jealous commanders sunk in dangerous and greedy apathy. It would have been a bitter pill to swallow but if he had realized that an invasion of Portugal was no longer feasible he might have brought himself to abandon the sink-holes of Andalucia and Estremadura in building a tight line of defense behind the Ebro river – in short a shift to a defensive strategy spiced with tactical offensives when necessary, not to mention systematic political and economic reforms, as prelude to annexing Biscay, Navarre and Catalonia to France, or at least establishing Prince Ferdinand as a cardboard king.

There is no indication that he even considered such a visit, and only one minor suggestion of the possible withdrawal of his troops from Andalucia to the Burgos area.[18] The news of Masséna's humiliating retreat which resounded throughout Europe was to Napoleon no more than a temporary setback soon repaired by the seizure of Badajoz fortress. He was convinced that this splendid achievement would be followed by Victor's capture of Cádiz and Suchet's of Valencia. Masséna meanwhile was being reinforced, and this time Lisbon surely would succumb to a two-pronged attack by Soult and Masséna.[19]

These fantasies were put on paper at the end of March 1811 when Napoleon still supposed Masséna to be at Coïmbra (he was licking his wounds at Salamanca). Even when Napoleon learned the true situation in April he refused to adjust his plans to reality. He continued to respect favorable reports, to reject unfavorable events. Most of his scores of orders were obsolete before they were dispatched to either a disgruntled king in Madrid or to equally disgruntled commanders in the field.

Relations with King Joseph had so deteriorated – poor performance and extravagance on Joseph's part, lack of funds, division of command, conflicting and obsolete orders on Napoleon's – that the king, suitably escorted, appeared in Paris in mid May to present the emperor with a lengthy written list of grievances and the notion of abdicating. Napoleon should have jumped at the chance to get rid of him – even a jerry-rigged government under the idiot Prince Ferdinand would have been preferable. Instead he left Joseph to cool his heels at Mortefontaine, then to participate in the ornate baptism of the King of Rome. Not until mid June did Napoleon finally agree to give Joseph command of the Army of the Center along with increased administrative support; in addition he would return with half a million francs and henceforth would receive a million francs a month. With that he sent the luckless monarch off to Madrid, content that Wellington would soon be removed from the peninsula.[20]

*

That was not to be. Determined to maintain the tactical offensive Wellington had turned to the recapture of the strategically vital fortresses of Badajoz in the south, Almeida and Ciudad Rodrigo in the north. The effort culminated in the important and bloody battles of Albuera southeast of Badajoz and that of Fuentes d'Oñoro southeast of Almeida. When the bodies were buried and the dust had settled, the English resumed the blockade of Badajoz, Wellington owned Almeida which opened the way for the siege of Ciudad Rodrigo, Soult was back in Seville, Masséna licking his wounds in Salamanca.

Masséna's failure to relieve Almeida cost him his command. His replacement, Marshal Marmont, had marched south to support Soult, an effort ended when after a sharp quarrel Soult had suddenly taken his army back to Seville. The situation changed little over the summer, Marmont finally returning north to protect communications in Léon. Although he succeeded in resupplying the garrison at Ciudad Rodrigo in September, he failed to disrupt Wellington's careful and elaborate preparations for a siege.

Napoleon's restless sights had already shifted back to the eastern coast of Spain. In late November he wrote Berthier "that the main business of the moment is the capture of Valencia." Soult was to send a division to Cuenca in support of Suchet: "The English have 18,000 sick in Portugal and are unable to undertake any offensive action."[21] Once Valencia was taken, Marmont would gain heavy reinforcements: "then the great movements of his army will begin . . . toward the end of January [1812], after the rainy season, in conjunction with the armies of Portugal and the South he should move on Elvas . . . while the Army of the North arrives on the Coa [river]."[22] (As Napoleon dictated these words, Wellington's impressive force was moving confidently toward Ciudad Rodrigo which would fall in mid January 1812 to open the way to Léon and the north.)[23]

As the year closed, Napoleon continued to denigrate the guerrilla threat. False reports had convinced him that Ballesteros' bands operating out of Gibraltar province had been neutralized.

Up north General Caffarelli was to march against the elusive and very destructive Mina "to pursue him everywhere until he is destroyed."[24] In Napoleon's mind his generals were going about this brigand business in the wrong way by concentrating large forces in the villages, thus continually exposing themselves to "disagreeable events." Instead, "some principal places should be occupied from which mobile columns could pursue the bands . . . the experience of the Vendée proved the superiority of mobile columns deployed everywhere in large numbers, as opposed to stationary corps."[25]

Comparison with the Vendée was particularly inept in view of Spain's immense coastline, the English navy's control of coastal waters, some of the most difficult terrain in the world and some of the best guerrilla leaders in history. Mobile columns occasionally neutralized or even destroyed a guerrilla band but the victim was soon replaced by another band which continued to fight hit-and-run actions, feinting here and there, clipper-like cutting of French communications, constant reporting of French strength and movements to Spanish and English commanders, constant unexpected whirlwind movements that baffled the French to keep them on constant and fatiguing alert.

General Thiébault had said it all two years earlier when Berthier insisted that to end the guerrilla threat "you have got to beat them and reduce them," to which Thiébault replied:

that in order to conquer the Spaniards you have to convince them . . . To beat them is easy, but how are you to reduce people who have information about everything, are never betrayed by anyone, show nothing but skirmishers, never masses of men, whom an army cannot get at, while individuals or weak detachments escape them only by miracle; against whom you cannot maneuver, who resist no more than they submit, and who, favored by the most broken ground, limit their warfare to alarms, excursions, surprises and assassinations . . . a struggle of this kind, if it

Bessières, Jean Baptiste 1768–1813 Marshal of France

looks like lasting, demoralizes troops and toughens the people. So few commanders understand it that it is bound to occasion many mistakes; lastly, armies are used up while populations renew themselves: it is like the hydra devouring and springing up afresh.[26]

Over two years later Marshal Bessières, who commanded the Army of the North and was relieved of his command in autumn of 1811, again stated the problem all too familiar to local commanders but one that Napoleon refused to recognize:

If I concentrate twenty thousand men all communications are lost, and the insurgents will make enormous progress. The coast would be lost as far as Bilbao. We are without resources, because it is only with the greatest pain that the troops can be fed from day to day. The spirit of the population is abominably bad: the retreat of the Army of Portugal had turned their heads. The bands of insurgents grow larger, and recruit themselves actively on every side . . . The Emperor is deceived about Spain: the pacification of Spain does not depend on a battle with the English, who will accept it or refuse it as they please, and who have Portugal behind them for retreat. Everyone knows the vicious system of our operations. Everyone allows that we are too widely scattered. We occupy too much territory: we are clinging on to dreams.[27]

Notes

1   Corr. XXII. Nr. 17553, Paris, 2 April 1811. See also Rose (*Life*), II, 234; Bingham, 97.

2   Miot de Melito, II, 494–5.

3   Corr. XXI. Nrs. 17452, Paris, 10 March 1911; 17411, Paris, 1 March 1811; 17434, Paris, 8 March 1811.

4   Bausset, 38–40; Vandal, III, 48–67.

5   Corr. XXI. Nr. 17395, Paris, 28 February 1811.

6   Corr. XXI. Nr. 17516, Paris, 24 March 1811. See also Vandal, III, 139–55.

7   Corr. XXII. Nr. 17832, St. Cloud, 21 June 1811.

8   Corr. XXII. Nr. 17847, St. Cloud, 23 June 1811.

9   Vandal, III, 211–15. See also Watson, 870; Corr. XXII. Nr. 18148, Breskens, 24 September 1811.

10   Corr. XXII. Nr. 18082, Trianon, 25 August 1811.

11   Corr. XXII. Nrs. 18139, Compiègne, 14 September 1811; 18241, Düsseldorf, 3 November 1811.

12   Corr. XXI. Nr. 17386, Paris, 25 February 1811. See also Vandal, III, 74–84.

13   Corr. XXII. Nr. 18230, Düsseldorf, 3 November 1811.

14   Corr. XXI. Nrs. 16807, St. Cloud, 19 August 1810; 16897, St. Cloud, 12 September 1810.

15 Corr. XXI. Nr. 17275, Paris, 8 January 1811. See also Thiébault, II, 296–307; Serramon, 81–101; Horta (*Estudios*), 99–115; Horta (*Merino*), 41–63; Priego, 25–37.
16 Corr. XXI. Nr. 17444, Paris, 9 March 1811.
17 Corr. XXII. Nr. 17943, St. Cloud, 25 July 1811.
18 Corr. XXII. Nr. 17740, Rambouillet, 21 May 1811.
19 Corr. XXI. Nr. 17531, Paris, 30 March 1811.
20 Corr. XXII. Nrs. 17561, Paris, 4 April 1811; 17752, Caen, 27 May 1811.
21 Corr. XXII. Nr. 18267, St. Cloud, 19 November 1811.
22 Corr. XXII. Nr. 18267, St. Cloud, 19 November 1811.
23 Thiébault, II, 356–71. See also Bryant (*Victory*), 424–31, 451–3.
24 Corr. XXII. Nr. 18267, St. Cloud, 19 November 1811.
25 Corr. XXII. Nr. 18276, St. Cloud, 20 November 1811.
26 Thiébault, II, 280–1.
27 Oman, III, 488–90.

CHAPTER TWENTY-ONE

THE RUSSIAN ADVENTURE – I: MARCH–JUNE 1812

I shall not fire the first cannon, but I shall be the last to sheathe my sword.

Czar Alexander of Russia to the French ambassador, General Caulaincourt, on the threat of war with France. Vilna, May 1812[1]

IN THE WINTER months of 1812 the question in Napoleon's mind was no longer *if* but *when* war would break out with Russia. Despite his frequent denials he was probably looking forward to it. He was convinced that his forces in Spain, somewhere around 250,000 troops, were more than adequate to contain if not eliminate the English threat, a chimerical belief reinforced in early January 1812 by Marshal Suchet's seizure of Valencia (a noteworthy achievement which won him the title of the duke of Albufera).

Napoleon heavily discounted Russia's fighting capability, as well he might considering his victories at Austerlitz and Friedland. Nor would he be without allies. A secret treaty with Prussia signed in February guaranteed him 20,000 troops, free passage of the country and logistic support for men and horses. A secret treaty with Austria signed a month later provided for 30,000 troops to protect his right flank in Poland. Davout's army in Germany would soon muster 200,000 men, Murat was coming from Naples to command a second army based on Stettin, General Junot would arrive from Italy with the vanguard of Viceroy Eugène's army of 80,000. A Bavarian force also 80,000 strong would be commanded by Gouvion St. Cyr. General Prince Poniatowski would command

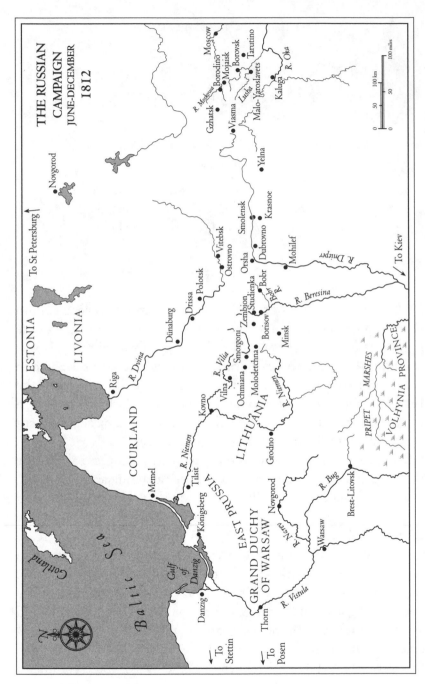

The Russian Campaign June – December 1812

60,000 Polish soldiers, the other confederation states would provide 70,000 more bodies – in all nearly 600,000 troops including the Imperial Guard, now a hefty 50,000. More French soldiers would soon arrive from Spain, and another 120,000 conscripts were to be raised in France.

Enormous supply depots in Germany and Poland were stocked during the early months of 1812. The French ambassador in Vienna was ordered to buy two million bottles of Hungarian wine (at no more than ten *sous* a bottle) for shipment to Warsaw; other sources were to stockpile 28 million bottles of wine and two million bottles of brandy as a year's supply for the army. A supplementary budget of 2.4 million francs was authorized for Danzig whose magazines were to hold 5,500 tons of wheat, the same of rye and a million bushels of oats. New and lighter wagons were to be built, 15,000 cavalry and artillery horses bought in Prussia, and 26 transport battalions formed and equipped with over 1,400 wagons. Hospitals and ambulances were ordered for a variety of cities and towns while marching orders were worked out to the last detail.[2]

Marshal Davout's Army of Germany became the new Grand Army, a massive behemoth to stretch from the Baltic coast to the eastern borders of Poland. Davout commanded the spearhead center corps, something over 70,000 strong, Oudinot a second force of 37,000 and Ney a corps of nearly 40,000. The left flank was given over to Macdonald's corps of about 32,000 including General Yorck's Prussians. Viceroy Eugène commanded an auxiliary corps of approximately 80,000 Italians and Bavarians echeloned behind Davout. The right flank would be guarded by King Jérôme's 70,000 Westphalians, Saxons, Hessians, Swiss, Dutch and Poles, along with Prince Schwarzenberg's Austrian corps of about 30,000. Marshals Victor and Augereau headed reserve corps numbering something over 80,000 men as a second line.[3]

Napoleon almost certainly had decided to invade Russia at this point, providing that life was not made easier for him by the Russians spilling over into Poland. In mid March he informed his

Davout, Louis-Nicolas 1770–1823 Marshal of France

director of artillery that "my intention is to open the campaign by besieging Dünaburg and Riga . . . get me indirectly and secretly some information on these two fortresses."[4]

By end of March, believing that Russia's war with Turkey would discourage any enemy movement, he began moving the army to the line of the Vistula river. A month later he sent a peace tentative to England, probably hoping to play on England's worsening relations with the United States (which shortly would lead to war). He probably hoped also to end the war in Spain, and he may even have intended to declare the current dynasty in Spain as independent, with the country ruled by a constitution as drawn up by the *cortes* in Cádiz. Portugal would retain its integrity under the house of Braganza, Naples would keep its present ruler and the kingdom of Sicily would be guaranteed under its current rulers.

Once all this was worked out, Spain, Portugal and Sicily would be evacuated by French and English troops. Other problems would be negotiated on the basis of *uti possiditis* or present possession. Napoleon hoped that this fourth effort to attain peace would succeed, but if not "France will at least have the consolation that England would be responsible for the spilt blood."[5]

A week later he learned that if the French army took up position on the Vistula the Russian army would deploy on the Niemen. Davout was instructed to act circumspectly since the army had not completed its deployment and the grass vital for forage would not be ripe until early June.[6] Napoleon also sent Count Narbonne with a rather fawning letter to Czar Alexander at Vilna who responded with a lengthy statement of his grievances and desire for peace while merely reiterating a host of earlier demands that included Napoleon evacuating Swedish Pomerania and recognizing Russia's right to receive neutral ships – demands which, when presented earlier by Prince Kurakine, had brought forth the angry response: "You are a gentleman, and yet you dare to present to me such proposals? You are acting as Prussia did before Jena."[7]

Czar Alexander and his generals, too well aware of "the nature of the beast," had a good idea of Napoleon's intentions owing to the recent theft of secret operational documents from the war ministry in Paris (Count Czernichev's caper hotly denounced by Napoleon).[8] The question in the czar's court was: what course should Russia take?

Despite minister of war Barclay de Tolly's efforts to reorganize the Russian army during the last two years, it was not a very imposing force – we are reminded of Archduke Charles' earlier effort to reshape the Austrian army after so many decades of neglect. Of an estimated 400,000 troops, large numbers were occupied in garrison duty in remote areas of the empire, one army being stationed in the recently acquired territory of Finland, another in the Danube valley at war with the Turks. Russia's newly acquired ally, Prince Bernadotte of Sweden, agreed to furnish a corps but this would not materialize until the following year (for which he would be rewarded with Norway). Secret negotiations were also under way with England, but this was a matter of money, not men.

The recent build-up along the western borders resulted in two armies: General Barclay's First Army of the West of six infantry and three cavalry corps, some 127,000 men supported by nearly 600 cannon and about 15,000 Cossacks under General Platov's command; and General Prince Peter Bagration's Second Army of the West, two infantry and one cavalry corps and 4,000 Cossacks, perhaps 66,000 strong.

Barclay's army based on Vilna was to hold the line of the Niemen river. Prince Bagration's force formed the left flank south of the Pripet marshes in Volhynia province. A smaller corps commanded by General Tormasov screened Galicia. These forces would be backed by armies coming from Finland and the Danube and by hordes of peasant conscripts and militia volunteers.

The weakest of the three commanders was Barclay de Tolly, a transplanted Scot-Lithuanian, although he had performed well in Finland. Bagration and Platov were flamboyant and sometimes reckless leaders but well knew their business. Officers and men were generally very brave, willing to fight to the death, but were not very well trained and in general lacked initiative. Nevertheless a spirited force held the right bank of the Niemen, patiently awaiting orders from its czar-god who would soon arrive in Vilna to take command of the army.[9]

Napoleon's hopes for a Russian invasion of Poland were in vain. Although Czar Alexander had seriously considered such a move, probably with the battles of Austerlitz and Friedland in mind he had finally decided on another kind of war. In spring of 1811 he had written to the Prussian king, "The system which has made Wellington victorious in Spain, and exhausted the French enemies, is what I intend to follow – avoid pitched battles and organize long lines of communication for retreat, leading to entrenched camps."[10]

This plan appeared to be the brainchild of his Prussian advisers, first General Scharnhorst, currently General von Phull, a staff theorist, "an émigré Prussian with a bogus reputation as a strategist," as a later historian described him.[11] Phull preached a modified Fabian strategy, first to exhaust the enemy, then to destroy him by enticing him into attacking an entrenched camp. This fortified camp was under construction at Drissa on the Dvina river where it overlooked the main roads to St. Petersburg and Moscow. In the event that the French invaded Russia, Barclay was to fall back directly on it while Bagration harassed the enemy's flank and rear before joining the larger army.

While Napoleon was studying background sources on the Baltic states and Russia, including the French translation of the English Colonel Wilson's book on the Russian army (not the most helpful text), and such histories as Voltaire's on Charles XII's ill-fated campaign of 1709, French and allied troops were daily arriving on the Vistula banks. Napoleon, Marie Louise and a large court reached Dresden in mid May to be joined by the emperor and empress of Austria, the Prussian king and numerous confederation rulers and their courts, Napoleon's idea being to show solidarity in the midst of elaborate social functions. He himself had little time for the niceties. Couriers arrived almost hourly with situation and supply reports, each read as avidly as Countess Montesquiou's assurances of the baby Napoleon's good health.[12]

Having ordered his troops to continue their march to the banks of the Niemen, he left Dresden at the end of May for a final inspection of his still strung-out units plodding through East Prussia, their supply lines in a tangle, the troops pilfering, plundering, violating and burning houses, a brutal and undisciplined march that according to a disgusted Captain Roeder soon turned Prussian peasants into implacable enemies.[13] None of this was new to Napoleon – for a man who loved order above all else he was singularly immune to temporary disorder during an exhausting few weeks of dealing with unit deployments, troop readiness, artillery and bridge trains, munition and provision dumps, intelligence reports on the enemy, countless regimental, brigade and division reviews and a host of other nuts and bolts that hold an army together. Somehow during this incredibly active period he evolved a final plan of operations based on what he knew of enemy locations and strengths.

With his left flank protected by Macdonald's corps, his right by Jérôme, Reynier and Schwarzenberg's corps, Davout's army with Eugène in support would push across the Niemen, seize Kovno and move up the left bank of the Vilia river to strike the czar's headquarters at Vilna. As he explained the plan to Jérôme, "first of all, make a feint as if entering Volhynia so as to hold the enemy [Bagration] there as long as possible, while by outflanking his extreme right I shall have gained twelve or fifteen marches on him toward St. Petersburg; I shall find myself on his right wing, cross the Niemen and seize Vilna which is the first object of the campaign." Once the enemy realized what had happened he "will take one of two courses: either he will withdraw to the interior to become strong enough to give battle, or he will take the offensive." If he chose to give battle he would be caught between the French center and left.[14] If he moved on the Vistula he would be checked by Jérôme and Schwarzenberg while Davout and Eugène fell on his flank and rear. We see here once again the "big battle" general thinking in terms of a "decisive victory," in this case a campaign of no more than 20 days.[15]

Napoleon was being dangerously optimistic – we are reminded of his less than careful preparations for the 1799 Syrian expedition. His troops were not in a high state of combat readiness. Although immense quantities of clothing and rations had been stockpiled at Danzig, transportation was difficult. Rations were in such short supply that the troops were forbidden to touch their personal issue until they had crossed the Niemen to begin the campaign. As one result many of the troops went hungry in trying to live off the inhospitable land and the sick-list steadily rose as did pillage and excesses of all kinds.[16]

Many of the French troops were scarcely more than conscripts who lacked sufficient training for a tough march into hostile country. His marshals and generals were a mixed bag. Davout, Gouvion St. Cyr and Murat, although difficult, were able enough as was Oudinot, but Macdonald less so. The bold and brave but not very bright Ney was getting old and tired but was still hard as iron. Viceroy Eugène with Desolles as chief of staff could be trusted as could General Reynier. King Jérôme was not reliable but had a capable chief of staff, General Marchand. Victor, commanding a rear area reserve, was only mediocre, Augereau crippled and worn out, General Yorck and Prince Schwarzenberg dubious quantities both professionally and politically. Many senior officers were brave and skilled veterans of previous campaigns but not all of them were able, nor were many officers of lesser ranks.

Over half of the army consisted of foreign troops, many of them untrained, unwilling and undisciplined, already sowing "terror and desolation" in Poland. Macdonald's corps consisted of Yorck's Prussian contingent, he later wrote, "and of a division formed by three Polish regiments, one Bavarian and one Westphalian; my staff was French."[17] Ironically only six years earlier Napoleon had instructed King Joseph in Naples not to worry about an Anglo-Russian force in Sicily because "an army composed of men of different nations will not take long to make some blunders. The art will be to wait and profit from them."[18]

How could he be so certain that his enemy would stand and fight? In view of Alexander's remarks to Count Narbonne he should have considered the possibility of a prolonged retreat, but there is little evidence that he did so. He made no arrangements for winter clothing, none for horses to be properly shod for ice and snow. Transport was sadly lacking – the new wagons and caissons were still on the drawing board. As was the case in Berlin in 1806 prior to his invasion of Poland, the medical services lacked doctors, surgeons, orderlies, bandages, medicines and ambulances. He had no real knowledge of the country, yet surely his experiences in Poland had given him a good idea of what to expect. "Find out how far upstream the Narev is navigable in June and July," he wrote Jérôme. "Could a ship sail right now to Novgorod?" – odd questions that should have been answered months earlier.[19]

What would he do if the enemy retreated? Without losing a great deal of face he would have to follow in the hope of bringing him to that "decisive battle" necessary to revive French fortunes. Meanwhile unrest would grow at home – and then of course there was Spain.

Although Napoleon refused to admit it, at least openly, the situation in the peninsula was anything but healthy. General Reille who now commanded the Army of the Ebro's four divisions had failed to eliminate increasingly serious guerrilla operations around Barcelona and in lower Catalonia and the Aragon. Joseph and Jourdan were in no more control of the army than ever. Napoleon, after scolding Marshal Marmont for a series of errors, ordered him to establish headquarters at Salamanca, reoccupy the Asturias, retake Ciudad Rodrigo and threaten the English at Almeida, all in preparation for another invasion of Portugal – tasks infinitely beyond Marmont's powers. Before the marshal could digest this order he was taken to task for other lapses such as not establishing himself at Salamanca so as to fulfill "the main role of the Army of Portugal . . . to hold in check five or six English divisions, to take the offensive in the north or, if the enemy has taken the initiative . . . to send as many divisions as necessary to raise the siege of Badajoz and force Lord Wellington to retreat."[20]

In mid March he again reversed command arrangements by declaring King Joseph commander in chief of all armies in Spain with Marshal Jourdan as his chief of staff, thus wiping out (in theory) the autonomous commands held by Suchet, Soult and Marmont. This order only created greater confusion and hard feeling in the command hierarchy without reducing the guerrilla threat in the Asturias and Galicia which Napoleon admitted was dominating "the rear areas of the army."[21]

Having so decreed, he nonetheless continued direct corre-spondence with individual commanders, once again reshaping the command in Aragon and Catalonia in order to put down the "brigands," continuing to smother Marmont with complicated orders for various contingencies – all presented to Joseph as a *fait accompli*, and all based on the assumption that the French armies were operating at a peak of efficiency while Wellington com-manded no more than 50,000 troops, over half of whom were Portuguese. Simultaneously additional troops were being sent to the south and more convoys of cash and paper money, some-where around 9 million francs, would continue to arrive in Spain.[22]

In Napoleon's mind the Spanish problem would soon resolve itself in the aftermath of a great victory in Russia. As units under-went final inspections, as *voltigeurs* prepared to cross the Niemen in small boats to establish bridgeheads and engineers loaded bridge-building equipment to follow them and as troops ate a final meal, commanders read aloud Napoleon's proclamation:

Soldiers! the second war of Poland begins . . . let us therefore march to the front, let us cross the Niemen, let us carry the war to the enemy's land. The second war of Poland will be as glorious for French arms as the first. But the peace that we shall make will be final, and will end the deadly influence that Russia has exercised for fifty years on European affairs.[23]

Notes

1   Caulaincourt, I, 335. See also Vandal, III, 183.
2   Rose (*Life*), II, 240–1. See also Marbot, III, 48; Vandal, III, 233.
3   Wartenburg, II, 108–9; Chandler (*Napoleon*), 754–6. These and following strength figures, French, allied and Russian, should be treated as estimates only.
4   Corr. XXIII. Nr. 18579, Paris, 14 March 1812.

5   Corr. XXIII. Nr. 18652, Paris, 17 April 1812. See also Fain (*Manuscrit*), 53–5.

6   Corr. XXIII. Nr. 18667, St. Cloud, 25 April 1812.

7   Rose (*Life*), II, 239. See also Fain (*Manuscrit*), 56–8; Vandal, III, 383, 429–31.

8   Corr. XXIII. Nr. 18541, Paris, 3 March 1812. See also Fain (*Manuscrit*), 27; Bausset, 56; Vandal, III, 234–5, 312–18, 377–81, 393.

9   Wartenburg, II, 110–11; Chandler (*Napoleon*), 750–3, 763–5.

10 Markham, 176.

11 Markham, 191. See also Vandal, III, 163–6, 235–9.

12 Corr. XXIII. Nr. 18715, Dresden, 23 May 1812. See also Caulaincourt, I, 332–6; Fain (*Manuscrit*), 60–6; Vandal, III, 402–29.

13 Rose (*Life*), II, 240–1.

14 Corr. XXIII. Nr. 18769, Thorn, 5 June 1812.

15 Corr. XXIII. Nr. 18781, Danzig, 10 June 1812. See also Caulaincourt, I, 346, 356; Chandler (*Napoleon*), 762–3.

16 Corr. XXIII. Nr. 18813, Königsberg, 16 June 1812.

17 Macdonald, 191.

18 Corr. XI. Nr. 9665, Munich, 12 January 1806; Corr. XXIII. Nr. 18760, Thorn, 4 June 1812.

19 Corr. XXIII. Nr. 18769, Thorn, 5 June 1812. See also Gotteri, 113–45.

20 Corr. XXIII. Nr. 18573, Paris, 12 March 1812.

21 Corr. XXIII, Nrs. 18583, Paris, 16 March 1812; 18621, Paris, 29 March 1812.

22 Corr. XXIII. Nrs. 18632, St. Cloud, 3 April 1812; 18640, St. Cloud, 8 April 1812; 18735, Dresden, 28 May 1812.

23 Corr. XXIII. Nr. 18855, Wilkowyski, 22 June 1812.

CHAPTER TWENTY-TWO

THE RUSSIAN ADVENTURE – II:
THE MARCH TO MOSCOW
JUNE–SEPTEMBER 1812

Every victory is a loss to us.

Captain Franz Roeder[1]

THE CAMPAIGN BEGAN well. Screened by light infantry carried across the Niemen by boat late on 23 June, engineers quickly bridged the river. Two days later most of the corps had crossed; only Viceroy Eugène's force was held up by slow progress of his supply wagons. Opposition was minimal, some Cossacks firing a few protest rounds before cantering off to the east.

What next?

Captured dispatches had now given Napoleon a good idea of enemy positions. Czar Alexander as commander in chief was with General Barclay de Tolly's army at Vilna on the left bank of the Vilia river about 60 miles southeast of Kovno. General Wittgenstein with two divisions was somewhere to the north shielding the fortresses of Memel and Riga while retiring on the Dvina river. General Bagration was reportedly marching north-ward from Volhynia to guard Barclay's left flank.

Napoleon's plan was to drive a wedge between Barclay and Bagration, giving separate battle to one or the other. Toward this end he sent Oudinot's two divisions northward to screen his left flank while Macdonald's corps marched toward the Dvina river, its mission "to garrison the Baltic coasts and to lay siege to Dünaburg and Riga."[2] Simultaneously the main army preceded by Murat's cavalry moved down the left bank of the Vilia, hoping to surprise Alexander and Barclay at Vilna. In the south King Jérôme's powerful force that included Prince Poniatowski's light Polish cavalry was to shadow Bagration's march.

As Murat was closing on Vilna the Russians were evacuating the town to fall back on an entrenched position at Drissa on the Dvina river. The French cavalry faced only spasmodic artillery fire before entering the town on 28 June. It was not much of a prize. Immense supply magazines which Napoleon had counted on – indeed depended on – were a pile of ashes, the bridge across the river destroyed. Until a bridge train arrived from Kovno the Grand Army had come to an unforeseen halt.

That army was already in an uncomfortable position. During the forced march to Vilna the mild weather suddenly changed to cold rain. As in Poland in 1807 the troops found themselves trying to negotiate primitive roads suddenly turned to quagmires that exhausted men and horses and were soon choked with overturned cannon, camions and wagons. The troops were wet, cold, tired and hungry. The meager rations carried by each soldier, bread, biscuit and flour, were soon eaten or thrown away.[3] The land was not rich, the few villages and farms were soon cleaned out, corn and grass were insufficiently ripe for proper forage and oats were in short supply.[4] "The rapid movement [to Vilna], without stores, exhausted and destroyed all the resources and houses which lay on the way," General Caulaincourt later complained. "The advance guard lived quite well, but the rest of the army was dying of hunger. Exhaustion, added to want and the piercingly cold rains at night, caused the death of 10,000 horses. Many of the Young Guard died on the road of fatigue, cold and hunger."[5] So many men and horses died that burial parties were working up to 5 miles from Vilna to avoid a serious epidemic.[6] By early July a large convoy of flour had failed to arrive, nor owing to a transport shortage had the bricks necessary to build ovens.[7] Marshal Ney was forced to send out strong cavalry patrols to round up stragglers, both to stop them from committing atrocities on local peasants and to prevent them from being killed by lurking Cossacks and peasants.[8]

Napoleon might well have gained some much needed assistance but for a diplomatic conflict. Vilna was the old capital of Lithuania which had been ceded to Russia by earlier nefarious partitions of Poland. Shortly after the emperor's arrival a delegation of elders wearing their former national dress paid court, as did a delegation from Warsaw which presented a petition for the independence of Poland. Napoleon had consistently refused to support this desire for independence (as Marie Walewska knew only too well), and now he had to wriggle out of a project that would have brought him thousands of allies but would have cost him the support of his Austrian ally.[9]

Was he tempted? Czar Alexander's negative reply to his last letter seemed to contradict any hope of a quick peace, as acknowledged by Napoleon's long and rambling response written at Vilna: if Alexander did not want peace then at least an arrangement should be made for rapid exchange of prisoners and direct communication between the rulers despite the hostilities.[10]

This communication signaled a distinct change in Napoleon's diplomatic style. Heretofore he had warned potential opponents of what they would lose by defying French arms. Now he was suggesting peace when the war had just started, but without the usual warning of the dire consequences awaiting an unbending opponent. Had the heavy toll of men and horses, with no shots fired, caused him to fear the future? Had the empty and sterile land given him second thoughts? Or was this still another attempt to bring Alexander back to the fold so that he could settle affairs in Spain and force England to the peace table? Any chance of that would have ended with his support of a Polish rebellion which moreover did not seem necessary in view of his predominant strength. Surely a "decisive victory" would force the czar to reason without introducing the complications certain to ensue from a Polish uprising.

The need for a "decisive victory" henceforth haunted him as the king's ghost of Elsinore haunted Hamlet. His first need was to eliminate Bagration who reportedly had reached Ochmiana. Believing that this prince was being tailed by Poniatowski's light cavalry followed by Jérôme's large corps, Napoleon sent three strong columns of infantry and cavalry under Davout, Grouchy and Nansouty to hold Bagration at Ochmiana while Jérôme moved in from the south to deliver the *coup de grâce*.[11]

This effort was no more than underway when Napoleon learned that Bagration had escaped the trap by withdrawing to the southeast, a dilatory Jérôme having failed to block his retreat. Berthier was ordered to inform the errant commander "that it is impossible to maneuver more badly . . . that the fruit of my maneuvers and the most beautiful opportunity of the war have been lost by the singular neglect of the basic concepts of war."[12]

Napoleon was momentarily stymied, but not for long. If Bagration and Barclay had escaped defeat they could still be destroyed further east, probably at the next river line, that of the Dvina. They were plainly on the run, it was only a matter of catching them up to force a battle. While the army waited for its supply trains Davout's columns remained on Bagration's trail, not an easy task since the wily prince knew the country very well and commanded some of the best horseflesh in the world. After heading south he cunningly doubled back to the northeast planning to join Barclay on the Dvina. His maneuver precipitated a serious quarrel between Davout and Jérôme, the latter again being negligent, but the damage was done. Jérôme in royal pique returned to Westphalia – a furious emperor transferred most of his corps to Marshal Victor's command.[13]

The main army marched from Vilna in mid July. The changeable weather had moved from wet cold to hot dry. The land offered little succor. Just as Portuguese peasants had done, Russian serfs turned much of it to burn while Cossacks buzzed in and around the columns like angry wasps to force the battalions to halt and form into defensive squares. Although the horsemen were invariably repulsed their nearby presence was always worrisome, their attacks tiring and time-consuming and sometimes very costly. "If the Russians want to send half our army to the dogs by winter," Captain Roeder sourly noted in his diary, "all they have to do is to make us march hither and thither with the individual units kept continually under arms. Then if they give us a few battles we shall be in a tough situation so long as they have plenty of light troops."[14]

Despite elongated supply lines and increasing troop hunger, Napoleon continued the march. General Grouchy's capture of "immense magazines" of flour at Orsha temporarily relieved the stomach crisis by providing the makings of a watery gruel.[15] The enemy retreat would soon expose the high roads to St. Petersburg and Moscow – surely Alexander would now turn and fight? If he were at Drissa as reported, then an end run south of Drissa toward Vitebsk, by threatening to cut the Moscow road while Oudinot in the north moved on the road to St. Petersburg, would bring on the desired battle.

Napoleon's spirits soared at the thought: "The entire Russian army is at Vitebsk," he inaccurately informed Maret on 25 July. "We are on the eve of great events." And a day later: "I am heading right now for Vitebsk . . . things could not go better. The light cavalry [of the advance guard at Ostrovno] has today taken twelve cannon and 600 prisoners . . . the country is beautiful, the harvest superb and we find food everywhere . . . the prince of Eggmühl [Davout] committed only ten battalions in repulsing Bagration's attack."[16]

Davout's victory ironically cost Napoleon the battle he so vehemently desired. Neither Czar Alexander nor General Barclay was pleased with Phull's "entrenched camp" at Drissa. Unlike Wellington's superb complex at Torres Vedras, it left flanks and rear exposed to a blockade by the much stronger French army and, considering the state of the camp and the Russian army, surrender sooner rather than later. Far better to let the French dig their own graves in the Russian hinterland, following Scharnhorst's advice to trade space for time, in this case time for Russian armies from Finland and the Danube to reinforce them. Turning over command of the army to Barclay, the czar departed first for Moscow to preach the need for a religious war, an appeal that brought thousands of peasant recruits to the flag; then, ever mindful of his neck he continued on to St. Petersburg to mend political fences. Barclay meanwhile had learned of Bagration's defeat by Davout at Mohilef and despite the protests of his generals ordered a further withdrawal to Smolensk on the banks of the Dnieper river.[17]

Napoleon has frequently been criticized for allowing Barclay to slip away. Considering the state of the French army it was perhaps just as well. "The heat is so intense and the army so weary," he wrote from Vitebsk, that it needed several days of rest.[18] These were not empty words. Despite the picture of plenty recently painted in his dispatch to Maret, his food wagons were far to the rear, more horses than ever were dying, the supply magazines at Vilna were empty. Sick-lists were daily rising as were the number of stragglers, hundreds of whom were daily routinely rounded up by cavalry patrols. A Russian general who came to imperial headquarters under a flag of truce reported that

> the roads were strewn with the carcasses of horses, and
> swarming with sick and stragglers. All [French] prisoners
> [at Russian army headquarters] were carefully questioned
> as to the matter of subsistence; and it was ascertained that
> already, in the neighborhood of Vitebsk, the horses were
> obtaining only green forage, and the men, instead of bread,
> only flour, which they were obliged to cook into soup.[19]

Not all the soldiers went hungry or thirsty. A veteran Guardsman, 27-year-old Sergeant Bourgogne, was billeted in a village outside Vitebsk in the house of a Jewish peddler. A scrounger of the *grondeur* school, he soon located a cauldron, barley and a grinding mill. His host was sent to procure hops (his good-looking wife and two daughters held hostage) and in short order Bourgogne and his troops had brewed five kegs of beer, two of which they tearfully had to turn over to Mother Dubois, the *cantinière*, who enjoyed a neat profit after their departure.[20]

This was an unusual cameo. General Caulaincourt later wrote that "the pillage and disorders of all kinds in which the army had indulged had put the whole countryside to flight." Outside of

Vitebsk, "we were in the heart of inhabited Russia . . . we were like a vessel without a compass in the midst of a vast ocean."[21] Another aide, Count Ségur, recalled that when the emperor's immediate entourage rejoiced at the "conquest" of Vitebsk he turned sharply on them and cried, "Do you think I have come all this way just to conquer these huts?"[22]

But as Napoleon had foreseen, a week or so of rest worked wonders as supply trains arrived along with troop reinforcements. But now the question of the next move arose. News from left and right was scarcely reassuring. In the south General Reynier's corps though holding its own was being pushed by General Tormasov and would soon need help from Schwarzenberg's Austrians and, further distant, Victor's corps. In the north Marshal Oudinot and General Gouvion St. Cyr continued to wrestle with Wittgenstein's Russians near Polotsk on the Dvina river. In trying to seize the town and its richly stocked Jesuit convent, Oudinot was wounded. He was replaced by Gouvion St. Cyr whose capture of the town won him a marshal's baton, an event he celebrated, Marbot tells us, by retiring into the convent to spend a day or two indulging his passion for playing the violin. Assured of his flank, at least for a time, Napoleon decided to push on to Smolensk.

Barclay was already in Smolensk, an ancient holy city divided by the Dnieper river, the "new" city on the right bank, the "old" city on the left bank. Joined by Bagration in the "new" city in early August he counted some 125,000 troops. Napoleon planned another enveloping attack by two columns which, crossing the Dnieper to outflank Barclay's left and threaten the Moscow road, would force a battle.

Napoleon got his battle but not the one he wanted when Murat opened the fighting in mid August by attacking the defenses around the old city. Despite numerous and costly charges the cavalry failed to break through a defensive shield and the army backed off.

After a brief interlude – despite a bad cold Napoleon celebrated his forty-third birthday by reviewing the troops – fighting resumed, a miserable two days of see-saw actions that cost the

Gouvion St. Cyr, Laurent 1764–1830 Marshal of France

French an estimated 10–15,000 casualties, the Russians considerably more. Thirty-five French generals were wounded, eight were killed (including Caulaincourt's brother). Fearful of his communications with Moscow, Barclay again overrode the protests of his generals and ordered a further retreat eastward, leaving a burning city behind.[23]

After an abortive attempt to block Barclay's retreat – the villain appeared to have been sluggish movement on General Junot's part – Napoleon spent almost a week in Smolensk, described by a young quartermaster clerk, Henri Beyle (known to history as Stendhal), as "this ocean of barbarism . . . coarse, dirty, stinking." Perhaps the surroundings formed a factor in Napoleon's shaping up his army for the march on Moscow, well over 200 miles distant. This was a dubious decision considering the lateness of the summer, his recent losses, the generally unsatisfactory condition of the army, the shaky state of its supply lines, increasing lack of forage for horses and the enemy's scorched-earth policy carried out mainly by Cossacks. Despite such adverse factors he remained supremely convinced that the enemy would come out to defend Moscow and that he would win his "decisive battle." As he confidently told General Caulaincourt, "We shall be in Moscow within a month; we shall have peace in six months."[24]

General Barclay's decision to evacuate Smolensk cost him his command. In mid August he was replaced by 67-year-old General Kutusov who was ordered to give battle at the first opportunity. We met Kutusov at the battle of Austerlitz which would never have been fought had Czar Alexander heeded his advice to retreat into Moravian wilds and let Napoleon destroy himself if he were so stupid as to pursue.

Kutusov did not want to give battle. Kutusov wanted peace, a surprising and very dangerous heresy for a general. As at Austerlitz he would have preferred a further retreat, this time into Russian spaces to give Napoleon and Alexander time to come to their senses and meet at the peace table. The imperial order however was not to be scorned and in early September he put his army, 130,000 strong including 17,000 untrained militia, some armed only with pikes, to work defending the town of Borodino only 75 miles from Moscow.[25]

Meanwhile the Grand Army revived to march in three columns, Eugène on the left, Davout in the center, Poniatowski on the right, in all about 124,000 infantry, 32,000 cavalry and nearly 600 cannon. Not far from Borodino a courier delivered letters and a portrait of the infant Napoleon from Marie Louise. That night in bivouac, shortly before one of the bloodiest battles in history, Napoleon called his generals and staff officers to view the portrait proudly displayed outside his tent.[26] We wonder as to his thoughts in the flickering light of a campfire?

The army reached Borodino on 5 September. Napoleon attacked almost at once. Furious fighting won an outlying redoubt but no more. Kutusov's main line of defense was first rate, a series of earthen redoubts surrounding the great redoubt, a massive affair bristling with angry cannon, his eager troops supported by 600 more guns, the undulating, cut terrain strongly favoring the defense, his right flank resting on hills and woods leading down to the Moskowa river, his left wing somewhat dangerously exposed. After an exhausting day spent in reconnoitring the position Napoleon issued his orders, his troops also on the *qui vive* wanting to avenge the weeks of slogging march on mostly empty stomachs.

Battle opened again early on 7 September and soon turned to massive slaughter as attack was followed by counter-attack, twelve hours of incessant cannon-fire, of unbroken fighting, of many brave deeds from one end to the other of the blood-soaked battlefield. French cannon alone fired 90,000 balls, French muskets nearly two million rounds, firepower answered in kind by the Russians who nevertheless ever so slowly were forced from the redoubts to a less defensible line. According to some observers Kutusov seemed almost disinterested in the slaughter, remote and uncaring, but as night fell he had seen enough. He had followed imperial orders, he had suffered over 40,000 casualties, and now he could retreat with some 90,000 survivors.[27]

Kutusov may have retreated but the French had little reason to celebrate having counted well over 30,000 dead and wounded – some accounts say 50,000. Ney, Murat, Poniatowski, Grouchy and many others had fought like lions. Ney, "the bravest of the brave" in Napoleon's words, won the title of the prince of the Moskowa. Forty-seven French generals including Davout were casualties, along with over 100 staff officers and aides. A modern authority has written that "almost thirty per cent of the contestants engaged had been hit."[28]

Napoleon has subsequently been criticized for his generalship, in particular for not allowing Davout to outflank Kutusov's left and for not committing the Old Guard at an especially critical moment, failures attributed to his so-called poor health.

Poor health? His reconnaissances on 6 September from early dawn to late dusk could not have been more thorough and left aides gasping for breath.[29] His orders were based on cogent facts, not on tactical dreams. A flanking movement followed by an attack on the Russian rear would have required a very strong force to succeed – the tactic was scarcely strange to Napoleon from yore. Even then it would have exposed the "holding" force to still another counter-attack which, if successful, would probably have killed the Grand Army. Similarly, had the Old Guard attacked and been defeated the Grand Army would probably have died.

Napoleon was in no position to run these risks. A week earlier he had received the ominous news from Spain of Marshal Marmont's defeat by Wellington near Salamanca, which forced Marmont to fall back on Burgos in considerable disorder. Although Marshal Soult had come up from Andalucia to force Wellington back to Ciudad Rodrigo, the door was now open to Léon and the north, and it was only a matter of time before the enemy walked through it. Is it any wonder that at times a few generals and staff officers found their commander distracted?

There was more. Platov's Cossacks, now nearly 30,000 strong, were seemingly everywhere, attacking small garrisons, raiding supply depots, striking convoys, picking off unfortunate stragglers. A general pervasive fear taken with severe food shortages had slowly infested French divisions to compound barbaric behavior of the troops: "the wholesale pillaging by the conquering army," the eyewitness Tarlé wrote, "by countless marauders, and sometimes by criminal bands of French deserters, caused the peasants' hatred of the enemy to grow from day to day."[30]

This hatred soon inspired the growth of guerrilla bands. Tarlé has given us the genesis of a partisan detachment. At the end of August a private in the Russian dragoons, an illiterate named Ermolai Chetvertakov, was taken prisoner but escaped. Joined by a friend, they killed two French stragglers, took their weapons and uniforms, then killed two French cavalry troopers and acquired their horses. These successes helped them to recruit 47 peasants, an ill-armed band that nonetheless killed 12 French *cuirassiers* and next a group of 59 careless French soldiers. In time Chetvertakov's band swelled to over 300 guerrillas operating in the country around Gzhatsk. (Later in the campaign he led more than 4,000 peasants against a French battalion supported by artillery and forced it to retreat.)[31]

Similar bands sprang up across the land. An infantry private taken prisoner at Smolensk, Stepan Eremenko, escaped and recruited a peasant band of 300 strong. A serf named Ermolai Vasilyev recruited some 600 of his fellows who armed themselves with muskets taken from the enemy.

Although Czar Alexander and his generals, most of whom were titled owners of vast estates, did not want to arm the peasants, the potential of this new force struck a young lieutenant colonel, the poet Denis Davydov, one of Prince Bagration's aides. A few days before the battle of Borodino, Davydov persuaded Bagration and Kutusov to give him 50 hussars and 80 Cossacks to work with peasant guerrillas in cutting French communications. This was the modest beginning of a subsequent Cossack-partisan campaign, the outstanding exploits of which were later published by Davydov in a seminal work, *The Journal of Partisan Actions*,[32] and, more indirectly, by the tragic accounts later related in the memoirs of their French victims.

Unlike Napoleon who regarded guerrillas as nothing more than verminous brigands Kutusov realized the immense potential of the weapon which henceforth he would so successfully exploit. For the nonce however he utilized his other weapon, that of retreat even beyond the holiest of holy cities, Moscow. A greatly reduced French army eventually followed him, another march of 75 miles. Aside from a few skirmishes the way was clear. Preceded by Murat's prancing cavalry Napoleon entered Moscow on 15 September. A day later the city was burning.

Notes

1 Roeder, 129.
2 Macdonald, 191–2.
3 Caulaincourt (*Mémoires*), I, 343; Corr. XXIII. Nr. 18840, Gumbinnen, 20 June 1812. See also Vandal, III, 501–50.
4 Corr. XXIV. Nr. 18935, Vilna, 9 July 1812.
5 Caulaincourt (*Mémoires*), I, 166. See also Vandal, III, 508–10.
6 Corr. XXIV. Nrs. 18885, Vilna, 2 July 1812; 18906, Vilna, 5 July 1812.
7 Corr. XXIV. Nr. 18884, Vilna, 2 July 1812.
8 Rose (*Life*), II, 245.
9 Marbot, III, 61–3. See also Seton-Watson, 129–30.
10 Corr. XXIV. Nr. 18878, Vilna, 1 July 1812.
11 Corr. XXIV. Nr. 18879, Vilna, 1 July 1812.
12 Corr. XXIV. Nr. 18905, Vilna, 5 July 1812.
13 Rose (*Life*), II, 248–9.
14 Roeder, 125.
15 Corr. XXIV. Nrs. 18974, 18975, Gloubokoïe, 19 July 1812; 18988, Gloubokoïe, 21 July 1812.
16 Corr. XXIV. Nrs. 19008, Biéchenkovitchi, 25 July 1812; 19011, Biéchenkovitchi, 26 July 1812.
17 Rose (*Life*), II, 250–1. See also Seton-Watson, 133–4.
18 Corr. XXIV. Nr. 19021, Vitebsk, 30 July 1812. See also Wartenburg, II, 134–5; Chandler (*Napoleon*), 778–9.
19 Clausewitz (*Campaign*), 110–11.
20 Cottin, 5.
21 Caulaincourt (*Mémoires*), I, 185; Caulaincourt (*Mémoires*), I, 375–9, 387.
22 Ségur, 30. See also Asprey (*War in the Shadows*), I, 151–2.
23 Cottin, 6–12; Wartenburg, II, 147–54; Chandler (*Napoleon*), 784–8.
24 Guyon, 222; Caulaincourt (*Mémoires*), I, 396, 408 ff. See also Marbot, III, 125–32.
25 Caulaincourt (*Mémoires*), 412–14, 418. See also Rose (*Life*), II, 254; Wartenburg, II, 146; Markham, 193; Chandler (*Napoleon*), 795. The strength figures vary considerably.
26 Caulaincourt (*Mémoires*), I, 420–1. See also Bausset, 77.

27 Caulaincourt (*Mémoires*), I, 422–35; Wartenburg, II, 160–9; Chandler (*Napoleon*), 794–807.

28 Chandler (*Napoleon*), 806–7. See also Caulaincourt (*Mémoires*), I, 432–3; Bausset, 78–87; Rose (*Life*), II, 254–6; Wartenburg, II, 161–9.

29 Caulaincourt (*Mémoires*), I, 422–5. See also Bausset, 78, who delivered the portrait to Napoleon and who found him "in no way disturbed by the excessive exertions" of this rapid-moving and complicated war.

30 Tarlé, 186.

31 Tarlé, 247–9. See also Seton-Watson, 138.

32 Tarlé, 186, 256–88, 326–56.

CHAPTER TWENTY-THREE

THE RUSSIAN ADVENTURE – III: THE LONG RETREAT AUGUST–DECEMBER 1812

Great numbers of [French soldiers] could be seen wandering over the countryside, either alone or in small groups. These were not cowardly deserters: cold and starvation had detached them from their columns . . . Now they met only armed civilians or Cossacks who fell upon them with ferocious laughter, wounded them, stripped them of everything they had, and left them to perish naked in the snow. These guerrillas . . . kept abreast of the army on both sides of the road, under cover of the trees. They threw back on the deadly highway the soldiers whom they did not finish off with their spears and axes.

Count Philippe Paul de Ségur[1]

WHAT A TRAGIC fire it was. Moscow was a beautiful city, a big, sprawling metropolis of numerous residential and business sections each architecturally unique sprouting amongst the cheerful green cupolas and onion domes lorded over by the majesty of the stolid Kremlin. About half of the residential palaces and mansions, smaller houses and shops were of wood. Governor Rostopchin had evacuated over 300,000 civilians and soldiers while arsonists, many of them dangerous criminals released from prison at the last moment, planted explosives and smashed the city's fire engines.

Marshal Duroc was still sorting out imperial headquarters in the luxurious rooms of the Kremlin when arsonists put match to fuse. The fire began on the night of 15 September, burned furiously and dangerously for three days and sporadically for another day or two until squelched by rain. Such was its intensity that imperial headquarters had to be temporarily moved outside the city proper. In addition to fighting the flames and shooting Rostopchin's convicts, the soldiers devoted themselves to an orgy of drunken looting of what they called "the Moscow fair." The great fire destroyed about three-quarters of the dwellings and shops. "The superbly beautiful city of Moscow no longer exists," Napoleon informed Czar Alexander two days after the fires were out. ". . . Four hundred arsonists were arrested in the act . . . They have been shot."[2]

Despite the fire the city still offered welcome comfort to hungry and tired soldiers, many of them nursing wounds. Sergeant Bourgoyne had skillfully billeted his company of grenadier Guards in a beautiful mansion complete with tailors, cook and two laundresses rescued from the streets. Subsequent discovery of its secret cellars yielded seven enormous chests of champagne, quantities of Spanish wine, port, 500 bottles of Jamaican rum, 100 panniers of sugar, a large number of hams and salted fish, some sacks of flour and plenty of beer – "all this for six non-commissioned officers . . . The rest of the company slept comfortably in the billiard room, warmed by sables, leopard, fox and bear furs." One squad discovered some cashmere shawls which they wore around their heads as turbans, "resembling sultans rather than grenadiers of the Guard; they only lacked some beautiful women."[3]

Governor General Mortier had soon restored order, Marshal Bessières had rounded up the unfortunate Russians and shipped them out of the city, the French colony including a troupe of actors was being looked after, General Lefebvre's military police were guarding the Kremlin, Eugène, Davout, Murat and Poniatowski's forces were posted on all roads outside Moscow, 1,000 supply wagons were on their way from Vilna. Nor had Rostopchin been able to evacuate all the military supplies: 150 field cannon, 60,000 new muskets, two million musket cartridges, tons of powder, saltpeter and sulfur, thousands of

cannon-balls – "three times what we have expended in battle,"
Napoleon informed Maret in Vilna.[4]

All well and good, but what did Napoleon intend to do with his
latest conquest? He probably did not know. He had not expected
the enemy to wantonly destroy not only an ancient and beautiful
city but one that was holy to all Russians in every sense of the
word. This could have been prevented, he informed the czar, had
Alexander responded favorably to his earlier letters and had the
French been met by a functioning administration common to their
entry in Vienna, Berlin and Madrid. This letter, an oblique suggestion for peace negotiations, was not answered.[5]

Not knowing the czar's political position Napoleon could not
appreciate its complexity, despite Caulaincourt and Lauriston's
analyses over the years. Barclay and Bagration's long retreat from
Vilna and the Pripet marshes had brought high-level criticism so
intense as to force Alexander to leave the army and return to St.
Petersburg, then to order Barclay and his replacement, Kutusov, to
give battle at Borodino. Seizure and burning of Moscow followed.
"The capture of Moscow has caused intense irritation," the czar's
sister had written him. "Dissatisfaction has reached the highest
point, and your person is far from being spared."[6] A false decision
had brought about his father's assassination. Even had he wished,
Alexander was in no position to acknowledge, much less accept,
Napoleon's tentative.

This scarcely suited the French emperor. Although mansion
cellars continued to yield quantities of delicacies, basic foods –
bread, flour, fresh meat, forage – remained in short supply.
Massive expeditions combing the countryside yielded meager
results, the peasants mostly having deserted, taking what animals
and provisions they could and destroying the rest. Working parties had to be escorted by more and more troops which sometimes
got the worst of it from omnipresent Cossacks and peasant bands.
Ninety thousand soldiers, several thousand camp-followers and
25,000 local civilians had to be fed daily. Supply convoys arrived

only irregularly, the result of a line of communications some 500 miles long which had become a Cossack playground. Convoys from Smolensk required an infantry-cavalry-artillery escort of at least 1,500 troops "who each night were to form a square around the precious wagons."[7] Horses were in ever shorter supply. "I have the greatest need for 14,000 cavalry remounts," Napoleon plaintively wrote Maret at end of September.[8]

Although it was autumn and daylight was shrinking, Napoleon did not appear to be overly disturbed. His frequent notes to Marie Louise (sometimes two a day), while lamenting the burning of Moscow, carried no suggestion of urgency. "The army here has very good cantonments and barracks," he wrote on 20 September, shortly after returning to the Kremlin, "my health is good, my affairs are going well."[9] Marshal Murat, whose cavalry occupied advance posts south and east of Moscow, reported that Kutusov's army showed little fight, indeed that his troopers were openly fraternizing with Cossacks and regular troops, that he had met with Kutusov who had agreed to an informal truce whereby one would notify the other at least three hours before the shooting started. Was an accommodation after all possible?

Still hoping for such, Napoleon sent General Lauriston, former ambassador to St. Petersburg, with a new peace tentative to the czar in early October. Lauriston was well received by Kutusov but was prevented from going on to St. Petersburg although Kutusov forwarded his letter by courier.

Napoleon might as well have saved himself the trouble. The Russian army was daily being reinforced from Finland and the lower Danube as well as by thousands of peasant recruits. Kutusov's armistice was designed merely to gain time, nor did it apply to Cossacks and guerrillas who continued to make life hell for French outposts. Captain Roeder graphically described the reaction of his regiment to an attack by a few hundred armed peasants and Cossacks near Viasma who "siezed the baggage of the Westphalian regiment and murdered the escort. This threw us into a state of unrest and vigilance." The commander of a punitive expedition was ordered to shoot any peasants he encountered and burn all dwellings. Roeder sardonically wrote, "I only hope that he omits at least the final measure for our sakes, in order that we may occasionally find somewhere to spend the night."[10]

Napoleon at last was becoming concerned with his situation, as evidenced in a lengthy memorandum probably written in early October. Having learned that Kutusov's army was advancing on Kaluga southwest of Moscow, he asked himself what should be done. Should he defend Moscow (not easily defensible) and take up winter quarters there, should he march on St. Petersburg to bring the czar to reason, or should he withdraw to winter quarters at Smolensk?[11]

Having received no reply to his most recent letter to the czar by mid October, he decided on winter quarters in the Smolensk area which he calculated the army would reach in early November. No further troop units or food convoys were to leave Smolensk and those underway were to halt at interim garrisons. Several thousand sick and wounded were to be evacuated. The army was to march within a few days either south toward the relatively unscarred area around Kaluga or due west to Viasma.[12]

Baron Jomini later portrayed Napoleon at this time as a nervous wreck, a sick man out of touch with reality. More to the truth he was angry with himself for having misread Alexander's character to such a disastrous degree. If on occasion he seemed hesitant he certainly had good reason: not since the awkward days of St. Jean d'Acre had he been in such a morbid situation, but that retreat was a matter of a single corps of several thousand troops, not a large, widely deployed army threatened by a powerful enemy, its transport facilities at a minimum for a march of hundreds of miles, days growing shorter and colder, nights longer and colder.

His orders for the march, not always practicable, show no signs of panic. Witnesses galore attest to his normal routine, busy days broken by a few relaxing hours reading novels sent from France, gazing at the portrait of his son, writing frequent notes to Marie Louise assuring her of his love for herself and his son. The day before he decided to retreat he promised the Countess Gudin, whose husband General Gudin, one of the heroes of Auerstädt, was killed on the march to Moscow, a generous pension and her sons pensions and titles. On the following day he wrote Countess Montesquiou his thanks for a favorable report on his infant son.[13] He frequently stressed his own good health to Marie Louise along with almost daily weather reports, cold and sunny but growing warmer.[14]

The day prior to the march Napoleon sent General Lauriston to Marshal Kutusov with a request for a peaceful withdrawal in accordance with the usual customs of war. Maret at Vilna was to purchase (at a reasonable price) flour for delivery to interim garrisons and ask the Prussian and Saxon kings for reinforcements. Marshal Mortier, commanding the rearguard, received detailed evacuation orders (that included blowing up the Kremlin). Equally detailed marching orders went to Davout, Ney, Lefebvre and other generals. All carriages and wagons were to be numbered and registered, and each was to carry at least two wounded soldiers – any vehicle not carrying wounded would be seized and burned. Commanders were to establish supply points along the roads with detachments deployed to defend against Cossack attacks.[15]

These and other documents suggest a state of order far from reality. How could he logically expect 40,000 wagons to be numbered and registered in a few days? How could units be brought to strength and supplied with provisions when the army was approaching anarchy? Just prior to the retreat a Russian officer noted that "every day the [French] soldiers streamed in thousands from the camps to plunder the city, and many thousand others were scattered throughout the countryside foraging and seeking for bread. Peasants armed with staves lay concealed in woods and marshes and slew hundreds of these marauders every day, and those who escaped fell into the hands of the Cossacks."[16]

Napoleon may have purposely exaggerated his demands for two reasons: first, to put the best face on an admittedly worsening situation, and second, in the hope that things would be sorted out once the gigantic retreat was underway. He was about to leave

Moscow on 18 October when he learned of a morning attack by several thousand Cossacks who caught General Sebastiani's light cavalry off guard in bivouac. In addition to heavy casualties the French lost 12 cannon and 65 wagons.

The main army marched early on 19 October, heading south-west, but owing to confusion and slow-moving artillery and baggage trains progress was slow. Ségur later described the columns as looking "like a caravan, a wandering nation, or rather one of those armies of antiquity returning with slaves and spoil after a great devastation." Sergeant Bourgoyne's company found itself entangled in a 3-mile string of sutler and merchants' wagons, three lines across the rude road, some of which were already broken down to turn the jabber of at least five languages into an ear-spliting cacophony. On the second day most of the wagons were broken down, the others stuck in the sandy road, "the French moaning, the Germans swearing, the Italians appeal-ing to the good lord, and the Spanish and Portuguese to the Holy Virgin." Soldiers were already beginning to discard valuable but heavy booty from their packs. On this same day partisans attacked the front of the convoy; Cossacks would attack on the following day and continue to do so.[17]

Despite such confusion and delay all went reasonably well for a few days. The weather was sunny and beautiful even if the nights were growing uncomfortably chilly, but then rain further slowed the lumbering columns. "The army is [marching through] extremely rich country, comparable to the best regions of France and Germany." Thus concluded an upbeat army bulletin sent to the folks in Germany and France.[18] The last troops were leaving Moscow, the Kremlin had been blown up.

Napoleon had intended to march to Kaluga on the Oka river and then through rich country to Yelna and Smolensk, but now he learned that Kutusov's advance guard had reached Malo Yaroslavets on the Lusha river less than 25 miles south of Borovsk. A day's fighting had cost Eugène and Davout some 2,000 casualties against a reported enemy loss of 7–8,000 killed or wounded. Davout had pursued the retreating Russians but was forced to halt by the cold, the burden of his wounded and the Cossack-partisan threat.[19]

Probably realizing that Kutusov was stronger than he had believed, Napoleon now made a curious decision to march due north to Mojaisk instead of moving northwest on Viasma or even west on Yelna.[20] Perhaps he preferred the known to the unknown but whatever the case the move cost him several days and his soldiers a great deal of unnecessary exertion.

The new route also proved particularly depressing:

> Everywhere we saw wagons abandoned for want of horses to draw them [one observer recalled]. Those who bore along with them the spoils of Moscow trembled for their riches; but we were disquieted most of all at seeing the deplorable state of our cavalry. The villages which had but lately given us shelter were level with the ground: under their ashes were the bodies of hundreds of soldiers and peasants . . . But most horrible was the field of Borodino, where we saw the forty thousand men who had perished there, yet lying unburied.[21]

Marbot too remarked on the field of Borodino "covered with the debris of helmets, swords, wheels, weapons, scraps of uniforms and thirty thousand corpses half eaten by wolves. The troops and the emperor passed by rapidly, casting a sorrowful glance at this immense tomb."[22]

Napoleon and the Guard reached Viasma only at the end of October. Although the army was now strung out for about 50 miles and was frequently under attack by guerrillas, Cossacks and regular army units, Napoleon did not seem to be upset although he continued to worry about the safe evacuation of the wounded. "The weather continues to be very good," he informed Maret in early November. None of his problems was mentioned in a flow of notes to Marie Louise which as usual continued to harp on the weather, his health and his love for her and their son, although this may have been as much for security reasons as to spare her from worry. Typical was a note from Viasma dated 1 November: "I am nearing Poland to establish my headquarters there . . . the weather is splendid, 3 or 4 degrees below freezing point, glorious sunshine. My health is perfect, my affairs in good shape . . . Write to your father [the Austrian emperor] that I request him [to have General Schwarzenberg] supported by the corps in Galicia and to reinforce him. When you write to the empress [of Austria] tell her I am at her feet."[23]

Only a few days later the favorable weather turned to a storm that covered the troops with snow and the roads with ice. The cavalry, unshod for winter except for Caulaincourt's Guard, was helpless. Fallen horses littered the roads, the poor creatures still in their death throes being butchered for food. Abandoned gun carriages, cannon, caissons, wagons and elegant carriages holding incredibly valuable treasures littered the primitive roads, the troops quickly stripping them of plunder only to abandon it in turn. As early as 6 November Ségur described the ghastly scene quoted at the beginning of this chapter. The human had become the animal. Even members of the Imperial Guard could not escape the terrible transmogrification. Our old friend, Sergeant Bourgoyne, in retreat with what was left of his grenadier company, morosely told a friend, "If I met anyone in the woods with a loaf of bread I would force him to give me half; no, I would kill him and take it all." Suiting action to word the sergeant investigated a nearby wood, found a servant boiling potatoes for his general and forced him to sell nine of the undercooked largesse – which he hid in his game bag and refused to share with his men.[24]

Napoleon's world was rapidly crumbling. Militarily he was in deep trouble. A few days earlier a Russian force had cut through dispersed French columns to isolate Davout's corps, a crisis resolved by Eugène sending two divisions to the rescue. On the extreme left or southern flank General Reynier, whose Saxons were under attack, was forced to call back Schwarzenberg's Austrians, thus allowing Admiral Tchitchagov to fall on Minsk

and its two million priceless rations. General Tormasov meanwhile was heading for Orsha to block the Dnieper crossings. On
the right or northern flank Victor and St. Cyr were hard pressed
by a reinforced Wittgenstein in the Polotsk area on the Dvina
river. If Wittgenstein broke through here he would join the southern armies on the Beresina river to cut off the French while
Kutusov closed in from flanks and rear.[25]

Nor was Napoleon pleased with the political situation, having
learned that an old, half-crazy republican general, Claude
François Malet, had escaped his Paris keepers, scraped together a
few followers, spread the word that Napoleon had been killed and
then arrested some pusillanimous officials in an unsuccessful
attempt to topple the government. Although Malet was shot,
Napoleon was upset by even the partial success of the revolt, bitterly commenting on the lassitude of his senior ministers and
officials.[26]

But that problem was remote from the present. The army had
lost an estimated 30,000 horses, with hundreds more falling daily
from cold and starvation. The right flank was again in jeopardy.
St. Cyr, forced by his wounds to return to France, handed over his
corps to Victor. "His Majesty orders that you attack the enemy
without delay, push him beyond the Dvina [river] and recapture
Polotsk," Berthier wrote Victor on 7 November, adding in cipher,
"The movement is most important. In a few days your rear could
be flooded with Cossacks; the army and the emperor will be at
Smolensk tomorrow, but very tired after a march of 120 leagues
without halt. Take the offensive, the salvation of the armies
depends on it; each day's delay is a calamity. The cavalry is on
foot, the cold has killed all the horses. March! – this is the
emperor's order."[27]

Smolensk was a disaster area. Cossacks and guerrillas had
recently driven off 1,500 oxen. Carefully stockpiled provisions
had been violated by Victor's soldiers and now a ravenous advance
guard finished the job to leave only smashed barrels and empty
bottles. Finding no forage in the desolate city, Napoleon ordered
one commissary officer after another put on trial until he learned

from its governor, Baron Jomini, "that a woman Praskovya led a small guerrilla troop that attacked and destroyed French foragers."[28] Sadly disappointed, Napoleon remained there only a few days waiting for the straggled columns to close and sending a stream of orders as urgent as they were impracticable to Maret in Vilna to procure the unprocurable, namely horses. Without horses there could be no reconnaissance to locate the enemy, no placement of cannon, no battle to destroy the enemy. To await that enemy was only to perish.

The army marched again on 12 November, but Kutusov had used the pause to bring his divisions parallel to the French line of march. Shadowed by this unwelcome presence, Napoleon lost patience. At Krasnoe a few days later he sent his Guard against the Russians, a stubborn fight and a victory that caused the cautious Kutusov, his troops also hungry, cold and tired, to back off to the south, enabling the French to reach Dubrovno and cross the Dnieper river to Orsha.[29]

Napoleon had left Ney's corps, now only about 3,000 strong, at Smolensk as rearguard, but owing to a mix-up of orders Ney had failed to march on schedule and subsequently found himself cut off by a Russian corps. Napoleon in despair at his silence had almost written him off when suddenly news arrived that by a herculean effort he had broken through the surrounding enemy to cross the Dnieper and, helped by reinforcements from Eugène's corps, to reach Orsha, an amazing but expensive feat that cost him most of his troops and all of his cannon.

The sad state of Ney's corps was shared by the Grand Army. Sergeant Bourgoyne, himself about dead, watched it pass. The advance guard had all but disintegrated, the foot soldiers, their frost-bitten feet wrapped in rags or skins, dying of hunger. Then came the debris of the Guard cavalry followed by the emperor on foot, cane in hand, wearing a thick fur cape and velvet hat of deep purple garnished by a round of black fox fur. On his right on foot, Murat; on his left, Eugène, then marshals Ney, Mortier and Lefebvre leading 7–800 officers and non-commissioned officers, marching in order and carrying, in profound silence, the regimental eagles. Next was the Imperial Foot Guard, the old grenadiers, followed by more than 30,000 men, almost all with frozen feet and hands, marching without weapons which they were unable to use, many hobbling along on sticks, dressed in tattered rags of filthy skins, trudging without complaint as one after the other fell out to die.[30]

This skeletal army's salvation now depended on its crossing the Beresina river at Borisov. Learning that General Dumbrowski, who was defending the bridgehead there with some 3,000 troops, had been attacked by Tchitchagov's Russians and forced to withdraw, Napoleon sent Oudinot's corps to recapture the bridge. Oudinot carved out a nice enough victory and pushed the enemy to the right bank but could not prevent the burning of the bridge.

Under normal circumstances this would not have been a major problem. Although the river was only about 85 yards wide the marshes on either side also had to be bridged, a matter of nearly 700 yards. At that time of year the troops usually could have crossed on the ice, but a sudden thaw – an all-too-familiar phenomenon to the *grognards* of the Polish campaign – filled the river with massive drifting chunks of ice which caused it to overflow its banks and turn the causeways to muddy quagmires. To worsen matters, Napoleon in a desperate attempt to hurry his march had sensibly ordered his commanders to burn all but the most essential wagons and accoutrements. Unfortunately in the subsequent rush the army's only bridge train had been destroyed.

The decimated French army now faced 34,000 enemy positioned north and south on the right bank of the river, with Wittgenstein's 30,000 approaching from the north, Tormasov closing on the Dnieper from the south and Kutusov's army lurking not too far away. Blocked by an angry water to the front, threatened by large forces on flanks and rear, the Grand Army seemed on the point of extinction.

Napoleon was always at his best under pressure. Learning of a ford near Studienka some 8 miles north of Borisov, he immediately went into action: Victor to seal his right flank from Wittgenstein, Davout to screen his rear while a series of feint attacks lured the Russians south toward Borisov. General Corbineau (who had discovered the ford) led his cavalry (each horse carrying a foot soldier on the rump) and a few cannon across the river to secure the bridgehead while Chasseloup and Éblé's engineers, many of them veterans of the Danube crossings, defied freezing waters strewn with deadly chunks of ice to throw up two rickety trestle bridges, one for troops and a wider one for artillery, the lumber coming from cannibalized houses in Studienka.

Marshal Oudinot's corps was the first to cross during the afternoon of 26 November, his 11,000 troops and guns a welcome reinforcement to Corbineau's meager defenses, the more so since they secured the vital causeway leading from the bridgehead to Zembion and the high-road to Vilna. Troops continued to cross during the night, as did Napoleon's meager headquarters staff the following day. Thousands of panic-stricken civilian refugees jammed the bridges either to be crushed to death or fall in the river to drown.

The enemy meanwhile had discovered Napoleon's ruse and began closing in on the area. Oudinot's corps supported by Ney and Mortier was attacked early on 28 November. Hard fighting lasted most of the day. Oudinot was wounded, but Ney took over in his inimitable fashion and a final charge forced the Russians to retire. Victor's corps, weakened by the capture of an entire brigade which got lost in falling back on Studienka, came under attack from Wittgenstein whose artillery fire caused the remaining refugee horde to once again storm the bridges with the same sad result as the previous day. Victor's battalions managed to cross during the night. General Éblé's engineers fired the bridges the next morning, a pathetic scene that left thousands of refugees either to drown in the river or starve to death on the land.

Napoleon had saved his remnant army but few armies could have been in worse shape to be saved. Led by Davout and Eugène's skeletal corps, followed by Napoleon and the remains of the Old Guard, then by Victor and Ney's survivors, the retreat in freezing weather and heavy snow made painfully slow progress frequently interrupted by skirmishes with Russian cavalry, Cossacks and guerrillas, the wounded Oudinot only just escaping capture, the road and bivouacs so crowded with dead as to remind Sergeant Bourgoyne of a battlefield.

In early December the army reached Molodetchna, to find only a few wagons of provisions sent from Vilna. "It is very cold and the army is very tired," Napoleon wrote Cambacérès in Paris.[31] Maret was informed that the exhausted troops needed bread, meat and brandy. "I have a hundred thousand isolated troops separated from the army and searching for food which exposes us to horrible dangers." On the other hand if these vagabonds could be corraled and looked after in Vilna, "ten days of rest and ample food will restore discipline."[32]

After sending off the wounded and what was left of the baggage to Vilna, Napoleon dictated a final army bulletin to be sent to Paris, a lengthy work which candidly described the terrible hardships, losses and virtual disintegration of the Grand Army, a disaster that he blamed mainly on the weather.[33] Two days later he was in Smorgoni for a meeting with his marshals.

Ever since General Malet's caper he had been toying with the idea of returning to Paris, a notion reinforced by insurrectionary rumors from both Paris and allied capitals. He had recently sent a senior aide to the capital "to contradict false rumors."[34] It was obvious that if the empire were to be saved a new army had to be called to the colors, an army that could only be mobilized by the emperor. In case anyone doubted his ability to form this army, he stressed in a final bulletin that despite the recent ordeal he had never been in better health, a fact also emphasized in private letters to Marie Louise, Cambacérès and Emperor Francis of Austria.[35] Privately he was worried about home affairs – General Clarke and General Savary, the minister of war and the minister of police, had had a terrible row over the Malet affair – and also about the situation in Spain where Burgos was now under siege by Wellington's army.[36]

The time had come, he told the marshals, for his return to Paris. Marshal Murat was henceforth to command the army with

Berthier as chief of staff. Hopefully they would find Vilna sufficiently provisioned to provide winter sanctuary or at least a
breathing space sufficient for the corps to recuperate. He knew
that each marshal, each general, each officer and each soldier
would do his best to carry on the retreat until a better day arrived.

That night Napoleon departed by sleigh with only a small party
that included Caulaincourt, Duroc and Roustam. Discarding his
uniform he traveled incognito as Caulaincourt's secretary. It was a
long, cold trip interrupted by modest meals and lodgings, stops at
Vilna, Warsaw and Dresden where the sledges were replaced by
carriages, then on to Leipzig and Mainz. He arrived in Paris on 18
December 1812. The Russian campaign was over – another was
soon to begin.

Notes

1   Ségur, 169.
2   Corr. XXIV. Nr. 19213, Moscow, 20 September 1812. See also
    Cottin, 16–25; Caulaincourt (*Mémoires*), II, 22–7; Bausset, 93–9.
3   Cottin, 45.
4   Corr. XXIV. Nrs. 19213, Moscow, 20 September 1812; 19214,
    Moscow, 21 September 1812.
5   Corr. XXIV. Nr. 19213, Moscow, 20 September 1812.
6   Seton-Watson, 135–6; Markham, 195.
7   Corr. XXIV. Nr. 19220, Moscow, 23 September 1812.
8   Corr. XXIV. Nr. 19234, Moscow, 29 September 1812.
9   Napoleon *Letters* (Roncière), 106.
10 Roeder, 155.
11 Corr. XXIV. Nr. 19237, Moscow, presumed early October 1812.
    See also Caulaincourt (*Mémoires*), II, 44–59, 66–9.
12 Corr. XXIV. Nrs. 19273, Moscow, 14 October 1812; 19275, 16
    October 1812. The latter ciphered letter was sent to Maret but
    later archivists could not decipher it. Maret however quoted impor-
    tant parts of it in clear to the French ambassador in Vienna
    (correctly remarking that the retreat "will make a sensation, espe-
    cially in distant countries.").

13   Corr. XXIV. Nr. 19276, Moscow, 16 October 1812.

14   Napoleon *Letters* (Roncière), 107–16.

15   Corr. XXIV. Nrs. 19277, Moscow, 16 October 1812; 19280, Moscow, 17 October 1812; 19283, 19284, 19285, 19286, 19287, Moscow, 18 October 1812; 19290, Moscow, presumed 19 October 1812.

16   Roeder, 169.

17   Chandler (*Napoleon*), 820; Cottin, 52–9.

18   Corr. XXIV. Nr. 19304, Borovsk, 23 October 1812. See also Napoleon *Letters* (Roncière), 117 ff.

19   Corr. XXIV. Nr. 19307, Borovsk, 26 October 1812.

20   Corr. XXIV. Nr. 19307, Borovsk, 26 October 1812; Napoleon *Letters* (Roncière), 118.

21   Rose (*Life*), II, 260.

22   Chandler (*Napoleon*), 823.

23   Corr. XXIV. Nr. 19313, Semlevo, 3 November 1812. Napoleon *Letters* (Roncière), 121.

24   Cottin, 69–72. See also Caulaincourt (*Mémoires*), II, 90–119; Bausset, 156–7.

25   Rose (*Life*), II, 262–4; Wartenburg, II, 202–33; Chandler (*Napoleon*), 828–30.

26   Caulaincourt (*Mémoires*), II, 122–9. See also Rose (*Life*), II, 265.

27   Corr. XXIV. Nr. 19326, Mikhaïlovka, 7 November 1812. See also Caulaincourt (*Mémoires*), II, 130–44.

28   Tarlé, 192–3. See also Bausset, 120.

29   Cottin, 118–22; Caulaincourt (*Mémoires*), II, 145–80.

30   Cottin, 201–5.

31   Corr. XXIV. Nr. 19366, Molodetchna, 3 December 1812; Marbot, III, 215–17; Cottin, 224–5.

32   Corr. XXIV. Nr. 19367, Molodetchna, 3 December 1812.

33   Corr. XXIV. Nr. 19365, Molodetchna, 3 December 1812. See also Caulaincourt (*Mémoires*), II, 193, 196.

34   Corr. XXIV. Nr. 19364, Sélitche, 2 December 1812.

35   Corr. XXIV. Nrs. 19365, Molodetchna, 3 December 1812; 19374, Benitsa, 5 December 1812; 19385, Dresden, 14 December 1812. See also Napoleon *Letters* (Roncière), 133–5.

36   Corr. XXIV. Nrs. 19371, Molodetchna, 4 December 1812; 19374, Benitsa, 5 December 1812.

CHAPTER TWENTY-FOUR

FIRE FROM THE ASHES
DECEMBER 1812–MARCH 1813

*I cannot take the initiative [in calling for peace talks], that
would be like capitulating as if I were a fort: it is for the others
to send me their proposals . . . If I concluded a dishonorable
peace, it would be my overthrow. I am a new man; I must pay
the more heed to public opinion because I stand in need of it.
The French have lively imaginations: they love fame and
excitement, and are nervous. Do you know the prime cause of
the fall of the Bourbons? It dates from [the French defeat in
1757 at] Rossbach.*

Napoleon to Count Metternich, April 1813[1]

DEFEAT AWAKENED NAPOLEON from an interminable nightmare.
Even before the final meeting with his marshals at Smorgoni he
had begun chivvying the courts of Saxony, Berlin and Vienna to
reinforce their contingents and stem the enemy advance, demands
repeated as he passed through Warsaw and Dresden on his way to
Paris.

Bad news awaited him in the French capital. Owing to zero-
degree temperatures and omnipresent Cossacks the Grand Army
was in a ghastly state. Although ample provisions and clothing
had awaited its arrival in Vilna, the starving men had savagely torn
into food and drink depots, many gorging themselves to death.

Murat also had panicked. Contrary to Napoleon's orders he
almost immediately continued the retreat, the remnants finally
stumbling into Königsberg. Only a few hours after arriving at the
Tuileries, Napoleon wrote Berthier, "I hope that you will have
taken position on the Pregel [river] . . . I hope that generals

Schwarzenberg and Reynier will have covered Warsaw. Prussia is preparing to send reinforcements to cover its territory."[2] The following day he informed Murat:

> I am extremely pleased with the spirit of the nation. The people are prepared to make every kind of sacrifice, and I am working without respite to reorganize all my resources. I already have an army forty thousand strong at Berlin and on the Oder. The king of Prussia intends to send reinforcements to his army and to promptly replenish all his cavalry; the king of Saxony has the same intentions.[3]

By end of December – only 13 days after his return – he notified Berthier that "on Sunday I reviewed about 25–30,000 troops."[4] He had bought nearly 5,000 horses and had contracted for 5,000 more in France, 2,000 from Warsaw, nearly 5,000 from Hanover with more to come from Prussia and Hamburg. "Come spring I shall march with an army larger than the Grand Army at the beginning of the [last] campaign," he wrote the Danish king in early January. ". . . I am assured of the favorable sentiments of Austria, I can only praise the king of Prussia."[5]

The renascence of military might continued despite two unforeseen blows. One was the treachery of General Yorck whose Prussian corps, at least 17,000 men and 60 guns, formed Marshal Macdonald's rearguard in his retreat to Tilsit. Having fought but little in the campaign Yorck defected to Wittgenstein's corps under terms said to have been negotiated mainly by Carl von Clausewitz who had joined the Russian service shortly after the Prussian-French treaty of 1812. Yorck shortly would take his force back to Prussia to form the nucleus of a new army allied with Russia.[6]

The other event was Marshal Murat's impulsive decision at Posen to leave the Grand Army and return to his Neapolitan kingdom. Each blow was disappointing, neither an immediate disaster. "I find Murat's conduct very extravagant – I can think of nothing similar," Napoleon wrote Viceroy Eugène. "This is a brave man in battle, but he lacks intelligence and moral courage."[7] Napoleon gave the command to Eugène: "I am annoyed at not having given it to you upon my departure." Eugène was to send as many redundant generals as possible to France along with battalion cadres necessary to build new regiments.[8]

By invoking both imperial and public wrath, General Yorck's treachery at least contributed to the national patriotic movement that gave the emperor virtual *carte blanche* in forming the new army. By end of January 250,000 conscripts and volunteers were being trained and equipped, mobile columns were rounding up an estimated 100,000 conscripts who had fled the colors, prosperous young gentlemen had volunteered as *chasseurs*, each with his own mount, weapons, accoutrements and servants, the gendarmerie had been culled to provide troops and horses, the artillery revitalized by 40,000 converted naval gunners, the Guard considerably enlarged. General Rapp was provisioning Danzig fortress to feed 20,000 soldiers for a year. General Lauriston at Hamburg commanded a new corps of observation on the Elbe, Marshal Marmont at Mainz another such on the Rhine, and General Bertrand at Verona a third force that soon would march northward.

Napoleon continued to massage his confederation allies, sending each a highly cosmeticized account of the Russian campaign in calling for continued support. Negotiations with Pope Pius VII, now at Fontainebleau under genteel house arrest, resulted in a second Concordat that seemed to settle the matter of appointing and consecrating new bishops. Under its terms the pope would take up residence at Avignon (not at all cheerfully).[9] In sending a copy of the document to Emperor Francis in late January, Napoleon added: "My troops are marching. France is an armed camp, and your Majesty can be certain that at the right time and with the aid of God I shall drive out the Russians more quickly than they have arrived."[10]

Frantic preparations continued throughout February as regiments, some newly formed, others recalled from Spain, were hustled to the Elbe and the Rhine, forward supply depots set up, new cannon, howitzers and mortars sent to artillery parks, recruits equipped and drilled – all cogs turning in that vast martial machine. In late February the imperial equipage was alerted to march, this time with half the usual number of chefs who would prepare simple meals only – soup, boiled beef, a roast and vegetables, no dessert. Imperial lodgings would consist of a mere two tents with two beds. The normal complement of 72 wagons was reduced to 10, 500 horses and mules to a mere 110.[11]

It is difficult to fault either Napoleon's or the French nation's incredible activity during these four months, but there were some major drawbacks. The officers and non-commissioned officers needed to train recruits (no matter their healthy spirits) were in very short supply. Equally serious was a shortage of horses. Napoleon's initial claims of availability soon proved chimerical. Contracts signed outside France failed to meet commitments in whole or in part, nor did the home country live up to expectations. By early February the army had received only 11,000 mounts, a very dangerous situation in view of cavalry, artillery and supply requirements. To worsen matters the troops lacked nearly everything from crossbelts to sabers, cooking utensils, water bottles, shoes, shirts, often muskets and bayonets. Quartermasters were short of wagons, cannon needed carriages and caissons.

Nor was the strategic situation healthy. Although Wellington had been rebuffed by Marmont at Burgos and forced to withdraw to Portugal, King Joseph's lot had not improved. He was at virtual swordpoint with Jourdan and the other marshals and generals, a military anarchy that brought him into catatonic funk deepened by his bankrupt government, constant conflict with his Cádiz officials, his own squabbling court and the emperor's disaster in Russia. In early January 1813, Napoleon ordered him to move his army headquarters to Valladolid, leaving only the extreme tip of his left flank in Madrid, and "to take advantage of

English inaction by pacifying Navarre, Biscay and the province of Santander," orders enlarged at month's end to include the Aragon. He should have no trouble "because the English are currently unable to do anything" – this when reinforcements were almost daily reaching Wellington while the Imperial Guard and other units were departing for France along with Marshal Soult.[12]

Joseph continued to receive less than helpful orders during February and March. In mid March, Catalonian guerrillas made a brief foray into France, a threat countered only with difficulty by local national guardsmen. Meanwhile the guerrilla leader Mina "was ravaging Navarre and Biscay, levying taxes . . . almost master of those two provinces," a situation so serious that General Clausel was ordered to form an expeditionary force 10,000 strong to put matters right.[13]

All of this was costing a great deal of money. In March still another convoy carried 4 million francs to the peninsula. A short time before Napoleon departed for *his* war he turned Spanish affairs over to General Clarke who was to inform the unfortunate Joseph that "he could expect nothing more [from Napoleon] in the current circumstances."[14]

Napoleon's military position in Germany was much more favorable. The rags of Eugène's Grand Army had fallen back from Vilna to Königsberg and finally to Berlin. They were not much to look at, a supposed 24 battalions under Ney's command, but they were slowly being reinforced and were backed by new French armies on the Elbe and the Main. So long as Prussia and Austria held firm in their alliances with France, the front should hold. Kutusov's Russians had also been hurt and needed rest and reinforcements.

Prussia however was an increasingly doubtful ally. Although King Frederick William was ostensibly shocked by General Yorck's defection to the Russians, he could not replace the loss of men, cannon and horses. The confederation states showed no signs of military enthusiasm. Neither were the Poles in Warsaw rushing to the colors, nor was the Bavarian king overly militant. Napoleon had made a peace of sorts with King Jérôme of Westphalia, but in view of his behavior in Russia there was little to be hoped for there.

Austria, in theory the right flank of the new Grand Army, was also proving difficult. Napoleon had written Emperor Francis from Dresden asking him to send a large corps to Galicia and Transylvania: ". . . such are the advantages of our alliance to our peoples that I think that your Majesty will do everything that he promised me . . . to assure the triumph of our common cause and lead us to a satisfactory peace."[15] But that common cause, which meant different things to each of the signatories, was forged before the Russian disaster. Napoleon's costly and humiliating retreat had greatly altered matters. The Vienna court was scarcely upset when Prince Schwarzenberg virtually defected from the alliance by marching his corps in Poland *away* from the enemy. Napoleon had since been alerted by his ambassador in Vienna that the court had entered into negotiations with England.[16]

What were these so-called allies up to? The short answer was the makings of a new coalition against their own ally, France, a coalition sponsored by Russia and financed by England. Russia's bellicosity stemmed in large part from the strident war party in St. Petersburg and particularly from the influence of the czar's civil adviser, Baron Stein, the reformist Prussian chancellor who ran afoul of Napoleon and was dismissed. Forced to take refuge in Austria, in 1812 he moved on to St. Petersburg as the czar's political adviser. Napoleon's retreat from Moscow prompted Stein to argue for the total defeat of France by inducing Prussia and the German states to mobilize and fight a war of liberation. It followed that Kutusov must advance to and beyond the Elbe.

Once the Grand Army had retreated across the Niemen river, Kutusov had halted his advance owing to casualties and a high sickness rate from lack of food and cold weather. His army now numbered only around 40,000 effectives (not counting Platov's Cossacks). Kutusov was old and tired (he would soon die), he had done his duty, Russia was free of enemy, it was time for peace.

Once again he was overruled by the czar. Yorck's treachery and Schwarzenberg's premature retirement from the field seemed to favor Stein's ambitions which melded nicely with Alexander's long-range desire to recover Poland. He accordingly sent Stein to join Yorck in East Prussia and arrange a military alliance. Yorck already was building a new army, its nucleus his veterans from Russia. Napoleon unwittingly had allowed the Prussian king to repair the losses of this contingent by recruitment. But unknown to Napoleon, for some years the Prussian military had been building a secret reserve army by prematurely retiring trained soldiers who were replaced by recruits to be trained and replaced in turn – the famous Krümper system devised by Scharnhorst to provide a ready reserve. Although not entirely successful, it did help build the Prussian army to around 65,000 effectives, not including a large *Landwehr* or militia.[17]

All this was too heady for the Prussian king who now left Berlin to join civil and military reformists at Breslau (today's Wroclaw), where he would shortly conclude a military alliance with Russia. So it was that within two months Prussia slipped from ally to neutral to enemy of France.

Austria's deceit was far more subtle. It was also prompted by hatred of France, evaluation of the situation in Spain and exuberance over Napoleon's disaster in Russia. But it was tempered with an inordinate fear of Russia and Prussia becoming future masters of Poland and Germany. Metternich accordingly played a very careful game, seeming to remain loyal to France while sliding quite gracefully into neutrality and a policy of armed mediation to assure Europe "a lasting peace" by establishing "a balance of power among the chief states" – as Prince Schwarzenberg, now Austrian ambassador to France, explained it in Paris.[18]

Napoleon reacted variously to these developments. His initial trust in the Prussian alliance had taken a knock with the news of

Yorck's treachery and Frederick William's failure to carry out his promises to repair the loss. In late January 1813, Eugène informed the emperor "that General Bülow has only 300 cavalrymen, and that thus Prussia, instead of joining with us to defend itself and repair General Yorck's treason, does nothing. There are 2,000 [Prussian] cavalry shut up in Silesian fortresses, as if they were afraid of us, instead of helping us and protecting their country."[19] In mid February Napoleon learned of a large "unauthorized recruitment" by Prussian officers not trusted by the king.[20]

Despite further rumors of Prussian war preparations and of the presence of Cossacks around Berlin, Napoleon was not unduly alarmed. After Russia and Prussia signed a preliminary treaty in early March he wrote Eugène to "stay in Berlin as long as you can. Make some disciplinary examples. Upon the least provocation by a city or village, burn it, even if it is Berlin which behaves badly."[21] Two days before the two powers signed a definitive treaty he reminded Eugène "that Prussia has only four million people." Discounting garrison requirements its effective army could not number more than 40,000. Both Russian and Prussian troops were suffering from sickness.[22] Apparently the maladies did not extend to the Cossacks who soon pushed Eugène out of Berlin back to the line of the Elbe and seized Hamburg.

Napoleon also treated the proposed Austrian mediation in somewhat cavalier fashion, probably because he trusted neither the Vienna court nor foreign minister Metternich. In early April he sent Count Narbonne to Vienna to ask Emperor Francis for 100,000 troops to fight Russia and Prussia. Prussia once defeated would be partitioned and Austria would regain Silesia (lost to Frederick the Great in 1740–1742).[23]

This proposal crossed with Prince Schwarzenberg's arrival in Paris to deliver Austria's offer of mediation to obtain peace. One reply deserved the other. As shown in the letter quoted at the beginning of this chapter, Napoleon maintained that Russia must take the initiative toward a peace. Metternich on the other hand quickly rejected Napoleon's request for troops, not surprisingly since he already was in secret talks with England, Prussia and

Russia. "If Napoleon will be foolish enough to fight," he wrote the Russian ambassador in Vienna, Count Nesselrode, "let us endeavor not to meet with a reverse, which I feel to be only too possible. One battle lost for Napoleon and all Germany will be under arms."[24] Continuing his deceit, Metternich declared that Austria would undertake *armed* mediation which in the chancellor's lexicon meant that it would withhold its alliance until it felt certain of joining the winning side.

Notes

1 Rose (*Life*), II, 281–2.
2 Corr. XXIV. Nr. 19386, Paris, 18 December 1812.
3 Corr. XXIV. Nr. 19388, Paris, 19 December 1812. See also Lavalette, II, 70–1.
4 Corr. XXIV. Nr. 19408, Paris, 30 December 1812.
5 Corr. XXIV. Nrs. 19422, 19424, Paris, 5 January 1813.
6 Macdonald, 194–7, 200–3; Henry, 301–3.
7 Corr. XXIV. Nr. 19490, Fontainebleau, 23 January 1813.
8 Corr. XXIV. Nr. 19474, Fontainebleau, 22 January 1813.
9 Corr. XXIV. Nrs. 19462, Paris, 18 January 1813; 19510, Fontainebleau, 25 January 1813.
10 Corr. XXIV. Nr. 19511, Fontainebleau, 25 January 1813.
11 Corr. XXIV. Nr. 19608, Paris, 23 February 1813; Corr. XXV. Nr. 19699, Trianon, 12 March 1813.
12 Corr. XXIV. Nrs. 19411, Paris, 3 January 1813; 19526, Paris, 31 January 1813; 19546, Paris, 7 February 1813. See also Miot de Melito, II, 587–90; Roederer (*Journal*), 296.
13 Miot de Melito, II, 589–90.
14 Corr. XXV. Nrs. 19725, Trianon, 16 March 1813; 19895, Mainz, 23 April 1813.
15 Corr. XXIV. Nr. 19385, Dresden, 14 December 1812.
16 Fuller, II, 451.
17 Craig, 49–50.
18 Rose (*Life*), II, 282–3.
19 Corr. XXIV. Nr. 19529, Paris, 3 February 1813.
20 Corr. XXIV. Nr. 19565, Paris, 10 February 1813.

21   Corr. XXV. Nr. 19664, Paris, 5 March 1813.
22   Corr. XXV. Nr. 19717, Trianon, 14 March 1813.
23   Asprey (*Frederick the Great*), 141–262.
24   Rose (*Life*), II, 283.

CHAPTER TWENTY-FIVE

THE MARCH TO THE ELBE – I: THE BATTLES OF LÜTZEN AND BAUTZEN APRIL–JUNE 1813

. . . being resolved to employ all means to restore peace, either general or on the continent, we have proposed a congress, be it at Prague or any other place convenient to the belligerent powers . . . consequently we are resolved to conclude an armistice . . . with the Russian and Prussian armies for the duration of the congress. Wishing to prevent the battle which, by the position that the enemy has taken [at Bautzen] appears imminent, and to mercifully avoid a needless spilling of blood, our intention is that you go to the advance posts and request an audience with Czar Alexander . . . to negotiate, conclude and sign any military agreement designed to suspend hostilities.

Napoleon to General Caulaincourt,
Dresden, 18 May 1813[1]

NAPOLEON ARRIVED IN Mainz in mid April to fight a new war. His original plan had been to cross the lower Elbe, march on Stettin, relieve the besieged fortress of Danzig, occupy Berlin and carry the war into central Prussia. He had been forced to abandon this plan, at least for the time being, by the enemy marching up the right or eastern bank of the Elbe toward Dresden, and by Cossacks crossing to the west bank and moving on Erfurt. Now, with 200,000 troops and over 450 cannon at his disposal, he intended to move on Leipzig, then to Torgau on the Elbe and finally up river to Dresden.

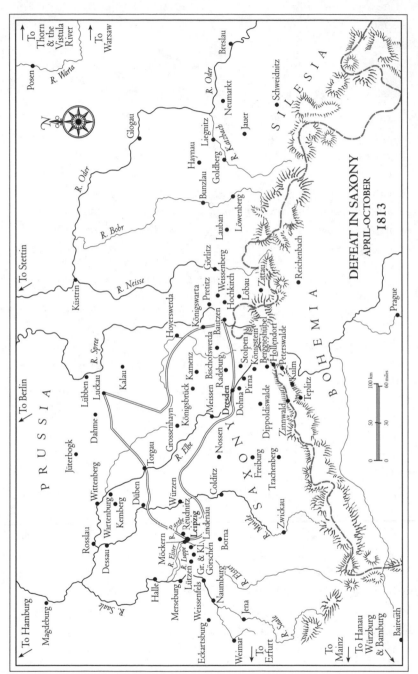

Defeat in Saxony April – October 1813

The major advantage of this revised plan was to secure the defense of the Elbe before the Russian-Prussian army could attack. The major disadvantage was that he knew precious little about the enemy and lacked sufficient cavalry to find out more. "I would be in a position to resolve matters very promptly if I had 15,000 more cavalry," he wrote the king of Württemberg.[2] Although he hoped to receive 30,000 horses in May, that seemed light years away when he was about to approach the enemy. It was Egypt all over again: "Of all the measures that I must recommend to you, the most important," he wrote Marmont, "is deployment into battalion square. Battalion commanders and captains must know how to make this movement in the fastest possible manner; this is the only way to defend yourself from cavalry charges and save the entire regiment."[3] He was also in doubt as to the attitude of his main ally, the king of Bavaria. Bavarian troops at Bamberg and Baireuth, he complained to Berthier in late April, "appear to have orders from their king only to guard their frontiers."[4]

Despite Napoleon's perennial optimism he was too skillful a tactician not to realize that he would be fighting, as in Russia, with one tactical hand – the cavalry – tied behind his back. There was a possibility however that he could avoid a difficult combat. Austria was still neutral as Metternich attempted to sell his policy of armed mediation to the belligerents. Although Napoleon remained suspicious of Austrian intentions he now favored Metternich's tentative. "A proposal has been made by Austria to convene a [peace] congress at Prague which I adhere to wholeheartedly, but it appears that Russia has not yet responded," he informed the Württemberg king.[5]

Czar Alexander had no intention of responding. Russia's new alliance with Prussia called for a combined army hopefully to be joined by Austria and the Rhenish confederation states in waging a "war of German liberation," the first step in crushing tyrant Napoleon. The army to accomplish this latterday crusade was to number an eventual 150,000 Russians and 80,000 Prussians not including Platov's Cossacks already operating in force and most effectively on the left bank of the Elbe, the burgeoning Prussian *Landwehr*, the independent cavalry or *Jäger* companies of well-off volunteers and a horde of Prussian civilian partisans who swore to do as much evil as possible to the French army.

By late April this grandiose effort consisted of a Russian corps marching from Pomerania to besiege the French-held Elbe fortress of Magdeburg and a main army that had marched from Silesia to concentrate at Dresden. The main army consisted of 88,000 Russian-Prussian troops of which 24,000 were cavalry and over 550 cannon, all under the command of Prince Peter of Wittgenstein (who had replaced the recently deceased Kutusov). The allied plan drawn up by General von Scharnhorst (once again chief of staff of the Prussian army) and by General von Gneisenau was relatively simple, indeed little more than a variation of Phull's "entrenched camp" tactic in Russia: let the French advance against one army which would fall back to entice the enemy to pursue, while neighboring divisions fell on its flanks and rear to isolate it for the *coup de grâce*.[6]

That moment seemed to have arrived in late April when advance posts reported French columns moving northeast of Jena on the road to Leipzig. Since this was to be the military event of the century Czar Alexander was on hand along with King Frederick William, each accompanied by large staffs.

With no real knowledge of enemy strength, location or intentions, but with Eugène and Macdonald's assault and seizure of Merseburg on his left and Oudinot coming up on his right, Napoleon marched on Leipzig. His army numbered about 145,000 effectives and nearly 400 guns but only 7,500 cavalry. In Naumburg at the end of April he learned that the previous day General Souham, commanding his advance guard, had defeated a large Russian corps at Weissenfels, news the more encouraging in that Souham had no cavalry but that his infantry squares had held against the Russian horse.[7] Inspired by this auspicious beginning the army continued on toward Leipzig, its right flank guarded by Marshal Ney's corps at Lützen, three divisions holding the town, two divisions the villages of Klein- and Gross-Görschen to the immediate south and southeast. His troops had no more than deployed on the Lützen plain (where 181 years earlier King Gustavus Adolphus had found death) than they were attacked by the allied army which had crossed the Elster river, five immense columns that debouched on the plain to strike Ney's advance posts, a nasty surprise but one fielded by the marshal though with heavy loss.

The fighting soon spread along a five-mile front of intense smoke and dust as Macdonald hurried up on Ney's left, Bertrand on his right, Oudinot circling to attack the enemy's reserve. Napoleon now committed Marshal Mortier's untried Young Guard while General Drouot deployed 80 guns in front of the Old Guard, a sudden killing cannonade followed by a bayonet charge that sent the enemy in a retreat pressed by the French for seven or eight miles, Napoleon and his staff reaching the hill where a few hours earlier Czar Alexander and King Frederick William had stood to witness the demise of their enemy.

Victory carried a sad price tag. Ney's corps suffered the bulk of the casualties, officially listed at 10,000 but probably double that (including those taken prisoner). Marshal Bessières was killed by a cannon-ball at the beginning of the battle; Ney's chief of staff, General Gouré, was also killed; General Girard, though several times wounded, refused to leave the field. The French claimed an enemy loss of 25--30,000 including several thousand prisoners, but this appears to have been highly exaggerated.[8] Two German princes were killed, General Scharnhorst and the young prince royal of Prussia wounded. Less than half of the French forces had taken part in the fight, but to Napoleon's fury "a good third of the howitzer shells failed to explode" due to old and faulty ammunition. On the credit side the troops fought as in the old days, the young conscripts, the old veterans, the sailors now soldiers.

"Nothing could equal the bravery, the determination and the passion that all these young soldiers are showing me; they are full of enthusiasm," Napoleon wrote Prince Cambacérès.[9] He failed to mention his own performance, "probably the day of all his career on which [he] incurred the greatest personal danger on the battlefield," Marbot later wrote. ". . . He exposed himself constantly, leading back to the charge the defeated troops of the IIIrd Corps."[10]

"Soldiers, I am pleased with you! You have fulfilled my hopes!" So began Napoleon's proclamation issued the following day: "In a single day you have overturned all these murderous conspiracies. We shall throw these Tartars back to their dreadful country that they ought not to have left. Let them stay in their frozen deserts, home of slavery, barbarism and corruption where man is reduced to the level of the beast."[11]

He also hurried to inform Emperor Francis of the victory, assuring him of his own good health despite repeated exposure to enemy fire. "I have daily news of the empress with whom I continue to be extremely pleased. She is presently my prime minister and performs the office to my great satisfaction." Details of the victory went to his ally, the king of Württemberg, the same day. It had been attained with only a third of his army, he proudly explained. "That does not surprise me, in view of the poor condition of the Russian infantry of today. The Russian emperor and the Prussian king are heading for Dresden; I am following. This will lead us to the Vistula."[12]

The battlefield had not been cleaned when Napoleon moved to exploit his victory, Ney to march on Leipzig to make "the most impressive entry possible," collect all possible intelligence on enemy movements and wait for reinforcements. Still not certain of his strategy Napoleon moved headquarters to Borna, possibly to take position on the Elbe, possibly to debouch from Wittenberg to march on Berlin – a great deal depended on how quickly Ney's torn corps could be repaired.

Meanwhile it was vital to keep up pressure on the beaten enemy. Eugène who won a sharp skirmish against the Russian rearguard east of Colditz was to press on to Nossen, General Lauriston to march from Würzen to Dresden, "making up to twenty miles a day" – the peasant carrying the order would receive 20 gold napoleons (a small fortune) if he brought a reply within six hours. Once Ney's losses were made up and he was joined by Sebastiani's cavalry he was to march on Torgau to unblock Wittenberg as soon as possible, "for the way things are going make it very possible that I shall march directly on Berlin." Meanwhile Ney was to send bread rations to Dresden and open hospitals to care for the wounded still at Lützen.[13]

Pursuit continued for several days as the Russians retreated eastward through Dresden (destroying the Elbe bridges), the Prussians on Meissen, each army leaving scores of their wounded and dead in the villages. Only six hours after the battle of Lützen (known to the Germans as the battle of Gross-Görschen), Napoleon reached Dresden from where he dispatched a scorching order to the Saxon king (now at Prague) either to fulfill his confederation obligations or to lose his crown.[14]

Not wanting to wait for the arrival of his bridge train Napoleon sent some light infantry to cross the Elbe at a nearby village. Covered by the fire of 60 cannon, the *voltigeurs* beat off an enemy attack while engineers set up a cable ferry, a raft bridge and a boat bridge for troops to fortify a bridgehead on the opposite bank. A supplementary boat bridge would be laid at Dresden and the main bridge repaired to withstand floods and ice floes, protected by a shield of piles upstream (*à la* the Danube four years earlier).

The stage was now set for further pursuit of the enemy: Ney's corps to Wittenberg to be joined by Victor's corps, Sebastiani's cavalry and Reynier's Saxon troops; Macdonald to march on Bischofswerda; Lauriston to deploy between Meissen and Torgau in support of Reynier; Eugène to cross the Elbe followed by Marmont's corps, Latour-Maubourg's cavalry and Oudinot's corps; Bertrand's division to screen the right flank between Dresden and Pirna.[15]

Having learned that the Russians were retreating into Silesia and that the Prussians had retrieved no more than 20,000 men from the battle, Napoleon with most of the army crossed the Elbe in pursuit. Headquarters would remain in Dresden. Apparently informed of Austrian machinations he ordered Viceroy Eugène back to Italy – a strong French-Italian corps on the Adige river would give the Vienna court a cautionary message.[16]

He now made clear his long-range plan in a letter to Marshal Ney who would soon command 100,000 troops at Torgau:

> You realize that with the considerable force under your command it is not a matter of remaining quiet. To relieve the [fortress of] Glogau, occupy Berlin in order to put Marshal Davout in a position to recover Hamburg and march on Pomerania with his five divisions, to seize Breslau, there are the three important goals that I am resolved on and that I would like to accomplish within the month. Because of your position we shall find ourselves concentrated, able to move on the right or left with maximum forces, according to the situation.

On the day Napoleon dictated these words, the king of Saxony arrived in Dresden and, more important, so did the advance guard of 3,000 Saxon cavalry. On the following day the elusive Prussians – Blücher, Yorck, Kleist and the king – reportedly joined the Russians at Bautzen, a rearguard of 30,000 troops rich in artillery, but this information was shortly contradicted by another report that the Prussians had left the town.[17]

Which report was accurate? Marshal Macdonald answered the question when he approached Bautzen on 15 May to find it defended by the main allied army.

Napoleon left Dresden four days later. The enemy's location having been confirmed, it was a matter of deploying for the attack, no easy matter considering the still dispersed corps. That was not the real reason for delay however. Napoleon had sent General Caulaincourt to Czar Alexander's headquarters with the armistice tentative quoted at the beginning of this chapter.

"Get him to talk to you," Caulaincourt was ordered:

In knowing his views you will come to understand each other. My intention in addition is to make him profitable concessions in order to free him from Metternich's intrigues. If I must make sacrifices, I would far prefer for Emperor Alexander and the Prussian king to profit from them rather than Austria which has betrayed the alliance and under the guise of mediator wishes to claim the right to settle everything after taking what suits her.

That aside, if Alexander were to lose the murderous battle, he would depart as a defeated enemy; if on the other hand he obtained "good conditions for his ally the Prussian king without Austria's intervention, [he] would prove to Europe that the peace is due to his efforts, to the success of his arms. In this way the prince will emerge from the struggle in an honorable way and will nobly make amends for the setback of Lützen."[18]

To a letter from Emperor Francis proposing a peace congress of the concerned powers, Napoleon replied: "I desire peace more than anyone . . . As soon as I learn that England, Russia, Prussia and the allies have accepted this proposal, I shall hurriedly send a plenipotentiary to the congress, and shall urge my allies to do the same. I would not even object to admitting representatives of the Spanish insurgents to the congress so that they can present their interests."[19]

If Napoleon opened the door if not to peace at least to an armistice, Alexander slammed it shut by refusing to receive Caulaincourt. Napoleon responded to this affront by issuing detailed orders for Dresden's defense before departing to fight the battle of Bautzen-Hochkirch.

*

The time necessary to deploy the French army had been well used by the Prussians (reinforced by von Kleist's corps) and the Russians (reinforced by Barclay de Tolly's force), a total of over 150,000 troops. The enemy's left rested on wooded hills rising from the Spree river 2–3 miles upstream from the entrenched center at Bautzen, the right on some wooded hills bordering the river. This first position was backed by a second line some 2–3 miles to the rear not far from Hochkirch. The center was formed by three villages heavily entrenched in marshy terrain, altogether a front of 3–4 miles.

Napoleon had deployed his corps in such a masterly fashion that the enemy could only guess at his total strength and intentions. Oudinot's corps held the right, Macdonald (under Soult's command) the center across the Dresden-Bautzen road, Marmont on the left and beyond him Bertrand. Ney's formidable force meanwhile had reached Hoyerswerda. Although the enemy knew of the French presence there, its strength was believed to be no more than 20,000, a threat that Yorck would contain with 30,000 men holding the left bank of the Spree.

The first clash ended in Prussia's favor with the collapse of an Italian division at Königswarta, owing to Bertrand's dalliance, but now Lauriston's corps suddenly appeared and within a few hours forced Yorck back to the other side of the river. Behind Lauriston came Ney's corps followed by Reynier's division, a force ordered to outflank the enemy's right.

The battle proper opened early on 20 May when Oudinot's people crossed the river to attack the enemy left deployed in the hills. Simultaneously Macdonald crossed on a stone bridge a mile or so above Bautzen, then Marmont's men bridged the river while Ney's army began to cross to strike the enemy's right. After considerable fierce fighting Bautzen was taken, and by seven in the evening the enemy was withdrawing to its second line of defense.

Battle was reopened early the next morning by Oudinot and Macdonald attempting to pin down the enemy's reinforced left as prelude to Soult and Marmont's main attack against the center.

Ney's force now on the east bank of the Spree seized Pretitz village to open the way to enemy headquarters. Heavy fighting continued along the entire line until mid afternoon when the hard-pressed defenders, seeing their right turned, beat the retreat to leave a field covered with dead and wounded, the survivors streaming into Hochkirch and Weissenberg.

Early the next morning Napoleon released the advance guard of his precious cavalry, 1,500 Polish lancers and Guard *chasseurs* who soon caught up the enemy. Surprised to see *any* French cavalry the enemy attacked only to be confronted with Latour-Maubourg's main force of several thousand horse which soon cleared the field. General Reynier's Saxons continued the pursuit, stopping that night only a mile or two from Görlitz.[20]

Bautzen was a very important victory, but another expensive one. Official French losses were put at 11–12,000 dead and wounded but undoubtedly were far greater. Napoleon also sustained a severe personal loss. The previous evening Marshal Duroc, a dear friend and confidant, was standing on a small hill speaking with Marshal Mortier and General Kirgener when a cannon-ball shattered a nearby tree and caromed off to graze Mortier, kill Kirgener and rip open Duroc's stomach. A stunned Napoleon later sat by the poor man's bed, holding his hand, until emotion forced him to spend an isolated night in his own tent. The marshal died soon after. "This is the only time in twenty years that he has not anticipated my desire," Napoleon wrote sadly to a friend.[21]

By evening of 23 May, General Reynier's division had crossed the Neisse river into Silesia. Napoleon's headquarters were in Görlitz on the Neisse, his army drawn up north and south enjoying a brief rest before continuing the pursuit into Silesia.

Thus the battle of Bautzen. Whatever its cost it was a victory that no doubt would have won the envy of Frederick the Great who 55 years earlier had ingloriously lost the battle of Hochkirch just a few miles down the road.[22]

*

There remained von Bülow's Prussian corps reportedly some-where between Luckau and Berlin. Corpses still covered Bautzen fields when Napoleon moved imperial headquarters to Bunzlau and turned his army toward Liegnitz and Glogau. "We are finally right in the middle of Silesia," he wrote Prince Cambacérès, "we are in hot pursuit of the enemy."[23] But now Czar Alexander, per-haps regretting his earlier intransigence, showed himself amenable to an armistice. As worked out in early June this called for a cease-fire until 20 July and a peace congress to open on 10 June in Prague.

Notes

1   Corr. XXV. Nr. 20031, Dresden, 18 May 1813. See also Caulaincourt (*Mémoires*), I, 132.
2   Corr. XXV. Nr. 19902, Mainz, 24 April 1813.
3   Corr. XXV. Nr. 19868, Mainz, 17 April 1813.
4   Corr. XXV. Nr. 19900, Mainz, 24 April 1813.
5   Corr. XXV. Nr. 19902, Mainz, 24 April 1813.
6   Rose (*Life*), II, 271–8; Görlitz, 38–40; Craig, 60–3.
7   Corr. XXV. Nr. 19929, Naumburg, 30 April 1813.
8   Fuller, II, 461.
9   Corr. XXV. Nr. 19962, Pegau, 4 May 1813.
10 Fuller, II, 460–1.
11 Corr. XXV. Nr. 19952, Lützen, 3 May 1813.
12 Corr. XXV. Nrs. 19963, 19964, Pegau, 4 May 1813.
13 Corr. XXV. Nrs. 19970, Colditz, 5 May 1813; 19972, Colditz, 6 May 1813.
14 Corr. XXV. Nr. 19984, Dresden, 8 May 1813.
15 Corr. XXV. Nrs. 19987, Dresden, 9 May 1813; 19989, Dresden, 10 May 1813.
16 Corr. XXV. Nr. 19998, Dresden, 12 May 1813. See also Gum, 155–8.
17 Corr. XXV. Nrs. 20006, 20007, 20008, 20009, Dresden, 14 May 1813.
18 Corr. XXV. Nr. 20017, Dresden, 17 May 1813.

19 Corr. XXV. Nr. 20019, Dresden, 17 May 1813.
20 Corr. XXV. Nr. 20042, Görlitz, 24 May 1813. See also Rose (*Life*), II, 291–5; Wartenburg, II, 258–62; Chandler (*Napoleon*), 890–8.
21 Corr. XXV. Nr. 20096, Haynau, 7 June 1813.
22 Asprey (*Frederick the Great*), 500–6.
23 Corr. XXV. Nr. 20051, Bunzlau, 26 May 1813.

CHAPTER TWENTY-SIX

THE MARCH TO THE ELBE – II: MAY–AUGUST 1813

I want peace which is of more concern to me than to anyone else . . . but I shall not make either a dishonorable peace or one that would bring an even more violent war within six months.

Napoleon to General Savary, Dresden, 13 June 1813[1]

CONSIDERABLE CONTROVERSY STILL surrounds the armistice signed by France, Prussia and Russia on 4 June, to remain in force for forty days (at Napoleon's insistence) – that is until 20 July while diplomats attempted to work out suitable peace terms at the congress of Prague. We don't want to get too involved with the sordid events that prefaced its demise, but since Napoleon has too often been named villain of the peace we feel obliged to mention some pertinent and often overlooked facts behind the tragedy.

Why did the emperor agree to an armistice after he had won two important battles and had the enemy on the run? Scores of his detractors, following Baron Jomini's malicious lead, have gleefully pointed out that, such was the deplorable state of the allied forces, had he continued his pursuit, had he carried on over hill, dale, river and ditch to outflank the enemy right at Schweidnitz he would have won his "decisive victory" to finish the war.

Whew!

Few would doubt that the allies had not taken kindly to defeat. During the battle the Russian czar had quarreled so violently with his army commander that Wittgenstein was relieved in favor of General Barclay, a man who preferred running to fighting and who, after the battle, insisted that the Russians retire into Poland to lick their wounds. This was strongly opposed by both Prussian generals and the czar. Another major quarrel was averted only by the armistice and allied withdrawal to Schweidnitz.

The allies had indeed suffered heavy casualties but the reverse side of this coin was that ample reinforcements would soon fill the gaps. Their armies moreover were far from being beaten rabble. Defeat had resulted in retreat, not rout. Despite Napoleon's vivid claims broadcast by an army bulletin, very few prisoners were taken, hardly any cannon, few if any ammunition caissons or supply wagons. The allied army was temporarily down – but not for long.

And the French army? Notwithstanding inspired and incredibly brave battle performances the cost in men, horses, weapons, ammunition and matériel had been heavy. Time was necessary to repair the damage and rest the troops. Above all Napoleon desperately needed more horses. He dared not risk what cavalry he had in standard tactics, which caused him to forfeit vital shock value during the fighting and normal exploitation of his victories during pursuit. He already had paid dearly for lack of long-range reconnaissance patrols, as witness Blücher's surprise attack at Lützen, Macdonald's sudden discovery of the allied army at Bautzen and more recently the success of an enemy ambush at Haynau. His base area was only relatively secure. Oudinot's march on Berlin had been defeated by a Prussian corps. Attenuated French supply lines were already threatened by Cossack and partisan attacks owing to lack of cavalry escort, his artillery had lost a great deal of mobility as had supply wagons at a time when he was very short of food and arms.[2]

So far he had won two battles but that did not mean he could win a third even against a disabled enemy. Without the tactical impetus provided by trained cavalry and fast-moving artillery Napoleon was unlikely ever to find that elusive "decisive battle." Even supposing his army was combat-ready, which it was not, an end-play around the enemy's right at Schweidnitz would have been not only a formidable but a very dangerous undertaking. Even a partial defeat would have placed him in great embarrassment in view of the distance from his Dresden base and the difficulty in bringing up supplies. Rumor also had it (accurately) that Prince Schwarzenberg was building a strong army at Prague. A serious defeat might well have tempted Austria to complete its treachery by Schwarzenberg marching on Leipzig to cut French lines of communication before striking from the rear.

On balance, then, each side needed to recover its strength before undertaking further military adventures. While it is probably true that both sides regarded the armistice as respite from war rather than as prelude to peace, it is also true that Napoleon alone did not slam shut the door to peace as has been so vigorously claimed by critics for nearly two centuries.

As we have seen, he welcomed the advent of a peace congress under Austrian auspices. Although his qualified trust in Austrian intentions may or may not have been genuine, he seemed to think that Emperor Francis would never turn on his own daughter and grandson. It was not like Napoleon however to let sentiment interfere with logic, which is why he had sent Eugène back to Italy to form a corps of observation on the Adige river. Emperor Francis already had turned *away* from his alliance with France – whom would he turn to next? But that was almost irrelevant because Napoleon was not dealing so much with the Austrian emperor as with a very shrewd, cunning, unscrupulous and altogether nasty piece of work named Klemens von Metternich.

Armed mediation was Metternich's ploy, with a very singular definition still to be revealed to the French emperor. But that emperor had evidently obtained proof of his duplicity for on 2 June he wrote General Clarke in Paris that he accepted the armistice for two reasons:

> First, because of my want of cavalry, which prevented me
> dealing great blows, and second, because of the assumption
> of a hostile attitude on the part of Austria . . . If I can, I
> shall wait for September to deal great blows. I wish then to
> be in a position to crush my enemies, though it is possible

that, when Austria sees me about to do so, she may make use of her pathetic and sentimental style, in order to recognize the chimerical and ridiculous nature of her pretensions.[3]

If Austria chose to play a double game he would answer in kind: "We must gain time," he cautioned his foreign affairs minister, Maret, on the same day, "and to gain time without displeasing Austria we must use the same language we have used for the last six months – that we can do everything if Austria is our ally . . . Work on this, beat about the bush, and gain time . . . You can embroider on this canvas for the next two months."[4]

This then was the situation when Napoleon took up temporary quarters at Haynau in early June. Here couriers hourly arrived and hourly departed for Paris carrying imperial decrees that ranged from matters of state to those of imperial dignity. Empress Marie Louise had received Prince Cambacérès in her bedroom: "My wish is that under no circumstances and under no pretext will you receive anyone while in bed. This is acceptable only after the age of thirty." Prince Cambacérès was to have a *Te Deum* sung only on the Sunday after news of a victory: "It would be ridiculous to sing a *Te Deum* for a victory when meanwhile one would have learned of a defeat."[5]

The emperor was still in Haynau when Metternich revealed his definition of armed mediation in the form of Austria's proposed bases of negotiation at the forthcoming peace congress: the grand duchy of Warsaw to be dissolved, with Russia the new overlord; Prussia to recover its 1806 boundaries including Danzig fortress, the Hanseatic cities to regain independence; and the confederation of the Rhine to be dissolved. So much for allied interests. Austria would regain the Illyrian provinces including Dalmatia; parts of Salzburg; the Tyrol, and the Venetian provinces.

Napoleon was understandably furious – if this was the result of his *winning* two important battles, what would have been the result had he lost them? "Everything makes me think that Austria holds some pretensions incompatible with the honor of France . . . and that she would like to profit from [present] circumstances to recover her losses in recent wars," he wrote Clarke from Dresden. ". . . It appears that in consequence she had deployed 60–80,000 soldiers at Prague." As one result he was forming a large corps at Würzburg under Marshal Augereau's command.[6]

Imperial headquarters were now in the spacious if uncomfortable Marcolini palace in Dresden where they would remain until the end of July. For the next few weeks the emperor's routine would be similar to that at Schönbrunn palace four years earlier. He reviewed troops in the morning, shut himself in his *cabinet* for hours at a time to deal with military and state affairs, relaxed in the evening by writing frequent repetitious and very tiresome notes to Marie Louise (who replied in kind), or by reading or watching a tragedy played by Talma and a troupe of actors imported from the *Théâtre Français*. Shortly after their arrival, Napoleon's former mistress, Madame George, turned up on her way home from St. Petersburg where, a tremendous success on the stage and in the boudoir, she had remained for five years. Now 26 years old, veteran of a series of lovers including a Polish prince (said to have paid her 5,000 francs a night), two Russian counts, Talleyrand, Metternich, probably Czar Alexander, and others, she was as lovely as ever. Napoleon greeted her warmly and received her on several occasions, but apparently the fire was out. She found him "very fat, complacent and self-assured" but serious and verbose.[7]

Napoleon had every reason to be serious and he always talked too much, even though he had a lot to say. He was under very heavy pressure. His priority need was for food, weapons and horses, and the quantities required were enormous. Marshal Davout who had recaptured Hamburg was to send him 1,100 tons of rice by land and water (the only way to prevent dysentery in the army); another 5,500 tons of rice and rye were to go to the Magdeburg depots. Erfurt was to ship 2,200 tons of flour in daily lots of 55 tons. He also needed thousands of muskets and bayonets. "The instant that hostilities recommence, I shall have 30,000 men without muskets."[8] His quartermaster was to distribute 1,000

Madame George

hand-grinding mills to the battalions, one mill being able to grind enough corn to make 200 rations of bread per day. Engineers were to reconnoitre roads from Bautzen to Königstein, Pirna and Dresden, the Elbe river from Dresden to the Bohemian frontier and that frontier to Baireuth. Ten thousand horses were to come from Denmark. Admiral Decrès in Paris was to prepare a new expedition of 20 frigates to sail at random "and harm the enemy as much as possible." The Americans wanted help in their war with England. Decrès was either to sell them six warships or send the ships to American ports if circumstances permitted.[9] Napoleon was displeased with the state of Dresden hospitals – corrective measures must be taken immediately. He was also concerned with the number of conscript soldiers wounded in the fingers and hand – were these self-inflicted wounds? (Investigation determined that they resulted from lack of training in loading and firing the cumbersome *fusil*.)

Meanwhile 10 June had come and gone with no sign of a peace conference. In mid June, Napoleon wrote the king of Württemberg: "The armistice is not necessarily followed by a [peace] congress. I have proposed it, but that is still not clear . . . according to my proposals the envoys of the belligerent powers would be called there."[10] This proposal jibes with an earlier statement to Caulaincourt as to why Napoleon insisted on a 40-day armistice: "If we did not intend to treat with a view to peace, we should not be so stupid as to treat for an armistice at the present time."[11] Taken singly or together these statements clash sharply with later accusations that – at least in mid June – Napoleon was bent on sabotaging the congress. It seems more likely that Metternich's delay in convening the congress, taken with further evidence of his duplicity and rumors of allied machinations, caused Napoleon to abandon any hope for an equitable settlement. Here is what was happening in the allied camp:

While Metternich's envoy at Dresden, Count Bubna, was assuring Napoleon of Austria's desire for a just peace, Count

Stadion, the Austrian envoy at allied headquarters, Reichenbach, was plugging for war and destruction of the French empire, goals heartily encouraged by the English envoy, Lord Cathcart. Although the English government had its hands full with wars in Spain and in the United States, it had not neglected the allies. In March it accepted the Russian-Swedish treaty of 1812 (which promised Norway to Sweden in return for alliance with Russia) and granted Sweden a subsidy of one million pounds (which caused Denmark to ally with France). Bernadotte in turn had landed 24,000 troops at Stralsund in mid May but had not moved rapidly enough to prevent Marshal Davout from seizing Hamburg. Cathcart now contracted to pay Russia over one million pounds annually to keep 160,000 soldiers in the field, Prussia half a million pounds annually to support 80,000 men. A few days later Metternich met with Czar Alexander who was assured that Austria would join the allies if Napoleon refused to accept mediation, or if he accepted it and it failed.[12]

"Metternich arrived at Dresden this afternoon," Napoleon wrote Marie Louise on 25 June. "We shall see what he has to say and what Papa François [the Austrian emperor] wants." Two days later he informed his wife that "I have had a long and wearisome talk with Metternich . . . I hope that peace will be negotiated in a few days time. I want peace but it must be an honorable one."[13] Two accounts of the meeting are extant, one by Napoleon and his secretary, Baron Fain, one by Metternich.

The first account quotes Napoleon as taking Metternich severely to task for playing a double role in favor of the allies. Metternich allegedly responded by offering a renewed alliance with France, but at the cost of most of the French empire, a settlement that in Napoleon's words "would be only a vast capitulation" imposed by Austria "without firing a shot, without even drawing the sword, deluding herself in thinking to force me to subscribe to such conditions . . . Ah! Metternich, how much [gold] has England given you to persuade you to play this role against me?" This tirade, the account continues, brought an embarrassing silence broken by a calmer Napoleon saying that he did not despair of peace "if in the end Austria wishes to consider her true interests." He then insisted that once the congress was convened its proceedings would not be interrupted by the resumption of hostilities "so that this door at least would always remain open to the reconciliation of the nations."[14]

Metternich's account of the audience differed considerably. He described Napoleon in semi-hysterical terms vis-à-vis relations with Austria. When Metternich reminded him that the French army consisted only of boys, the emperor allegedly replied: "You do not know what goes on in the mind of a soldier; a man such as I does not take much heed of the lives of a million men" (a highly suspect statement, but one possibly made in a moment of pique to emphasize his determination). Metternich also claimed that his final words to Napoleon were: "You are lost, Sire; I had the presentiment of it when I came: now, in going, I have the certainty." He further wrote that Berthier, upon escorting him to his carriage, asked if he were satisfied with Napoleon. "Yes, he has explained everything to me: it is all over with the man."[15] Something like this may have been said but it is highly doubtful that Metternich would so address the emperor, nor was it characteristic of Marshal Berthier to ask such a question.

Whatever the accuracy of either version, the audience was obviously not a success. Metternich departed at once for the allied camp at Reichenbach, where on the following day he signed a secret treaty that pledged Austria to join Russia and Prussia if Napoleon did not agree to evacuate all Polish and Prussian fortresses. Austria would be paid a £500,000 subsidy by England should its army join the allies.[16] "Count Metternich has just arrived," Napoleon wrote Prince Eugène two days later. "We shall see if the congress can be convened at Prague, but in all probability there will be war."[17]

A few days after the unfortunate meeting with Napoleon, Metternich reappeared in the Saxon capital with a letter from Emperor Francis. This four-hour audience was much more pacific. Napoleon agreed to Austrian mediation provided that the

Berthier, Louis-Alexandre 1753–1815 Marshal of France

mediator (Metternich) would be impartial and would not conclude a convention with any belligerent party during the
negotiations; also that the mediator "presented himself not as
arbitrator but as conciliator to remove differences and reconcile
the participants."[18] Metternich having agreed to these conditions,
Napoleon accepted his proposal to open the Prague congress on 5
July and, accordingly, to extend the armistice to 10 August. "I
think the peace conference will begin before 5 July, at Prague," he
wrote Marie Louise. "Metternich . . . strikes me as an intriguer
and as directing Papa François [Emperor Francis] very badly. The
man has not enough sense for his position."[19]

Whether Napoleon really wanted peace or whether he needed
more time for military preparations is debatable. A modern military historian holds that Austria wanted the delay in order to

complete its secret mobilization,[20] and this could explain Napoleon's cold, brief and somewhat threatening reply to the letter delivered by Metternich: "I want peace. If the Russians are as moderate as I, it will be made promptly . . . I hope that [you] will not allow [yourself] to become involved in a war that would bring misfortune to [your] country and increase the world's evils."[21]

A few hours after Metternich departed to gain allied approval of the armistice extension, a courier arrived in Dresden with a dispatch from Spain: the duke of Wellington had won a crushing victory over King Joseph and Marshal Jourdan at Vitoria, close to the French border in northern Spain.

Napoleon had made a major error in leaving the defense of Spain in Joseph and Jourdan's hands. As Wellington recovered from his unsuccessful foray into northern Spain and as his strength increased, French strength contracted, in part because of some regiments having been called home.

Wellington now had well over 100,000 troops – British-Portuguese-Spanish – at his disposal. With his advance masked by swarms of guerrillas and his supply assured by British and American ships, he began what would prove to be his final drive across Léon into northern Spain. Joseph with less than 50,000 troops under his direct command, quarreling constantly with his ailing chief of staff, fell back under threat of Wellington's columns pressing his center and flanks. After yielding Burgos fortress to retire behind the Ebro river, he frantically called in Clausel's force from Navarre, Foy's from Biscay. With his right flank and communications with France threatened, he next retired into the trap of Vitoria to set up a dispersed and disorganized defense in the surrounding steep hills, the small town with its narrow dirt streets packed with thousands of wagons, hundreds of guns and caissons, scores of carriages loaded with rich loot, and thousands of dispirited French officers and men.

Wellington did not hesitate. Early on 20 June his divisions, superbly commanded by such as Thomas Picton and Rowland Hill, struck the center, flanks and finally the rear of the fugitive army to win a total victory, guns, caissons, wagons and carriages abandoned as troops fled in all directions. Marshal Jourdan narrowly escaped capture – his baton was taken and sent to the prince regent of England. Joseph had hastily departed in his carriage but was soon forced on horseback, finally arriving in St. Jean de Luz with 20 francs in his purse, before continuing in disgrace to his Mortefontaine estate.

The defense of Spain was now up to General Clausel, who had not reached the defeated army, and to Marshal Suchet still in the Aragon – in all perhaps 150,000 men.

Napoleon reacted to the catastrophic news by attempting to keep it a secret from the allies, and by sending Marshal Soult to take command of the remaining French forces "in lieu of the king," he informed Marie Louise, "who is no soldier and knows nothing about anything." A few days later he instructed his regent wife:

If [Joseph] comes to Mortefontaine, it must be incognito and you must ignore him; I will not have him interfere with the government, or intrigues set up in Paris . . . Peace would be made if Austria were not trying to fish in troubled waters. The [Austrian] emperor is deceived by Metternich who has been bribed by the Russians; he is a man, moreover, who believes that politics consist in telling lies.[22]

After furiously ordering Joseph's arrest (never carried out), Napoleon as usual accommodated himself to the situation, sending numerous directives to Clarke in Paris that he supposed would enable Soult to repair the damage. Not doubting its impact once the enemy learned the news, he doubled efforts to prepare for battle. Fortifications were rushed at Königstein and Dresden, the wounded evacuated. In mid July he traveled to Wittenberg, Magdeburg and Leipzig, reviewing numerous divisions and ordering Magdeburg fortress – "one of the strongest places in the world" – to be turned into a gigantic arsenal equipped to repair muskets and manufacture ammunition.

The peace congress had still not convened, the fault of the allies who, according to Napoleon, had accepted Metternich's proposal only on 11 July, but had yet to sign a formal agreement extending the armistice. Whether or not the congress convened was now irrelevant. The news of the French defeat at Vitoria reached allied commanders on 12 July at the Silesian village of Trachenberg, where they had summoned Prince Bernadotte to explain his seeming reluctance to fight. The czar at once called for a *Te Deum* to be sung, Bernadotte agreed to take more vigorous action and a plan of operations was decided upon once the armistice expired.

The main allied army was to face Napoleon east of Dresden, avoiding prolonged battle, while Bernadotte marched a Russian-Prussian-Swedish force 70,000 strong from the north to fall on Leipzig. The main army meanwhile was to move cautiously, falling back if necessary to let subsidiary units strike enemy flanks and rear area installations, an attrition strategy designed to weaken the enemy until the time came, in the words of Schwarzenberg's chief of staff, Count Radetzky, "to strike the final blow with assurance."[23] Although Emperor Francis had not yet committed Austria to the alliance, the Prussian ambassador reported to Berlin "that Metternich looked on war as quite unavoidable, and on the [peace] congress mainly as a means of convincing Emperor Francis of the impossibility of gaining a lasting peace." A week later Lord Cathcart agreed to pay Austria a £5,000 monthly subsidy to support a rebellion in the Tyrol and northern Italy.[24]

On the same day that Napoleon's fate was sealed by the Trachenberg agreement, the long-delayed peace conference opened at Prague, but with only two diplomats present, the Russian Anstett and the Prussian Humboldt. Although Napoleon's envoy, Caulaincourt, was to have joined Count

Narbonne at Prague on 16 July, Napoleon delayed his departure on grounds that the allied representatives had not yet signed the agreement to extend the armistice.

The peace congress was still inert when Napoleon departed for Mainz in late July to meet with Empress Marie Louise. Only now did he authorize his two envoys to present their *pleins pouvoirs* and take their seats. His instructions were brief: "If they wish to extend the armistice, I am prepared to do so; if they wish to do battle, I am ready."[25]

Considering the situation, Napoleon's letters and orders from Mainz are remarkably calm as apparently was his brief stay, enjoying a reunion with the empress who, following his orders, for some time had been urging her father not to be drawn into allied intrigues. News from Spain was good. Marshal Soult with 100,000 troops and plenty of artillery was marching to the relief of Pamplona – the English were surprised by this rapid reaction and were retreating.[26] News from Prague was discouraging but negotiations were to open on the first day of August. "Will they succeed? – this is a problem," he noted to Admiral Decrès.[27]

Back in Dresden he learned that Metternich was sticking to his demands of early June, what Napoleon regarded as a vast capitulation of empire, undoubtedly prelude to even greater sacrifices that Russia and England would impose. He would not ever consider dissolving the confederation of the Rhine which was under his protection. To walk away from its member states would forever sully French honor by exposing them to a return of all the old evils of feudalism, thus destroying the foundations of Napoleon's nebulous "grand design" for a prosperous Europe – as yet obscure and unformed. Not once but several times in past years he had emphasized that his accomplishments (however striking) were only the beginnings of a unified Europe, presumably under French hegemony, a sentiment remarked by Marshal Duroc's whispered reply on his deathbed to Napoleon's assurance that they would meet again: "Yes, Sire, but this will be in thirty years when you will have triumphed over your enemies and realized all the hopes of our country."[28]

In view of mutual intransigence the present impasse could not be overcome. Actors and actresses were sent home from Dresden. Corps commanders were alerted to expect marching orders. A few innocuous gestures to save the peace were made at Prague but these were show not substance.

"The army celebrated my birthday today," Napoleon wrote Marie Louise from Dresden on 10 August, "I had a very fine parade of 40,000 men . . . This evening I am going to the court banquet, and afterwards to the display of fireworks."[29]

The armistice expired at midnight while the emperor no doubt was watching fireworks. Austria declared war on France the following day. Fighting was to resume on 17 August.

Notes

1   Corr. XXV. Nr. 20119, Dresden, 13 June 1813.
2   Fain (*Mémoires*), I, 421–2; Fuller, II, 464–5. See also Craig ("Coalition Warfare"), 2–4.
3   Wartenburg, II, 268; Rose (*Life*), II, 295.
4   Rose (*Life*), II, 295.
5   Corr. XXV. Nrs. 20093, 20094, Haynau, 7 June 1813.
6   Corr. XXV. Nrs. 20108, 20110, Dresden, 11 June 1813.
7   Saunders, 151–2.
8   Corr. XXV. Nrs. 20139, Dresden, 17 June 1813; 20149, Dresden, 18 June 1813.
9   Corr. XXV. Nr. 20121, Dresden, 13 June 1813.
10 Corr. XXV. Nr. 20123, Dresden, 13 June 1813.
11 Rose (*Life*), II, 295.
12 Rose (*Life*), II, 304–5, 315–18. See also Seton-Watson, 145–6.
13 Napoleon *Letters* (Roncière), 169.
14 Corr. XXV. Nr. 20175, Extract of Baron Fain's *Manuscrit de 1813*.
15 Rose (*Life*), II, 319–20. See also Metternich, II, 462–3.
16 Rose (*Life*), II, 317.
17 Corr. XXV. Nr. 20194, Dresden, 28 June 1813.
18 Corr. XXVI. Nr. 20330, Dresden, 5 August 1813.
19 Napoleon *Letters* (Roncière), 170–1.

20   Chandler (*Napoleon*), 900.

21   Corr. XXV. Nr. 20198, Dresden, 30 June 1813.

22   Napoleon *Letters* (Roncière), 171–4. See also Miot de Melito, 600–17; Roederer (*Journal*), 296–321.

23   Craig ("Coalition Warfare"), 5–6. See also Thiébault, II, 84.

24   Rose (*Life*), II, 321–4, 326.

25   Corr. XXV. Nr. 20317, Mainz, 29 July 1813.

26   Corr. XXV. Nr. 20317, Mainz, 29 July 1813.

27   Corr. XXV. Nrs. 20317, 20318, Mainz, 29 July 1813.

28   Corr. XXV. Nr. 20042, Görlitz, 24 May 1813.

29   Napoleon *Letters* (Roncière), 181.

CHAPTER TWENTY-SEVEN

THE BATTLE OF THE NATIONS: DRESDEN AND LEIPZIG AUGUST–OCTOBER 1813

I hope to make Austria repent of its foolish pretensions and of its infamous betrayal [of the alliance with France].

Napoleon to Prince Cambacérès, Dresden,
9 August 1813[1]

A DAY AFTER Austria declared war on France, Napoleon informed Marshals Ney and Marmont of his *tentative* plans based on a very inadequate knowledge of the enemy.

In the north Oudinot with 110,000 men, Davout from Hamburg with 40,000 and General Girard from Magdeburg with 10,000 were to seize Berlin and Stettin, their combined force sufficient to check if not subdue Bülow and Bernadotte's corps. Napoleon's own command, numbering nearly 300,000 troops, was to take position "between Görlitz and Bautzen to secure my communications with and command of the Elbe, to determine the designs of the Russians and Austrians, and to profit from circumstances." After discussing pros and cons of alternate arrangements, he uncharacteristically wrote: "Let me know what you think of all this . . . It seems to me that the current campaign can not produce a good result unless we first fight a major battle." Because Austria had to field armies against Bavaria and Italy he doubted if their Army of Bohemia could muster more than 100,000 troops; the Prussians and Russians including their corps at Berlin he reckoned to be 200,000 strong.[2]

His orders were reasonable enough, even though he fielded them for comment. But then he wrote Marmont: "I would like to know if there is a good position in front of or behind Bunzlau from where a well-deployed corps of 200,000 men could fight an enemy army that debouched in force from the Bohemian and Saxon frontiers and if there is a good road from Bunzlau to Hoyerswerda."[3] He also ordered his chief engineer to reconnoiter "three good positions where the army could concentrate, one behind Görlitz . . . the second in front of and the third behind Bautzen. The left wing should above all be supported, this army being subject to attack by the Russians and Austrians."[4] This was not the Napoleon of old who never forgot the location of a twig on a former battleground.

The action began prematurely by the Prussians Blücher and Kleist violating the grace period and marching on Liegnitz. Then came news that the French turncoat General Moreau had returned from the United States and was serving as adviser to Czar Alexander so as to be in on the kill. Finally, Marshal Ney's chief of staff, Baron Jomini, filled a briefcase with secret papers including current ciphers and joined the enemy. Jomini, wrote Napoleon, "who has published some books on campaigns, and who the Russians have been after for a long time . . . has yielded to corruption. He is no soldier. He is however a writer who has grasped some sound notions of war. He is Swiss." (Jomini was to be judged, condemned and executed *in absentia*.)[5]

Napoleon moved his "small" headquarters to Bautzen on 14 August. Two days later he confidently wrote Maret in Dresden: "Things look quite favorable. The enemy maneuvers as if he believed that I had evacuated the right bank of the Elbe."[6] He also wondered if Löwenberg, where Macdonald's corps was deployed, was not a better place to meet the enemy than Bunzlau where he had deployed Marshal Ney with 130,000 men.[7]

Before this was resolved, a spy assured him that the Russians minus one corps had departed for Bohemia. This caused him to move another large corps to the Eckartsberg behind Zittau. "Once I am assured that Blücher with Yorck, Kleist and Sacken (the

Army of Silesia), with a force of less than 50,000 men, moves on Bunzlau, and that Wittgenstein and Barclay de Tolly's [two Russian corps] are in Bohemia in order to march on Zwickau or Dresden, I shall march in force to wipe out Blücher," he wrote Macdonald. ". . . Moreover, I hold high hopes from all this. It seems to me that the enemies are engaged in some strong actions, which should in a few weeks give us some great results. Let me know what you think of all these things."[8]

Instead of taking up a solid defensive position, as he had outlined to Ney and Marmont a few days earlier, Napoleon was steadily advancing east and south in pursuit of his great battle. This would have been more logical had his intelligence been accurate. Far from that it was almost non-existent, he had no real idea of enemy movements and intentions, nor of aggregate enemy strength. In keeping with its basic strategy the enemy was tiring him out by various shunts and shuffles. Imperial headquarters next moved to Reichenbach, then Görlitz, Zittau and back to Görlitz, all within six days, his idea now being to build a "grand chain" around Dresden and the Elbe. "What matters to me," he wrote Gouvion St. Cyr at Pirna, "is that we are not cut from Dresden and the Elbe; it is not important if we are cut from France."[9] Although enemy movements were still not clear, "what is clear is that 400,000 soldiers based on a complex of strong fortresses, on a river such as the Elbe, and able to debouch equally from Dresden, Torgau, Wittenberg and Magdeburg, cannot be turned."[10]

As few enemy showed themselves, his confidence continued to grow to what might charitably be called ridiculous proportions. On 20 August he moved his headquarters to Lauban prior to joining Macdonald and Lauriston in order to lead an attack on the enemy at Löwenberg. "I have ordered what was necessary," he wrote Berthier. "It is doubtful that the enemy would dare to undertake a struggle that would become fatal to him. If this happens however I shall return rapidly, attack him in turn, move into Bohemia and march on Prague."[11] So much for his initial plan of waiting to be attacked, so much for his cardinal rule of never dispersing his corps to a dangerous degree in the presence of an enemy.

His pulse jumping at the thought of battle – "The intention of the emperor is to fight to extinction," he wrote Berthier – he moved on to Lauban and Löwenberg, spewing out attack orders on the way: "The main business of the moment," he informed Ney and Marmont at Bunzlau, "is to join together and march on the enemy." His grand attack, scheduled for 22 August, was pre-empted the previous day by Blücher's Army of Silesia which attacked Bunzlau and Goldberg. Napoleon rushed to the action, directed a successful counter-attack and sent troops in pursuit as far as Jauer. He then left Macdonald with 120,000 men – what he henceforth called *his* Army of Silesia – to hold this flank and retired the rest of the army on Görlitz, the first step in a general withdrawal to Dresden.[12]

Napoleon believed that his successful counter-attack was due to the "extremely poor" performance of enemy infantry and to their surprise in meeting the French who were supposed to be retiring behind the Elbe. Perhaps so, but this was also in keeping with the allied plan because, as Blücher was withdrawing his troops, the Austrians and Russians were marching into Saxony from Bohemia. "If the enemy has actually ordered a major move on Dresden," Napoleon wrote to St. Cyr, "I regard it as an extremely fortunate event that in a few days will enable me to fight a great battle which will decide a great many things."[13]

Just where this battle was to take place was problematical, but at Stolpen, where he was concentrating the army, he learned of General Lauriston's victory over Blücher between Goldberg and Jauer, the enemy allegedly suffering 7,000 dead at a cost of 800 French.[14] Napoleon now intended to march on Königstein, seize Pirna and, his right flank secure, march into Bohemia, even to Prague. This offensive maneuver was interrupted by an enemy advance which resulted in a two-day battle, another hard-fought and costly victory for the French. "I am so tired and so busy," Napoleon wrote Cambacérès late on 27 August, "that I can't write at length . . . Things are going very well here."[15]

The emperor now sent Murat westward to strike enemy flanks and rear. General Vandamme next defeated a Russian corps near Hollendorf and pursued it to Teplitz in Bohemia. Marmont meanwhile marched on Dippoldiswalde to eliminate any threat from there, and to join with Murat and St. Cyr to attack the enemy as he tried to negotiate the difficult pass of Zinnwald back into Bohemia. To top this good fortune came news of General Moreau's death from a cannon-ball, the unfortunate end of an unfortunate traitor.

So much for the credit side of the ledger. Came now the red ink. Oudinot had failed to occupy Berlin, the result of General Reynier's Saxons having been defeated by Bülow's Prussians, a shock that caused Oudinot to abandon his march and fall back on Wittenberg. "It is truly difficult to find anyone more scatter-brained than Oudinot," Napoleon sourly noted to Berthier in turning the luckless marshal's command over to Ney.[16]

Before this setback had played out, Vandamme in hot pursuit of Russians and Prussians retreating into Bohemia had marched into a clever trap set by the Russian General Ostermann and closed by Kleist's Prussians suddenly appearing *behind* the pursuers to capture Vandamme and some 13,000 of his men, the other 19,000 eventually struggling back to friendly lines. Macdonald in turn chose to ignore orders by going after Blücher's army, an effort that resulted in the battle of Katzbach which cost Macdonald 15,000 men taken prisoner and 100 cannon in addition to heavy casualties.[17]

There were other problems. Too many French commanders were tiring their troops and wasting ammunition in tilting at windmills: "They see large enemy forces when I am not pres ent."[18] The bogey here stemmed mainly from countless Cossack, *Landwehr* and partisan actions which continued to increase and to cause troops to be diverted to garrison duties at Meissen and other towns while flying columns scoured partisan areas in an attempt to eliminate them. The perennial problem of adequate supplies would not disappear despite Napoleon's frequent adjurations to commanders to use local resources in baking their own bread and in supplying vegetables and meat to the men. Clothing and shoes were running dangerously low, there were not enough ambulances to remove the wounded from the last battlefield.[19]

In Napoleon's mind the general picture was nevertheless more favorable than not, owing both to his continued belief in the superiority of French arms and to his operating on interior lines which offered him considerable freedom of movement. At month's end he drew up a lengthy memorandum as to the better of two offensive actions. Should he march on Prague or should he aim for Berlin, seize Stettin and relieve the besieged fortress of Küstrin (Oudinot's original mission)?

After considerable thought he opted for Berlin. He would move imperial headquarters to Magdeburg to oversee the operation designed to draw the Russians north. There he would fight and defeat them, then rush back to Dresden to fall on the Austrians and end the campaign and the war by "a great battle."

We need offer no further details because this ambitious plan already had been preempted by the recent tactical setbacks that were prelude to his ultimate disaster. Hurrying to Bautzen to repair Macdonald's losses he pushed the enemy back across the Neisse, modestly reporting to Maret that "as soon as the enemy learned that I was present he raced off in all directions."[20]

Ney simultaneously had only begun the proposed march on Berlin when he suffered a severe defeat between Jüterbogk and Dahme and fell back on Torgau. Napoleon was now fighting at Dohna west of Pirna in challenging still another advance, this by the Russians whom he forced back into Bohemia, his troops occupying the Peterswalde and Zinnwald passes. On 11 September he informed Maret that "we are masters . . . of all the Bohemian passes."[21]

Meanwhile however Macdonald had retreated unnecessarily on Bautzen which exposed his two principal commanders, Lauriston and Poniatowski, to attacks. Communications with Leipzig had also been cut and those with Torgau threatened by omnipresent Cossacks. The Dresden garrison had nearly run out of food.

At this critical juncture a large enemy corps commanded by the turncoat prince of Württemberg debouched from Teplitz to push Mouton out of Berggieshübel, an action which brought Napoleon running to the scene to again force the intruder back into Bohemia, a several day action fought in miserable weather. Macdonald however had been pushed out of Bautzen and was being threatened by a large corps closing on Radeburg northeast of Dresden. Heavy rains continued, morale was low, the troops were tired and hungry and poor old Berthier, worked nearly to death, fell ill.

As September drew to a close Napoleon's situation was complex and dangerous. The enemy though beaten time and again in local battles refused to stand, and if one or two corps fell back into Silesia or Bohemia one or two fresh corps suddenly appeared to start the whole dreary attrition process all over. This strategy had given Bülow and Bernadotte's corps time to come from the north to close on the Rosslau area uncomfortably close to Leipzig and Dresden while bridging the Elbe when and where possible. Blücher with 70,000 troops was marching on Wartenburg north of Leipzig via Königsbrück and Grossenhayn. Other Russian corps, sometimes singly, sometimes joined with Prussian and Austrian corps in Bohemia, continued to threaten Dresden from the east, southeast and south in carrying the encirclement westward to be joined by the Austrian Army of Bohemia whose forces reached southwest of Leipzig. Russian Cossacks and bands of Prussian partisans continued to roam the countryside, spreading disruptive rumors while falling on weak French detachments and garrisons when possible.

Although healthy reinforcements were steadily reaching the enemy, the French were not so fortunate. Napoleon's only immediate assets were Augereau's corps coming from Würzburg and the Bavarian army, vapid at best, loitering on Bavarian frontiers but at least holding one Austrian army in check. Eugène's army in northern Italy was facing another Austrian army and would go nowhere. Davout's divisions were stumbling around the countryside south of Hamburg and would soon retire inside its walls.

Girard's corps having been isolated by Oudinot's retreat and Ney's defeat had returned to the security of Magdeburg. Garrisons in Danzig, Stettin and Küstrin fortresses might as well have been on the moon. The combat troops were generally exhausted, hungry, their uniforms in tatters, many lacking shoes. "The army is not being fed," Napoleon complained to his chief quartermaster on 23 September. "It would be an illusion to think otherwise." The daily ration had dropped to 8 ounces of bread, 3 ounces of rice and 8 ounces of meat. At this rate "the soldier would perish."[22] Persistent rainy, cold weather hindered mobility already limited by lack of horsepower. Units were running low on ammunition which could only be replaced from depots at Erfurt and Magdeburg.

Napoleon must have been on the verge of exhaustion. For weeks he had been almost constantly on the move, fighting a dozen battles often in miserable weather, all in futile pursuit of that nebulous "decisive battle." "It appears that the enemy has definitely given up his plan of entering Dresden or any other offensive operation," he despondently wrote Berthier and Gouvion St. Cyr at the end of September, "being content to wage skirmish warfare."[23]

Why then did he persist in his discredited strategy? The short answer is because he did not believe that it *was* discredited. We are dealing here with disparate and complex factors working on a strange amalgam of past and present caught in the fearful coils of the arrogance of ignorance, trapped in his belief of enemy impotence and cowardice, failing to recognize that his once omnipotent and beautiful army had weakened and withered into halting old age, that the political elixir which he had brewed to save Europe from itself had turned poisonously bitter and impotent. Professionally he was failing to respect the interplay of quantitative and qualitative factors that govern the battlefield, the basis of the formula which when applied to his immense strategic and tactical skills explained his former military mastery. That was the real key to his disjointed actions and spurious decisions and it is at once terribly sad, yet in another sense strangely noble – a defeated man refusing to accept defeat.

No recognition of this yet shows in the scores of orders and directives hurled to his minions, only because he was not quite defeated. If the enemy seized a bridge, French regiments recaptured it. Blücher's army moved on Wittenberg, Macdonald went after it. If enemy forces arrived north and south of Leipzig, Ney and Marmont would secure the Elbe and Mulde bridges, Augereau soon would garrison the city, Murat would deploy Victor, Poniatowski and Lauriston's corps to guard southern and southeastern approaches.

Napoleon moved headquarters to Würzen on 8 October. "Nothing new," he reported to Maret. "All goes well here."[24] Glorious memories were blinding him to present facts: he would march most of the army to relieve the siege of Wittenberg, then move west to Rosslau, seize Bülow's immense baggage depots, recross the Elbe and bring the enemy to battle. "Either I shall give battle to the enemy," he wrote Count Narbonne, the governor of Leipzig, on 9 October, "and with the aid of God hope to enjoy a complete success, or I shall oblige the enemy to raise the siege of Wittenberg." And to Cambacérès on the same day: "[Raising the siege of Wittenberg] will possibly occasion a battle for which I hold success as certain, and which would have a great influence on things."[25]

The new operation began well. The Wittenberg garrison was relieved, Blücher's army dispersed and Dessau taken by Ney. In the south Murat defeated Wittgenstein at Borna to send the Russians and Schwarzenberg's Austrians in retreat. Augereau's corps had reached Leipzig, and Gouvion St. Cyr at Dresden had defeated an attack by the Russian Bennigsen. But a strong enemy force marching on Halle *northwest* of Leipzig again changed matters and caused Napoleon, now at Düben, to call in Ney and his other corps from the north. "The decisive moment appears to have arrived," he wrote Marmont on 12 October.[26]

He was correct. A new tidal wave was racing across his sea of troubles. His hesitant ally, the king of Bavaria, had gone over to the allies. Suddenly an entire Austrian army was free to join Schwarzenberg's already imposing force, suddenly the Bavarian army was at the disposal of the allies, suddenly the quantitative factor swept all before it.[27] The enemy must be attacked before he could be reinforced. Increasingly intense, somewhat frantic and at times confusing orders called in all corps to join an attack scheduled initially for 15 October, but then delayed a day.

Napoleon was too late. On 14 October he notified Ney and Macdonald that "tomorrow the 15th we shall be attacked by the Army of Bohemia [Schwarzenberg from the south] and by the Army of Silesia [Blücher from the northwest]."[28] Even as he was dictating this message, General Wittgenstein with some 80,000 troops and 80 cannon was moving on Murat's position.

Murat was all fight. Six attacks along the line were repulsed with the help of some "beautiful cavalry charges" and a brilliant performance by Poniatowski who received his marshal's baton on the field of battle. Now came a report of Bernadotte's arrival in Merseburg with 70,000 troops, apparently to be joined by the Army of Bohemia coming from the south. Early on 15 October, Prince Schwarzenberg, commanding the allied armies, announced that "a general and decisive battle" would take place the following day.[29]

Schwarzenberg was good for his word. The allied attack opened at 9 a.m., the evident plan being to outflank the French right which was defended by Murat's force of Lauriston, Poniatowski and Victor's corps. Three enormous columns preceded by 200 cannon struck the French line no fewer than six times during the morning, each attack beaten off with heavy enemy losses. A final Austrian attempt was shattered by Drouot's artillery firing *mitraille* almost point-blank on enemy flanks. Murat's casualties were said to number 2,500, enemy casualties an alleged 25,000 including over 3,000 prisoners.

Elsewhere on this stinking, smoke-covered field Bertrand beat off a cavalry-partisan attack at Lindenau while Marmont, though wounded, threw Yorck's Prussians out of Möckern and managed to re-establish his line by the time darkness ended the action. The day finished with no one the winner. The human cost was heavy, an estimated 25,000 French and 30,000 allied troops.[30] French cannon alone had fired 80,000 rounds.

The following day was quiet. The French were joined by General Reynier's small Saxon corps, but Schwarzenberg was reinforced by Bennigsen's 40,000 Russians coming from Dresden while Bernadotte was at last moving in from Merseburg with some 70,000 men. Upset by reports of heavy enemy reinforcements Napoleon shifted Murat's force into a semi-circle about two miles south and southwest of Leipzig. He also dispatched one of Bertrand's corps to clear the Weissenfels plain of enemy light horse and secure the Saale river crossings to ensure communication with Erfurt.

The enemy struck again on the morning of 18 October, only to be repeatedly repulsed by Lauriston, Poniatowski and Augereau backed by the Old and part of the New Guard – a fearful day's to-and-fro mêlée ended that evening by massive French artillery fire which forced the enemy to withdraw two or three miles from the field. Ney meanwhile fought off Blücher's attacks in the north, a success stained in mid afternoon by most of Reynier's Saxon corps along with the Württemberg cavalry and the Hessians joining the enemy to open the way to Reudnitz, a crisis finally resolved by Nansouty's Guard cavalry and infantry.[31]

Despite a precarious situation Napoleon seemed determined to fight on, that is until that evening when his artillery generals reported that in five days the hungry cannon had eaten more than 220,000 rounds and that no more than 16,000 rounds remained, scarcely enough for two hours of fighting. Ammunition could only be replaced from depots in Erfurt and Magdeburg. Cut from Magdeburg, it was Erfurt or nothing, and speed was vital if the Bavarians were not to get there first.

It was not an easy retreat. A 5-mile-long defile from Leipzig to Lindenau had to be crossed by half a dozen bridges. Nevertheless by early morning of 19 October two-thirds of the army including artillery, supply dumps, baggage, the cavalry and the Guard had crossed the defile. This left Macdonald and Poniatowski's rearguard (along with some 8,000 wounded and sick who could not be moved). Napoleon had rejected the suggestion of lining the town ramparts with troops and cannon and burning the suburbs "of one of the most beautiful cities of Germany" to cover the rear-guard's final exit. Instead the main bridge between Leipzig and Lindenau was mined and a colonel charged to blow it the moment the last soldier crossed.

Sadly the colonel turned the mission over to a corporal and disappeared. Enemy troops had gained the ramparts by mid morning and were firing down on the rearguard. The corporal at the bridge panicked and ordered the engineers to light the fuses. Within minutes over 12,000 soldiers and several hundred wagons found themselves stranded. Thousands tried to swim the Elster. Although it was a short distance the current was strong and the banks steep and slippery. Only a few made it. Marshal Macdonald was one who lived to tell the tale. The brave General Lauriston and Marshal Poniatowski drowned.[32]

Notes

1   Corr. XXVI. Nr. 20343, Dresden, 9 August 1813.
2   Corr. XXVI. Nr. 20360, Dresden, 12 August 1813.
3   Corr. XXVI. Nr. 20361, Dresden, 12 August 1813.
4   Corr. XXVI. Nr. 20366, Dresden, 12 August 1813.
5   Corr. XXVI. Nrs. 20382, Bautzen, 16 August 1813; 20410, Görlitz, 18 August 1813. See also Macdonald, 335; Miot de Melito, III, 261–2, Alger, 142–8; Elting ("Jomini"), 247–51.
6   Corr. XXVI. Nr. 20383, Bautzen, 16 August 1813.
7   Corr. XXVI. Nr. 20389, Bautzen, 16 August 1813.
8   Corr. XXVI. Nr. 20390, Bautzen, 16 August 1813.
9   Corr. XXVI. Nr. 20398, Bautzen, 17 August 1813.
10 Corr. XXVI. Nr. 20398, Bautzen, 17 August 1813.
11 Corr. XXVI. Nr. 20419, Zittau, 20 August 1813.
12 Corr. XXVI. Nrs. 20421, 20425, Görlitz, 20 August 1813; 20445, Görlitz, 23 August 1813. See also Macdonald, 217–19.
13 Corr. XXVI. Nr. 20455, Görlitz, 23 August 1813.
14 Corr. XXVI. Nr. 20468, Stolpen, 25 August 1813.
15 Corr. XXVI. Nr. 20482, Dresden, 27 August 1813.
16 Corr. XXVI. Nr. 20502, Dresden, 2 September 1813.

17   Rose (*Life*), II, 345–50; Wartenburg, II, 293–304; Chandler (*Napoleon*), 904–12. See also Macdonald, 219–22, who fails to mention his own major tactical errors and also minimizes his losses; Marbot, III, 276–80.

18   Corr. XXVI. Nr. 20437, Löwenberg, 22 August 1813.

19   Corr. XXVI. Nrs. 20451, Görlitz, 24 August 1813; 20481, Dresden, 27 August 1813; 20493, Dresden, 30 August 1813.

20   Corr. XXVI. Nr. 20521, Bautzen, 6 September 1813.

21   Corr. XXVI. Nr. 20540, Breitenau, 11 September 1813.

22   Corr. XXVI. Nr. 20619, Hartau, 23 September 1813.

23   Corr. XXVI. Nrs. 20618, Hartau, 23 September 1813; 20659, Dresden, 29 September 1813.

24   Corr. XXVI. Nr. 20724, Würzen, 8 October 1813.

25   Corr. XXVI. Nrs. 20733, 20734, Würzen, 9 October 1813.

26   Corr. XXVI. Nr. 20782, Düben, 12 October 1813.

27   Klang, 22–41.

28   Corr. XXVI. Nrs. 20801, 20802, Düben, 14 October 1813.

29   Corr. XXVI. Nrs. 20807, 20815, Leipzig, 16 October 1813.

30   Chandler (*Napoleon*), 932.

31   Macdonald, 228–9. See also Marbot, III, 320.

32   Corr. XXVI. Nr. 20830, Erfurt, 24 October 1813. See also Macdonald, 231–3.

CHAPTER TWENTY-EIGHT

THE STORM BREAKS
OCTOBER–DECEMBER 1813

One year ago all of Europe marched with us. Today all of Europe marches against us.

Napoleon to the senate, Tuileries,
14 November 1813[1]

IF EVER A beaten army was held together by the will of one man it was the French army in the last days of October 1813. Napoleon had lost many thousands of soldiers – the dead rudely interred in Saxon earth or drowned in Saxon waters; the wounded and sick who remained in Dresden, Leipzig and Magdeburg; the garrisons of Stettin, Küstrin, Glogau, Hamburg, Danzig; the thousands of stragglers and deserters worming their way homeward. Thousands of caissons and wagons had been destroyed, food and ammunition often lacking, the marching troops exhausted. Yet Napoleon refused the word defeat in that by escaping *total* defeat he was victorious – and he had a point.

He still had an army, rag-tag yes, but still an army. And he also had France. Perhaps with the glorious year of 1793 in mind he wrote Cambacérès from Gotha on 25 October, "When all Europe is under arms . . . and everyone pushing to take them up, France is lost if it does not do the same."[2] He would soon call on France to furnish the men, arms and money necessary to topple the Fourth Coalition. "It is possible that, when you receive this letter," he wrote General Clarke on 25 October, "I shall be on the Frankfurt plains with 30,000 cavalry, 100,000 infantry and four or five hundred cannon." The general was to send 100,000 artillery

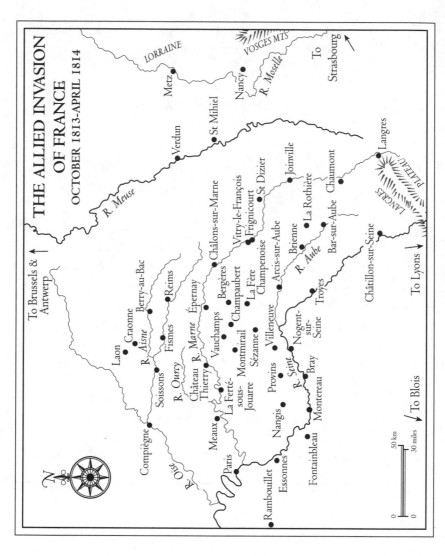

The Allied Invasion of France October 1813 – April 1814

rounds to Mainz and to arm that city along with Wesel, Juliers, Venlo and other towns. For this it was necessary to call up 140,000 conscripts and round up 100,000 evaders. Marshal Kellermann at Mainz was to clear the right bank of the Rhine of all but mobile forces. The old marshal was also to intercept, feed, equip and arm thousands of fugitive soldiers coming from Germany and return them to their units.[3]

Meanwhile the long retreat continued, the men having regained some strength and spirit from Erfurt supply depots and a brief rest at Gotha. Five days later the army came on a strong Austrian-Bavarian force at Hanau deployed to block the French retreat to the Rhine. Napoleon attacked at once, a five-hour action that sent the enemy running after suffering heavy casualties and losing several thousand men taken prisoner plus a large number of cannon and some battle standards. Another three days and the army was at Mainz from where the emperor wrote Prince Cambacérès, "I am trying to rally, rest and reorganize the army from here."[4]

He not only had to bolster army spirits but also the nation's. More than ever he needed that nation behind him. He already had sent a score of enemy standards to General Clarke who was to parade them ostentatiously before presenting them with appropriate fanfare at court – "This is a compliment that I love to offer you," he wrote the empress. "I want you to see this as a token of my great satisfaction for your conduct during the regency that I entrusted to you."[5]

Although his communiqués and army bulletins had informed the public of a severe setback they never once suggested final defeat. "Your fears and terror at Paris make me laugh," he scolded his police minister, General Savary. ". . . Start from the principle that my infantry, artillery and heavy cavalry are so superior that I fear nothing."[6] And to his finance minister, Count Mollien: "I want the ministers to display calm and confidence . . . I shall have no difficulty in putting an end to this coalition as I have to the others."[7]

Napoleon spent nearly a week at Mainz, sending directives hither and yon, setting up Rhenish defenses, getting the torn divisions back to France, sending Eugène in Italy a flow of instructions, trying to cope with reverses in Spain, raising provincial national guard units in France, ordering neglected border fortresses repaired – all intensive, nerve-racking, time-consuming efforts continued from his *cabinet* in St. Cloud soon after his arrival in Paris on 9 November.

Military and home affairs necessarily took priority, and of military affairs unit reparations, supply and deployments. His supply depots were nearly exhausted, yet he had to clothe and arm what in time would amount to another 300,000 replacements. In early November he promised General Clarke two million francs to settle government debts with gunsmiths and a million a month to manufacture 30,000 *fusils* every 30 days and repair 90,000. In mid December he again was complaining of shortages of muskets and uniforms. Guard workshops alone were to tailor 2,000 uniforms a day, unemployed carriage-makers to produce 1,000 new model wagons and several hundred ambulances in a very short time.[8]

Home affairs concentrated on raising conscripts, money and morale. His proposed budget for 1814 ran well over a billion francs, and even with increased revenues he was looking at a deficit of 32 million.[9] If fighting resumed the sum would undoubtedly swell which would mean asking the burdened country to make even greater sacrifices.

Conscription was not living up to expectations. In late December, Napoleon appointed 20 councillors of state, each with an accompanying auditor, to serve as *commissaires extraordinaires*, one to each military department. Similar to the despised *représentants en mission* of "Terror" days (except in political beliefs), they were mostly retired generals with virtually unlimited powers to conscript men, then clothe, equip and arm them; complete and provision fortresses, requisition necessary horses; and raise national guards – tasks which, perhaps lacking in zeal, they seemed for the most part to have failed in carrying out.[10]

Spain was a major and uncomfortable problem. Although General Suchet's corps remained in Catalonia, Wellington's army had crossed the northwestern border and was approaching Bayonne. Napoleon could do little more than hope that Marshal Soult would hold the enemy until he was free to deal with the situation or until peace was somehow made. Meanwhile an army of reserves was to be formed on the French side of the Pyrenees, but that order seems to have been issued more in desperation than anticipation. Soon enough he would have to take the step that he dreaded; he would have to place the idiot Ferdinand on the Spanish throne.

The situation in Italy was slightly happier thanks to Eugène's herculean effort in building a new Italian army. He now commanded a sizeable force on the Adige river and King Joachim of Naples (Marshal Murat) promised to march an army of 30,000 to defend the line of the Pô river. The Bavarian king, Eugène's father-in-law, prompted by Metternich, was trying to buy Eugène's loyalty, but that was not going to work. Eugène was not the brightest person in the world but he was loyal and would remain so. This was not the case with Murat who while professing loyalty to Napoleon had been welcoming Metternich's blandishments (as had Queen Caroline for some time). Suspecting as much, Napoleon ordered Fouché (then at Naples) to persuade Murat to march, to inform Queen Caroline of Napoleon's wishes, "and to do everything possible to prevent the Naples court from being misled by Austria's fallacious promises and by Metternich's oily language."[11]

Holland constituted another major concern, and Napoleon devoted reams of directives and orders to its security. The key here was Antwerp and the Scheldt which he made largely a naval matter though with supporting troops. Vice-Admiral Allemand, the only admiral Napoleon respected, was given command of the Flushing flotilla, Vice-Admiral Missiessy the Antwerp flotilla, altogether 150 ships. General Lebrun commanding ground forces at Antwerp was also to be reinforced – "Antwerp has nothing to be afraid of," Napoleon assured him. ". . . Show yourself cool and energetic."[12]

Would the war continue or would there be peace?

The negotiating waters rising from a slimy bottom composed of ambition, greed, fear, arrogance and deceit, remained deep and dark. From these murky depths generations of historians have pulled factual fish suitable to their particular theses, either ignoring or obscuring similar fish swimming in the opposite and therefore unpalatable direction.

In mid November, Napoleon ordered Marshal Marmont to discuss terms of capitulation of the besieged fortresses, including Dresden, with the enemy, and to request the traditional "honorable surrender" which would allow the troops to march home with arms and equipment. Prior to this move but unknown to Napoleon, Metternich had summoned the French minister at Gotha, Baron St. Aignan, for peace talks at Frankfurt with himself and the British and Russian ambassadors to Austria, Lord Aberdeen and Count Nesselrode (also speaking for Prussia). St. Aignan was politely received and was assured "of the moderation of the allies, especially of England, and of their wish for a lasting peace founded on the principle of the balance of power." Such was allied altruism that France would only have to return to its "natural" frontiers – the Rhine, the Alps and the Pyrenees. Lord Aberdeen assured the French diplomat that England was prepared to relax the maritime code and sacrifice many of its colonial conquests in order to build a durable peace, and Count Nesselrode stressed that Prussia also approved the offer.[13]

This was a curious tentative. The day following the meeting, Metternich wrote General Caulaincourt: "Monsieur Saint-Aignan will speak to you of my conversations. I expect nothing from them, but I shall have done my duty. France will never sign a more fortunate peace than that which the Powers will make today."[14]

A few days after Napoleon's arrival in Paris, St. Aignan verbally reported that "the allies' general and abridged conditions are a peace founded, (1) on the balance of power of Europe; (2) on the recognition of all nations within their natural limits; (3) on the recognition of the independence of all nations without any nation able to claim the right of supremacy or sovereignty, and, in whatever guise, either on land or sea." These bases were apparently confirmed in a following letter from Metternich who allegedly stressed allied demands for a quick acceptance. Following Napoleon's orders, Maret responded favorably on 16 November and suggested that Metternich convene a peace congress at Mannheim. Maret's letter in turn drew a complaint from Metternich that the French had not specifically "accepted the proposed terms as a basis for negotiation."[15]

While this scenario was playing out, Maret had been replaced as foreign minister by Caulaincourt who replied to Metternich's letter on 1 December: "His Majesty adheres to the conditions communicated by Monsieur Saint-Aignan. They will entail great sacrifices on the part of France. His Majesty will make them without regret, providing that similar sacrifices are made by England, in order to thus reach a general peace on land and sea which your Excellence asserts to be the aim not only of the continental powers but also of England."[16]

The operative words of this very important letter are "a general peace on land and sea" agreed to by England. In other words, Napoleon would yield his claim to European hegemony if England yielded its claim to supremacy of the seas – what Napoleon had been fighting for ever since the rupture of the peace of Amiens in 1803.

Caulaincourt's letter reached Metternich on 5 December. The Austrian minister replied only on 10 December, in general favorably but stating that before the congress could open at Mannheim it was necessary to confer with his allies. It would seem then that the Frankfurt proposals presented to St. Aignan by Metternich, Nesselrode and Aberdeen had yet to be accepted by their own governments. Such was the rampant hatred of these governments for Napoleon that, taken with ensuing allied delays, we wonder if this was not a contrived attempt, however awkward, to justify the invasion of France. Or was it a unilateral effort on Metternich's part stemming from his fears of a Russian-Prussian dominated Europe? If so, then this fear must have been shared at least partially by Nesselrode (representing Russia and speaking for Prussia) and Aberdeen (representing England).

The mystery deepens because we know that Czar Alexander was adamant in his insistence that France would be reduced, not to its natural frontiers, but to those of 1791 (thus losing Holland, Belgium, the Rhineland, Italy, Savoy and Nice). Prussia's prime minister, Count Hardenberg, greeted the Frankfurt proposals (contrary to Nesselrode's pledge of Prussian concurrence) with a succinct diary entry: "Propositions of peace without my assent – Rhine, Alps, Pyrenees: a mad business." Britain's foreign minister, Lord Castlereagh, prior to learning of the proposals had written Aberdeen that "this nation is likely to view with disfavour any peace which does not confine France within her ancient limits."[17] Nor, as we shall see, did Britain have any intention of yielding its mastery of the world's waters. Allied reaction to Metternich's tentative may have been so violent that perforce he had to swiftly backtrack by means of blaming the fiasco on Napoleon's indolence.

Napoleon on the other hand undoubtedly held secret intentions contrary to his stated willingness to accept the natural frontiers. Even had he proved willing to yield his empire he would never have accepted the old 1791 limits, just as Britain would never have accepted maritime parity. To surrender Belgium, taken at the cost of so much blood during the revolution, probably would have brought a Jacobin revolution, nor could he dream of allowing Austria to control the Savoy and Nice.

Whatever the case, neither side had stopped its martial movements. Prince Schwarzenberg broke his word and to Napoleon's fury claimed Marshal Gouvion St. Cyr's garrison of Dresden as legitimate prisoners-of-war. Wellington continued to move cautiously on Soult defending Bayonne. Marshal Suchet remained on the defensive in Catalonia. In a belated effort to remove Spain from the war Napoleon finally recognized Ferdinand as king of Spain, the idea being to clear the peninsula of French and British troops, thus cutting Wellington's communications with Portugal and bringing French troops home as much needed reinforcements.

This might have worked three or four years earlier – the Spanish detested the English as much as they did the French – but as it was, the *cortes* rejected the treaty and Ferdinand remained in France. Blücher and Schwarzenberg were preparing to cross the Rhine. Bülow's army with a small English force had overrun Holland.

By late December peace was a forgotten word, a forlorn orphan whose whimperings were drowned in the cadenced drill of marching feet. Napoleon was deploying his feeble corps along northern and eastern borders. Fired by allied invasion of the empire, the army, if not all of its marshals and generals was on his side and so were millions of common folk. When a committee of the *Corps législatif* mounted a minor rebellion against one of his *ukases*, he disbanded the body and sent its members home.

These awesome days however offered the emperor more losses than gains. Seduced by months of allied blandishments King Joachim (Marshal Murat) of Naples, who had promised the emperor to deploy 30,000 troops on the banks of the Pô river, defected to the enemy to increase pressure on Viceroy Eugène and end any thought of sending reinforcements to France. A few days later Napoleon's last ally, Denmark, was invaded by Bernadotte's Swedish troops. The price of survival was allegiance to the allied cause, not to mention the cession of Norway to Sweden, Heligoland to England. In the hope of winning renewed Italian support Napoleon authorized Pope Pius VII to return to Rome albeit under certain restrictive conditions. The pope refused to accept all of them and got only as far as Tarrascon.[18]

The powerful new armies that Napoleon visualized did not and would not appear. Suchet and Soult could not march north, Davout was locked in Hamburg. Fortress garrisons in Prussia, Germany, Holland and Belgium were either now or about to become prisoners-of-war.

French defenses were pathetic. General Maison with 15,000 troops at Antwerp; Macdonald defending the lower Rhine so weak that in his words, "I could only watch the Rhine, not defend it"[19];

on Macdonald's right, Morand with a supposed 13,000; then Marmont around Kaiserlautern with 16,000, Victor at Strasbourg with 10,000; Ney at Nancy, Mortier at Langres, Augereau at Lyons, each with a small corps – in all something over 65,000 mostly ill-trained, ill-equipped and ill-fed soldiers, many of them recovering from typhus, facing victorious armies nearly five times stronger.[20]

Blücher's advance guard crossed the Rhine at the end of December. Victor immediately evacuated Strasbourg, fell back on Nancy and, joined by Ney's meager force, was huddling behind the Meuse river by mid January. The precipitate retreat shattered Napoleon's already tenuous defensive plans. Marmont at once had to withdraw, first to Metz and then to the Meuse. Napoleon relieved Victor of sector command, giving it to Marmont with orders to hold the line of the Meuse.[21] Macdonald had fallen back before Bülow's march and by mid January was approaching Châlons-sur-Marne.

Schwarzenberg meanwhile with an army some 150,000 strong had marched through neutral Switzerland to cross the border and deploy on the flatland of Langres, waiting to be joined by Blücher who had continued southwest, crossed the Marne and marched on Brienne.

Now it was necessary for Napoleon to move. In late January he appeared at a state reception in the Tuileries. Here he named Marie Louise the regent in his absence, this time supported by redeemed brother Joseph whom he appointed lieutenant-general of France responsible for the defense of Paris. His three-year-old son was by his side, wearing a national guard uniform. Taking him by the hand Napoleon circled the large room, stopping to ask officers and officials to form a united political front in support of the regent. He then said goodbye to wife and son, climbed into his carriage and departed for war. He would never see them again.

Notes

1 Corr. XXVI. Nr. 20886, the Tuileries, 14 November 1813.
2 Corr. XXVI. Nr. 20833, Gotha, 25 October 1813.
3 Corr. XXVI. Nrs. 20835, 20837, Gotha, 25 October 1813.
4 Corr. XXVI. Nr. 20846, Mainz, 2 November 1813.
5 Corr. XXVI. Nr. 20844, Frankfurt, 1 November 1813.
6 Corr. XXVI. Nr. 20851, Mainz, 3 November 1813.
7 Corr. XXVI. Nr. 20853, Mainz, 3 November 1813.
8 Corr. XXVI. Nrs. 20855, Mainz, 3 November 1813; 21010, Paris, 15 December 1813; 21015, Paris, 17 December 1813. See also Roederer (*Mémoires*), 264–73.
9 Corr. XXVI. Nr. 20947, Paris, 26 November 1813.
10 Corr. XXVI. Nrs. 21040, 21041, the Tuileries, 26 December 1813.
11 Corr. XXVI. Nr. 20896, St. Cloud, 15 November 1813. See also Gum, 158–62.
12 Corr. XXVI. Nrs. 21013, Paris, 16 December 1813; 21016, Paris, 17 December 1813; 21051, Paris, 28 December 1813.
13 Rose (*Life*), II, 370–1.
14 Rose (*Life*), II, 374.
15 Rose (*Life*), II, 371.
16 Corr. XXVI. Nr. 20956, Paris, 1 December 1813.
17 Rose (*Life*), II, 372–3.
18 Rose (*Life*), II, 380.
19 Macdonald, 259.
20 Corr. XXVII. Nrs. 21055, Paris, 1 January 1814; 21056, Paris, 2 January 1814; 21089, Paris, 12 January 1814. See also Wartenburg, II, 370–6; Chandler (*Napoleon*), 948–9. As usual there is a considerable discrepancy in figures. Marshal Macdonald, for example, is usually credited with having 10,000 or 12,000 troops but later wrote that he had scarcely 3,000 men. As we have earlier pointed out, strength reports of these years are always suspect, particularly in times of great confusion.
21 Corr. XXVII. Nrs. 21105, Paris, 17 January 1814; 21115, Paris, 19 January 1814.

CHAPTER TWENTY-NINE

DEFEAT AND ABDICATION
JANUARY–APRIL 1814

You, my friends – continue to serve France. Its welfare was my
single thought and will always be the object of my wishes. Do
not pity me . . . I want to write about the great things that we
have done together. Farewell, my children.

Napoleon's farewell address to the Old Guard,
Fontainebleau, 20 April 1814[1]

NAPOLEON REACHED IMPERIAL headquarters at Châlons-sur-Marne
on 26 January 1814, to take command of the army. Politically he
was at a dead end. In early January he had sent his foreign minister, Caulaincourt, to allied headquarters at Chaumont to try to
determine the real allied goals, "to listen to and observe everything."[2] Caulaincourt never got the chance. Refused entrance by
the allies he was left cooling his heels at the French advance posts.

Some three weeks later Napoleon was facing the combined
forces of four major powers. Although his own strength was not
slight it was dangerously dispersed. If the allies could not at once
seize the northern fortresses, neither could the garrisons leave
those fortresses. If the Spanish *cortes* did not ratify the treaty of
Valençay which would place Ferdinand on the throne, neither
could Soult at Bayonne nor Suchet in Catalonia march their corps
northward. Eugène's Army of Italy was facing a separate Austrian
army (shortly to be reinforced by turncoat Murat's Neapolitans)
and could not move north. Strategically Napoleon was out-
manned, out-maneuvered and out-gunned, on the defensive, his
major corps withdrawing on Vitry-le-François shadowed on the

east by Blücher's corps which had reached St. Dizier on the Marne. His troops lacked food, clothing and shoes. Volunteers were many, but he had few and often no arms for them. The weather was vile, the men tired and discouraged, many down with or recovering from the dreaded typhus.

A bleak picture, yes, but not without some merits. The allies had not marched all this way without losses of their own. They had suffered heavily in Saxony, they were forced to leave substantial garrisons and siege forces in Germany, Holland, Belgium and northern France, their ponderous supply lines were uncomfortably stretched and they were not agreed as to a strategic objective. Czar Alexander, strongly influenced by his militant advisers who were Napoleon's old nemeses, the Prussian Stein and the Corsican Pozzo di Borgo, and King Frederick William, influenced by Alexander and by his own General Gneisenau, wanted to march straight on Paris. Prince Schwarzenberg commanding the large Austrian force was reluctant to do so. Although Napoleon dangerously minimized allied strengths he was correct in writing to one of his marshals that the enemy "are scattered in all directions."[3]

Napoleon also held the decided advantage of fighting on interior lines. Even with a limited number of cavalry and artillery horses he had so far retained tactical mobility, he had a large number of cannon and, most important, the army could still fight. As was usual his presence worked its magic, not least because of his obvious concern for the troops. "Get 2–300,000 bottles of wine and brandy to Vitry," he ordered Berthier, adding (no doubt with a doleful smile), "If there is no other bottled wine than champagne, take it. It is better for us to have it than the enemy."[4]

Two days before his arrival the Old Guard had defeated an allied force at Bar-sur-Aube. Two days after his arrival he attacked Blücher at St. Dizier, forcing him to retreat southwest to Brienne (of Napoleon's schooldays). He followed with 10,000 men wallowing through mud owing to a sudden thaw to face Blücher and Sacken's 30,000-strong corps plus cavalry. The French attacked late in the day, seized the all-important château and fought through the night to push Blücher in retreat, this time to the southeast. The emperor now took up a strong defensive position in front of Brienne from where he wrote Joseph: "I have reason to believe that Caulaincourt has arrived at the general headquarters of the emperors at Chaumont. The effect of this action at Brienne and the position of our armies should accelerate the conclusion of the peace."[5]

His optimism was decidedly premature. Pursued by Gérard, Victor and Marmont on the following day, the hunted suddenly turned on the hunters to win a sharp victory at La Rothière. Each side lost an estimated 5,000 men killed and wounded, the French 70 or more guns and 3,000 troops taken prisoner.[6]

A far worse defeat would shortly follow. Napoleon still believed that France would make peace on the Frankfurt bases since diverse allied objectives could not but threaten the so-called equilibrium of Europe, the balance of power preached by England and Austria. Had he had ears in allied councils he would have been heartened by his own perspicacity.

God in the form of the English foreign minister, Lord Castlereagh, had arrived in the allied camp in late January. No more than Metternich did he want Russia to acquire Poland nor Prussia to gain Saxony. Unlike Metternich but like Czar Alexander he *did* want France confined to its 1791 borders. Unlike Czar Alexander he along with Prussia and Austria wanted Louis XVIII placed on the French throne. But unlike the other players Alexander wanted Bernadotte to have that throne. Metternich argued for a negotiated peace as soon as possible. Russia and Prussia insisted on seizing Paris to dictate peace terms. Castlereagh held the purse-strings, Schwarzenberg commanded the allied army. Metternich agreed to humble France but threatened to remove Austria from the coalition if peace talks did not take place. Metternich won. The congress of Châtillon-sur-Seine (southeast of Paris) opened on 5 February 1814.

If the allies wished peace, Napoleon wrote Caulaincourt, they must settle matters promptly, "for in a few days a general battle will decide everything . . . As the allies already have stated the conditions you should have them by now. Accept them if they are acceptable. If not we shall run the risk of a battle and even the loss of Paris and everything which would follow."[7]

But now, rather than finding himself negotiating on the bases of the Frankfurt proposals, Caulaincourt instead was handed a *fait accompli*: France would return to its 1791 borders, maritime freedom was not to be discussed. Although empowered to accept the *ukases*, Caulaincourt understandably sent them to Napoleon who received them only on 8 February.

French headquarters were now at Nogent-sur-Seine in order to shield Paris. Almost nothing was going well. "The army is dying of hunger," Napoleon wrote his chief quartermaster. "Lacking bread, flour must be distributed."[8] Bülow's Prussians occupied Brussels. Alexander's Russians were close to Troyes. Macdonald, pushed by Yorck, had fallen back on Épernay. Enemy cavalry were flooding the country. General Sacken's 15,000 Russians of Blücher's corps had reached Montmirail.[9]

Paris was in a state of growing ferment nurtured by such as Talleyrand, King Joseph and his deposed brothers, Louis of Holland and Jérôme of Westphalia, who with a number of ministers and councillors were plugging for peace at any price. The regent, Marie Louise, was writing her husband lengthy letters, almost daily stressing her undying love and devotion and relating their son's antics while cataloguing the capital's ills including her endless list of physical problems – in the space of ten days "such a headache that I can't see properly," repeated stomach-aches, possible "sciatica in my right leg," "twinges of rheumatism," "pain in the small of my back," very feverish with more rheumatism, leeches to be applied for being "too full-blooded."[10] The treasury was nearly empty, extreme discontent and fear were running rampant, the citizenry leaving in droves.

Napoleon tried his best to strengthen weak spirits. "I had meant to launch an attack on Bar-sur-Aube against Emperor Alexander," he wrote Joseph on 6 February, "but I am sacrificing everything to the necessity of covering Paris." On the following day he replied to a dejected note from Marie Louise: "Your letter grieves me deeply; it tells me you are discouraged. Those who are with you have lost their heads. I am quite well and I hope my affairs will take a turn for the better, but I do beg you to cheer up and take care of yourself . . . You know how much I love you." Joseph was to ensure that the empress, her son and the royal family would be evacuated from Paris, but only as an emergency measure: "We must not shut our eyes to the fact that the consternation and despair of the populace might have disastrous and tragic results."[11]

For the moment he could do little to change allied minds. Swallowing his fury he instructed Caulaincourt to try to keep negotiations open in a play for time. At this point however, at Czar Alexander's instigation, the allies broke off negotiations at Châtillon.

Only force remained. Napoleon planned to attack Blücher's Army of Silesia first because it moved considerably faster than Schwarzenberg. After knocking out the Prussians and Russians he would retrace his steps and strike the Austrians. With an agility enhanced by desperation and brilliant leadership the army reached Sézanne the evening of 9 February. Napoleon believed that the most efficacious way to handle the enemy beast now at Montmirail in a drive on Paris was to cut off its tail – Sacken's rearguard of about a dozen regiments with 40 cannon at Champaubert.

He struck early the next day, a surprise attack that captured a large assortment of generals, colonels and other officers along with 6,000 soldiers, 40 cannon and 200 wagons. Having eliminated the tail he turned to the body, marching the Old Guard west on Montmirail and on the following day falling on Sacken and Yorck's main force, killing or wounding several thousand, taking thousands more prisoner and sending the rest running north to take refuge at Château-Thierry, leaving 120 cannon and thousands of muskets on the field – another splendid victory won by only half of the Old Guard at the cost of perhaps 1,000 French casualties. "The Army of Silesia no longer exists, I have put it in total flight," Napoleon jubilantly wrote Joseph. ". . . I believe that these two days have cleared Paris of all dangers, for this was the best army of the allies."[12]

Jubilation was premature. He was not strong enough to exploit what amounted to a local victory. While he was fighting at Montmirail, Schwarzenberg began moving on Nogent-sur-Seine. Victor perforce was falling back but Oudinot's corps, recently arrived from the south, held Montereau on Victor's right.

Napoleon was digesting this news when he learned that Blücher, reinforced by 20,000 Germans and Russians, was making another move on Montmirail and Vauchamps to force Marmont's withdrawal. Napoleon marched at once to attack Wittgenstein's main force at Vauchamps. This brief but fierce battle resulted in still another victory, an estimated 4,000 enemy casualties and 8,000 prisoners at a cost of 300 French, the enemy retiring in confusion on Bergères.[13]

Blücher's defeats and serious losses had not only caused Czar Alexander to reopen peace negotiations at Châtillon, but also to persuade Schwarzenberg to march on Victor's force holding the line of the Seine. Moving as ponderously as ever Schwarzenberg crossed the river at Nogent and Bray, his center moving on Nangis, his right on Nogent and his left toward Fontainebleau. Napoleon responded by leaving Marmont to hold Montmirail while he marched the rest of the army south to Nangis. From here he attacked the Austrians and on 16–17 February put them into disorganized flight back to Troyes capturing, as he claimed in letters to Caulaincourt, Eugène and Marie Louise, 20 generals, 5–600 officers, 30–40,000 soldiers, 150–200 cannon, "almost without firing a shot."[14]

The whirlwind victory, taken with the reopening of the peace negotiations, convinced Napoleon that he was on the verge of evicting the enemy from all of France. Marshal Augereau at Lyons was to march on Geneva to threaten Schwarzenberg's communications. Caulaincourt at Châtillon was to press for peace, but a "solid and honorable peace" fashioned on the bases of the

Frankfurt proposals.[15] His optimism seemed to be confirmed when Schwarzenberg suddenly proposed an armistice. "These wretched creatures fall on their knees at the first check," Napoleon scornfully wrote Joseph. ". . . I shall accord no armistice until they have left my lands."[16]

The allies were not going to leave France, there would be no armistice, Napoleon was to have no peace with honor. Despite the dramatic series of French victories, despite continuing quarrels between the Russian and Austrian emperors and their marshals and generals, the allies with the possible exception of Austria seemed no more inclined toward peace than ever. Soon after negotiations reopened at Châtillon, Lord Castlereagh knocked petulant heads together to bring about a declaration of renewed solidarity among the four allies, and it soon became clear that they and not Napoleon were negotiating from strength.

Allied generals had good reasons for their belief. Ever since the invasion Napoleon had been reacting rather than acting. If he knocked out one corps here another popped up there – a repeat of allied strategy and tactics in Saxony: muscle over mind, quantity over quality. Napoleon had dealt no knockout blow. He had hurt Blücher and Schwarzenberg but each had been reinforced and soon returned to the offensive. He had also hurt himself because replacements were not easy to come by and good commanders were becoming increasingly rare. He also was paying a price – ill on occasion, sometimes exhausted: "I was so tired last night," he wrote Marie Louise on 19 February, one of the rare times when he did not claim the best of health, "that I slept eight hours on end."[17]

Marshal Victor had been a great disappointment. First had come his precipitate retreat across the Meuse, then his failure to contest Schwarzenberg's recent crossing of the Seine. He had lost his sector command; now he lost his corps command. (To his credit he begged to remain with the army even as a private. Napoleon relented and gave him command of two Guard divisions.) Augereau at Lyons was proving difficult, excusing inactivity by lack of uniforms and equipment. "I have destroyed 80,000 enemy with some battalions of conscripts lacking cartridge pouches and proper uniforms," Napoleon wrote him. "You say that the national guard are pitiful: I have four thousand here from Angers and Brittany, in round hats, without cartridge pouches, wearing wooden shoes, but carrying good muskets . . . I am ordering you to take to the field within twelve hours after the receipt of this letter. If you are still the Augereau of Castiglione, keep your command; if your sixty years are weighing on you, leave it and turn it over to your most senior general."[18] Admiral Ganteaume was so paralyzed at the thought of an enemy attack on Toulon that Napoleon relieved him of command. Caulaincourt who was in public and private correspondence with Metternich thought it futile to continue the struggle, a defeatism that drew a withering reprimand from his master: "I consider you as being kept in the dark, knowing nothing of my affairs, and influenced by lies."[19] A British officer at allied headquarters noted that Caulaincourt "works tooth and nail for peace, as far as it depends on him. He dreads Bonaparte's successes even more than ours, lest they should make him more impracticable."[20] Marshal Soult was another broken reed in Napoleon's mind, letting himself be pushed back by Wellington for want of "a little more resolution and energy." Marmont was fighting his own war owing to his "excessive vanity," forever failing to keep Napoleon informed of his movements.[21]

Napoleon's hoped for weapon, the French people, were behaving variously. Royalist agents aided by the likes of Talleyrand had won over large numbers of citizens once loyal to the emperor by spreading defeatist rumors and preaching the virtues of rule by the doddering old pretender. His officials were also letting him down. "The minister of interior [Montalivet] is a milksop," he wrote Joseph on 24 February, "neither he nor the police minister [Savary] knows France any better than I know China."[22] Joseph's secret intrigues and desire for peace were growing ever stronger. Marie Louise, often since portrayed as "a brave little thing," was nothing of the sort, forever feeling sorry for herself, daily bombarding Napoleon with court quarrels and petty but divisive gossip.

The army continued to support him as in general did peasants and workers, particularly in northern and northeastern France where Cossacks and Russian soldiers were committing hideous atrocities. "It would be impossible for the disposition of the inhabitants and peasantry [of Burgundy] to be better," he wrote Marie Louise in late February. "They come forward to a man."²³ Some local national guard and partisan units had been formed, and more would have appeared had officers and weapons been available. Had the country risen in righteous wrath, as Napoleon begged it to do, the war might well have taken a different course. That this did not happen was in part the result of obstructionist local prefects who favored the Bourbons, in part to a lack of officers and weapons, in part to a tired people who had suffered and given too much for too long. Napoleon would continue to call for *levées en masse* almost to the end of his rule – the results would continue to be minimal.

Military poverty brought about a sharp change in tactics. Heretofore he had met the enemy head-on in an attempt to destroy first Blücher's army, then Schwarzenberg's. Hoping to be reinforced by fortress garrisons and civilian partisans, he now ate professional crow by reverting to a form of what he had always held in contempt, guerrilla warfare, the refuge of "brigands" and *canaille*. Henceforth he intended to strike the enemy's rear and, by destroying parks and depots, to threaten his lines of communication so as to force him to halt his advance or even to retreat.

In early March Napoleon was at La Ferté-sous-Jouarre preparing "to carry the war into Lorraine," as he informed King Joseph, "where I shall rally all the troops in my Meuse and Rhenish fortresses." Once he brought Blücher to terms he intended a similar maneuver, in conjunction with Augereau marching northeast from Lyons, to fall on Schwarzenberg's rear areas and force him to about-face.²⁴

He began this operation by causing Blücher to retreat north of Fismes. But now Bülow's Army of the North arrived from

Belgium to join Blücher behind Laon. Napoleon next seized Reims and marched north on Berry-au-Bac. A few days later he beat the Russians at the battle of Craonne and marched on Laon. This movement was interrupted by a night attack which forced Marmont to retreat for several miles, "an accident of war," Napoleon informed Joseph, but also "a blunder" on the part of Marmont "who has acted like a second lieutenant."[25] Finding Blücher's position at Laon too strong to be turned Napoleon retired on Reims.

Despite recent victories he was not much closer to his goal of reinforcing the army before torching enemy vehicle parks and supply dumps. His own losses had been heavy. "The Young Guard is melting away like snow," he wrote Joseph. ". . . My mounted Guards are also melting away very rapidly."[26] "For God's sake," he wrote Clarke, "order Maison [in Belgium] to take to the field . . . [along with] General Durette at Metz, General Morand at Mainz and other generals."[27]

Augereau had finally marched from Lyons – but not very far. Soult had lost a battle to Wellington and retreated east to leave Bordeaux open to the English. The Dordogne had to be defended, Poitou and Rochefort covered, the task of Marshal Suchet hurriedly recalled from Catalonia to form the Army of the Garonne. To add to his burdens he had become suspicious of a growing intimacy between Marie Louise and King Joseph. "Do not be too familiar with the king," he cautioned his wife. "Keep him at a distance, never allow him to enter your private apartments . . . do not let him play the part of adviser." He wrote again the following day: "You trust [Joseph] too much . . . Everyone has betrayed me . . . Mistrust the king: he has an evil reputation with women." Two days later: "The king is intriguing; he will be the first to suffer; he is a pygmy, swelling with his own importance."[28]

These suspicions aside, Napoleon continued to confide his military plans to Joseph as well as his fears. "If the enemy advanced on Paris in such strength that all resistance became impossible," Joseph was to evacuate the court, ministers, councillors of state, other dignitaries and what was left of the treasury to the Loire. "Do not abandon my son – remember that I would prefer him drowned in the Seine rather than in the hands of the enemies of France."[29]

Such gloom was momentary however. He was still dreaming of gaining a favorable or at least an acceptable peace. Caulaincourt at Châtillon was authorized "to make concessions necessary to the continuance of negotiations with the understanding that the treaty would call for evacuation of our lands and mutual return of all prisoners-of-war."[30] Two days after this letter was dictated, the allies summarily terminated the congress.

The enemy forced Napoleon's next move. At Épernay he learned that Prince Schwarzenberg had crossed the Seine and was marching on Provins and Villeneuve. Napoleon at once turned south, his intention being to cut Schwarzenberg's communications between Nogent and Troyes. As he anticipated, this move caused the Austrians to hurriedly fall back on Bar-sur-Aube. Somewhat ironically his new tactics were beginning to achieve their aim. "I am struggling with the greatest want of provisions," Marshal Blücher wrote Schwarzenberg on 17 March, "the soldiers have been for some days without even bread; and I am cut off from Nancy, so that I have no means of procuring any."[31]

Once again Napoleon's primary task was to prevent Blücher from joining Schwarzenberg. While Marmont and Mortier withdrew south on Châlons and Épernay, he marched north on Vitry, Frignicourt and St. Dizier, his supposition being that Schwarzenberg would head northwest toward Brienne in order to attack him at St. Dizier. Still hoping to receive 12,000 troops from his fortresses, he sent some light cavalry east to St. Mihiel to open communications with Verdun and Metz while French agents circulated through Lorraine, Alsace and the Vosges alerting loyalists to prepare to "sound the tocsin of rebellion." His own army would march on Metz, over 70 miles to the northeast, to carry the war to the eastern frontiers. Prior to this adventurous move however, he seized Bar-sur-Aube and Chaumont which forced Schwarzenberg to retreat to Châtillon. "In only four or five hours," he wrote

Berthier on 25 March, "I will have some clear notions of what the enemy is doing."[32]

The enemy was scarcely idle. Despite hungry troops Blücher had pushed back Marmont, crossed the Marne and on 24 March joined Schwarzenberg's advance guard. The previous day the allies had intercepted a letter from Napoleon to Marie Louise informing her of his intended march to the Marne. At an allied council of war the following day Czar Alexander persuaded Schwarzenberg to join Blücher in an attack on Napoleon's much smaller force. But now the allies intercepted an official dispatch from Paris to Napoleon that spoke of an empty treasury, general discontent and the sensation caused by Wellington's seizure of Bordeaux. Using this incentive the czar won Prussian and Austrian approval to march directly on Paris.[33]

Events moved rapidly. On 25 March enemy cavalry smashed Marmont and Mortier near Fère-Champenoise, forcing their remnants, no more than 12,000 strong, to retreat on Paris. Four days later the allied advance guard crossed the Marne at Meaux. Thousands of citizens had already fled from the capital. Marie Louise, her son, Joseph, most of the royal family and the government were on their way southwest (with what was left of the treasury), leaving Marmont and Mortier's savaged corps and a supposed 12,000 national guards, half without muskets, to defend Paris. On 30 March, Marmont surrendered the city in return for honorable evacuation of his and Mortier's troops.

What of Napoleon?

Having learned on 27 March of the allied move he at once marched west, but confusion was great and he only reached Troyes two days later. Here he learned that Paris was *in extremis* and that Augereau at Lyons had gone over to the allies. On 30 March news arrived at Fontainebleau that the court had left the capital and that Marmont had surrendered the city and moved his troops south. In a state of shock the emperor sent Caulaincourt to negotiate a peace, but there was to be no negotiation.

Fontainebleau "From Top to Bottom"

The allies already had decided that Louis XVIII was to be the new king of France. Until his arrival a provisional government headed by Talleyrand would rule the country under allied direction. Czar Alexander coldly turned down Caulaincourt's petition for an armistice, but did not seem opposed to Napoleon abdicating in favor of his son and a regency under Marie Louise.

Caulaincourt reported this distressing result to the emperor at Fontainebleau on 4 April, but Napoleon refused to consider abdication, saying that he had decided to march on the capital. His marshals rebelled. To his angry assertion that the army would obey him, Marshal Ney responded, "No, it will obey its commanders."[34] Thus stymied, Napoleon signed a decree of conditional abdication which was taken to the czar by Caulaincourt, Ney, Macdonald and Marmont. The czar debated the issue for several hours, but had still to make up his mind when Marshal Marmont turned himself and his corps over to the allies. Alexander now rejected the proposed conditional abdication but he and the other allied leaders offered favorable terms if Napoleon agreed to *unconditionally* abdicate: he would retain the title of emperor, gain sovereignty of Elba island along with an annual allowance of two million francs (to be paid by France), and be allowed to take 600 soldiers of the Old Guard with him; Marie Louise would keep her title of empress and be given three Italian duchies, one being Parma.[35]

Hoping still to persuade his marshals and generals to march, this time to the Loire to join Soult and Suchet's corps, Napoleon did not immediately accept the offer. But while he held off, five of his marshals – Oudinot, Victor, Lefebvre, Ney and Berthier – went over to the enemy. He and Marie Louise had stayed in close correspondence but she had not seriously fallen in with any of his plans to join him in exile. Using illness and her father's prohibition as excuses, she had not come to see him, nor had his brothers, nor any of his ministers.

On 11 April a forlorn and dejected Napoleon dictated and signed his abdication.[36] Caulaincourt and Macdonald remained with him but could not bring him out of a deep depression. On the

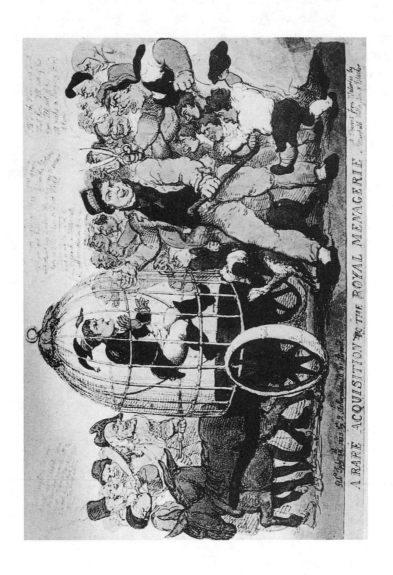

A Rare Acquisition in the Royal Managerie, 1815

night of 12 April the emperor attempted suicide by swallowing the contents of a phial that he had worn around his neck during the retreat from Russia. A combination of opium, belladonna and white hellebore made him very sick but did not kill him. After a ghastly night he recovered sufficiently to prepare himself for exile.

It was not an easy departure. He wrote several times to Marie Louise, reportedly ailing at Rambouillet, still hoping that she and their son would join him, but in vain. He also wrote a sad farewell to Joséphine at Malmaison. His emotional farewell to the Old Guard, quoted in part at the beginning of this chapter, brought shameless tears running down scarred and furrowed faces of those standing at attention in the courtyard at Fontainebleau.[37]

Accompanied by generals Bertrand and Drouot and escorted by Austrian, Russian, Prussian and English keepers and a small mounted guard, he left Fontainebleau on 20 April. The procession, and above all the emperor, were well received by the people until they neared the coast. So threatening was an armed mob near Avignon that Napoleon allegedly changed into civilian clothes complete with white cockade. After further uncomfortable incidents the party reached Fréjus to board a British frigate. On 28 April 1814, HMS *Undaunted* weighed anchor for the journey to Elba.

Napoleon Bonaparte was 44 years old.

Notes

1   Corr. XXVII. Nr. 21561, Fontainebleau, 20 April 1814.
2   Corr. XXVII. Nr. 21062, Paris, 4 January 1814.
3   Corr. XXVII. Nr. 21138, Vitry-le-François, 26 January 1814. See also Craig ("Coalition"), 13–17; Craig (*Prussian Army*), 63–5.
4   Corr. XXVII. Nr. 21135, Châlons-sur-Marne, 26 January 1814.
5   Corr. XXVII. Nrs.. 21150, 21160, Brienne, 31 January 1814.
6   Rose (*Life*), II, 381–4. See also Wartenburg, II, 378–83; Chandler (*Napoleon*), 959–64.
7   Corr. XXVII. Nr. 21179, Troyes, 5 February 1814.

8   Corr. XXVII. Nr. 21214, Nogent, 8 February 1814.

9   Corr. XXVII. Nrs. 21190, Troyes, 6 February 1814; 21226, Nogent, 9 February 1814.

10 Palmstierna, 42–59. See also Lavalette, 81–5.

11 Napoleon *Letters* (Roncière), 208–9.

12 Corr. XXVII. Nrs. 21229, Champaubert, 10 February 1814; Épine-au-Bois farm, 11 February 1814. See also Napoleon *Letters* (Roncière), 214–15.

13 Corr. XXVII. Nrs. 21254, Château-Thierry, 14 February 1814; 21255, Montmirail, 14 February 1814. See also Rose (*Life*), II, 393–405; Wartenburg, II, 392–9; Chandler (*Napoleon*), 979–83.

14 Corr. XXVII. Nrs. 21285, Nangis, 17 February 1814; 21295, Nangis, 18 February 1814. See also Napoleon *Letters* (Roncière), 219–21, 224.

15 Corr. XXVII. Nrs. 21285, Nangis, 17 February 1814; 21315, Château de Surville, 19 February 1814.

16 Corr. XXVII. Nr. 21293, Nangis, 18 February 1814.

17 Napoleon *Letters* (Roncière), 223.

18 Corr. XXVII. Nr. 21343, Nogent, 21 February 1814. Augereau was 56 years old at this time.

19 Napoleon *Letters* (Roncière), 222.

20 Rose (*Life*), II, 410.

21 Corr. XXVII. Nrs. 21353, Châtres, 23 February 1814; 21426, Bézu-Saint-Germain, 4 March 1814.

22 Napoleon *Letters* (Roncière), 226.

23 Napoleon *Letters* (Roncière), 228.

24 Corr. XXVII. Nrs. 21420, La Ferté-sous-Jouarre, 2 March 1814; 21426, Bézu-Saint-Germain, 4 March 1814.

25 Corr. XXVII. Nr. 21461, Chavignon, 11 March 1814.

26 Wartenburg, II, 405.

27 Corr. XXVII. Nr. 21452, Berry-au-Bac, 6 March 1814.

28 Napoleon *Letters* (Roncière), 237–9; Palmstierna, 113–24.

29 Corr. XXVII. Nr. 21497, Reims, 16 March 1814. See also Miot de Melito, II, 679–80; Lavalette, II, 86–8.

30 Corr. XXVII. Nr. 21505, Reims, 17 March 1814.

31 Macdonald, 285.

32 Corr. XXVII. Nrs. 21534, Château du Plessis, 23 March 1814; 21538, Dizier, 23 March 1814; 21541, Doulevant, 25 March 1814.

33 Rose (*Life*), II, 418–19.
34 Rose (*Life*), II, 427. See also Macdonald, 286–93.
35 Rose (*Life*), II, 431.
36 Corr. XXVII. Nr. 21558, Fontainebleau, 11 April 1814.
37 Corr. XXVII. Nr. 21560, Fontainebleau, presumed 19 April 1814.

CHAPTER THIRTY

THE EMPEROR OF ELBA
JUNE 1814–FEBRUARY 1815

Oh, it's a snug little island,
A right little, tight little island.

Thomas Dibdin[1]

FOR A SMALL island (86 square miles) Elba had enjoyed a turbulent existence over the centuries, its folk having been ruled by Etruscans, Greeks, Romans, Italians, Spanish and French, its iron ore exported hither and yon, its residents the frequent prey of Barbary pirates. In 1802 it had been ceded to France and in 1814 it was given to Napoleon.

No inhabitant past or present had seen the likes of its new ruler who was landed at Porto Ferrajo, courtesy of a British frigate, in early May 1814. The island greeted him and he greeted the island, an event consecrated by the new governor, General Count Antoine Drouot, who announced a public holiday to the delight of Elba's 11,380 subjects. This was followed by a dozen or so officials appearing in Napoleon's new palace, a dilapidated two-story building, *Il Mulino* (the Mill), to be quizzed in detail as to their functions.

Napoleon was not pleased with the condition of his new realm. Elba needed roads, buildings, schools, hospitals, even churches. Its one worthwhile industry, mining of ore and granite, was losing money, its citizenry lived in Mediterranean torpor seemingly content to exist on olives, citrus, fowl, occasional meat and bad wine. The island lacked sewers, many cisterns were contaminated, malarial marshes needed drainage, idle land wanted cultivation. In short he had inherited a colony neglected both by the mother country and by its own deeply religious, conservative and very backward inhabitants.

Napoleon's first concern was his own security. Five or six hundred of the Old Guard had followed him into exile along with 80 faithful Polish cavalrymen. The island's garrison – soldiers, gendarmerie and artillerymen – numbered about 1,100 more bodies. The Guard remained close to the emperor. There was no doubt in Napoleon's mind that a large number of royalists would welcome his demise, and he was right. Louis XVIII's brother, Comte d'Artois, made no secret of his desire to rid the world of this evil creature.[2] This sentiment would increase as the French people began to resent the new dynasty and as thousands of prisoners-of-war returned home to find no work. Such was the fear of Napoleon's attraction to the discontent that there was talk in allied circles of transferring him to the Azores, even to St. Helena. Assassination would have been an easier solution and Napoleon was probably correct to fear either that or being kidnapped.

Thus it was that he quickly reorganized island defenses almost as if the combined armies of the world were ready to strike. Naval officials responsible for a total five craft manned by 100 seamen were quizzed as if they were about to challenge the British fleet. Orders to seize and garrison the small neighboring island of Pianosa a few miles south of Elba were more detailed than those written to capture a fortress on the Elbe. For additional security, including defense against marauding Algerian corsairs, he ordered the acquisition of another two ships that would require 100 more sailors.[3]

Meanwhile he had established his court with as much pomp as ever existed at the Tuileries: General Bertrand as grand master of the palace, General Drouot as governor and minister of war, Monsieur Peyrusse as treasurer, Baron Fain as secretary. Suitable uniforms were procured for the various underlings and lackeys. A new flag bearing the arms of the Medicis topped by

The Arrival at Elba, 1814

Napoleonic bees was unfurled. Several imperial carriages were at his disposal along with three riding horses and several small boats.

He applied the same energy and care to civil projects. Hardly had property owners recovered from celebratory hangovers than they were shocked to learn that within two months they were to have latrines dug and nightly emptied "in a place that will not be noxious to promenades." Those who did not comply would be fined. The commissioner of streets was to furnish "two trash wagons" to keep the streets clean and fines would be levied on offenders. Benches were to be provided along the quays and the streets lighted.[4]

Napoleon's initial *ukases* set the pattern for his brief reign. Almost daily he was demanding new roads, wells, forts, schools, hospitals, a cemetery, new crops, trees planted, idle land cultivated, the fishing fleet reorganized and licensed, the theater repaired until a new one could be built. *Il Mulino* was soon undergoing massive rehabilitation, its center raised to the level of its wings, rooms refurbished, kitchen paths cleaned, the road paved, an underground sewer dug, new gardens laid out and others improved.

This flurry of activity was momentarily and sadly broken in June when news of Joséphine's sudden death reached the emperor. The restoration of the crown had brought her back into the social whirl, Malmaison being frequented by Czar Alexander, who had taken a strong fancy to its mistress, and by other important personages. While riding in an open carriage with the czar in mid May she had caught a bad cold but refused to cancel a ball a few nights later. Lightly garbed she had walked in the gardens with Alexander which brought on severe throat and chest complications. When she died four days later, presumably from pneumonia, Hortense and Eugène were with her. Eugène informed Napoleon of the tragedy – "at noon you lost the best of friends, and my sister and I the most devoted of mothers . . . She died with the courage, serenity and resignation of an angel. Everything she said to us about you in the last moments of her life showed us clearly how sincerely she was devoted to you." After reading the letter Napoleon reportedly muttered some telling words, "Ah, now she is indeed happy."[5]

With that he went back to work. An extensive reconnaissance on horseback led him to discover two villages that he liked: Porto Longone (today's Porto Azzura) about seven road miles southeast of Porto Ferrajo, and Marciana, a fishing village about eight miles west of the capital, each connected to the capital by very poor roads. Porto Longone was to house a second palace of three large suites on the first floor, and ten suites on the ground floor including "a beautiful apartment" for the Bertrands, a salon and a billiard room.

The tiny port of Marciana led to Marciana Alta, a village on the surrounding cliffs known for its cool air and sparkling drinking water. This in turn led to steps hewn from granite and marked by 14 stations of the cross to an ancient shrine, the *Madonna del Monte* (Our Lady of the Mountain), about an hour's climb to an old church and a hermitage inhabited by a few monks. Being high up in the mountains this was an ideal summer retreat shaded by chestnut trees in the cool air scented by rosemary and the *maquis* familiar to Napoleon's youth.[6]

A primitive road connected Porto Ferrajo to Procchio but the road west to Marciana was little more than a track. This became one of Napoleon's pet road-building projects but progress was slow. In late August he complained to Bertrand of the delay: "Order the *intendant* to pay twenty *sous* a day to forty laborers to widen this road by a meter so as to accommodate pedestrians and wagons."[7]

These and many more projects were underway when the first visitors arrived on the island in early August.

The first arrivals were refugees, a large number of French officers discharged on half-pay. "It is difficult to refuse bread to officers who have served me for a long time," Napoleon noted sadly to General Drouot. The best he could do was to form them into a guard, put them in a caserne, feed them and pay each 50 francs a month.[8]

Bonoparte, Letitia 1750–1836 Napoleon's mother,
known as Madame Mère

His mother, Madame Mère, arrived in mid August accompanied by two valets, two footmen and a chef. Napoleon installed her in the mayor's house at Marciana Alta to relieve her from the oppressive heat. She would soon be followed by sister Pauline and by Marie Walewska and 4-year-old Alexander.

Napoleon had assumed that the Empress Marie Louise and their son, once settled in Parma, would come to see him, perhaps to remain, a wish repeated in several notes written from Fontainebleau and Elba. Initially Marie Louise embraced the notion, or at least claimed to do so, but since landing on Elba he had not heard from her, a disappointment he correctly blamed on official interception of their letters.

When Napoleon departed from Fontainebleau, Marie Louise was at Rambouillet by orders of her father, Emperor Francis.

She was under Doctor Corvisart's care and was about to depart for the waters at Aix-les-Bains before taking up residence in Parma. Her father and Metternich, having already decided that she and the child were never to see Napoleon again, immediately shot down this plan by hustling her off to Vienna and the confines of Schönbrunn palace. There she remained for two months before departing for the baths, leaving her son tucked away in Schönbrunn, prior to going on to Parma. To watch over her [read: intercept any letters from Napoleon], Metternich and her father sent a dashing military officer, Count Neipperg, 42 years old, handsome, suave, a hussar wearing a black patch over a missing eye plucked by an enemy lance. Neipperg, who had negotiated Murat's treachery, quickly made the easiest conquest of his life. (The affair led to a 15-year relationship. They returned to Vienna, Marie Louise had two children by him and finally married him.)

News of this twist in events naturally circulated rapidly, at least in aristocratic circles. Almost unbelievably Napoleon was not informed of it, probably because his followers were greatly dispersed, correspondence was difficult and they also knew that he did not like bad news, especially if it were personal.

Unlike his empress, Marie Walewska did come to see him at Fontainebleau to say goodbye. Unfortunately he was then temporarily *hors de combat*, having been deposed and still ill from his suicide attempt. Having waited all night, she had departed without seeing him. He was extremely contrite and continued to keep in touch with her when she and Alexander moved to Florence. In early August her brother Theodore had visited Elba to arrange a tryst.

Marie's biographer, Christine Sutherland, tells the story in charming detail. Marie and Alexander, accompanied by Theodore and Marie's sister, landed on the first day of September and were clandestinely hustled to the old shrine, the *Madonna del Monte*, where Napoleon had set up light housekeeping (the monks being relegated to the basement of the hermitage). Marie was said to have had hopes of a permanent union, apparently assuming that

Napoleon had learned of his wife's infidelity. This is difficult to believe in that her husband and their child were still alive, but in any case Napoleon had personal and dynastic reasons for keeping the marriage intact. Only three days before Marie's arrival he had received news of the empress up to 10 August. This was the last letter he would receive from her – it contained her usual declarations of undying love but also the unwelcome news that she was returning to Vienna by order of her father. Napoleon had been hoping for her arrival at Elba for the September grape harvest, and at once sent her a message to keep writing to him through secret channels.[9] Having been a victim of political vicissitudes he knew only too well that today's enemy may be tomorrow's friend, that should France rise in rebellion against the Bourbons he might well be recalled to the throne, in which case he would need his empress.

Whatever the political complications, his reunion with Marie was brief but rapturous. His servant, the Mameluke Ali, later wrote that Napoleon personally carved the meat and poured wine for dinner: "He took great pleasure in serving the ladies himself; during the entire meal the emperor was very gay, gracious and charmingly gallant. He was happy." The lovers spent only two nights together, Napoleon in a dressing-gown leaving his tent at night and returning in the morning. The days were gorgeously idle, the emperor playing with four-year-old Alexander who called him Papa Emperor, the ladies taking long walks, entranced with the magnificent views of the island and neighboring Corsica.[10]

Unforeseen circumstances rudely interrupted the idyll: the good people of Porto Ferrajo were celebrating in the belief that they were being visited by the Empress Marie Louise and the king of Rome. First came Napoleon's doctor to pay his respects to "the Empress," then a note from Count Bertrand reporting on the excited populace. This was a real blow to Napoleon. Should the truth emerge he would never see Marie Louise or his son again, and the French court which had not paid him one *sou* of the promised allowance would pounce on the scandal as one more excuse to disown him.

At Napoleon's insistence the solemn party that evening made its way down the rugged steps, a driving rain announcing the approach of a heavy storm. An angry sea prevented the passengers from boarding their ship at Marciana Marina. They would have to be taken to the more sheltered Port Longone. The lovers said a sad goodbye, briefly embraced – and the carriages departed.[11]

Some accounts of this period have Napoleon in a deep malaise, presumably for having sent his loved one away. His correspondence however shows him deeply immersed in a wide variety of domestic projects such as the importation of 500 mulberry bushes to start a silk industry, contracting for the sale of mineral rights for 1815, ordering armchairs and sofas shipped in for his palaces, exploring the new acquisition of Pianosa island for horticultural and mining possibilities, arranging the gift of uncultivated ground around the salt bogs to the officers of his Guard – 2 arpents (about 2½ acres) to each in perpetuity – for kitchen gardens, and arranging the interior of his palaces. A heart-broken man does not generally concern himself with strengthening wooden cross-beams by "three iron bands, each four feet long."[12] In short, he remained as active as ever in a host of projects covering almost every facet of life on Elba. It would seem that at this point he intended to retain his new empire despite the increasingly perilous state of his finances and reports of rising political turbulence in France.

In exiling Napoleon the allied powers had agreed that he should retain his title and be given an allowance of two million francs a year by France. King Louis, undoubtedly influenced by the comte d'Artois, Talleyrand, Fouché and others, almost at once reneged on the financial commitment. As the year wore on and despite a certain amount of pressure from Austria and England the French paid nothing to the exiled emperor.

Estimates vary as to how much money Napoleon took with

him. He probably lost all of his secret horde in the cellars of the Tuileries, but who knows? If he got away with as much as four or five million francs he was fortunate. It is possible that he received funds from private interests in France. Madame Mère was said to have arrived with a considerable fortune, but Madame Mère was as tight as they come and it is doubtful if she offered substantial help or, such was Napoleon's pride, if he requested it. Pauline had wanted to give him her jewels after his defeat at Leipzig but he had politely refused to accept them. Marie Walewska was said to have arrived with her jewels to give to him, but apparently he refused them also. Income from island domains was minimal – as of mid April revenue from the mines and the sale of salt and fish amounted to a mere 135,000 francs, mostly from the mines. Estimated income for the year was just over 400,000 francs.[13]

The military budget amounted to something like a million francs a year. Napoleon's projected household budget for 1815 came to 380,000 francs. He was also spending constantly on palace improvements and public works so it is little wonder that his eagle eye, all too familiar to 15 years of terrified auditors, scrutinized and often challenged even the smallest expenses.[14]

By late 1814 he was in an obvious state of penury, to the extent that Madame Mère and Princess Pauline were vociferously complaining to the British commissioner-keeper, Colonel Neil Campbell (without effect). Since there was no indication that his allowance would ever be paid it seems reasonable to assume that he was facing ultimate bankruptcy, a prospect that could only make him wish for any feasible alternative. One cannot help but wonder what would have happened had the allied powers proved good for their word and had Marie Louise and their son joined him in his empire by the sea.

Napoleon had many enemies but he also had numerous admirers who regarded him as the consolidator – the savior, if you will – of the humanistic fruits of the French revolution. King Louis had seemed to get the restoration off on a good footing by declaring a constitutional charter of individual rights and establishing a quasi-parliamentary government. "The charter was to have been the palladium of our liberties," wrote one witness, "it had been solemnly sworn to, and the first legislative act of the government [designed to correct the abuses of power] was to violate it."[15]

The king had not been long on the throne when ugly rumors began circulating throughout France that, despite his proclaimed constitutional monarchy, he and his ultra-conservative advisers intended to reinstate what amounted to a feudal regime, that lands sequestered from *émigrés* and sold to commoners and peasants were to be reclaimed, even that he wished to reinstate the hated tithe. Those officials – ministers, legislators, generals and marshals – who accepted the new regime were generally provided for and some, such as Talleyrand and Fouché, greatly prospered.

Most of those who had fought for their country did not prosper. Battle-scarred officers found themselves subordinated in rank and perquisites to court favorites who had never heard a shot fired in anger. Thousands of officers and soldiers who returned from distant garrisons, tens of thousands of prisoners-of-war, other thousands of surplus officers and men found themselves mere flotsam floating in an ocean of bureaucratic favortism and corruption with no jobs, half-pay or none at all, no future.[16]

Nor did the people prosper. Everything they had sacrificed for, their sons, their own livelihoods, was gone. Their beautiful country was reduced to its 1791 borders, occupied by Russian, Prussian, Austrian and English troops, their emperor replaced by a fat, doddering old man of 59 years, so gout-ridden he had to be helped to the throne, so figuratively blind and so ideologically beholden to the past that he refused to see much less heed the sufferings of his people, the moribund state of industry, the enormous unemployment.

Napoleon would have learned of at least some of these developments from the discharged officers who flooded Elba in August and from sympathizers who were in covert contact with him. He would have learned of Bourbon doings from Madame Mère, Marie Walewska and Princess Pauline. One of his trusted servants, Cipriani Franceschi, was in Vienna from where he reported the discordant proceedings of the allied congress.

Had he always thought of returning to France as liberator or did his decision result from the plight of his soldiers, his own disappointment at not hearing from Marie Louise, his penury? His correspondence and the testimony of those around him suggest that, at least in the winter of 1814–15, he intended to remain on Elba. After returning from the exploration of Pianosa island he busied himself with remodeling the Porto Ferrajo palace for winter use. He was laying in stacks of wood and he had received at least two large shipments of books from Leghorn. He wanted Bertrand to have an inn of 20 beds built in Porto Ferrajo to attract important visitors. As winter approached and Pauline arrived his social activities increased. In early January the two were planning six balls for January and February, more celebrations for Mardigras in March. The ice house was to be filled with snow for the coming summer. The imperial huntsman was to buy three setters for the hunt, the same for wild boar and five or six for hare. As late as 19 February he was arranging for houses in Marciana suitable for Madame Mère, Princess Pauline and the Bertrands for July, August and September.[17]

This may have been deception but if so it was overkill. Napoleon had continued to receive reports on the dismal state of affairs in France. Cipriani reported from Vienna that the allies were discussing the probability of moving the exile to St. Helena island.[18] That alone would have made him contemplate an escape attempt, but in late February two events seemed to supply the powder necessary to explode his perhaps suppressed desires. One was the arrival of an ousted sub-prefect whose testimony, along with that in a letter brought from the former foreign minister, Maret, confirmed the turbulent situation at home. The second was Colonel Campbell's departure in mid February for a holiday with his mistress in Leghorn.

Ten days later Napoleon sailed for France with about 1,000 troops and a few cannon loaded on the *Inconstant* and several smaller craft. North of Corsica the brig was hailed by a French cruiser whose captain, spotting the Elban flag – Medici red stripes topped by Napoleonic bees – inquired as to Napoleon's health. *"Très bien,"* was the response, no doubt causing much giggling among the Guard crouched out of sight below the bulwarks.[19]

The liberator stepped ashore at Golfe Juan near Antibes on 1 March 1815.

Notes

1   Thomas Dibdin, *The Snug Little Island.*
2   Rose (*Life*), II, 439.
3   Corr. XXVII. Nr. 21598, Porto-Ferrajo, 28 July 1814.
4   Corr. XXVII. Nr. 21567, Porto-Ferrajo, n.d. See also Sutherland, 212–13.
5   Palmstierna, 235–6. See also Bruce, 478; Lavalette, II, 184–7.
6   Sutherland, 217–19.
7   Corr. XXVII. Nr. 21618, La Madone, 26 August 1814.
8   Corr. XXVII. Nr. 21607, Porto-Ferrajo, 9 August 1814.
9   Corr. XXVII. Nr. 21624, La Madone, 28 August 1814. See also Napoleon *Letters* (Roncière), 275–9; Palmstierna, 213–23.
10 Sutherland, 220–2.
11 Sutherland, 225–6.
12 Corr. XXVII. Nr. 21625, La Madone, 30 August 1814.
13 Corr. XXVII. Nr. 21581, Porto-Ferrajo, 24 June 1814.
14 Corr. XXVII. Nrs. 21631, Porto-Longone, 6 September 1814; 21662, Porto-Ferrajo, December 1814.
15 Macdonald, 346–7, 418.
16 Macdonald, 341–8, 354–9, 370–1.
17 Corr. XXVII. Nrs. 21643, 21644, Porto-Longone, 19 September 1814; Nr. 21668, Porto-Ferrajo, 17 January 1815; 21677, Porto-Ferrajo, 19 February 1815.
18 Korngold, 100.
19 Rose (*Life*), II, 442.

CHAPTER THIRTY-ONE

RETURN TO THE THRONE
FEBRUARY–JUNE 1815

*There is no historical precedent that induces me to venture
on this bold enterprise: but I have taken into account the
surprise that will seize on men, the state of public feeling,
the resentment against the allies, the love of my soldiers, in
time all the Napoleonic elements that still germinate in our
beautiful France.*

Napoleon to his staff aboard the *Inconstant*,
late February 1815[1]

IT WAS SURELY one of the boldest acts in history. Napoleon landed
on the southern coast of France with 1,000 soldiers, two cannons
and some very fiery words set forth in three proclamations, one to
the French people, one to the French army and one to the Old
Guard. These somewhat verbose messages amounted to a denunciation of the military traitors, Marmont and Augereau, who had
cost France a victory over the allies; a denunciation of the
Bourbon puppets who had nothing in common with French aspirations; and an appeal to throw off the white cockade, take on the
tricolor and fight for the future of the country.[2]

The first target, the nearby garrison of Antibes, failing to
respond favorably to the emperor's arrival – his messengers were
arrested – he cut out to the north toward Grenoble, a long march
over extremely hilly and difficult terrain but one that avoided
probable challenge from Rhone royalists. Five days later at Gap,
Napoleon issued a fourth and similar proclamation to the people
of the upper and lower Alps. This was more pithy and to the

point: "My return puts all your concerns at rest; it guarantees the preservation of all your private properties. Social equality and the rights that you have enjoyed for twenty-five years, those so desired by your forefathers, today constitute a part of your life."[3]

This message was well received in the sparse Alpine villages whose younger men at once left hearth and home to go with the liberator. His next hurdle was Grenoble, that beautiful city tucked in Alpine folds, but now commanded by General Marchand who had gone over to the Bourbons and who, upon hearing of the landing, had sworn to exterminate this "band of brigands." The brigands first encountered Marchand's authority in the form of a battalion defending a southern defile. The royalists seemed apprehensive, the front ranks drew back. In a show of courageous bravado Napoleon put his troops at parade rest and alone walked toward the menacing muskets. The master of those muskets ordered his men to fire. They did not do so.

'Soldiers!" Napoleon barked, "if there is one among you who wishes to kill his emperor, he can do so. Here I am." His words produced repeated shouts of *Vive l'Empereur* and Marchand lost a battalion. A garrison regiment next joined the brigands, Grenoble gates were beaten down, Marchand and his royalist staff fled and the brigands, strengthened in body and spirit, marched on toward Lyons – but not before Napoleon issued a brief message of gratitude: "Dauphinois, you have fulfilled my hopes . . . before leaving your country to go to the good city of Lyons, I must express my appreciation for the inspiration provided by your noble sentiments."[4]

Napoleon had always been popular in Lyons, if only because of his efforts to revive the famous silk industry. The city had become headquarters of the comte d'Artois, the king's younger brother, its garrison commanded by Marshal Macdonald. Artois, who embraced fear like a mistress "until he might be called a very dare-devil of cowardice,"[5] immediately fled, shortly followed by Macdonald. Any doubts held by the emperor as to his course must have vanished in the enthusiastic welcome given him and his troops who now numbered around 14,000 with more volunteers arriving daily. Such was his growing strength that he now decreed the end of a Bourbon government composed of traitors intent only on reinstating feudal rule with all its evils. This brave document (considering his still meager army) scrapped the *fleur-de-lys* in favor of the tricolor, called for seizure of all lands held by Bourbon nobility and for a future meeting of electoral colleges on the *Champ de mai* in Paris.[6]

Learning that Marshal Ney who commanded a royalist corps was marching against him, he responded with a brief note ordering Ney to fly the tricolor and join him at Châlons: "I shall receive you as [I did] the day after the battle of the Moskowa." Ney, who had promised King Louis to bring the emperor to Paris in an iron cage, abruptly changed heart and soon joined his own corps to the fledgling army.[7]

Paris meanwhile had exploded into a series of anti-Bourbon riots. When it became clear to the king that he would soon see Napoleon at the head of a highly spirited army and not in a cage, he, his court, the palace guard and senior officials hastily decamped, some north to the border eventually to find sanctuary in Ghent, some to the Vendée. On 20 March, as Napoleon had prophesied aboard the *Inconstant*, he arrived in Paris to celebrate the king of Rome's birthday "without a shot being fired."

The Congress of Vienna had convened the previous September when principals from Russia (Czar Alexander and Count Nesselrode), Great Britain (Lord Castlereagh to be followed by the duke of Wellington), Austria (Count von Metternich) and Prussia (Count von Humboldt), arrived to redraw the map of Europe. France not having been invited, King Louis sent his foreign affairs minister, Talleyrand, to the Austrian capital to look after his interests. Talleyrand's cunning and intricate diplomacy coupled with a lavish entertainment budget won France admission to the club in November.

Although the congress had not formally opened, the major powers were already quarreling over the spoils. Russia was determined to acquire the grand duchy of Warsaw, Prussia was equally insistent on gaining Saxony, ambitions strongly opposed by Great Britain and Austria. France soon joined the latter countries in a secret agreement signed in early January to go to war if necessary against Prussia and Russia.

By a miracle owing in part to strong Jacobin rumblings in France, in part to general exhaustion, vocal fire replaced gunfire, a complicated period of negotiations well told from the French standpoint in Talleyrand's correspondence with King Louis.[8] A compromise reached in early February gave most of western Poland to Russia, western Saxony to Prussia, and partially restored Austrian hegemony in southern Germany and Austrian control over a large part of Italy. As a final insult to France, the Savoy, Nice and Genoa were given to the king of Sardinia.

Having planted the seeds for another century of warfare the diplomats comfortably sat back to work out details in the few hours of the day not devoted to the limitless hedonistic pleasures offered by the city on the Danube.

Napoleon's unexpected landing in France replaced frivolity with fear. The tyrant of course would have to be put down like some rabid beast but that would take time. The allied army had scattered. Russian and Austrian troops had returned home, most of Wellington's victorious army was back in England. Blücher still commanded some 120,000 troops, many of them recruits, based on Liège. Wellington commanded a polyglot force of British, German and Dutch-Belgian troops, many untrained, based west of Brussels.

By the time the newcomer reached Paris however, the allies had agreed to field another immense army (in return for a three million pound subsidy from England). They had also declared Napoleon an outlaw to be seized and deported or, if the Prussians had their way, shot.

Napoleon's first task was to establish a new government: Maret, secretary of state; Caulaincourt, foreign minister; Cambacérès, justice; Mollien, treasury; Gaudin, finance; Fouché, police;

Carnot, interior; Davout, war; Decrès, navy. Within days a host of former officials – Montalivet, Denon, David, Desmazis, Fontaine, Corvisart and Boyer – had resumed their offices.

He next turned to the Sisyphean prospect of consolidating his rule. He was looking at a tired and dispirited nation, its existence threatened by subversion from within, allied arms from without. Tens of thousands of citizens, mainly in the Vendée and the south, remained loyal to the royalist cause; but hundreds of thousands more, particularly peasants and soldiers, supported Napoleon's return. The fence-sitters in whose hands lay the key to success or failure counted in the millions. If they had not forgotten the strains of Napoleonic adventurism, they had soon grown to loathe Bourbon rule by foreign-bought reactionaries wanting to plunge the nation back into feudal darkness. Winning them over would have been difficult even in normal circumstances. But now the job had to be done while simultaneously restoring order in a torn country and rebuilding a greatly weakened and ideologically insecure army.

Napoleon dealt with local insurgencies in the usual manner. Dependable regiments were sent into the Vendée where they soon broke up insurgent bands and caused the main instigator, the duke of Bourbon, to sail for England. Believing that area to be under control he next sent General Clausel with a strong force to deal with southern insurgents. Thanks to Marshal Masséna's cooperation, in but a few weeks the tricolor once again flew over Marseilles, Toulon and Antibes.

The gains proved all too ephemeral. Bourbon royals might have been forced from the country but numerous followers and sympathizers remained. Agents in English pay continued to pour into the west and south as did partisans from Paris, Lyons, Poitiers and elsewhere, their activities frequently supported by money and arms delivered by the Royal Navy. Repressive measures that steadily grew more intense worked only a temporary effect. "The fact of civil war in the Vendée cannot be denied, nor can we delay in . . . forming an army to fight the rebellion," Napoleon told his ministers in late May.[9]

This increasingly serious situation continued into June with ramifications in every principal city in France. It was perhaps the main reason why Napoleon chose to meet the allied military threat outside the country rather than await the inevitable invasion. It was also the reason why he had to defer certain civil reforms until the crisis was favorably resolved. Fearing general rebellion he hoped to stifle it by harsh counter-measures and by leaving an army 20,000 strong in the Vendée – troops which he could well have used to meet the allied armies.

Directly related to the insurgency problem were his political promises. As stated in numerous proclamations, decrees, addresses to ministers, the council of state, judges and provincial delegations, he promised to rule under a constitutional monarchy, to fight no wars abroad unless necessary to repel unjust aggression, to invoke no arbitrary acts from the throne, to guarantee ownership of personal property and free speech. "I have renounced the notion of a great empire," he informed the council of state, "of which I have only laid down the bases. Henceforth the welfare and the consolidation of the French empire will be the object of all my thoughts."[10]

For nearly two centuries Napoleon's critics, pointing to his years of autocratic rule, have written off these pledges as mere verbiage to be discarded once the present crisis had passed and he was firmly in power. Such was his character, goes the "leopard and spots" argument, that he would never change.

Some evidence exists to support this gloomy prognostication. The interim constitution, a lengthy document called the *Acte Additionnel aux Constitutions de l'Empire*, signed on 22 April 1815, did grant the emperor considerable arbitrary powers, particularly of legislative and juridical appointments, but it also guaranteed legislative liberties and such individual rights as equality before the law, freedom of speech, religions and individual petition – moreover it was interim legislation subject to future council, ministerial and legislative debate and modification.[11] Napoleon's cynical remarks attributed to such as Lavalette and others suggested intended deceit, but they may or may not have been said.

That aside, *never* is a dangerous word and to state that Napoleon would *never* change is to claim unwarranted omniscience. The emperor had regained his throne in circumstances entirely foreign to those of his earlier rule, when up to 1812 he could literally do no wrong in extending the tentacles of French power to the north, east and south of Europe. His sudden fall from power and the defection of most of his government and army marshals had been a soul-searing experience. During those long nights on Elba could he have asked himself what went wrong? Could he in the night's darkness privately have admitted personal responsibility, at least in part, for his fall (as he would do on several occasions in exile on St. Helena)? Could he have realized that a compromise peace in 1811 or in 1813 was essential to save France, that his continental system had been a disastrous failure, that the French people no longer approved of an expansionist policy, that this policy was not what France needed?

His critics have supposed him incapable of change without perhaps realizing that self-doubt may be the beginning of an intricate process that can make a weak man stronger or a strong man weaker. He already had made a sea-change in military strategy and tactics. Having denigrated guerrilla and partisan warfare for two decades, he embraced it in 1814 and intended to do so in 1815 with all the passion of a convert to the faith. Why then should he be unable to make a sea-change in foreign and domestic policies?

Had Napoleon defeated the allies, he would not have had much to account for in his subsequent rule if he had only issued a few proclamations designed to mobilize the country. A proclamation made in a moment of urgency is not necessarily a guarantee of future behavior. But add to those proclamations the guarantee of a constitutional monarchy – rule by law, not by whim – add the guarantee of a host of civil rights promised to legislative and other official bodies, words published in the *Moniteur* and reprinted throughout France and Europe. Those words were not ambivalent mumbo-jumbo, they firmly committed the emperor to radical change. The legislative and ministerial bodies, the council of state, the courts, provincial councils – they all quoted his promises as the basis for their support of the imperial throne. Napoleon would have found it very difficult if not impossible to have reneged once the crisis had passed.

There were other indications of a possible character change. Although on occasion he breathed fire and brimstone when challenged by subordinates (in itself an interesting development), these outbursts seem to have been few, as if the ignominy of inelegant exile had dampened the imperial fire of old. Mollien, his devoted minister of the treasury, later wrote: "He seemed habitually calm, pensive, and preserved without affectation a serious dignity, with little of that old audacity and self-confidence which had never met with insuperable obstacles . . . A kind of lassitude, that he had never known before, took hold of him after some hours of work."[12]

He seemed softer, much more human, at times even humble. He seemed to want to regain the former admiration, support and devotion of his people. He formally pledged himself to the dictum that "all power comes from the people, is exercised for the sake of the people."[13] He wrote gently to Emperor Francis to ask for the return of Marie Louise and his son in expressing hope that the temporary peace would continue. Though desperately short of money he awarded the duchess of Bourbon, who remained in France, a generous pension, and he tried to find money to help impoverished Spanish refugees. He persuaded a heretofore implacable enemy, the republican liberal Benjamin Constant, to return to France to oversee the writing of the new constitution. He named probably the most genuine republican of all, Lazare Carnot, minister of the interior and charged him with making extensive improvements in Paris, notably to the Louvre. He ordered compensation to be paid to the people of Champagne, Lorraine and Alsace whose houses had been destroyed in the previous year's fighting.

Bonaparte, Lucien 1775–1840 Prince of Canino

His orders to subordinates began to read differently. *My corps, my cavalry, my* artillery gave way to the pronouns *our* and *your*. The large number of individuals who refused to swear allegiance to the new government were neither summarily imprisoned nor deported. Instead they became the subject of a plaintive note to the justice minister asking his opinion as to what should be done to them – a suggestion of compromise and reconciliation.[14]

He allowed the disgraced King Joachim (Marshal Murat) of Naples – who, contrary to his agreement with Napoleon, had prematurely attacked the Austrian army in Italy and had been thrashed – to take refuge in France, an act of considerable magnanimity. Prince Lebrun was forgiven for serving in the royalist legislature and was restored to the office of arch-treasurer of the empire. Prince Joseph was reinstated as personal adviser to the emperor. Prince Lucien was appointed to the council of state. Prince Jérôme received command of an army division.

None of these acts taken singly perhaps amounted to much, but in aggregate they would seem to have pointed to an important character change – whether temporarily or permanently we shall never know.

There remained the daunting task of rebuilding an army reduced by the Bourbons on grounds of economy and allied demands to somewhere between 150,000 and 200,000 troops of varying efficiency and loyalty. In large part it consisted of redesignated old imperial regiments, some of whose officers and men welcomed the emperor's return, some who did not. Several marshals and a good many generals and senior officers had readily served the Bourbons. A number returned to the Napoleonic fold, others did not. Berthier had fled to his wife in Bavaria, his physical and mental health shattered – he was shortly either to jump or be pushed to his death from a hotel balcony in Bamberg. Soult replaced him as chief of staff, not the most judicious appointment but the choice was limited.

Macdonald, Augereau, Victor, Oudinot and Gouvion St. Cyr stayed with the Bourbons – no great loss. Ney had rejoined the emperor, perhaps unfortunately as it turned out. Masséna, whose passive performance at the time of Napoleon's landing probably saved the expedition, was later welcomed back, though old and ailing. Suchet, the ablest of the marshals, was given command of the Army of the Alps, his mission to screen the eastern border. Corps commands went to Reille, Drouot, Vandamme, Jérôme Bonaparte, Gérard, Mouton, Rapp, Brune, Decaen and Clausel. Marshal Grouchy and generals Pajol, Exelman, Kellermann (the younger) and Milhaud commanded cavalry corps.

Manpower was the first problem. In the hope of immediately raising 100,000 heads, Napoleon broadcast an appeal to non-commissioned officers and men who had left the army, to retired troops of the Guard and to discharged soldiers in the Rhineland and Belgium "to hurry to their country's defense," promising immediate retirement once peace was achieved.

Realizing that the navy was useless he ordered Admiral Decrès to put ships' officers in command of the 60–80,000 troops who were to be raised as coastguards.[15] In addition local departments were to raise national guard units to garrison border fortresses. He could also count on 130,000 conscripts from the class of 1815, but such was the fragile state of public opinion that he did not immediately issue the call.

The army was plagued by shortages of almost every item, in part owing to indolent and corrupt civil *commissaires*, in part to an almost empty treasury. Such was the lack of muskets that some national guard units had to be issued pikes.[16] Thousands of old muskets could not be repaired because there was no money to pay the artisans. Horses were in very short supply. Three or four thousand had been acquired from the Bourbons, but Napoleon wanted a minimum of nearly 35,000. "The II Corps lacks a battery of light artillery as does the cavalry reserve," Napoleon complained to Davout on 10 May. "The guns and caissons are ready but there are no horses . . . The bridge trains at Douai lack rope . . . Most of the northern forts do not have the wood necessary to construct defenses." By late May, Davout was still trying to procure an additional 8,000 mounts with little success, the fault (according to Napoleon) of apathetic bureaus.[17]

"The greatest misfortune would be for us to be too weak in the north and suffer an initial attack there," he wrote Davout in mid May. ". . . The sixteen regiments [of the Army of the North] are apparently very weak and have but few resources to strengthen themselves." His troops urgently needed uniforms and shoes. Food rations were scarce: "War is coming," he wrote Davout a few days later, "and the soldier will not be able to take the field with four days of bread."[18]

*

Although the allied behemoth had still to be formed, the allied plan had meanwhile jelled: Wellington and Blücher to move into northern France and march directly on Paris, supported by Barclay de Tolly's 150,000 Russians coming up on the central Rhine; Schwarzenberg's 210,000 Austrians crossing the upper Rhine to move into eastern France; General Frimont's 75,000 Austrian-Italian troops to march on Lyons from the south.

The Austrians and Russians could not be properly deployed until early July, if then, which left immediate matters in the hands of Blücher and Wellington. Blücher's Prussians were encamped between Liège and Charleroi, Wellington's polyglot force was strung out between Brussels and Ostend on Blücher's right, altogether a line about 100 miles long.

Despite the problems of dispersal and lack of trained troops the aggressive Blücher had argued for a push into France since early May. The less than aggressive Wellington insisted on waiting for the arrival of the other allied armies. Wellington's strategy was chosen by the military council in Vienna – and there the matter rested.[19]

Napoleon had to decide whether to wait for the allied horde to strike or to try to prevent the assault by a surprise attack of Wellington and Blücher's forces. He has often been criticized, not least by Wellington, for not remaining on the defensive, but he had good reasons for not doing so.

One reason, as we earlier suggested, was the unstable condition of the country – an attack of the northern and eastern provinces might well have brought a general rising against which he had little defense. Another reason was the disparate parity of numbers and the poor condition of his troops. Even if they had been in top shape their chances would have been slim against five armies attacking from three or four different directions. A third reason was his belief that, if he could surprise Wellington and Blücher, he could hope to defeat one army first, then the other – a victory that might well topple the allied coalition and lead to a satisfactory peace.

We do not know when he decided on a pre-emptive attack. In late April he ordered Bertrand to have his field equipage in Compiègne by the first of May since he intended to command the Army of the North. The build-up of troops continued during May, as did an espionage effort "to learn what is happening beyond the Rhine, mainly at Mainz." At end of May the Guard was alerted to march on 5 June – "There will probably be a battle soon," he noted to General Drouot.[20]

By the first of June, the day the *Champ de mai* was celebrated with great glitter and gold in Paris, six infantry and four cavalry corps were guarding the northern and eastern frontiers of France with a reserve – the Guard – at Compiègne. It was not a formidable force, probably no more than 110,000 infantry and 10–15,000 cavalry. In addition to the field army, troops (mostly national guards) garrisoned the frontier fortresses and formed an outer ring of Paris defenses. Voluntary free corps of irregulars and partisans were being formed to infiltrate behind allied forces in Belgium.

In early June, Marshal Grouchy was appointed to command the cavalry. On 7 June, Napoleon addressed the opening of the legislature: "I come to begin the constitutional monarchy," but he warned the legislators that the approaching crisis would demand their approval of repressive measures if the nation were to be saved.[21]

His decision to attack had been made. The French-Belgian frontier was to be sealed. Old Marshal Mortier was to command the Guard cavalry and Masséna was entrusted with Metz fortress. On 11 June, Marshal Ney was ordered to appear at general headquarters, Avesnes, within three days. Suchet was to be notified that hostilities would commence on 14 June.

Notes

1   Rose (*Life*), II, 445.
2   Corr. XXVIII. Nrs. 21681, 21682, 21683, Golfe Juan, 1 March 1815.

3   Corr. XXVIII. Nr. 21684, Gap, 6 March 1815.

4   Corr. XXVIII. Nr. 21685, Grenoble, 9 March 1815.

5   Thiébault, I, 74.

6   Corr. XXVIII. Nr. 21686, Lyon, 13 March 1815. See also Macdonald, 362–84.

7   Corr. XXVIII, Nr. 21689, Lyon, (presumed) 13 March 1815.

8   Talleyrand, II, 275–490. See also Seton-Watson, 149–52.

9   Corr. XXVIII. Nr. 21945, Paris, 21 May 1815. See also Miot de Melito, II, 726–7, 730–2.

10 Corr. XXVIII. Nr. 21716, the Tuileries, 26 March 1815. See also Corr. XXVIII. Nrs. 21715, 21717, the Tuileries, 26 March 1815; 21839, Paris, 22 April 1815; 21905, the Tuileries, 14 May 1815; 21906, Paris, 14 May 1815; 22035, 22039, the Tuileries, 11 June 1815. See also Miot de Melito, II, 715–17.

11 Corr. XXVIII. Nr. 21839, Paris, 22 April 1815. See also Miot de Melito, II, 724–6.

12 Rose (*Life*), II, 449–50. See also Miot de Melito, II, 732, who later wrote of his final audience in mid May: "The emperor was no longer what I had seen him formerly . . . The confidence that of old had manifested itself in his speech, the tone of command, the lofty ideas that directed his words and gestures, had disappeared."

13 Corr. XXVIII. Nr. 22037, Paris, 9 June 1815.

14 Corr. XXVIII. Nr. 21820, Paris, 18 April 1815.

15 Corr. XXVIII. Nrs. 21737, the Tuileries, 28 March 1815; 21836, Paris, 22 April 1815.

16 Corr. XXVIII. Nr. 21840, Paris, 24 April 1815.

17 Corr. XXVIII. Nrs. 21887, Paris, 10 May 1815; 21961, Paris, 26 May 1815.

18 Corr. XXVIII. Nrs. 21896, Paris, 12 May 1815; 21915, Paris, 16 May 1815.

19 Rose (*Life*), II, 456–7; Fuller, II, 496–8; Chandler (*Napoleon*), 1015.

20 Corr. XXVIII. Nrs. 21851, Paris, 27 April 1815; 21861, Paris, 1 May 1815; 21938, Paris, 20 May 1815; 21994, Paris, 30 May 1815.

21 Corr. XXVIII. Nr. 22023, Palace of the Representatives, 7 June 1815. See also Miot de Melito, II, 742–3.

CHAPTER THIRTY-TWO

THE BATTLE OF WATERLOO
18 JUNE 1815

Day inconceivable . . . a series of unprecedented accidents . . .
Ah! poor France.

Napoleon's outburst to Las Cases on the anniversary
of Waterloo, St. Helena Island, 18 June 1816[1]

NAPOLEON REACHED AVESNES on 13 June from where he issued detailed orders for the deployment of the Army of the North. This army consisted, at least on paper, of around 125,000 troops, the bulk infantry, with well over 300 guns.[2]

He faced two armies, Wellington's on his left, Blücher's on his right. Wellington commanded a mixed force perhaps 67,000 strong of which some 30,000 were British troops. Blücher was better off with around 120,000 men. Distance severely diluted these strengths however, the cantonments of two armies stretching about 100 miles from Ostend southeast to Liège.

Napoleon held a general idea of enemy deployments. His was a central position by choice, his the option of attacking whichever army offered the most advantageous target before dealing with the second one. He had initially thought to strike Wellington first but fresh intelligence changed his mind. "Tomorrow the 15th I shall march on the Prussians at Charleroi," he wrote Joseph, "which will either bring the enemy to give battle or to retreat. The army is beautiful and the weather fair enough."[3] And to the army:

Soldiers, today is the anniversary of Marengo and
Friedland . . . Soldiers, we have forced marches to make,

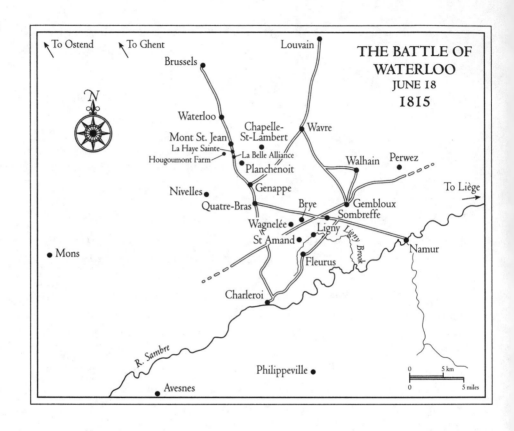

The Battle of Waterloo, June 18 1815

battles to fight, dangers to run; but with steadfastness
victory will be ours. The rights, the honor and the
happiness of the country will be regained. For every brave
Frenchman the moment has arrived to conquer or perish![4]

Detailed marching orders were issued for the following day. The
divisions were to move rapidly – all wagons with the exception of
ammunition caissons and ambulances found in the columns were
to be burned.[5]

Napoleon departed from Avesnes on horseback at 3 a.m. on 15
June after informing Joseph that "the enemy making some movements to attack us, I march to meet him. Thus the battle begins
today."[6] And a busy day indeed as he buzzed from on corps headquarters to another, assessing the latest information on the enemy,
reconnoitering the terrain, straightening out twisted communications and command arrangements and, as always, haranguing the
troops whenever a moment offered. Arriving at Charleroi around
noon he pored over maps while forming his plan of operations,
and a very good plan it was.

Marshal Ney caught up with him in mid afternoon and was
given command of the left wing with orders, according to at least
one witness, to chase the enemy northward and occupy Quatre-
Bras.[7] He next received Marshal Grouchy, gave him command of
the right wing with orders to march northeast on the Prussians.
Ney failed to seize Quatre-Bras but Grouchy, propelled by
Napoleon's temper in late afternoon, finally managed to drive
Ziethen's outposts back to Fleurus, taking 1,500 prisoners and six
cannon.

Napoleon who had been on horseback most of the day returned
exhausted to Charleroi late that evening, issued hurried instructions to his secretary, Baron Fain, and flopped down on his iron
cot for a much needed three hours of rest.

The day was a definite gain for the French. While Napoleon
slept, Fain informed Joseph of the latest developments, noting
that "it is possible that there will be a very important battle tomorrow."[8] A subsequent army bulletin enlarged on events, in main the

seizure of Fleurus with light casualties. General Bourmont and two senior officers of Gérard's corps had defected to the enemy and Marshal Mortier was forced to take to bed because of sciatica, but otherwise the situation was favorable: "The delight of the Belgians could not be described. Some villages have held dances at the sight of the liberators, and everywhere there is heartfelt enthusiasm . . . No one can describe the good spirit and zeal of the army."[9]

Shortly after midnight Napoleon received Marshal Ney for a two-hour discussion of future operations, the conclusions of which were later confirmed in writing. Ney would command 45–50,000 troops of the left wing, Grouchy about the same number of the right wing. The Guard would be kept in reserve at Fleurus to be committed as necessary. Ney was to march on Brussels come evening, hopefully to arrive the following morning, probably followed by Napoleon and the Guard, the plan being to cut communications between Wellington and Blücher. Grouchy was to continue his advance northeast, seizing Sombreffe and Gembloux in the shortest possible time, thus barring the road from Quatre-Bras to Namur – reports indicated that the Prussians could not number more than 40,000.[10]

While Napoleon and Ney were having their *tête-à-tête* shortly after midnight on 16 June, the duke of Wellington was in prominent attendance at the duchess of Richmond's elegant ball in Brussels along with a number of his richly clad generals and officers. Myths abound as to his professional judgment at this point, but in the words of a distinguished modern British military historian, "the only certain fact which has emerged is that he was totally unprepared to face the situation."[11] He did not anticipate an immediate attack by Napoleon, but if the latter did attack he would surely strike the Mons area in order to cut Wellington's communications with the English Channel. Informed that there had been some fighting that afternoon south of Quatre-Bras and east around Fleurus, and that Blücher was concentrating his army at Sombreffe, Wellington nevertheless kept the bulk of his forces west of Brussels and north of Mons to protect his lines of communication. Upon learning that Napoleon's army was at Charleroi, he saw his error and at once ordered his people to march on Nivelles, west of Quatre-Bras, allegedly telling the duke of Richmond that he would have to fight Napoleon at Waterloo.[12]

By the time Wellington left Brussels for Quatre-Bras early on 16 June, his wounded men of the previous day's fighting against Ney's cavalry were in despondent retreat northward, convinced that all was lost. Numerous accounts describe the confused state of Wellington's army at this crucial point, but owing to Ney's indolence and despite some severe miscalculations it nevertheless managed to reach Quatre-Bras before the French.[13]

Ziethen's Prussians had not been as badly hurt in the previous day's fighting as Napoleon supposed. They now held a salient, a lopsided semi-circle – Wagnelée, St. Armand, Ligny – and were being reinforced by two corps. Blücher's other corps were either in or approaching Sombreffe. Instead of falling back as Napoleon expected, Blücher was determined to meet and defeat the French army, but with 84,000 troops, not the 40,000 estimated by the emperor.

Around 8 a.m. on 16 June, Napoleon shrugged off a report from Grouchy that Prussian columns were approaching Sombreffe from the direction of Namur. Only after he reached Fleurus and made his own reconnaissance did he realize that Blücher intended to stand and fight. This more than suited Napoleon who planned to attack once Gérard's corps arrived.

His plan was simple and deadly. While cavalry pinned down the Prussian left, he would hit the center and right. Ney would come from Quatre-Bras to fall on the right rear, at which point the Guard would smash through the center to deliver the *coup de grâce*. This plan was not dissimilar to that of the battle of Bautzen and it was to meet with just as many snags, the result of over-confidence on Napoleon's part, poor intelligence, confused orders, inadequate communications, slow-moving commanders and a determined enemy defense.

The battle began in mid afternoon, the French cavalry containing Blücher's left, Gérard attacking Ligny, Vandamme and Girard moving on St. Armand. Resistance proving far stronger than Napoleon supposed – probably the reason why he had left Mouton's corps standing idle at Charleroi – he soon ordered Ney to march on Blücher's right: "The fate of France is in your hands."[14]

Ney had his own problems, the result of his having failed to march early in the day, thus giving Wellington time to reinforce the prince of Orange's weak force defending Quatre-Bras. By the time Ney received Napoleon's newest order, General Reille's corps still had not won the town. Ney was waiting impatiently for Drouet's divisions of his command to come up, but Napoleon, equally impatient, had sent an order to Drouet to direct his approach march so as to fall on Blücher's right rear at Ligny. Upon learning of this pre-emption Ney lost his temper, furiously countermanded the emperor's order and plunged himself into battle which ended only in a draw that night, each side suffering 4–5,000 casualties.

The battle of Ligny meanwhile was proceeding favorably, albeit with heavy casualties including General Girard's death. Anticipating Drouet's early arrival on Blücher's right, Napoleon was preparing to launch the Guard against the Prussian center when, around 5 p.m., Vandamme's rearguard mistook Drouet's advance guard for the enemy. This error caused near panic in Vandamme's less than secure ranks, a dangerous confusion not sorted out until Drouet had received Ney's counter-order and reversed his march. As one result neither Drouet nor Mouton, who had been ordered to march far too late, participated in what could have been a knock-out blow of Blücher's Prussians.

The Guard finally swept into Ligny in late evening, a bayonet attack owing to a violent thunderstorm that prevented musket fire, and moved northward toward Brye. Blücher still refused to admit defeat. While riding to the attack at the head of some 30 cavalry squadrons, his horse fell dead from a bullet and nearly killed its master by rolling on him. An aide finally managed to extricate him and dragged him to safety while the shattered corps on his right wing escaped into darkness.

Thus ended the battle of Ligny, a definite French victory but a costly one. Estimates wildly vary, but the Prussians probably suffered about 15,000 casualties (including those taken prisoner) with another few thousand Belgians and Germans deserting the army and heading for Liège. The French suffered somewhere around 10–12,000 casualties.[15]

Command confusion and ignorance did not end with victory. After a brief and well-deserved rest at Fleurus, Napoleon congratulated himself on having sent the Prussians running back to Liège. Having completed the first goal of his strategy he could now lash out at Wellington. Overlooking Ney's insubordination (which must have been difficult) he now ordered the errant marshal to attack the English to his front while he, Napoleon, moved on the enemy left. Grouchy's cavalry were to pursue the Prussians to determine if they were continuing their retreat or if they intended to join Wellington.[16]

General Gneisenau had little use for Wellington and would have preferred the army to withdraw to its Liège base, but Blücher, slowly reviving from his painful fall, and General Grölmann, his quartermaster-general, overrode him and ordered the army back to Wavre so as to keep contact with Wellington. The duke learned of this early on 17 June and ordered his army to withdraw on Mont St. Jean where he would stand against the French providing that Blücher supported him with an infantry corps.[17]

Wellington's withdrawal began in mid morning, 17 June.

Marshal Ney as usual had not obeyed orders. While the enemy force was moving out in considerable confusion, the French were cooking midday dinner oblivious to the tactical opportunity presented. This idyll was rudely interrupted by Napoleon who led whatever cavalry he could get his hands on in pursuit of Wellington's rearguard, Lord Uxbridge's cavalry, a thrilling but futile chase hindered by still another violent thunderstorm that confined the French to the Quatre-Bras-Brussels road, just possibly saving Uxbridge's bacon. The pursuit continued until about 6.30 p.m. when the French vanguard reached La Belle Alliance, a range of hills about 2 miles south of Mont St. Jean. A similar range across the valley paralleled the French positions, and there Wellington had deployed his army on the reverse slopes – as Milhaud's cavalry soon discovered.

Napoleon could go no further until his infantry arrived. In headquarters south of La Belle Alliance he managed a short rest before touring outposts for several hours in driving rain. He returned to headquarters to find a dispatch from Grouchy dated the previous night: one Prussian column was apparently retiring on Wavre, a second one on Perwez (presumably *en route* to Liège) and a third on Namur. Once his patrols had reported further, "if I find the mass of the Prussians is retiring on Wavre I shall follow them so as to prevent them gaining Brussels and to separate them from Wellington."[18]

For one reason or another – possibly Napoleon's waiting for a second report from Grouchy, or the pressure of preparing to attack the English, or Soult's ineptness – a reply to this message was not sent until 10 a.m. on 18 June, that is until the battle of Waterloo was about to begin.

This was sloppy but not necessarily crucial. After a belated start Grouchy, with Vandamme and Gérard's corps, had reached Walhain on the Gembloux-Wavre road. From here he sent Napoleon a message stating that the Prussians apparently intended to concentrate some miles south of Louvain (about 15 miles east of Brussels); accordingly he would concentrate his troops at Wavre to interpose them "between the Prussian army and Wellington." Shortly after noon however he and Gérard heard heavy cannon-fire in the direction of Mont St. Jean.

Heeding one of Napoleon's basic axioms – always march to the sound of guns – Gérard insisted on a change of course which Grouchy, having misinterpreted his orders, refused to consider. As a result the right wing of Napoleon's army was marching *away* from battle while Bülow's corps (to be followed by those of Pirch and Ziethen) was marching *toward* battle.[19]

Napoleon was partly responsible for this disastrous scenario. Despite the suggestions of Marshal Soult and General Jérôme Bonaparte that the Prussians intended to join Wellington, he remained convinced that at least for the time being they were *hors de combat*. He also believed that Grouchy understood the tactical position and would respond accordingly, thus in mid morning of 18 June he sent Marbot's hussars on patrol to the northeast (Bülow's approach route) to keep an eye out for Grouchy.[20]

Heavy rains during the night had caused Napoleon to delay the attack from 9 a.m. to 1 p.m. so that the ground would be dry enough to support artillery limbers. His attack plan was simple enough: Drouet's corps to strike Wellington's center which was defending the ridge north of La Belle Alliance; simultaneously Prince Jérôme's division of Reille's corps to move on Hougoumont farm to threaten Wellington's right sufficiently to cause him to weaken his center.

Napoleon's line stretched about 3 miles east from the Nivelles-Brussels road, the allied line about 2¼ miles northeast from Hougoumont. Opposing strengths have been variously cited but Napoleon probably mustered around 70,000 effectives with nearly 250 guns, Wellington perhaps 65,000 with 150 cannon.[21] If Napoleon had weakened himself by sending off Grouchy's right wing, Wellington had reciprocated by leaving a corps 17,000 strong to guard what he still feared to be his vulnerable extreme right south of Mons.

The French cannonade opened sometime before noon while Jérôme's division moved through the woods in front of Hougoumont farm, a large walled château overlooking extensive orchards held by the English. What Napoleon intended as a feint to draw troops from Wellington's center soon turned into a separate battle as Jérôme, perhaps hoping to redeem past errors, repeatedly attacked a valiant and stubborn enemy. As J.F.C. Fuller pointed out in his detailed and excellent account of the battle, instead of drawing enemy troops the battle of Hougoumont farm consumed French troops as Reille was forced to commit Foy's division in support.

Neither did the initial massive cannonade live up to expectations, partly because the soft ground prevented the cannon-balls from ricocheting but mainly because of Wellington's tactic made famous in Portugal and Spain of sheltering his main body on the reverse side of a slope, generally impervious to anything but howitzer fire, while waiting for the enemy to come into musket range.

Drouet's infantry had no more than begun their advance when Napoleon learned that Bülow's vanguard was closing on Chapelle St. Lambert some 4–5 miles to the northeast. He at once sent a message to Grouchy: "Do not lose a minute to draw nearer to us and to join us and crush Bülow, whom you will catch in the very act."[22] He followed this by deploying some light cavalry and Mouton's reserve corps to the threatened flank.

Drouet's columns continued forward to clamber up the enemy-held ridge, only to see Sir Thomas Picton's infantry suddenly rise to pour volley after volley of musket fire into the massed ranks while cannon firing grapeshot cut huge holes in the columns before they could deploy in line. Drouet's people did what they could to sustain the attack – the brave Picton was killed in the *mêlée* – but then they were hit by Uxbridge's cavalry charge which claimed 3,000 prisoners and two eagles but which, blood up, continued across the valley to attack and be severely mauled by French artillery batteries before limping back to their lines to close the first phase of the battle.

Although each side had suffered heavily, Wellington held the upper hand provided he could hold on until Blücher's corps arrived. Napoleon already had learned that Grouchy was too far off to reach the battlefield in time – it was Bülow who held the key to victory or defeat.

But Bülow was not to be hurried. He had marched from Chapelle St. Lambert about 4 p.m., soon to be delayed by French light cavalry and Mouton's infantry. Hoping to pre-empt his arrival Napoleon ordered Ney to seize La Haye Sainte in preparation for an all-out assault against the enemy center.

Ney with only two brigades attacked the village and was repulsed, but believing that Wellington had decided to retreat he took it upon himself to lead a cavalry charge 5,000 strong. The unexpected attack fell on allied squares and gun batteries. Most of the cannon were taken but almost immediately recovered when the French were routed by Uxbridge counter-attacking with his remaining 5,000 horse. A second effort impetuously supported by *all* of the remaining French cavalry including the Guard's, perhaps a total 10,000 troopers, jammed the field between Hougoumont and La Haye Sainte and soon was put to rout. A final advance by infantry managed to seize the fought-over village but then halted owing to lack of reinforcements.

In the interim Bülow's advance guard had closed on the French right to push Mouton's force out of Planchenoit village, a crisis resolved by the hastily deployed Young Guard who recaptured it only shortly to lose it. With communications thus threatened, Napoleon committed several battalions of the Old Guard whose bayonet attack overwhelmed the Prussian defenders.

It was now nearly 8 p.m. The smoke-covered battlefield was a horrible mélange of dead and dying humans and horses. On the left, Jérôme who had been wounded was still stymied at Hougoumont despite the heavy losses of the defenders. On the right the Young Guard again held Planchenoit. Ney in the center held La Haye Sainte, his artillery thundering against Wellington's center. But now Ziethen's vanguard was closing on the allied left with Blücher's main force not far distant.

Napoleon now turned over the last nine battalions of the Guard to Ney. Strengthened further by units from Reille's divisions and supported by heavy artillery fire, the troops moved out in two columns between Hougoumont and La Haye Sainte.

The grenadiers of the Old Guard led the way across several

hundred yards of blood-soaked fields, drums beating, the sinking sun reflecting off their bayonets, the horse-drawn field guns firing murderous case shot.

The defenders, a brigade of English Guards, remained crouched behind the crest until the French were but 25–50 yards to their front. Then, suddenly, they rose to pour forth the accurate fire for which they were famous. Within minutes thousands of musket balls shredded the attackers who, losing all semblance of order, turned and fled. The second column on their left, the Middle Guard, similarly advanced only to be met by soldiers of a light brigade appearing as if by magic to send the *chasseurs* in wild retreat behind La Haye Sainte.

At Wellington's signal 40,000 soldiers raced in pursuit of the broken enemy, but such was the general exhaustion that they soon came to a halt. Wellington met briefly with Blücher around 9 p.m. at La Belle Alliance. The Prussian marshal agreed to his cavalry continuing the pursuit, but this effort petered out by midnight.[23]

Notes

1   Las Cases, IV, 272.
2   Fuller, II, 496, whose figures I have rounded off. Almost every historian presents a different set of figures, some founded on highly suspect official before- and after-action reports, others on equally suspect personal accounts, still others seemingly on divine inspiration, none of which are more than estimates, in some cases educated, in others not. See also Rose (*Life*), II, 189–90; Wartenburg, II, 414; Chandler (*Napoleon*), 1014–16, 1020; Meyers, 75–89.
3   Corr. XXVIII. Nr. 22050, Avesnes, 14 June 1815.
4   Corr. XXVIII. Nr. 22052, Avesnes, 14 June 1815.
5   Corr. XXVIII. Nr. 22053, Beaumont, 14 June 1815.
6   Corr. XXVIII. Nr. 22054, Beaumont, 15 June 1815.
7   Fuller, II, 500.
8   Corr. XXVIII. Nr. 22055, Charleroi, 15 June 1815.

9   Corr. XXVIII. Nr. 22056, Charleroi, 15 June 1815.

10 Corr. XXVIII. Nrs. 22058, 22059, Charleroi, 16 June 1815.

11 Fuller, II, 502.

12 Fuller, II, 503.

13 Fuller, II, 503–4. See also Thackeray, Chapters 29–32, for a splen-
    did fictional treatment of the British army in Brussels at this time.

14 Fuller, II, 506.

15 Fuller, II, 509. See also Rose (*Life*), II, 464–82; Wartenburg, II,
    426–35; Chandler (*Napoleon*), 1034–57.

16 Fuller, II, 515–17. See also Rose (*Life*), II, 481, for a slightly dif-
    ferent version; Wartenburg, II, 435.

17 Fuller, II, 516–17.

18 Fuller, II, 519–20.

19 Fuller, II, 521–3.

20 Fuller, II, 523.

21 Fuller, II, 524. See also Rose (*Life*), II, 487–509; Wartenburg, II,
    437–41; Las Cases, IV, 272–3.

22 Fuller, II, 526.

23 Rose (*Life*), II, 487–511; Wartenburg, II, 430–41; Fuller, II,
    492–542; Chandler (*Napoleon*), 1064–90.

CHAPTER THIRTY-THREE

ABDICATION AND EXILE
JUNE–AUGUST 1815

*If the Admiral [Hotham], in consequence of the demand that
you have addressed to him, sends you the permits for the
United States, His Majesty [Napoleon] will go there with
pleasure; but in default of them, he will go voluntarily to
England as a private individual to enjoy the protection of the
laws of your country.*

General Count Bertrand to Captain Maitland of the
Royal Navy, Ile d'Aix, July 1815[1]

NAPOLEON ESCAPED CAPTURE only by taking refuge in a battalion
square of the Guard which allowed him to reach Charleroi early
on 19 June. It was a matter now of picking up the pieces. The
allied pursuit having stalled, Prince Jérôme and other generals
were to intercept retreating fugitives at Philippeville and Avesnes
and reform them into an army. From Philippeville the emperor
wrote Joseph in Paris of the need to rally the nation in order to
raise a new army 300,000 strong.[2]

After transferring command to Marshal Soult and stealing a
short rest the emperor continued on to Laon where he spent the
night and from where he dispatched a final bulletin, a lengthy
document that presented only a confused version of events from
16 June through the final battle (which he held to be "glorious and
yet so fatal to French arms").[3]

Napoleon arrived at the Élysée palace in Paris on 21 June to
closet himself with his ministers. Such was the political ferment
that Prince Lucien Bonaparte urged him to dissolve the chambers

and declare Paris in a state of siege. Cambacérès, Carnot and Maret advised him either to dissolve the chambers or confront the legislators in person. He refused to consider a prorogue which he believed would bring on a civil war. Probably because of fatigue he sent Carnot to the chamber of representatives and Lucien to the chamber of peers with appeals for a final national effort against the invading enemy.[4]

The emperor still commanded a fair amount of military muscle. A modern military historian has calculated that despite a loss of some 40,000 men in casualties, prisoners and deserters in the recent campaign, Marshal Soult would soon rally more than 55,000 troops, including 25,000 ably salvaged by Grouchy; this figure would rise to a total 117,000 by the addition of fortress garrisons, various militias and national guard units, not including 170,000 conscripts then in training.[5]

Wellington and Blücher had also suffered heavy casualties, perhaps a total 25,000, to reduce Wellington's strength to slightly over 50,000, Blücher around 65,000. Marshal Suchet meanwhile had defeated an Austrian army in the Piedmont, General Rapp's small force had checked Schwarzenberg on the Rhine and General Clausel had pacified the Vendée (at least temporarily).

If the odds were not entirely hopeless militarily, they were politically. Military defeat at Waterloo was the final straw. Fouché's treachery had already turned such powerful members of the chambers as Lafayette into enemies who proclaimed that dissolution of the chambers would be an act "of high treason." In a swift reversal of recent pledges to the emperor, the two houses overrode the protests of dissenters to inform Napoleon the following day that he had one hour in which to abdicate or be stripped of his title. His ministers with the exception of Carnot urged him to abdicate. Lucien, Davout and supporters in the legislature wanted him to fight on.

Shock and exhaustion told. In a declaration to the French people Napoleon formally renounced the throne in favor of his son (virtually a prisoner at Schönbrunn).[6] The chambers happily accepted the abdication but refused to accept the king of Rome.

Instead a provisional government was formed of five members which included Carnot and Caulaincourt with Fouché as president to rule until further notice. Ordered by Fouché to leave Paris on 25 June, Napoleon and a few intimates traveled to Princess Hortense Bonaparte's court at Malmaison.

Napoleon did not find it easy to climb out of the wreckage of state. The allied armies had reached Compiègne and their blood was up. A French request for an armistice brought little more than a sneer. Blücher and Gneisenau were intent not only on capturing the fugitive outlaw but on executing him. Wellington did not agree and a nasty quarrel with his enemy Gneisenau took place. There seems little doubt however that Napoleon's life was in danger, which may have prompted Fouché's peremptory order for him to leave Paris. At any rate Fouché sent him a keeper the next day, General Becker, with the advice to move to Rochefort on the coast in a bid to leave France.[7]

Where could he go?

He seems to have favored North America. From Malmaison he ordered his librarian to send him "several works on the United States," and to prepare a large library which "should be consigned to an American agency and shipped from Le Havre."[8] The provisional government had asked Wellington for the necessary passports, and two French frigates were made available for the voyage.[9]

Napoleon still had not made up his mind. General Becker found him at times jovial, at times pensive, eating well, discussing a variety of plans including a final attempt to rally an army to defeat the invaders. Blücher unknowingly solved the problem of indecision by sending a flying column to seize him, an attempt temporarily stymied by Marshal Davout's quick action. Fouché now ordered him to leave Rochefort and sail even without passports.[10] That he intended to do so was suggested by the immense amount of luggage taken to the coast – not only a large wardrobe and cartons of books but also cases of gold and silver tableware, serving dishes, precious china and crystal, family portraits and valuable memorabilia, not to mention some official records and maps and a library of back copies of the *Moniteur*. Upon his departure from Malmaison a tearful Princess Hortense pressed on him a valuable diamond necklace (which Las Cases sewed in his uniform for safe keeping).

Napoleon and his small party – Count Bertrand with wife and children, generals Savary, Gourgaud and Becker – reached Rochefort on 3 July. Perhaps the party, joined now by brother Joseph, Count Montholon with wife and child, General Lallemand and Las Cases with his son, realized their plight. Various plans of escape were hashed over: the two French frigates could slip him out at night; he could be smuggled onto a fishing boat and later transferred to a larger vessel; a Danish captain offered to stow him away in a beer cask. But these and other notions were just as quickly discarded owing to the efficient British naval blockade of the few exit points.

Meanwhile the hunt for the quarry remained very lively as it was joined by numerous royalists. On 8 July the party was put on a small ship that anchored off the tiny island of Aix on the French coast, and on the following day orders arrived from the provisional government to sail within 24 hours. Four days later King Louis XVIII arrived in Paris, the provisional government was dissolved, the Bourbons controlled the country, the Prussians and royalists more than ever wanted Napoleon's blood.

Somewhat frantically Napoleon contacted the local British naval commander, Captain Maitland of HMS *Bellerophon*, asking if his passports had arrived, and if not could he sail without them. The passports had not arrived. They never would. The allies did not want Napoleon to live in England or the United States. They already had decided to exile him as a prisoner to St. Helena island. Maitland's orders were to prevent his departure unless it was on the *Bellerophon*.

Time was running out. Napoleon now dictated a brief note to the prince regent of England asking for temporary asylum from "the most powerful, the most steadfast and the most generous of my enemies."[11] Maitland at once sent off Gourgaud with this letter. Napoleon and his party could follow on the *Bellerophon* but with the stipulation, according to Maitland, that the ex-emperor "would be entirely at the disposal of our government."[12]

This was a verbal declaration which Las Cases may or may not have quoted correctly. In view of subsequent events it is important to quote from Bertrand's *written* note to Maitland announcing that the emperor would come on board on 15 July: "If the Admiral [Hotham], in consequence of the demand that you have addressed to him, sends you the permits for the United States, His Majesty [Napoleon] will go there with pleasure; but in default of them, he will go voluntarily to England as a private individual to enjoy the protection of the laws of your country."[13]

The voyage to Torbay [Torquay] was pleasant enough. Napoleon dressed in the uniform of the Guard *chasseurs* was well received though without the customary cannon salute. He did not know that henceforth he was to be addressed as "the general" – so far as the allied powers were concerned, the emperor had disappeared. Maitland described him as a "remarkably strong, well-built man," cheerfully inquisitive, prowling about the ship, asking innumerable questions, eating like a horse, joking with the crew who soon worshipped him.[14]

Gourgaud rejoined the party at Torbay but brought no response from the prince regent or Whitehall. Somewhat ominously the party was not allowed to land before the ship sailed for Plymouth. There the secretary of the admiralty and Admiral Lord Keith, commanding Plymouth station, personally delivered the written order for his exile to St. Helena "in order to prevent any further disturbance to the peace of Europe." Up to this point Napoleon had been "entirely at ease" but now his anger surfaced as his jailers listened impassively to his arguments that he had boarded the *Bellerephon* as a private citizen, not as a prisoner-of-war, that he would never survive on St. Helena, that he would prefer death to this unjust exile – all of which, subsequently written and sent to Keith, brought no response from the executioners.[15]

Napoleon on Board the Bellerephon

Ironically the good people of England came from many miles around hoping for a glimpse of this incredible man. Some days, Maitland later reported, over a thousand people in small boats rowed as close as possible to the surrounding guard boats, women waving handkerchiefs when Napoleon appeared on the quarter-deck. Keith had warned Maitland that Whig tempers were running high and that an attempt might be made either by Napoleon and his party or by sympathizers on shore to get him off the ship.

For this reason Maitland sailed on 4 August to rendezvous with HMS *Northumberland*, Rear Admiral Sir George Cockburn's flag, to which Napoleon and his party were transferred. Following orders from Whitehall, Cockburn and a customs official searched their possessions, confiscating 4,000 gold napoleons (about 80,000 francs) from Napoleon's personal luggage but not disturbing other valuables.[16] All but Napoleon were required to surrender their swords. Savary and Lallemand were removed from the party (and later imprisoned), the surgeon backed out and was replaced with Maitland's, Barry O'Meara.

The voyage lasted 67 relatively uneventful days. Most accounts credit admiral, captain and crew as being good hosts. Napoleon was given comfortable if small quarters and was paid every courtesy other than being addressed as emperor, majesty or sire. Acting on orders, Admiral Cockburn and his officers addressed him only as general and did not remove their hats when he appeared on deck, petty and unnecessary humiliations from which grew many future troubles.

What Napoleon called his court was a mixed bag. We met the Bertrands earlier on Elba. General Count Bertrand, veteran of many battles and grand marshal of the palace since Duroc's death, was 42 years old. A refined, intelligent, brave and capable officer, he was a great favorite of Napoleon. Not so his small and restless wife. The countess was of Irish-Creole stock (the mind boggles). She had done everything possible to prevent Bertrand from

accompanying the emperor, including an attempt to throw herself
overboard at Plymouth. She might well be excused for not wanting to raise three children on an island in the middle of nowhere,
but as her husband probably pointed out to her, that would be
better than living as a penniless widow once the Bourbons had put
him before a firing squad.

Next in the pecking order were Count and Countess
Montholon and their three-year-old son. General Montholon was
a 33-year-old converted royalist whose professional career was as
mediocre as his social career was execrable. The countess, whose
reputation was also sordid, was three years older. Each had been
previously married. Having run through his first wife's fortune
Montholon was a virtual bankrupt. His wife although aging was
not unattractive physically, she played the piano and sang well.
She was also a true schemer, easily insinuating herself first into
Napoleon's favor and then his bed. Rivalry between the two
countesses was keen, and Napoleon would greatly enjoy himself
by playing on the contest.

General Baron Gaspard Gourgaud was a year younger than
Montholon. Commissioned in 1802, he had carved out a
respectable enough military career before being appointed an
orderly officer to Napoleon in 1811. He always claimed to have
saved the emperor's life on one occasion during the allied invasion
of France, and he may well have done so. He also served at
Waterloo and was promoted to brigadier general. A rather unattractive bachelor, in or out of drink he was a braggart, conceited,
childishly petulant and dangerously jealous of his position.

The oldest member of this weird group was the marquis de
Las Cases, 49 years old. From a noble family, he had become a
royalist naval officer, had emigrated and spent 10 years in
England, becoming something of a celebrity as author of a
scholarly and very profitable historical atlas. Upon return to
France under Napoleon's amnesty he became a respected councillor of state, a position he retained under the Bourbons. He
returned to the fold however and begged to accompany the
emperor into exile as amanuensis, his plan being to return to

France and sell the memoirs at vast profit. His idolatry and greed caused him to leave behind wife and children with the exception of 15-year-old Emmanuel, a very bright lad who soon became a favorite of the emperor.[16]

Finally there was Barry O'Meara, a Royal Navy surgeon formerly of HMS *Bellerophon*, and recruited at the last minute, whose fluency in Italian caused Napoleon to name him personal physician.

In addition the party included eleven servants: a *maître d'hôtel*, four valets, chef, steward, grooms and footmen. We met the *maître d'hôtel*, Cipriani Franceschi, briefly as Napoleon's secret agent in Vienna when the emperor was on Elba. First valet Marchand had also served him on Elba and had become a great favorite, as had second valet Louis Etienne St. Denis, known as Ali, each of whom later wrote patchy but often interesting and amusing memoirs of life with the emperor.

Napoleon's shipboard routine was simple enough. Breakfast in his quarters was followed by several hours spent in reading books from his portable library or in dictating his memoirs to Las Cases who also undertook to teach him English, at first with little success. In mid afternoon and again after dinner he appeared on deck, walking briskly, talking with officers and crew who were favorably impressed with his professional knowledge of matters nautical. He frequently conversed with Cockburn, insisting on one occasion that he had fully intended to invade England in 1803–5, on another vigorously defending the duke d'Enghien's execution and inveighing against French liberals and "the danger of representative institutions on the continent," no matter how well that political system suited the more staid English. He also prophesied that once the allied armies left France there would be a general insurrection owing to the people's hatred of the Bourbons.[17]

He remained generally in good humor, never complaining, according to Las Cases. In passing the equator the oppressive heat made it difficult for him to sleep, and on one occasion when the vessel was being painted he kept to his cabin for two days to escape the odor which made him ill. Aside from that and one or two brief stomach upsets his health was excellent, which he attributed to eating a great deal of meat plus exercise.[18]

The party dined at the admiral's table, Napoleon occupying the place of honor, the others seated by rank along with six naval officers. Twenty bottles of one wine or another – sherry, claret, madeira, port and champagne – were consumed nightly, an average of over 1½ bottles per person per dinner, a comfortable enough liquid intake in that some of the bottles may have been flagons and since wine was also drunk at breakfast and luncheon.[19]

In the evenings he often conversed with his guests or listened to Madame Montholon sing or to the reading of a play, frequently playing cards or chess to pass the time. It was a boring enough routine, but after the repeated traumas of the last three years probably salutary. The admiral's secretary noted that upon passing the equator, "his spirits are even and he appears perfectly unconcerned about his fate."[20]

Not so his companions. Infighting for his favor had begun even before the ship was underway. It continued to such a noticeable degree during the voyage that Sir George Bingham, colonel of the 53rd Regiment, noted in his diary: "It is not difficult to see that envy, hatred and all uncharitableness are firmly roted in Napoleon's family, and that their residence in St. Helena will be rendered very uncomfortable by it."[21]

Notes

1   Rose (*Life*), II, 521.
2   Rose (*Life*), II, 512.
3   Corr. XXVIII. Nr. 22061, Laon, 20 June 1815.
4   Corr. XXVIII. Nr. 22062, Élysée palace, 21 June 1815. This is Napoleon's message to the representatives. That to the peers has not been found but presumably was along the same lines. See also Rose (*Life*), II, 513–14.

5   Chandler (*Napoleon*), 1090–5. See also Fuller, II, 540, for a variance in figures.

6   Corr. XXVIII. Nr. 22063, Élysée palace, 22 June 1815.

7   Las Cases, I, 24–9.

8   Corr. XXVIII. Nr. 22064, Paris, 25 June 1815.

9   Rose (*Life*), II, 516. See also Metternich, II, 523; Lavalette, II, 196–9.

10 Rose (*Life*), II, 517–18. See also Las Cases, I, 30–1.

11 Corr. XXVIII. Nr. 22066, Ile d'Aix, 14 July 1815. See also Las Cases, I, 37–47.

12 Rose (*Life*), II, 520–1.

13 Rose (*Life*), II, 520–1.

14 Rose (*Life*), II, 521–2.

15 Las Cases, I, 78–9.

16 Las Cases, I, 84–5.

17 Las Cases, I, 111–17. See also Korngeld, 56–9; Rose (*Life*), II, 532–3.

18 Las Cases, I, 195 ff., 256–7.

19 Rose (*Life*), II, 534. Rose's figures are based on a nice piece of research into secret Admiralty files that showed a total consumption of 1,344 assorted bottles. There is no mention of who picked up the tab.

20 Rose (*Life*), II, 532–3.

21 Rose (*Life*), II, 536.

CHAPTER THIRTY-FOUR

ST. HELENA ISLAND
OCTOBER 1815–APRIL 1816

There is an island in the silent sea,
Whose marge the wistful waves lap listlessly –
An isle of rest for those who used to be.

Thomas Samuel Jones, *The Island.*[1]

MILLIONS OF YEARS ago an angry volcano gave birth to St. Helena island in the middle of the South Atlantic ocean. Discovered by the Portuguese at the beginning of the sixteenth century, the island lay dormant until the mid seventeenth century when it became a port of call for ships sailing to and from the East Indies. It was soon taken over by the English East India Company from whom in 1815 it was "borrowed" by the English government as a fitting place for Napoleon's exile.

From the standpoint of security it was an excellent choice. Twelve hundred miles west of the African coast, 1,700 miles northwest of Capetown, its nearest neighbor was Ascension island 700 miles to the northwest. A little longer than 10 miles and 6½ miles at its widest point, it is ringed on three sides by cliffs over 2,000 feet above sea level.

In 1815 artillery batteries protected the four possible landing places, while strategically placed outposts along the cliffs notified government headquarters by semaphore within minutes of a ship approaching from up to 60 miles away. Its only port, Jamestown, was defended by a well garrisoned fort studded with cannon ports. Several Royal Navy frigates and brigs constantly patrolled surrounding waters. The native population was a mélange of several thousand Europeans, Chinese, East Indians and negroes. The latter numbered 1,800 of whom three-quarters were slaves indentured to work in the plantation fields of a few large landowners.

The *Northumberland* dropped anchor in Jamestown bay on 15 October 1815. Napoleon was taken ashore to spend the night in Jamestown. The only town on the island it was little more than a country hamlet of one street giving on to a string of houses overlooked by two barren mountain ridges. Here he was placed in a grubby boarding-house with armed sentries posted outside his door – welcome to St. Helena.

The next morning he and Admiral Cockburn were driven to Plantation House for a meeting with the East India Company's governor, Colonel Mark Wilks, who was waiting to be relieved by a governor of the Crown. Wilks was 55 years old, "a military officer, a man of letters, a diplomat and a chemist," but unfortunately relieved of his duties by Cockburn.[2]

It was Cockburn's responsibility to enforce the ground rules of Napoleon's imprisonment. His inelegant status had been determined by the allies who in August had signed a convention making him a prisoner of all the powers who were to send commissioners to St. Helena to confirm Napoleon's imprisonment, but not to interfere with Cockburn's security measures. The prisoner would be under watch day and night by armed sentries. A country house about 6 miles from town, Longwood, was being prepared for him and his "family." Meanwhile the family would lodge in Jamestown while the prisoner occupied a bungalow about 2 miles inland. He could receive only those visitors authorized by Cockburn. Letters, coming and going, would be censored. He could move by foot, horse or carriage only within a limited area. Should he wish to go beyond the limits a British officer would have to accompany him. If Napoleon weren't actually locked *up*, he was locked *in* – and so began a six-year ordeal.

*

The first seven weeks of the ordeal were spent in what Cockburn euphemistically described in his diary as "a pretty little bungalow" called Briars. This structure occupied a small plot on the property of a local merchant, William Balcombe, who lived in a modest house close by. The aptly named Briars was a one-room hut used by the Balcombes as tea-house for adults, play-house for children. The room was square with two doors and two windows, no curtains, no blinds, a chair or two, no couch, no beds, no stove, no plumbing. "Never in his campaigns, perhaps never in his life could the emperor have had a smaller lodging or so many privations," Las Cases later wrote in describing the property and subsequent existence.[3]

Napoleon moved in immediately. Marchand and Ali arrived with his folding camp-beds and a few necessaries, and Las Cases and his son were summoned so that he could continue dictating his account of the Italian campaigns. Aside from the primitive conditions – his meals had to be brought from town, the restriction of movement and presence of armed sentries – the surroundings were quite pleasant. Tucked away in the rocks the cottage bordered on a kitchen garden and overlooked an orchard of fruit trees and a flower garden. It being late spring south of the equator the weather was variable, some days fair, the air soft with fragrant country scents, some days unpleasantly damp from mists and rain brought by the trade winds.

The emperor soon become friendly with the Balcombes and their two daughters, 16-year-old Jane and 14-year-old Betsy, the latter a little devil who loved playing tricks on him. Most of his time was spent either in reading or dictating but he also took long walks and frequently played blindman's bluff with the children who adored him. He was sometimes a guest at family dinners and much enjoyed conversations with the senior Balcombes even with the language difficulty. Cockburn finally respected repeated complaints of inadequate lodging by having a tent erected in front of the cottage to serve as a combined office and dining area. Gourgaud and Bertrand joined Las Cases in taking down the emperor's memories and keeping him company. The chef arrived, linen and silver

The Sorrows of Boney

covered the rude table and the sentries were eventually moved to less conspicuous posts thanks to Balcombe's intercession.

In not many weeks the routine palled and the complaints increased. A cold spell in early December prevented the emperor from taking evening walks and from dining in the tent. "He was sad," Las Cases noted, "silent, his face had something hurtful and harsh."[4]

Isolation was beginning to tell and this was partly Napoleon's fault. The Wilks did what they could to make life more pleasant for the new arrivals. They were invited to Plantation House for dinners and balls which most of them enjoyed. Gourgaud became so smitten with the governor's beautiful daughter that he almost forgot to be jealous of Las Cases. Napoleon stubbornly refused all such invitations. As long as he was not addressed as emperor and given liberty of the island he would have nothing to do with local society. Since Cockburn could not or would not relax the allied rules, the result was unpleasant impasse.

His refusal to compromise title and freedom stemmed not only from a deepset imperial arrogance. As he had informed Cockburn during the voyage, it would not be long before the French nation rose in protest against the Bourbons. His thinking did not stop there however. He was well aware of his English sympathizers grouped around the Whig party leader, Lord Holland. If somehow the Tories could be voted out of office, he reasoned, almost certainly the Whigs would allow him a more comfortable exile, perhaps even freedom to return to France if the throne should become vacant. In pursuit of these dreams he intended to discredit the English government and by extension its allies for humiliating him in cruel imprisonment. Thus his frequent clashes with Cockburn, thus his virulent letters smuggled to influential sympathizers in England and France.[5]

Imperial spirits revived with the move to Longwood accomplished with considerable ceremony in mid December. The former residence of the lieutenant-governor, it was a converted barn of four rooms and outbuildings hastily being enlarged by the *Northumberland*'s carpenters to house Napoleon, his suite and servants. Almost six miles from Jamestown, it was located in the middle of a barren plateau which made it ideal for surveillance undertaken by a regiment encamped a short distance away.

Las Cases left us a detailed floor plan of Longwood. Carpenters had fashioned large reception and drawing rooms, the latter giving onto a spacious dining room. Napoleon's apartments consisted of a work room, library, small sitting room, small bedroom and a jerry-built bathtub. The Montholons occupied three rooms, Las Cases and his son two rooms. Staff were closeted in various attics and rude outbuildings with the exception of Ali who, armed with a wicked-looking scimitar, slept before the emperor's door. The Bertrands occupied a small house about a mile distant but normally dined in the big house.

The Bertrands were wise. Carpenters who no doubt could expertly repair a splintered mast or plug a leak in a shattered hull apparently knew little about houses, although the result was not altogether their fault. They had few materials to work with, the existing buildings were decrepit with no cellars. Lack of underground ventilation taken with frequent rains and high humidity resulted in foul air, damp and musty closets, mildewed clothes and rotted shoes. Damp drafts tore through jerry-built rooms, tarpaper and slat roofs leaked. Insects flew everywhere. Large and ravenous rats which infested the island also infested the floors, walls and ceiling of Longwood and were so vicious that the hired help gave up trying to keep chickens. Water was piped in by conduit and had to be boiled, drinking water had to be brought from distant springs. Workmen would hammer away for another two or three months. Armed sentries were posted some distance from the house during the day, but come dark they took station immediately under the windows.[6]

Neither the location nor a variable climate helped matters. Violent winds swept across a plateau nearly 2,000 feet above sea level. Although clouds normally obscured the sun, the days were intensely hot with high humidity come evenings. There were no shade trees, only a small and feeble garden and virtually no grass thanks to the hot winds. On one side an uncultivated bleak plateau ended in a deep ravine backed by bare mountains. On the other side valleys and ravines cut through some sparsely settled green land backed by more mountains. Such was the heat that outings were confined to early mornings and late afternoons, but heavy rains sometimes for days on end prevented outdoor exercise.

We know a great deal about the dreary day-to-day life at Longwood owing to a spate of often conflicting memoirs by such as Las Cases, Gourgaud, O'Meara, Bertrand, Montholon, Marchand and Ali (not to mention numerous lesser-fry "I was there" accounts). These works, however patchy and distorted, none the less contain some interesting insights on Napoleon's personality, character and career, many of which are confirmed by other sources.

Briefly: Napoleon's daily routine was perforce limited. Marchand awakened him early and served coffee in bed. One or more of the valets washed him and helped him shave, then rubbed him down with a coarse brush and doused him with *eau de cologne* (which soon ran out and was replaced with homemade lavender water) and finally helped him dress, an elaborate process that required one or two hours.

Weather permitting, he and Las Cases usually went for a long walk or horseback ride before breakfast. The emperor breakfasted late, either in his room or, in fair weather, in the small garden. When in the mood he followed this with dictation to Las Cases, Gourgaud or Bertrand. On occasion he received guests, usually lunched alone in his room, conversed in Italian with O'Meara and toward evening walked or rode with the ladies in a small open carriage in good weather but otherwise stayed by the fireplace reading. He often interrupted this routine with steaming baths that sometimes lasted for three or four hours.

Dinners were formal. The carefully coiffured and gowned ladies and uniformed generals gathered in the drawing room, everyone standing to await the emperor's arrival after which the ladies only were permitted to sit until dinner was served.

The Rats Won't Have Him, 1816

Although the food was poor it was eaten off precious china while equally inferior wine was drunk from exquisite crystal goblets. Table talk was restrained. If the emperor did not speak no one else spoke. Dinner normally lasted for forty minutes before the company returned to the drawing room. Pleasantries there consisted of Madame Montholon warbling a few French ballads followed by someone, often Napoleon, reading a play, usually one of Racine, Molière or Voltaire's tragic dramas. Conversation was normally light, the emperor twitting the ladies, sometimes rudely, but on occasion reminiscing, often to the company's delight. Cards or chess also whiled away the hours until the emperor retired, usually around eleven.

Even with enjoyable company this basic routine would soon have palled. The company was not enjoyable. Bertrand by virtue of living away soon yielded most of his overlord duties to Montholon only to become intensely jealous of the latter's new standing with the emperor. Bertrand, Montholon and Gourgaud bitterly resented Las Cases who daily spent hours with Napoleon and was clearly the new favorite (a fact that gives considerable spice to his memoirs). Nearly everyone complained about their crude apartments and cheap furnishings and the poor quality of food and wine. Not surprisingly the evenings grew increasingly tense as innuendo ruled, and it is little wonder that Napoleon often dined privately in his study, preferring badinage with Marchand and Ali.

Napoleon struggled against boredom as best he could and indeed the days were not all doom and gloom. He truly enjoyed pre-breakfast rides with Las Cases. The trails were so poor that they often dismounted, frequently stopping to chat with cottagers and their children, who invariably received a coin or two, or with British officers and soldiers. On one occasion they encountered a cottager's beautiful young daughter whom Napoleon named the Nymph. He was sufficiently smitten to pay her repeated calls and to rename the particular valley in her honor.[7]

Early in his residence he often entertained important visitors, ship captains, army officers, civil officials, who informed him of affairs in France and England. He also enjoyed the company of younger officers who listened in awe as he recalled a great battle or the high points of a difficult campaign.

He started English lessons again with Las Cases, often studying up to five hours a day in bad weather, made excellent progress and by February was reading English with the aid of a dictionary. More books arrived from France and England. Cockburn supplied him with newspapers which by the time they reached St. Helena were about three months old. In February 1816 he learned from the papers of King Joachim's (Marshal Murat) execution in Calabria. Having double-crossed Napoleon only to be deceived by his Austrian ally, Murat landed a small force on the Calabrian coast where it was immediately captured by Austrian troops who summarily shot him. Napoleon was not surprised to learn his fate for which he showed no sympathy.[8]

A month later he learned that Ney and Labédoyère had been tried for treason and executed. Ney's wife had obtained passports for his escape and begged him to leave. "Upon my word, Madame," the old marshal replied, "you are in a great hurry to get rid of me!"[9] Instead of escaping he chose to stand trial. Napoleon had earlier learned of Ney's prosecution which he thought was unfair, but according to Gourgaud he showed little sympathy with his execution, remarking that "one ought never to break one's word . . . I despise traitors . . . Labédoyère acted like a man without honor," and "Ney dishonored himself."[10]

He often enjoyed playing with the Montholon and Bertrand children. In time creature comforts arrived: a proper bath-tub, a billiard table, some decent furniture. After a hiatus of several weeks he resumed dictation, recounting the Egyptian campaign to Bertrand, not a very successful effort since he lacked proper sources and maps. Working with Las Cases and young Emmanuel, he edited and re-edited his work on the Italian campaigns. He tried to keep peace among his officers, sharing dictation, joking and reminiscing with each, assuring each of his devotion, pulling their ears to show his pleasure.[11]

Ney, Michel 1769–1815 Marshal of France

It was not an easy time for him. He was already ill when he moved to Longwood. Las Cases reported that a one-mile walk exhausted him. Although he slowly regained strength and took longer walks and rides, he still suffered from bouts of sickness and depression. At times he shut himself in his apartments for a day or more, gazing stonily at a portrait of his son perched on a sheep and Isabey's portrait of Marie Louise, the room gloomy, light from the fireplace playing over its squalid furnishings, Frederick the Great's alarm clock ticking out life. Some nights he could not sleep and asked to be read to or wandered back and forth from one bed to the other in the two small rooms.

Longwood was not the real problem, imprisonment was. He did not like his jailer's assumed familiarity, his ignorance of protocol, his inflated ego and supercilious treatment of the French officers. As his bleak existence continued, his resentment rose. He continued to complain vigorously about the discomforts of Longwood, the shortage of such essentials as coffee, white sugar, firewood, even paper, the obtrusive and humiliating presence of sentries. He demanded a proper lodging in a comfortable location, better provisions, freedom to ride where he wished, an end of surveillance.

Admiral Cockburn did relax some rules as time went on. Bertrand was given permission to issue visitor passes without consulting the admiral. At year's end Napoleon's pistols and muskets were returned to him. After inflicting further restrictions on the emperor's movements, Cockburn suddenly turned round and gave him freedom of the island.

But these seemingly altruistic acts were subject to sudden changes of whim and in some cases were meaningless. Pistols and muskets were of no use since there was no game to shoot except some turtledoves who lived in distant gum trees (but soon moved away). No cartridge pouches were sent with the weapons and, another humiliation, the muskets had to be turned in to the duty officer each night.[12] Shortly after Cockburn withdrew travel restrictions, Napoleon and Las Cases were met at the end of a long ride by an officer who insisted on escorting them back to Longwood, an insult that caused Napoleon to refuse to receive Cockburn in the future.

The break solved nothing. It was evident to the occupants of Longwood that every "favor" bestowed by the admiral – and there weren't many – was followed by a new and restrictive regulation which brought home the sordid fact that they were an isolated group of prisoners subject to his every whim.[13]

Notes

1 Jones, Thomas Samuel, "The Island."
2 Las Cases, III, 76.
3 Las Cases, I, 272–81.

4   Las Cases, II, 11, 19.
5   Rose (*Life*), II, 566. See also Las Cases, I, 283–6.
6   Las Cases, II, 35–48.
7   Las Cases, II, 111–13; Korngold, 106–8.
8   Las Cases, II, 242–4.
9   Macdonald, 447.
10 Rose (*Life*), II, 541. See also Las Cases, II, 28–31; Korngold, 115; Macdonald, 393–4.
11 Las Cases published Napoleon's account of numerous battles and campaigns as well as treatises on such as Caesar and Frederick the Great in the *Mémorial*. See also Corr. XXIX and XXX for the original manuscripts, often with corrections in Napoleon's handwriting. These works are patchy and sometimes inaccurate owing to a lack of proper sources, maps and an aging memory. Their merits however far outweigh their defects, and we should be grateful for Napoleon's effort during difficult years.
12 Las Cases, II, 106–7.
13 Las Cases, II, 106 ff.; III, 64–7.

CHAPTER THIRTY-FIVE

DEATH OF AN EMPEROR
APRIL 1816–MAY 1821

*Your nation, your government, you yourself will be disgraced
by your treatment of me; your infants will share it; thus will
posterity judge it.*

Napoleon to the governor of St. Helena, General Sir
Hudson Lowe, St. Helena, May 1816[1]

SIR HUDSON LOWE was the son of an English army surgeon. The
same age as Napoleon, he early began what became a mediocre
army career nearly terminated in 1808 when he prematurely surrendered the isle of Capri to the French. An accomplished linguist
he henceforth served variously in police and espionage activities
on the continent, including a tour as commanding officer of a
company of turncoat Corsicans. Appointed British army representative to Marshal Blücher's headquarters in 1813 (in which
capacity he surveyed Napoleon through a field glass giving final
orders to his marshals at Bautzen), he carried the news of the
final French defeat to the prince regent who in the tradition of the
day rewarded him with a knighthood. Facing uncomfortable
retirement as a brigadier general, he was saved by appointment to
the lucrative post of governor of the Crown of St. Helena.

According to surgeon O'Meara, Napoleon's first impression
after a brief meeting (from which Admiral Cockburn was
excluded), was neutral: "The new governor is a man of very few
words, but he appears to be a polite man. However it is only from
a man's conduct for some time that you can judge of him."[2] Baron
Las Cases was not so charitable, describing him "as of normal

height, thin, gaunt, wizened; red hair and freckled face; oblique eyes, rarely looking one full in the face, topped by blond, thick and very prominent eyebrows." According to Las Cases, Lowe struck Napoleon as "hideous with the face of a hangman," but conceded that they had to get along with him.[3]

Lowe's first moves were agreeable enough. He inspected Longwood, was shocked by the condition of its private apartments – more "bivouacs than rooms" – and promised immediate repair. He also said that his French library of nearly 2,000 volumes would be at the household's disposal, and he later sent "material covering the Grand Army and official documents relating to the Egyptian campaign" for Napoleon's possible interest.[4]

That was the end of the good news.

As a modern historian, Ralph Korngold, has explained in his well researched and written book, *The Last Years of Napoleon*, Lowe's mandate from Britain's war minister, Lord Bathurst, gave him full authority of action, but he also was "to allow every indulgence to General Bonaparte which may be compatible with the entire security of his person . . . Many things however must be determined by local circumstance." The task called for keen judgment which Lowe did not possess. The duke of Wellington had transferred him from his staff in 1815 because of his pusillanimous character. "I knew him very well," Wellington told Lord Stanhope. "He was a stupid man . . . like all men who know nothing of the world, he was suspicious and jealous." He was also aware that, if Napoleon escaped, he would lose his job, his temporary rank of lieutenant general, a salary of £12,000 a year, a free residence complete with servants and 60 negro slaves, stables, carriages, gardens, entertainment allowances and numerous other perquisites.[5]

Lowe's fears were constantly fed by a Tory ministry in London, in particular by Bathurst who sent him various reports of alleged escape plots generally hatched in the United States. These seemed somewhat chimerical in view of the island's remoteness, British ships on constant patrol and the defensive strength of the army

garrison, but Lowe's overriding fear was that of Napoleon inciting
the garrison to mutiny (there had been two mutinies in the past).
Although such an effort was totally foreign to Napoleon's character, not to mention the integrity of the 53rd English regiment, it
became an obsession with Lowe whose solution was total isolation
of his prisoner in so far as possible.

Some two weeks after the governor's arrival he rejected
Napoleon's request to abolish the 12-mile travel limit. He next
canceled Bertrand's authority to issue visitor passes. That was followed by a generally unsuccessful effort to frighten the staff into
returning home. It soon became clear that under guise of security
measures he was also bent on humiliating his prisoner, indeed on
breaking his spirit.

Longwood was left in a state of shocking disrepair. Although
Lowe agreed to build a new house he insisted that it be close to the
old one rather than in an area that offered the "trees, water and
vegetation" desired by the emperor. British officers anxious for an
audience with the military genius of the age were discouraged
from calling. Sentries were neither to salute nor speak to him
under pain of being flogged (but some continued to do so). Lowe's
promise to supply French books resulted in his sending Napoleon
the recently published memoirs of one of his inveterate enemies,
Abby de Pradt, a work which vilified the emperor in every possible way. The governor's other offering was equally insulting, a
distorted collection of Napoleon's official writings brought out
by an English lampoonist.

Ignoring protocol in the Cockburn fashion, Lowe turned up at
Longwood at the end of April which led to a long and unpleasant
audience. "What a base and sinister figure is that of the governor," Napoleon remarked to Las Cases. "In my life I have never
encountered anything like him." Lowe returned a week later in
visibly bad humor, "his manners becoming sullen and rude," Las
Cases noted.[6]

By mid May an impending break was obvious. After another
long and stormy audience Napoleon complained to Las Cases
that "I have been sent more than a jailer. Sir Lowe [sic] is an

executioner . . . I received him angrily today . . . we looked like two rams about to gore each other; I must have been very angry because I felt my left calf pulsing. This is a sure sign with me and has not occurred in a long time."[7]

Two months after Lowe's arrival in spring of 1816, Rear Admiral Sir Pulteney Malcolm relieved Cockburn. The same ship brought the allied commissioners. France was represented by the marquis de Montchenu, 59 years old, a royalist *émigré* maliciously selected by Talleyrand. "I know that Montchenu," Napoleon told O'Meara. "He is an old fool, a gossip, an armchair general who has never smelt powder."[8] The Russian commissioner, Colonel Count Alexander Balmain, was 35 years old, a cultured diplomat. Baron Barthelemy von Stürmer, 29 years old, carried the Austrian flag.

In theory their presence (with the exception of Montchenu) should have improved Napoleon's situation, but this was not the case. Napoleon was partially at fault because he refused to consider himself a prisoner of the allied powers and thus would not see them. Moreover they held no executive powers. Balmain and Stürmer disapproved of Lowe's more extreme measures and wanted them altered, but dared not make an issue out of it. Although Malcolm soon gained disfavor by arguing for softer conditions he did not dream of carrying his case to the Admiralty.

A new crisis arose in August when Lowe, acting on orders from London, informed Napoleon that his annual household allowance was reduced to £8,000 (from about £18,000), a ludicrous figure in view of the island's high prices. Bertrand so hotly protested the cut that he was placed under house arrest with sentries in attendance. This led to another angry audience and a furious and insulting outburst from Napoleon.

Not surprisingly Lowe countered with additional restrictions, particularly on travel limits, but Napoleon got something of his own back by dictating an indictment against his cruel and vicious imprisonment. Called "the Remonstrance," copies were smuggled to England and the continent where they were published greatly to the allies' embarrassment. Meanwhile the war continued but the two opponents never met again.

Napoleon's troubles did not end with Hudson Lowe. Longwood had become a cockpit of jealousy, deceit, spite, hatred and extreme unhappiness which increased as living conditions worsened and approaching winter tended to keep people indoors. A particular target of resentment was Las Cases who had won the rank of chamberlain for his labors. In between quarreling with Lowe, Napoleon tried to keep the peace at home, patiently encouraging Montholon and Gourgaud to cease their vendetta against Las Cases. This was like asking dogs to stop barking, and the result was the same.

Las Cases solved the problem by going home. Napoleon had more or less finished dictating his memoirs and would soon start repeating himself. Las Cases' eyes had bothered him for some time, his son was bored, he was tired of being taunted by intellectually inferior persons, fed up with the confined and uncomfortable existence at Longwood. The only way he could leave was to get himself deported, a complicated process which brought about his arrest and the confiscation of his precious manuscripts. Much to Napoleon's regret, he and Emmanuel finally sailed in late November.

Eventually reaching Frankfurt, Las Cases rewrote the work from memory. Published only in 1823 under the title, *Mémorial de Sainte-Hélène*, the work was a great success; it was translated into several languages and was said to earn him over 2 million francs. The several volumes offer lengthy accounts of various campaigns along with a recital of the tragic events on St. Helena and Napoleon's candid thoughts on a wide variety of subjects, including his opinions of various marshals, generals and civilian officers.

Unfortunately we can offer only a few of the more lively character appreciations which, according to the author, were made very objectively with no sign of bitterness. Napoleon believed that a great general must share a large amount of intelligence, character and courage, what he called equilibrium. Equilibrium was the sole merit possessed by Viceroy Eugène and was sufficient to make him a very distinguished person. Physical and moral courage were not sufficient. It was impossible to be more brave than either Murat or Ney but neither had any brains. Augereau's poor behavior resulted from few brains and bad company. Berthier compensated for all his faults by being always at hand and indefatigable – "no one else could have replaced him." Kléber had great talent but sought only glory and had no belief in his country, the result of his Prussian service as a youth. Desaix possessed the "necessary equilibrium" to a very superior degree. Moreau was a second-rate general – nature had not finished his creation, he had more instinct than genius. Lannes originally showed more courage than intelligence but grew wiser every day and had attained "a very superior equilibrium" when he died: "I found him a pygmy, I lost a giant." Suchet's character and spirit grew to a surprising degree to give him the necessary equilibrium. Masséna's equilibrium showed only in the midst of battle. A host of generals, Gérard, Clausel, Foy, Lamarque and others, met the requirement and would have been "the new marshals." Drouot possessed every quality of a great general and had reasons to consider himself superior to some of the marshals. Junot, to whom Napoleon had always been very generous, ran through vast sums without paying debts, spending "without discernment or taste," often indulging in crude excesses. His poor performance in the Russian campaign cost him the governorship of Paris. His physical excesses led to insanity and suicide.[9]

The Longwood wars unfortunately did not end with Las Cases' departure. The previous month the Bertrands had moved to a new house close to Longwood which enabled the count to try to enforce his rank as grand master of the palace, the Montholons having considerably gained the emperor's favor. Gourgaud, having lost his favorite target, turned on Montholon with an almost inexplicable vengeance, almost like a lover claiming that the count was usurping the emperor's affection. Napoleon did his best to reassure him of his friendship, even sending money to his mother, but Gourgaud continued to behave like a spoiled child.

At times amused, at times upset, at times bored with the whole scene, Napoleon spent more time in his quarters, on occasion dictating to Bertrand, Gourgaud or Montholon, chatting with O'Meara or his valets and reading innumerable books and four-month-old newspapers. Although Gourgaud's diary is at times suspect, the picture he drew at this time of a tired, bored and physically flagging Napoleon was all too true. Although he continued to dictate his memoirs, he began repeating what he already had told Las Cases and also to embroider the facts, stating for example that the Lyons Academy had awarded him a gold medal for his prize essay. But there also were flickers of his old self as the following examples testify:

On Gustavus Adolphus: "Here then is the great Gustavus. In eighteen months he won one battle, lost another and was killed in a third. This is the way to acquire fame in a hurry." On the duke of Wellington: "an ordinary man who has been prudent and lucky, but no great genius." On brother Joseph: "We were beaten at Vitoria because Joseph slept too much. If I had slept on the night of Eggmühl, I would never have made the superb maneuver, the most beautiful I ever made."[10]

If we can believe Gourgaud, Napoleon was beginning to lose interest in women, but that did not prevent occasional reminiscences of happier days. He recalled spending a night 12 years earlier with a German girl procured by Murat. Although she spoke no French and he no German, "She was one of the most pleasant women I have known, she didn't smell . . . I never saw her again." The mysterious Madame D. who was his mistress at one point would accept no gifts from him, "not even a diamond necklace," but he had to send Duroc to her to retrieve his love letters. He preferred blondes to brunettes, which is why he quickly discarded Madame Grassini. "When I knew that Marie Louise was blonde, I was very pleased." Although he loved Marie Louise, "I think I loved Joséphine more . . . she was a real woman . . . graceful even in retiring to bed, even in dressing herself."[11]

*

In late June a visiting English diplomat described the emperor as dignified, affable and pleasing, seemingly in good health. The last bit was an act. He had been frequently ill, anything from stomach upsets to moods of despair – what he termed the *chat noir* (*black cat*) – to insomnia when he had to be read to while alternating between his two camp-beds.

Owing to Lowe's restrictions he was gradually giving up walks and rides, to O'Meara's despair. He could live in the past during talks with Gourgaud and others, but he still had to return to an increasingly uncomfortable present. His patience grew shorter, his temper flared more often (not surprisingly in view of Lowe's malice, Gourgaud's constant whining and Bertrand's complaints of lost fealty). The Countess Albine de Montholon was pregnant, which was inconvenient to whatever sexual drive was left to him. (She delivered a daughter in January, the father a toss-up between Montholon, Napoleon and one or two other suspects.) Taken with domestic turmoil, the lack of exercise soon told on his health. In late 1817 he complained of a pain in his side (not the first time) and swollen legs, the latter an interim affliction that had begun in Russian cold.

O'Meara diagnosed the pain in his side as "chronic hepatitis" but Lowe, who had been feuding with the surgeon for some time, refused to accept the diagnosis and insisted that there was nothing wrong with the prisoner. An angry letter from Bertrand to Lowe in October – "The question is, do you or do you not wish to kill the emperor?" – brought some respite. Lowe restored the 12-mile travel limit and authorized Napoleon to speak with whom he wished when riding. Sentries surrounding the house were moved back to the garden.

Napoleon did not trust these and other gestures and did not respond to O'Meara's urgings for him to resume walks and rides. He was right – the insults continued. It was not long before the governor even installed two sergeants disguised as gardeners which caused the emperor to stop walking in the garden. Lowe next reissued an order that forbade anyone to correspond or communicate with Longwood without his authorization. By

November, Napoleon was visibly suffering, convinced that he had less than a year to live.[12]

Napoleon suffered another blow in early 1818 when his trusted *maître d'hôtel*, Cipriani Franceschi, suddenly died under somewhat mysterious circumstances, an event that gave rise to later, often fanciful theories that he was poisoned for knowing too much. Then a month later the Balcombes left for England, to Napoleon's great distress. Gourgaud meanwhile had gone nearly round the bend, threatening to fight a duel with Montholon and accusing everyone of conducting a vendetta against him. To the relief of all he departed for England in March.[13]

In April the emperor was again seriously ill. Montchenu reported to Paris that "it appears that he suffers from an obstruction of the liver. The proof is that he has finally decided to take mercury in such large doses that his nerves are affected." In late July, Bertrand informed the governor that the emperor "had not left the house for one hundred days." He was suffering severely from a combination of fever, bronchitis, swollen legs, bleeding gums and the pain, now acute, in his right side. He rarely ventured out, frequently kept to his bed during the day.[14]

To worsen matters the quarrel between Lowe and O'Meara came to a head to the extent that the surgeon departed for England in August 1818. Napoleon was sorry to see him go. In addition to valuable gifts including the manuscript of the 1815 campaign, he was said to have given him a credit of 100,000 francs on his London account.[15] Lowe replaced O'Meara with an army surgeon whom Napoleon refused to see so that for several months he received no professional treatment.

Early in January 1819, while dictating to Montholon, the emperor fainted. Bertrand was summoned as was the surgeon of the flagship, John Stokoe. To ward off apoplexy Stokoe persuaded his patient to be bled. "I took this opportunity of more particularly examining the liver," he reported, "and am fully persuaded of the diseased state of that viscus, having distinctly felt a degree of hardness . . . I therefore advised the immediate adoption of a course of mercury, with other medicines in such form as best suited the constitution of the patient."[16] Since this and a subsequent report conflicted with the English government's stand that Napoleon was in good health (as steadily reported by Lowe and confirmed by Gourgaud upon his arrival in London), Stokoe was soon declared *persona non grata* and was eventually courtmartialed and dismissed from the service on meaningless grounds. Prior to his departure he was liberally rewarded by Napoleon and later by the Bonapartes – the disgusting saga is well told in Ralph Korngold's book.[17]

Napoleon's health was on the downslide. He was not well enough to walk or ride, not even to take more than a short outing in the *calèche*. He suffered a severe setback in July when Madame Albine Montholon and her two children departed for Europe on grounds of her poor health. To the Bertrands' fury, Napoleon gave her a large amount of cash in addition to expensive gifts, and persuaded her husband to stay on by a hefty increase in salary, allowances and bonuses.

Two months later a ship delivered a French doctor, two priests, a *maître d'hôtel* and a cook sent by Cardinal Fesch at Napoleon's request. One priest was old and useless, the other, Vignali, young and ignorant although claiming to be a doctor of medicine.[18] The two servants were hopeless. The young French-Corsican doctor, Francesco Antommarchi, was trained in dissection of corpses and not much else. He was loutish, conceited, a gossip and a sex maniac who consorted with island whores when he should have been attending the emperor. While in London however he had conferred with O'Meara and Stokoe and now, after examining the patient, confirmed their diagnoses of a liver problem. When Napoleon refused to exercise by riding horseback, Antommarchi persuaded him to take up gardening which was feasible since Lowe in one of his generous moments had had a reservoir built for water piped from the hills.

It was a brilliant idea. Napoleon's health dramatically improved as he flung himself into the project, daily summoning the

servants at 6 a.m. to do the digging, planting innumerable flowers, trees and shrubs, constructing a fountain, a walk, a summer
house, often interrupting labors to post servants along ditches in
order to demonstrate military tactics. Lowe, relieved by reports of
his prisoner's seeming recovery, provided plants, seeds and
garden furniture and toward the end of 1819 relaxed travel
restrictions to the extent that Napoleon once again began to enjoy
long walks and rides.

As his health improved his interest in life revived. He was soon
reading more books that Lady Holland, wife of the opposition
leader, was sending from England, discussing them with Bertrand
and Montholon, dictating more memoirs, eating and sleeping with
more regularity. His health remained stable enough for the first six
months of 1820, but in July he suffered a serious attack described
by Antommarchi as "shivering, fever, pain in the head, nausea,
dry and frequent coughing, and vomiting of a bilious quality,
extremely bitter."[19]

Once recovered he continued to garden and ride, but not without pain. In October he suffered another fainting spell. Once
again he was deteriorating with attacks occurring more frequently.
Although he still went for drives in the two-wheeled *calèche*, these
grew fewer as he spent more time in bed, often taking dinner
there, or being read to as his eyesight deteriorated.

Montholon noted in early December that "for several days now
his stomach has failed to retain anything. His pulse can be felt
only with the greatest difficulty. His gums, his lips, his nails are
quite discolored. His feet and legs, although wrapped in flannel
and hot towels, are ice-cold, as are his hands . . . when he says,
'There is no more oil in the lamp,' it is unfortunately but too
true."[20]

The lamp flared for the last time in January 1821. Bertrand was
reading to him from Bernadotte's memoirs alternately with a life
of Cromwell, each session marked by long and intelligent conversations often enlivened by Napoleon reliving many of his

campaigns in analyzing his political victories and defeats. He had a seesaw built in the billiard room with a saddle for himself on one end and the Bertrand children on the other. Although the exercise soon tired him his health continued to improve. He grew noticeably more cheerful and active. Morning buggy rides gave him a healthy appetite for lunch. "If this keeps up," Bertrand wrote in late January, "he will be quite recovered in a fortnight."[21]

It was but a brief remission. In mid February he was very sick, suffering "pains in his spleen and kidneys." In early March he was digesting his food only with difficulty while visibly growing weaker. After managing to shave himself one morning he remarked to Bertrand that "it was like accomplishing one of the labors of Hercules. How exhausting." Though still going for drives, he could not retain food and was suffering severe stomach pains. By mid March he was no longer strong enough for the daily drive, much less for the move into the recently completed new house. A few days later he suffered a feverish convulsion and found it difficult to breathe. Antommarchi was sent for and explained it away by "wind [gas] in the stomach and the lower abdomen."[22]

A few weeks earlier the governor had volunteered the services of a regimental surgeon, Archibald Arnott, whom Napoleon refused to see. Bertrand nevertheless called him to confer with Antommarchi. Arnott was not worried about the fever, which in his opinion had no connection with the old liver problem and with proper medication should run its course in a couple of weeks or so. He prescribed emetic pills, small doses of opium and a blister on the lower abdomen.

The day after Arnott's prognosis (made without seeing the patient), Napoleon was much worse. "If I should end my career now," he told Bertrand, "it would be a great happiness to me. At times I have longed to die, and I have no fear of death. It would be a great joy to me if I were to die within the next two weeks." A few hours later he sensed himself at "death's door . . . I am very glad that I have no religion. I find it a great consolation, as I have no imaginary terrors and no fear of the future."[23]

Arnott finally examined the patient in early April. Napoleon's suggestion that the pain could be connected with the pylorus (his father allegedly having died from a cancerous tumor there) drew a negative response. Arnott diagnosed "an infection of the stomach" with the pain coming from "gas in the intestines." A week or so later the omniscient surgeon informed Bertrand "that he saw no danger whatever," an opinion shared by Antommarchi who continued administering emetics and quinine, often over the violent remonstrations of the patient.

Despite pain and weakness Napoleon was often alert, hurling questions at Bertrand and Montholon, and forcing Arnott to give him an anatomical lecture on the stomach and its suburbs, paying close attention to whatever was said or read to him, refusing to see Madame Bertrand (with whom he was angry for not being his mistress). At times he was calm and lucid, at times angry and hurtful. When Antommarchi appeared late one morning Napoleon flew into a rage, accusing him of being only interested in his whores. "Very well," he shouted to Bertrand, "let him spend all his time with his whores. Let him fuck them from the front, the rear, in the mouth and ears, but get rid of that man for me, he is stupid, ignorant, pretentious and utterly devoid of any sense of honor . . . I have made my will: in it I have left Antommarchi twenty francs to buy himself a length of rope with which to hang himself."[24]

With Montholon's willing collaboration Napoleon had destroyed a will written in 1819 and had written a new one. Still under the impression that his Paris banker was holding six million francs in addition to the funds Joseph controlled, he now willed far more money than he possessed along with extensive properties that were no longer his. His principal beneficiary was Count Montholon to whom he left two million francs, a circumstance that in our day has given rise to dubious theories that Montholon murdered him by lacing his wine with arsenic, an ingenious theory that Sherlock Holmes at once would have torn to shreds if only on the grounds of Napoleon's constant exposure to paint with a high lead content, his frequent infusions of deadly mercury and his extremely limited intake of wine – at most a teaspoon diluted with water – during his illness. Bertrand was left 500,000 francs, Marchand 400,000 (in addition to the spontaneous gift of Hortense's diamond necklace), Las Cases 100,000, with 100,000 each to twenty generals or their survivors and smaller sums to the servants. As in the first will, he left numerous personal possessions to family and friends including a gold snuffbox to Lady Holland, his English benefactress. He continued to dictate further codicils until shortly before his death.[25]

Despite Arnott's reports to the contrary, his patient was daily growing weaker. He had ceased being shaved and had grown a beard. Marchand and Ali moved him from his bedroom to the large anteroom. Once settled in an armchair by the east window he would look up to greet the day: "Good morning, sun; good morning, my friend." If not well enough for a drive he spent the days being read to or napping. He ordered the young priest, Vignali, to set up a *chapelle ardente* or funeral chapel in the neighboring room and to conduct religious services up to and after his death. Bertrand was told that if his body were not allowed to be returned to France he should be buried close to his favorite spring in a nearby valley.[26]

The end came in early May. He had been confined to bed for some days, existing mainly on arrowroot and gentian, occasionally taking a sip of flavored water or a spoonful of wine mixed with water, frequently dozing, his physical needs attended to by Marchand and Ali with daily and sometimes hourly visits by the doctors. Occasionally he could take food. One evening he enjoyed soup, an egg and a spoonful of wine and asked Montholon to tell him some bawdy stories. Such moments were rare. "I know that I have none of the symptoms of death," he told Arnott, "but I am so weak that it would not take a cannon-ball to kill me; a grain of sand would suffice." Severe vomiting continued, his mind began to wander, evoking ghosts from the past, his appetite virtually ceased, he repeated questions already answered, his hearing sharply deteriorated. At end of April, Arnott in an abrupt change of mind warned that death was near. At Lowe's insistence

Antommarchi and Arnott were joined by Lowe's personal physician and the admiral's surgeon; the latter two, without seeing the patient, recommended 10 grains of calomel taken in a biscuit dipped in wine, and this was duly administered.[27]

Early on 5 May, after a night of frequent vomiting, Napoleon opened his eyes and muttered a few inarticulate words variously interpreted by those about him. He remained unconscious for the rest of the day. Surrounded by what remained of his court, Montholon, the Bertrands and their children, Antommarchi and Arnott, Marchand, Ali and the remaining servants, he died that evening.

He was 51 years old.

As Vignali transformed the death room into a chapel, the body was washed and shaved, sprinkled with lavender water and laid out on a camp-bed covered with a sheet, a silver cross once given to him by his mother on his chest, candles burning on either side of the bed.

By morning his sallow, emaciated face with folds of flesh was said to have changed to that of a much younger man. "At that moment," Bertrand wrote, "the emperor's face made him look . . . about forty. By four o'clock he looked older than he really was."[28]

According to Montholon, Napoleon had asked for an autopsy "believing it might be of great value to his son." The body was taken to the neighboring room and placed on the table where the emperor had spread his maps while dictating. No fewer than 17 persons including 7 English doctors watched Antommarchi perform the unpleasant task. His bladder and penis were described as small, which helped to explain his urinary difficulties. The pylorus was surrounded by tumors and presumably cancerous ulcers which had eaten into the stomach. Although the doctors agreed that this was the cause of death they disagreed when it came to the condition of the liver, a subject that need not concern us except to remark that Hudson Lowe wanted it to be declared normal so as to contradict earlier diagnoses by O'Meara and others of chronic hepatitis. Following Napoleon's instructions, Antommarchi removed the heart and placed it in a silver vessel filled with wine to be given to Empress Marie Louise. He also removed the stomach which was placed in a vessel of wine.[29] Subsequently he was accused of cutting off the penis (for later sale), but this would have been difficult in the presence of so many witnesses (although he might have been alone in sewing up the cadaver).[30]

An elaborate funeral followed a few days later. Hundreds of people, islanders, sailors and soldiers, filed by the body dressed in the colourful uniform of the Guard *chasseurs*, many leaving flowers. That evening the corpse was laid in a tin coffin, the head having been shaved in accordance with his wishes, the hair to be woven into a watch chain for his son and bracelets for his brothers and sisters.[31] The coffin, with lid soldered on, was placed in a mahogany coffin, then in another lead coffin and finally a fourth mahogany coffin, and loaded onto a converted carriage. Led by priest Vignali the procession moved slowly down a road flanked by soldiers and sailors standing at attention, behind them most of the island's population.

Accompanied by volleys of musket and cannon fire the overweight coffins were lowered into a specially constructed concrete-lined grave, sealed with a large boulder and then cemented over – in Chateaubriand's sardonic words, "as though they feared that he could never be sufficiently imprisoned."

Notes

1   Las Cases, III, 301. See also Gourgaud, II, 214.
2   Rose (*Life*), II, 547.
3   Las Cases, III, 68.
4   Las Cases, III, 91.
5   Korngold, 135–7.
6   Las Cases, III, 97, 133, 210 ff. In a later work which Napoleon never saw, Pradt apologized for his treatment of the emperor in his *Histoire de l'ambassade dans le grand-duché de Varsovie*.

7   Las Cases, III, 300.

8   Korngold, 167, citing O'Meara.

9   Las Cases, I, 367–8; II, 16–19; III, 309, 370. See also Rose (*Life*), II, 360–1; Korngold, 213–33.

10   Gourgaud, II, 122, 150, 156.

11   Gourgaud, II, 167, 170, 275–7, 312.

12   Korngold, 291–2; Gourgaud, II, 374.

13   Gourgaud, 483–5. See also Korngold, 281–3. Once in London Gourgaud presented himself as a royalist hero, spreading all sorts of lies about the Longwood group. When this earned him no reward he reverted to the role of Napoleonic protector, writing to Marie Louise, Czar Alexander and Emperor Francis of Lowe's viciousness and Napoleon's "prolonged agony," a turn-around that forced him to leave England for Hamburg where he wrote his memoirs.

14   Korngold, 291–303.

15   Korngold, 303–4.

16   Korngold, 326.

17   Korngold, 322–9.

18   Bertrand (Henri), 8.

19   Korngold, 359, citing Antommarchi.

20   Korngold, 366–7, citing Montholon.

21   Bertrand (Henri), 2–19.

22   Bertrand (Henri), 65, 113, 131.

23   Bertrand (Henri), 132–3.

24   Bertrand (Henri), 148–9.

25   Bertrand (Henri), 180–93, 195–7, 210–11, 215–6, 227, 236–7. See also Korngold, 379–81; Coston, II, 525 ff. for the will in full.

26   Bertrand (Henri), 167, 182, 262–3.

27   Bertrand (Henri), 164, 166.

28   Bertrand (Henri), 261. See also Korngold, 393–4.

29   Bertrand (Henri), 219, 244, 264.

30   Bierman, 579–80. If the organ were amputated – and this is a very big *if* – it would seem more likely that Vignali was the culprit since he was often alone with the body during the post-mortem vigil. Napoleon died on 5 May and was not buried until 9 May. The body was not embalmed. The famous death mask was made on 7 May when Bertrand noted that "he was already disfigured, and the body omitted an extremely unpleasant smell." (Bertrand, Henri, 264.)

The organ, later described as mummified, could not have been so treated on St. Helena and would have to have been carefully preserved to prevent putrefaction. Its subsequent alleged travels are described in Dr. Bierman's amusing account. In the 1920's it was put up for auction in New York and was described in the newspapers as "looking like a maltreated strip of buckskin shoelace or shriveled eel." It was acquired some ten years ago by a leading New York urologist.

31 Korngold, 399.

SELECTIVE BIBLIOGRAPHY

Abrantès *see* Junot.

Abrantès, Laure Junot, Duchesse d'. *Mémoires.* 10 vols. Paris, n.d.

Adams, Henry. *History of the United States of America During the Administrations of Thomas Jefferson and James Madison.* N.Y.: Library Classics of the United States, 1986. 2 vols.

Adye, John. *Napoleon of the Snows.* London: Nash and Grayson, 1931.

Aldington, Richard. *Wellington.* London: Heinemann, 1946.

Alger, John I. "Jomini: A Man of Principle." *The Consortium on Revolutionary Europe,* 1980.

Ali *see* Saint-Denis.

Allgemeine Deutsche Biographie. Vols. I and II. Leipzig, 1875.

Altamira, Rafael. *A History of Spain.* N.Y.: Van Nostrand, 1949.

Antommarchi, François. *Mémoires . . . ou les derniers moments de Napoléon.* Paris: Barrois, 1825. 2 vols.

Arnold, Eric P. Jr. *Fouché, Napoleon and the General Police.* Washington (D.C.): University Press of America, 1979.

Asprey, Robert B. "The Peninsular War," *Army Quarterly,* April 1959.

———. *War in the Shadows: The Guerrilla in History.* Garden City, N.Y.: Doubleday, 1975. 2 vols.

———. *Frederick the Great: The Magnificent Enigma.* N.Y.: Ticknor & Fields, 1986.

Aubry, Paul V. *Monge – Le Savant Ami de Napoléon Bonaparte*. Paris: Gouthier-Villars, 1954.

Bainville, Jacques. *Napoleon*. Boston: Little, Brown, 1933. Tr. Hamish Miles.

Barahona, Renato. "The Napoleonic Occupation and its Political Consequences in the Basque Provinces (1808–1813)." *The Consortium on Revolutionary Europe*, 1985.

Bartel, Paul. *La jeunesse inédite de Napoléon*. Paris: Amoit-Dumont, 1954.

Bartual, Carlos Diaz. "Tropas Españolas al Servicia del Imperio." *Revista de Historia Militar*, Num. 38, 1975.

Bausset, L.F.J. de. *Mémoires . . .* Paris: Baudoin Frères, 1820–1827. 2 vols.

Beaucour, Fernand Émile. "Le Grand Projet Napoléon en l'Expédition en Angleterre: Mythe ou Realité?" *The Consortium on Revolutionary Europe*, 1982.

Belloc, Hilaire. *Napoleon*. Philadelphia: Lippincott, 1932.

Bellune, Duc de. *Extraits de Mémoires Inédits*. Paris: Dumaine et Laquionie, 1846.

Benoist-Méchin, J.G.P.M. *Bonaparte en Égypte*. Lausanne: Clairfontane, 1966.

Bernoyer, François. *Avec Bonaparte en Égypte et en Syrie 1798–1800*. Abbéville: Les Presses Françaises, 1976.

Berthier, le Général de Division. *Relation des Campagnes du Général Bonaparte en Égypte et en Syrie*. Paris: Didot, An VIII [1799].

Berthier, Louis-Alexandre. *Mémoires*. Paris: 1827. 2 vols.

Bertrand, Henri-Gratien. *Napoleon at St. Helena – the Journals of General Bertrand*. N.Y.: Doubleday, 1952.

Bertrand, L., and Petrie, C. *The History of Spain*. London: Eyre & Spottiswoode, 1934.

Beyle, Henri *see* Stendhal.

Biagi, G. *see* Masson, Frédéric.

Bierman, Stanley M. "The Peripatetic Posthumous Peregrination of Napoleon's Penis." *The Journal of Sex Research*, November 1992.

Bigelow, John. *Principles of Strategy*. Philadelphia: Lippincott, 1894.

Bingham, D.A. *The Letters and Despatches of the First Napoleon*. London: Chapman and Hall, 1884. Vol. 3.

Blond, Georges. *La Grande Armée 1804–1815*. Paris: Laffont, 1979.

Blythe, Legette. *Marshal Ney: A Dual Life*. N.Y.: Stackpole, 1937.

Bond, Gordon C. "Louis Bonaparte and the Collapse of the Kingdom of Holland." *The Consortium on Revolutionary Europe*, 1974.

Bosher, J.F. *The French Revolution*. London: Weidenfeld & Nicolson, 1989.

Boswell, James. *An Account of Corsica, The Journal of a Tour to that Island; and Memoirs of Pascal Paoli*. London: 1852.

Botzenhart, Manfred. "Metternich and Napoleon." *Francia*, 1: 584–594, 1973.

Boulay de la Meurthe, Comte. *Le Directoire et L'Expédition d'Égypte*. Paris: Hachette, 1885.

——— (ed.). "Correspondance de Talleyrand avec Le Premier Consul pendant la Campagne de Marengo." *Extrait de la Revue d'Histoire Diplomatique*, April 1892.

Bourcet, Pierre. *Principes de la Guerre des Montagnes*. Paris: Imprimerie Nacionale, 1775.

Bourgogne *see* Cottin, Paul.

Bourrienne, Louis Antoine Fauvelet. *Memoirs of Napoleon Bonaparte*. N.Y. Crowell, 1885. 4 vols.

Bouvier, Félix. *Bonaparte en Italie 1796*. Paris: Cerf, 1902.

Boyer, Ferdinand. "Quelques Considerations sur les Conquêtes Artistiques de Napoléon," *R. Italiana di Studi Napoleonici*, 1968.

Brett-James, Antony. *Wellington at War, 1794–1815*. London: Macmillan, 1961.

Broadley *see* Wheeler.

Browning, Oscar. *The Boyhood and Youth of Napoleon*. London: John Lane, 1906.

Bruce, Evangeline. *Napoleon & Josephine – An Improbable Marriage*. London: Phoenix, 1996.

Bryant, Arthur. *The Years of Endurance 1793–1802*. London: Book Club Associates, 1975.

———. *Years of Victory 1802–1812*. London: Book Club Associates, 1975.

Burton, R.G. *Napoleon's Campaign in Italy 1796–1797 and 1800*. London: George Allen, 1912.

Byrd, Melenie, S. "Denon and the Institute of Egypt," *The Consortium on Revolutionary Europe*, 1989.

Caird, L.H. *The History of Corsica*. London: Unwin, 1899.

Callwell, E.C. *Small Wars – Their Principles and Practice*. London: HMSO, 1899.

Carnot, Lazare N.M. *Mémoires Historiques et Militaires.* Paris: Baudouin Frères, 1824.

Carr, Raymond. "Spain and Portugal – 1793 to c. 1840." *The New Cambridge Modern History.* London: Cambridge University Press, 1965. Vol. 9.

————. *Spain 1808–1975.* Oxford: Clarendon Press, 1982.

Carrington, Dorothy. "Les Parents de Napoléon d'Après des Documents Inédits." *Annales Historiques de la Révolution Française,* Vol. 52, 1980.

Castelot, André. *Bonaparte.* Paris: Librairie Academique, 1967.

———— *Napoleon.* N.Y.: Harper & Row, 1967. Tr. Guy Daniels.

Cate, Curtis. *The War of the Two Emperors: The Confrontation Between Napoleon and Tsar Alexander, Russia 1812.* N.Y.: Random House, 1985.

Caulaincourt, Général de. *Mémoires du Général de Caulaincourt, Duc de Vicenze,* Paris: Plon, 1933. 3 vols.

Caulaincourt, Duke of Vicenza, *Memoirs.* London: Cassell, 1950. 3 vols. Tr. H. Miles.

Chandler, David. *The Campaigns of Napoleon.* London: Weidenfeld & Nicolson, 1967.

————. "Fire Over England: Threats of Invasion That Never Came." *The Consortium on Revolutionary Europe,* 1986.

Chaptal, Comte de. *Mes Souvenirs sur Napoléon.* Paris: Plon, 1893.

Charles-Roux, F. *Bonaparte: Governor of Egypt.* London: Methuen, 1937.

Chateaubriand, Vicomte de. *Mémoires d'outre-tombe.* Paris: Flammarion, 1948. 4 vols.

Christiansen, Eric. *The Origins of Military Power in Spain 1800–1854.* London: Oxford University Press, 1967.

Chuquet, Arthur. *La Jeunesse de Napoléon.* Paris: Armand Colin, 1897. 3 vols.

————. *Inédits Napoléoniens.* Paris: 1913. 2 vols.

Clausewitz, Carl P.G. von. *Clausewitz on War.* London: Penguin, 1968.

———— *The Campaign of 1812 in Russia.* London: John Murray, 1843.

Cobham, Alfred. *History of Modern France.* London: Penguin, 1957. 3 vols.

Colin, Jean. *L'Éducation militaire de Napoléon.* Paris: R. Chapelot, 1900.

Constant (Wairy). *Mémoires de Constant.* Paris: Michel, 1909.

Cooper, Duff. *Talleyrand.* London: J. Cape, 1934.

Coston, Baron de. *Biographie des Premières Années de Napoléon Bonaparte*. Paris: Marc Aurel, 1890. 2 vols.

Cottin, Paul, and Heyault, Maurice. *Mémoires du Sergent Bourgogne*. Paris: Hachette, 1914.

Craig, Gordon A. *The Politics of the Prussian Army 1640–1945*. Oxford: Clarendon Press, 1955.

———. "Problems of Coalition Warfare: The Military Alliance Against Napoleon 1808–1814." *U.S. Air Force Academy*, 1965.

Crefeld, Martin Van. *Supplying War – Logistics from Wallenstein to Patton*. London: Cambridge University Press, 1977.

———. *Command in War*. Cambridge, Mass.: Harvard University Press, 1985.

Daline, V. "Napoléon Et Les Babouvistes." *Annales Historiques de la Révolution Français*, 1970.

Delderfield, R.F. *The Retreat from Moscow*. N.Y.: Atheneum, 1967.

Denon, Dominique Vivant, Baron. *Voyages dans la Basse et la Haute Égypte pendant les campagnes de Bonaparte en 1798 et 1799*. London: 1807. 2 vols.

Description de l'Égypte, ou recueil des observations et des recherches qui ont été faites en Égypte pendant l'expédition de l'armée française. Paris: 1809–1828. 24 vols.

Desgenettes, R. *Histoire Médicale de l'Armée d'Orient*. Paris: Chez Craullebois, 1802.

———. *Souvenirs d'Un Médecin de l'Expédition d'Égypte*. Paris: Calman-Lévy, 1893.

Doppet, Général. *Mémoires politiques et militaires*. Paris: 1820.

Driault, J.E. *Napoléon en Italie*. Paris: Félix Alcan, 1901.

Du Teil, Baron Joseph. *Napoléon Bonaparte et Les Généraux Du Teil*. Paris: Alphonse Picard, 1897.

Dufraisse, Roger. *Napoleon*. N.Y.: McGraw-Hill, 1992. Tr. Steven Englund.

Dumas, Mathieu. *Souvenirs du Lieutenant-Général Comte Mathieu Dumas, de 1770 à 1836*. Paris: Gosselin, 1839. 8 vols.

Dupont, Amiral Marcel. *L'Amiral Decrès et Napoléon*. Paris: 1991.

Dupuy, Trevor N. *A Genius for War – The German Army and Central Staff 1807–1945*. London: Macdonald and Janes, 1977.

Dupuy, Trevor N. et al. *The Harper Encyclopaedia of Military Biography*. New York: HarperCollins, 1992.

Elgood, P.G. *Bonaparte's Adventure in Egypt*. London: Oxford University Press, 1931.

Elting, John R. *see* Esposito.

———. "Jomini and Berthier." *The Consortium on Revolutionary Warfare*, 1989.

Epstein, Robert M. "Eugene de Beauharnais: A Military Commander or Macdonald's Puppet?". *The Consortium on Revolutionary Europe*, 1983.

———. "The Army of Italy at the Battle of Wagram: Turning Point of the Napoleonic Wars." *The Consortium on Revolutionary Europe*, 1989.

——— *Napoleon's Last Victory and the Emergence of Modern War*. Lawrence, Kansas: University Press of Kansas, 1994.

Esposito, Vincent J., and Elting, John R. *A Military History and Atlas of the Napoleonic Wars*. N.Y.: Praeger, 1964.

Fain, Baron. *Manuscrit de Mil Huit Cent Douze*. Paris: 1827.

———. *Mémoires du Baron Fain*. Paris: Plon, 1908.

Falk, Minna R. "Stadion, Adversaire de Napoléon (1806–1809)," *Annales Historiques de la Révolution Française*, Vol. 34, 1962.

Finley, Milton C. Jr. "Reynier, Menou and the Final Siege of the Egyptian Campaign." *The Consortium on Revolutionary Europe*, 1983.

Fisher, H.A.L. *Napoleon*. London: Oxford University Press, 1945.

Flayhart, William H. "The United Kingdom in the Mediterranean: The War of the Third Coalition and the Anglo-Russian Invasion of Naples." *The Consortium on Revolutionary Europe*, 1980

Flayhart, William Henry III. *Counterpoint to Trafalgar: The Anglo-Russian Invasion of Naples 1805–1806*. Columbia (S. Carolina): University of South Carolina Press, 1992.

Forester, C.S. *Nelson*. London: The Bodley Head, 1929.

———. *The Naval War of 1812*. London: 1957.

Forrest, Alan. *The Soldier of the French Revolution*. Durham (N. Carolina): Duke University Press, 1990.

Fortescue, B. *Napoleon's Heritage*. London: John Murray, 1934.

Fortescue, John. *Wellington*. London: Ernest Benn, 1925.

Fouché, Joseph. *Les Mémoires de Fouché*. Paris: Flammerion, 1945.

Fournier, August. *Napoleon I*. N.Y.: Henry Holt, 1911. Vol. I. Tr. A.E. Adams.

Fuente, Francisco de la. "Portuguese Resistance to Napoleon: Don Miguel Forjaz and the Mobilization of Portugal." *The Consortium on Revolutionary Europe*, 1983.

Fugier, André. *Napoléon et l'Espagne 1799–1808*. Paris: Felix Alcan, 1930. 2 vols.

———. *Napoléon et l'Italie*. Paris: Panin, 1947.

Fuller, J.F.C. *A Military History of the Western World*. N.Y.: Funk & Wagnalls, 1955. Vol. 2.

———. *The Conduct of War 1789–1861*. Rutgers (N. Jersey): Rutgers University Press, 1961.

Gates, David. *The Spanish Ulcer: A History of the Peninsular War*. N.Y.: Norton, 1980.

Gaxotte, Pierre. *The French Revolution*. N.Y.: 1932.

Geer, Walter. *Napoleon and His Family*. London: Allen and Unwin, 1923.

Geyl, Pieter. *Napoleon For and Against*. London: Jonathan Cape, 1949.

Gillespie, Charles. "The Scientific Importance of Napoleon's Egyptian Campaign." *Scientific American*, September 1994.

Godlewski, Guy. "Napoléon et Les-États-Amis," *La Nouvelle Revue Des Deux Mondes*, Juillet–Septembre, 1977.

Goldstein, Marc A. *The People in Counter-Revolutionary France*. London: Peter Long, 1988.

Görlitz, Walter. *The German General Staff – Its History and Structure 1657–1945*. London: Hollis & Carter, 1953.

Gotteri, Nicole. "La Lorgne d'Ideville et le service de renseigne-ments . . . pendant la campagne de Russie (juin 1812–mars 1813)." *Revue d'Histoire Diplomatique*, 1984.

Gourgaud, Général Baron Gaspard. *Campagne de Dix-Huit Cent Quinze . . .* Bruxelles: Aug. Wahlen, 1818.

———. *Mémoires pour servir à l'histoire de France sous Napoléon*. Paris: Didot, 1823. 2 vols.

———. *Sainte-Hélène: Journal inédit de 1815 à 1818*. Paris: Flammarion, 1899.

———. *The St. Helena Journal of General Baron Gourgaud 1815–1818*. London: John Lane, 1932.

Grab, Alexander I. "Popular Uprisings in Napoleonic Italy." *The Consortium on Revolutionary Europe*, 1989.

Grandmaison, Geoffrey De. *L'Espagne et Napoléon*. Paris: Plon, 1908 ff. 3 vols.

Guedalla, Philip. *Napoleon and Palestine*. London: Allen & Unwin, 1925.

Gum, Ert. "Eugene de Beauharnais and an Affair of Honor." *The Consortium on Revolutionary Europe*, 1974.

Guyon, Edouard-Felix. "Stendhal et la Campagne de Russie de 1812," *Revue Historique D'Histoire Diplomatique*, Vol. 98, 1984.

Hall, H.F. *see* Napoleon.

Harford, Lee S. Jr. "Bavaria and the Tyrol Under Napoleon." *The Consortium on Revolutionary Europe*, 1989.

Headley, J.T. *Napoleon and His Marshals*. N.Y.: Baker and Scribner, 1846. 2 vols.

Heles, Edward E.Y. *Napoleon and the Pope . . .* London: Eyre & Spottiswoode, 1962.

Henry, Peter A. "Clausewitz and the Campaign of 1812 in Russia." *The Consortium on Revolutionary Europe*, 1989.

Herold, J. Christopher. *Bonaparte in Egypt*. London: Hamish Hamilton, 1963.

Heyault, Maurice *see* Cottin, Paul.

Horne, Alistair. *How Far From Austerlitz? Napoleon 1805–1815*. London: Macmillan, 1996.

Horta, Nicolás Rodriguez. "Dos Estudios Sobre Las Guerrillas en La Guerra de la Independencia." *Revista de Historia Militar*. Numero 8 (15), 1964.

———. "La Guerrilla del Cura Merino." *Revista de Historia Militar*. Numero 12 (25), 1968.

———. "Un Capuchino Vasco en la Guerra de la Independencia Española." *Revista de Historia Militar*. Numero 22 (44), 1978.

Hortense [Bonaparte]. *The Memoirs of Queen Hortense*. N.Y.: Cosmopolitan Book Corporation, 1927.

Horward, Donald D. "Napoleon and Berthier." *The Consortium on Revolutionary Europe*, 1980, Vol. II.

———. *Napoleon and Iberia: The Twin Sieges of Ciudad Rodrigo and Almeida*. Tallahassee [Florida]: Florida State University Press, 1984.

———. "Wellington and the Defense of Portugal (1808–1813)." *The Consortium on Revolutionary Europe*, 1987.

Howarth, David. *Waterloo: Day of Battle*. N.Y.: Atheneum, 1968.

———. *Trafalgar: The Nelson Touch*. London: Collins, 1969.

Iung, Th. *Bonaparte et Son Temps 1769–1799*. Paris: Charpentier, 1880–1881. 3 vols.

———. *Lucien Bonaparte et Ses Mémoires 1775–1840*. Paris: Charpentier, 1802.

Jackson, W.A.F. *Attack in the West. Napoleon's First Campaign*. London: Eyre & Spottiswoode, 1953.

Johns, Christopher M.S. "Portrait Mythology: Antonio Canova's Portraits of the Bonapartes." *Eighteenth-Century Studies*, Vol. 28, Nr. 1 (1994).

Jonquière, C. de la. *L'Expédition de l'Égypte*. Paris: 1900–1907. 5 vols.

Jomini, Antoine Henri, Baron de. *The Political and Military History of the Campaign of Waterloo*. N.Y.: Redfield, 1860.

———. *The Art of War*. Philadelphia: Lippincott, 1862.

Junot, Madame. *Memoirs of Madame Junot*. N.Y.: 1883, 3 vols.

Junot, Madame. *see* Abrantès.

Keegan, John. *The Mask of Command*. N.Y.: Viking, 1987.

Kircheisen, Friedrich M. *Memoirs of Napoleon Ier*. N.Y.: Duffield, 1929. Tr. Frederick Collins.

Kirchiesen, Gertrude. *Die Frauen um Napoleon*. Munich, 1912.

Klang, Daniel. "Bavaria and the War of Liberation, 1813–14." *French Historical Studies*, Vol. 4, 1965.

Knight, George D. "Lord Liverpool and the Peninsular Struggle, 1809–1812." *The Consortium on Revolutionary Europe*, 1989.

Koch, Général. *Mémoires de Masséna (1796–1797)*. Paris: Paulin et Lechevalier, 1848.

Korngold, Ralph. *The Last Years of Napoleon – His Captivity on St. Helena*. N.Y.: Harcourt Brace, 1959.

Lacour-Gayet, Robert. "Napoléon et les États-Unis," *Revue d'Histoire Diplomatique*. Vol. 83, 1969.

Larchey, Lorédan. *Les Cahiers du Capitaine Coignet (1799–1815)*. Paris: Hachette, 1883.

Larrey, D.J. *Mémoires de Chirurgie Militaire et Campagnes*. Paris: chez J. Smith, 1812. 4 vols.

Las Cases, Comte de. *Mémorial de Sainte-Hélène*. Bruxelles: P.J. de Mat, 1828. 4 vols.

Lavelette, Comte. *Mémoires et Souvenirs du Comte Lavelette*. Paris: Fournier, 1831. 2 vols.

Lefebvre, Georges. *Napoleon from Tilsit to Waterloo, 1807–1815*. N.Y.: Columbia University Press, 1970. Tr. J.E. Anderson.

Lloyd, E.M. *A Review of the History of Infantry.* London: Longmans, Green, 1908.

―――. "The Third Coalition." *The Cambridge Modern History.* London: Cambridge University Press, 1904. Vol. 9.

Longford, Elizabeth. *Wellington – The Years of the Sword.* London: Weidenfeld & Nicolson, 1969.

Lucas-Dubreton. *Le Maréchal Ney 1769–1815.* Paris: Librairie Arthème Fayard, 1941.

Ludwig, Emil. *Napoleon.* Garden City (N.Y.): Garden City Publishing Company, 1926. Tr. Eden Cedar Paul.

Macartney, C.A. *The Habsburg Empire 1790–1912.* N.Y.: Macmillan, 1969.

Macdonald, Marshal. *Recollections of Marshal Macdonald.* London: Richard Bentley, 1893. Tr. S.L. Simeon.

MacDonald, J.R.M. "The Terror." *The Cambridge Modern History.* London: Cambridge University Press, 1904. Vol. 8.

Macdonell, A.G. *Napoleon and His Marshals.* London: Prion, 1996.

Mackesy, Piers. *Statesmen at War: The Strategy of Overthrow, 1798–1799.* London, 1974.

―――. *War Without Victory: The Downfall of Pitt, 1799–1802.* Oxford, 1984.

―――. *British Victory in Egypt, 1801.* London: Routledge, 1995.

Madelin, Louis. *Histoire du Consulat et de l'Empire.* Paris: Hachette, 1937–1954. 16 vols. Vol. 1: *La Jeunesse . . .*

―――. *Histoire du Consulat et de l'Empire.* Vol. 3: *De Brumaire à Marengo.* Paris: Hachette, 1938.

―――. *The Consulate and the Empire.* London: Heinemann, 1934. Tr. E.F. Buckley.

Mahan, Alfred. *The Influence of Sea Power upon the French Revolution and Empire 1783–1812.* London: Sampson, Low, Marston, 1892. 2 vols.

―――. *The Influence of Sea Power upon History, 1660–1783.* London: Sampson, Low, Marston, 1900.

―――. *Sea Power in Its Relations to the War of 1812.* London: Sampson, Low, Marston, c. 1905.

Maras, Raymond. "Napoleon and Levies on the Arts and Sciences." *The Consortium on Revolutionary Europe,* 1987.

Marbot, Général Baron de. *Mémoires du Général Baron de Marbot.* Paris: Plon, 1891. 3 vols.

Marcaggi, Jean Baptiste. *Le Souvenir de Napoléon à Ajaccio*. Ajaccio, Corse: Rombaldi, 1921.

Markham, Felix. *Napoleon*. London: Weidenfeld & Nicolson, 1963.

Marmont *see* Raguse.

Martin, Marc. "Les Journaux Militaires de Carnot." *Annales Historiques de la Révolution Française*. Vol. 49, 1977.

Martineau, Gilbert. *Napoleon's St. Helena*. N.Y.: Rand McNally, 1966.

Masséna, Marshal *see* Koch.

Masson, Frédéric. *Napoleon at Home*. Philadelphia: Lippincott, 1894. 2 vols. Tr. J.E. Matthew.

———. *Napoleon and the Fair Sex*. London: Heinemann, 1894.

———. *Napoléon et sa Famille*. Paris: Ollendorff, 1898 ff. 14 vols.

———. *Napoléon dans sa Jeunesse*. Paris: Ollendorf, 1907.

———. *Joséphine de Beauharnais 1763–1796*. Paris: Ollendorff, 1913.

——— et Biaggi, Guido. *Napoléon inconnu . . . Papiers Inédits*. Paris: Ollendorff, 1895.

Mathiez, Albert. *La Réaction Thermidorienne*. Paris: Armand Colin, 1929.

———. *Le Directoire*. Paris, 1934.

———. "Robespierre L'Histoire et la Légende." *Annales Historiques de la Révolution Française*. Vol. 49. 1977.

Maurois, André. *Napoleon – a pictorial biography*. London: Thames & Hudson, 1963. Tr. P.J.S. Thomson.

McLynn, Frank. *Napoleon*. London: Jonathan Cape, 1997.

Melchoir-Bonnet, Bernardine. *Le procès de Louis XVI*. Paris: Librairie Académique Perrin, 1992.

Méneval, Baron Claude François de. *Napoléon et Marie-Louise*. Paris: Amyot, 1844.

———. *Mémoires . . .* Paris: Dentu, 1893–1894.

———. *Memoirs to Serve for the History of Napoleon I from 1802 to 1815*. London: Hutchinson, 1894. Tr. R.W. Sherrard.

Metternich, Klemens, Prince de. *Mémoires Documents et Écrits Divers laissés par le Prince de Metternich*. Paris: Plon, 1886. 2 vols (ed. Prince Richard de Metternich).

Meurthe *see* Boulay de la Meurthe.

Meyer, Jack Allen. *Wellington's Generalship – A Study of his Peninsular Campaign*. Columbia (S. Carolina): University of South Carolina Press, 1984.

Meyer, Frank. "Thirteen Critical Decisions at Waterloo." *Parameters,* Spring 1991.

Miot, Jacques-François. *Mémoires pour Servir à l'Histoire des Expéditions en Égypte et en Syrie.* Paris: Demonville, 1804.

Miot de Melito, Comte. *Mémoires du Comte Miot de Melito.* Paris: Michel-Lévy Frères, 1858. 2 vols.

————. *Memoirs of Count Miot de Melito.* N.Y.: Charles Scribner's Sons, 1881. 2 vols. Tr. C. Hoey and J. Lillie.

Mollien, Nicolas-François, Comte de. *Mémoires d'un Ministre du Trésor Public.* Paris: Guillaumin, 1898. 2 vols.

Montholon, C.F.D., Comte de. *Récits de la captivité de l'Empereur Napoléon à Sainte-Hélène.* Paris: Paulin, 1847. 2 vols.

Montgomery, Frances. "General Moreau and the Conspiracy Against Napoleon in 1804: The Verdict of the Court and History." *The Consortium on Revolutionary Europe,* 1988.

Muller, Charles. *The Darkest Day: 1814.* Philadelphia: Lippincott, 1963.

Napier, W.F.P. *History of the War in the Peninsula and in the south of France from the Year 1807 to the Year 1814.* London and N.Y.: Routledge and Sons, 1878. 3 vols.

Napoléon. *Lettres de Napoléon à Joséphine pendant la première campagne d'Italie et Lettres de Joséphine à Napoléon et à sa Fille.* Paris: Fermin Didot Frères, 1833. 2 vols.

Napoléon I. *Correspondance de Napoléon Ier.* Paris: Plon/Dumaine, 1858 ff. 32 vols.

Napoleon. *The Letters and Dispatches of the First Napoleon.* London: Chapman and Hall, 1884. 3 vols.

Napoléon IER. *Lettres Inédites de Napoléon Ier.* Paris: Plon, 1897. 2 vols.

Napoleon. *Napoleon's Letters to Josephine 1796–1812.* London: J.M. Dent, 1901. Ed. and tr. F. Hall.

Napoléon. *Dernières Lettres Inédites de Napoléon Ier.* Paris: Honoré Champion, 1903. 2 vols.

Napoléon Bonaparte. *Lettres inédites de Napoleon Ier à Marie-Louise, écrites de 1810 à 1814.* Paris: 1933.

Napoleon Bonaparte. *The Letters of Napoleon to Marie-Louise.* London: Hutchinson, 1935. Commentary by Charles De La Roncière.

Napoléon. *Lettres d'Amour à Joséphine.* Paris: Fayard, 1981. Presentées par Jean Tulard.

Napoleon Bonaparte. *Supper at Beaucaire*. London: Cockerel Press, 1945. Tr. S. De Clair.

Nasica, T. *Mémoires sur l'enfance et la jeunesse de Napoléon*. Paris: Ledoyen, 1852.

Ney, Michel. *Mémoires du Maréchal Ney . . .* Paris: Fournier, 1833. 2 vols.

Nicolson, Harold. *The Congress of Vienna. A Study in Allied Unity: 1812–1822*. N.Y.: Harcourt Brace, 1946.

Oman, Carola. *Napoleon's Viceroy Eugene de Beauharnais*. N.Y: Funk and Wagnalls, 1966.

Oman, C.W.C. *A History of the Peninsular War*. London: Oxford University Press, 1902–1930. 7 vols.

———. *Studies in the Napoleonic Wars*. London: Methuen, 1929.

O'Meara, Barry E. *Napoléon en Exil*. Paris: Seignot, 1823. 4 vols.

———. *A Voice from St. Helena*. London: Simpkin and Marshall, 1922.

Palmstierna, C.F. *My dearest Louise. Marie-Louise and Napoleon 1813–1814*. London: Methuen, 1958. Tr. E.M. Wilkensen.

Paret, Peter. *Yorck and the Era of Prussian Reform 1807–1815*. Princeton (N. Jersey): Princeton University Press, 1966.

———. "Napoleon as Enemy." *The Consortium on Revolutionary Europe*, 1983.

Parker, Harold T. "Why did Napoleon Invade Russia? . . ." *The Consortium on Revolutionary Europe*, 1989.

Passant, E. *A Short History of Germany 1815–1945*. London: Cambridge University Press, 1962.

Petre, F. Loraine. *Napoleon's Campaign In Poland 1806–1807*. London: John Lane The Bodley Head, 1907.

Petrie, C. *see* Bertrand, L.

Pinaud, Pierre-Français. "Guerre et Finances de 1792 à 1815: Le service de la Trésorerie aux Armées." *Revue Historique*, Vol. 283, 1990.

Platonov, S.F. *History of Russia*. London: Macmillan, 1925. Tr. E. Arensberg.

Pokrovsky, M.N. *Brief History of Russia*. London: Martin Lawrence, 1983. 2 vols. Tr. D.S. Mirsky.

Pratt, Fletcher. *The Empire and the Glory – Napoleon Bonaparte 1800–1806*. N.Y.: William Sloane, 1949.

Priego, Juan Lopez. "Dos Acciones de Guerra del Cura Merino, Relatadas Por El Merino (16 y 28 De Abril De 1812)." *Revista de Historia Militar*, Número 12(25), 1968.

Priestley, E.C. *see* Cole, D.H.

Quimby, Robert S. *The Background of Napoleonic Warfare. The Theory of Military Tactics in Eighteenth Century France*. N.Y.: Columbia University Press, 1957.

Ragsdale, Hugh. "Russian Influence at Luneville." *French Historical Studies*, Nr. 3. 1968.

Raguse, Duc de. *Mémoires du Duc de Raguse*. Paris: Perrotin, 1857. 2 vols.

Rapp, Jean, Comte. *Mémoires du Général Rapp . . .* Paris: Gernier frères, 1895.

Ratcliffe, Bertram. *Prelude to Fame – An Account of the early life of Napoleon up to the battle of Montenotte*. London: Frederick Warne, 1981.

Reddaway, W.F. *A History of Europe from 1715 to 1814*. London: Methuen, 1959.

Reeves, Craig A. "Command and Control: Napoleon's Aides-de-Camp and Orderly Officers." *The Consortium on Revolutionary Europe*, 1990.

Reinhard, Marcel. *Avec Bonaparte en Italie – d'après Les lettres Inédites de son Aide de Camp Joseph Sulkowski*. Paris: Hachette, 1946.

Rémusat, Paul D. (ed.). *Mémoires de Madame Rémusat 1802–1808*. Paris: Calmann Levy, 1880. 3 vols.

Ribiera, Aileen. *Factions in the French Revolution*. N.Y.: Holmes & Meier, 1989.

Roeder, Franz. *The Ordeal of Captain Roeder*. London: Methuen, 1960. Ed. and tr. Helen Roeder.

Roederer, Count P.L. *Journal du Comte P.-L. Roederer*. Paris: H. Daragen, 1909.

Roederer, Pierre-Louise. *Mémoires Sur La Révolution, Le Consulat et L'Empire*. Paris: Plon, 1942. Ed. Octave Aubry.

Rogers, H.C.B. *Napoleon's Army*. London: Ian Allen, 1974.

Roider, Karl A. *Baron Thugut and Austria's Response to the French Revolution*. Princeton (N. Jersey): Princeton University Press, 1987.

Rose, J. Holland. "The Despatches of Colonel Thomas Graham on the Italian Campaign of 1796–7." *The English Historical Review*, Nr. 53, Vol. XIV. January 1899.

————. *The Life of Napoleon.* London: George Bell & Sons, 1903. 2 vols.

————. "The Second Coalition." *The Cambridge Modern History.* London: Cambridge University Press, 1904. Vol. 8.

————. *Napoleonic Studies.* London: George Bell & Sons, 1904.

————. *The Personality of Napoleon.* London: George Bell & Sons, 1912.

————. *Pitt and Napoleon. Essays and Letters.* London: George Bell & Sons, 1912.

Ross, Steven T. "The Military Strategy of the Directory: The Campaign of 1799." *French Historical Studies,* Vol. 5, Nr. 1, 1967.

Rothenberg, Gunther E. *The Art of Warfare in the Age of Napoleon.* Bloomington (Indiana): Indiana University Press.

————. *Napoleon's Great Adversaries: The Archduke Charles and the Austrian Army.* Bloomington (Indiana): Indiana University Press, 1982.

————. "The Case of Archduke Charles." *The Consortium on Revolutionary Europe,* 1983.

Roustam, Raza. *Souvenirs de Roustam Mamelouck de Napoléon Ier.* Paris: Ollendorff, 1911.

Rovigo, Duc de. *Mémoires du Duc de Rovigo pour Servir à l'Histoire de l'Empereur Napoléon.* Paris: A. Bossange, 1828. 8 vols.

————. *Memoirs of the Duke of Rovigo . . .* London: H. Colburn, 1828. 4 vols.

Saint-Denis, Louis-Etienne "Ali". *Souvenirs du mameluck Ali sur l'Empereur Napoléon.* Paris: Payot, 1926.

Saint-Hilaire, M. *Napoléon au Conseil d'État.* Paris: Victor Magen, 1843.

Saunders, Edith. *Napoleon and Mademoiselle George.* London: Longman Green, 1958.

Savant, Jean. *Les Mamelouks de Napoléon.* Paris: Calmann-Lévy, 1949.

————. *Napoleon In His Time.* London: Putnam, 1958. Tr. K. John.

Savary, Général. *Memoirs of the Duke of Rovigo.* London: Henry Collins, 1828. 4 vols.

Savary, Jean-Marie-René *see* Rovigo, Duc de.

Savary, Jean-Julien. *Guerre des Vendéens et des Chouans contre la République Française . . .* Paris: Baudouin frères, 1824–7.

Schevill, Ferdinand. *The History of the Balkan Peninsula. From the Earliest Times to the Present Day.* N.Y.: Harcourt Brace, 1933.

Schom, Alan. *One Hundred Days: Napoleon's Road to Waterloo*. N.Y.: Atheneum, 1992.

———. *Napoleon Bonaparte*. N.Y.: HarperCollins, 1997.

Schroeder, Paul W. "The Collapse of the Second Coalition." *Journal of Modern History*. The University of Chicago Press, Vol. 59, June 1987.

Ségur, Le Général Comte de. *Histoire et Mémoires*. Paris: Firmin Didot, 1873. 3 vols.

Ségur, Count Phillippe Paul de. *Napoleon's Russian Campaign*. London: Michael Joseph, 1958. Tr. J.D. Townsend.

Serramon, Jean. "Operaciones en El Reino de Léon (Mayo a Septiembre de 1811)." *Revista de Historia Militar*. Número 9(19), 1965.

Seton-Watson, Hugh. *The Russian Empire 1801–1917*. Oxford: Clarendon Press, 1967.

Shanahan, W.O. *Prussian Military Reforms 1786–1813*. N.Y.: 1945.

Showalter, Dennis E. "Manifestation of Reform: The Rearmament of the Prussian Infantry, 1806–13." *Journal of Modern History*, University of Chicago Press, September, 1972.

Sloane, William. *Life of Napoleon Bonaparte*. N.Y.: 1909. 4 vols.

Soult, Jean de Dieu. *Mémoires du maréchal général Soult*. Paris: Anyot, 1854.

Standing, Percy Cross. *Guerrilla Leaders of the World*. London: Stanley Paul, 1912.

Stendhal (Henri Beyle). *Journal de Stendhal, 1801–1814*. Paris: Garnier, 1888.

———. *A Life of Napoleon*. London: The Rodale Press, 1956. Tr. Ronald Gant.

Stschepkin, E. "Russia Under Alexander I, and the Invasion of 1812." *The Cambridge Modern History*. London: Cumbridge University Press, 1904. Vol. 9.

Suchet, Louis-Gabriel. *Mémoires du maréchal Suchet* . . . Paris: Bossange, 1928. 2 vols.

Sutherland, Christine. *Marie Walewska – Napoleon's Great Love*. London: Weidenfeld & Nicolson, 1979.

Talleyrand-Périgord, Charles Maurice de. *Mémoires du Prince de Talleyrand-Périgord* . . . Bruxelles: Société Belge de Libraire, 1838. 2 vols.

———. *Lettres Inédites de Talleyrand à Napoléon, 1800–1809*. Paris: Perrin, 1889. Ed. Pierre Bertrand.

————. *Mémoires du Prince de Talleyrand*. Paris: Calman Lévy, 1891–1892. Vols 1 and 2.

Tarlé, Eugène. *Napoleon's Invasion of Russia, 1812*. London: Allen & Unwin, 1942. Tr. G.M.

Teil *see* Du Teil.

Thackeray, William Makepeace. *Vanity Fair*. N.Y.: The Modern Library, n.d.

Thibaudeau, Antoine Claire. *Histoire de Napoléon*. Paris, 1827 ff. 5 vols.

————. *Mémoires sur le Consulat et l'Empire*. Paris, 1835 ff. 10 vols.

————. *Histoire de la campagne d'Égypte sous le règne de Napoléon-le-Grand*. Paris, 1839, 2 vols.

Thiébault, Paul, Baron. *The Memoirs of Baron Thiébault*. London: Smith, Elder, 1896. 2 vols. Tr. and condensed by A.J. Butler.

Thiers, Louis-Adolphe. *Histoire du Consulat et de l'Empire*. Bruxelles: 1845 ff. 20 vols.

————. *History of the Consulate and the Empire of France under Napoleon*. Philadelphia: Lippincott, 1861.

Thiry, J. *Aube du Consulat*. Paris: Berger-Levrault, 1948.

————. *Le Concordat et le Consulat à Vie*. Paris: Berger-Levrault, 1956.

————. *Napoléon en Italie*. Paris: Berger-Levrault, 1973.

————. *Napoléon en Egypte*. Paris: Berger-Levrault, 1974.

————. *Années de Jeunesse de Napoléon Bonaparte*. Paris: Berger-Levrault, 1975.

Thomazi, Auguste Antoine. *Napoléon et ses marins*. Paris: Berger-Levrault, 1950.

Thompson, J.M. *Napoleon Bonaparte. His Rise and Fall*. Oxford: Basil Blackwell, 1952.

Tolstoy, Leo N., Count. *The Physiology of War: Napoleon and the Russian Campaign*. N.Y.: Crowell, 1888. Tr. H. Smith.

————. *War and Peace*. London: Heinemann, 1971. Tr. C. Garrett.

Tortel, Christian *see* Bernoyer.

Trenard, Louis. *La Révolution Française dans la Région Rhône-Alpes*. Paris: Perrin, 1992.

Trevelyan, George. *George the Third and Charles Fox*. London: Longman Green, 1914. 2 vols.

Turner, Martha L. "French Art Confiscation in the Roman Republic, 1798." *The Consortium on Revolutionary Europe*, Vol. II, 1980.

Tute, Warren. *The True Glory*. London: Macdonald, 1983.

United States Military Academy. *Atlas to Accompany Napoleon As A General* by Count Yorck von Wartenburg. West Point (New York), 1942.

———. *Great Captains Before Napoleon*. West Point (New York), 1948.

———. *Jomini, Clausewitz and Schlieffen*. West Point (New York), 1948.

Vallejo-Nágera, Antonio. *Yo El Rey*. Madrid: Planeta, 1985.

Van Crefeld *see* Crefeld.

Vandal, Albert. *Napoléon et Alexandre Ier*. Paris: Plon, 1891 ff. 3 vols.

———. *L'Avènement de Bonaparte*. Paris, 1911.

Vann, James Allen. "Habsburg Policy and the War of 1809." *Central European History*, Vol. VII, 1974.

Vernadsky, George. *A History of Russia*. New Haven (Conn.): Yale University Press, 1945.

Vicenza *see* Caulaincourt.

Victor, Marshal *see* Bellune.

Volney, Constantin. *Voyage en Syrie et en Égypte*. Paris: 1787. 2 vols.

Volney, Count C.F. *Oeuvres Complètes*. Paris: Bossange, 1821. Vol. 1.

Wairy *see* Constant.

Walach, Isser. *The French Veteran from the Revolution to the Restoration*. Chapel Hill (N. Carolina): University of North Carolina Press, 1979.

Walter, Jakob. *A German Conscript with Napoleon*. Lawrence (Kansas): University of Kansas, 1938.

Warner, Oliver. *The Battle of the Nile*. London: 1960.

Wartenburg, Count Yorck von. *Napoleon as a General*. London: K. Paul, Tench, Trubner, 1902. 2 vols. Ed. and tr by W.H. James.

Watson, G.E. "The United States and the Peninsular War. 1808–1812." *The Historical Journal*, Vol 14, 4, 1976.

Wheeler, H.F.B., and Broadley, A.M. *Napoleon and the Invasion of England*. London: John Lane, 1908. 2 vols.

Wilkinson, Spenser. *The Rise of General Bonaparte*. Oxford: Clarendon Press, 1930.

Williams, David Hamilton. *Waterloo: New Perspectives: The Great Battle Reappraisal*. N.Y.: Wiley, 1994.

Williams, E.N. *The Ancien Régime in Europe 1648–1789*. London: The Bodley Head, 1970.

Wright, G.N. *Life and Campaigns of Arthur, Duke of Wellington*. London: Fisher, 1841. 4 vols.

Zawadzki, W.H. "Prince Adam Czartoryski and Napoleonic France. 1801–1805. A Study in Political Attitudes." *The Historical Journal*, Vol. XVIII, 1975.

Ziegler, Philip. *Addington*. London: Collins, 1965.

Zweig, Stefan. *Napoleon*. London: Allen and Unwin, 1927.

INDEX